CW00540798

ISRAEL VICTORY

HOW ZIONISTS WIN ACCEPTANCE AND PALESTINIANS GET LIBERATED

DANIEL PIPES

A WICKED SON BOOK
An Imprint of Post Hill Press
ISBN: 979-8-88845-629-3
ISBN (eBook): 979-8-88845-630-9

Israel Victory:
How Zionists Win Acceptance and Palestinians Get Liberated

Cover Design by Jim Villaflores

This is a work of nonfiction. All people, locations, events, and situations are portrayed to the best of the author's memory.

Post Hill Press
New York • Nashville
wickedsonbooks.com
posthillpress.com

Published in the United States of America
1 2 3 4 5 6 7 8 9 10

To Barre Seid

Who honors me with faith in my work
and trust in my judgment.

There is only one way to defeat the enemy,
and that is to write as well as one can.
The best argument is an undeniably good book.

—Saul Bellow, 1956

TABLE OF CONTENTS

Author's Note ix
Foreword: Creating a New Paradigm xi
Preface xiii
Abbreviations xxi

Part I: Palestinian Rejectionism

1 Explaining the Virulence 3
2 Explaining the Tenacity 30

Part II: Israeli Conciliation

3 Enriching the Enemy 55
4 Placating the Enemy 85

Part III: Diplomacy Fails

5 The Oslo Accords: Israel's Nakba 109
6 Plans Galore 131

Part IV: Defeat and Victory

7 Universal Patterns 151
8 Victory After 1945 165

Part V: Approaching Victory

9 Reinterpreting the Conflict 183
10 Positive Developments 194
11 Israeli Overconfidence 226

Part VI: Victory Attained

12 Defeating the Palestinians 245
13 Victory's Benefits 279

Conclusion: The Impact of October 7 297
Appendices 306
About the Author 314

AUTHOR'S NOTE

The completed manuscript of this book went off to the publisher on the relative quiet of September 30, 2023. The Hamas attack on Israel on October 7 upended both the Palestinian-Israeli conflict and the debate about it, requiring the manuscript to be withdrawn and revised, with an entirely new conclusion. The new version went off on the final day of 2023.

FOREWORD

CREATING A NEW PARADIGM

ISRAEL VICTORY SHEDS NEW LIGHT on an emotionally charged, deeply entrenched conflict that has confounded all who approach it.

Daniel Pipes' work mainly consists of two discernible insights: the identification of everlasting distinct and opposite Palestinian and Israeli mentalities, namely rejectionism and conciliation; and his creative policy recommendations.

He characterizes *rejectionism* as the Palestinian attitude from the 1880s until today, and highlights how it consists not just of a refusal to recognize Israel, but also of a stubborn, unwavering commitment to its destruction. This 140-year-old mindset, Pipes argues, emerged at the dawn of Zionism, became an ideology under past Arab leaders and continues today with present Arab leaders. Rejectionism drives the Palestinians to wallow in perpetual conflict, even at their own expense.

He states that *conciliation*, its polar opposite, has defined the Zionist approach for just as long. It seeks to win Israel's acceptance from Palestinians not through coercion but via enrichment and placation. Pipes astutely documents the faith in this eccentric approach by Theodor Herzl, as well as by past and present leaders of Israel. He states that due to its reversal of normal war strategy, conciliation has time and again proven a monumental failure. Nevertheless, it remains the dominant approach among Israel's security establishment and among the country's allies.

Pipes' proposition replaces the illusion of conciliation with "Israel Victory," or the goal of imposing a sense of defeat on the Palestinians. "Ending the conflict," he writes, "means one side wins, the other loses." "Israel Victory" requires Israel to abandon the old, failed pursuit of conciliation. For Palestinians, it implies an even more profound change, one away from obsessive genocide toward coexistence.

But how is that to be achieved? Here, drawing on his fifty-five years of studying Middle Eastern history and a deep understanding of the Palestinian condition, Pipes offers a compelling and comprehensive roadmap for Israel, and reaches the conclusion, that counter-intuitively and ironically, while "both parties need the collapse of rejectionism," this "would bring even greater benefits to Palestinians than to Israelis."

As a long-time follower of Pipes' work and a personal friend for over a decade, I have benefited from our intense discussions, his thought-provoking insights, and a joint dedication to finding solutions for the Middle East's challenging reality. It is therefore unsurprising that Daniel has transformed his many writings on the Palestinian-Israeli conflict into a compelling book which will ignite in the reader a process of reflection and reevaluation, and will serve as a catalyst for renewed conversations about the conflict.

As readers embark on the engrossing journey through *Israel Victory*, they will find themselves challenged, enlightened, and inspired.

Danny Danon
Member of Israel's Knesset
Chairman of World Likud
Former Ambassador of Israel to the United Nations

PREFACE

Palestine is not a picnic. Two powerful forces are colliding. Blood is inevitable. It has flowed in the past; it is flowing today; it will flow in the future until one side emerges victorious.

—ALBERT VITON, American journalist, 1936

CHEERFUL ISRAEL. THE UN'S WORLD Happiness Report asks residents of 137 countries subjectively to assess their contentment, then it factors in objective measures, such as income levels, government services, individual freedom, and corruption. In March 2023, it found Israel to be the fourth-happiest country on Earth, following three Nordic countries, Finland, Denmark, and Iceland. In contrast, the "State of Palestine" ranked ninety-ninth.

To the extent that such numbers mean anything, and it is a serious study, a fourth-place ranking points to a remarkable ability to live the good life, an obviously healthy attribute. Israel's burgeoning birth rate, the rich world's only one above replacement (and it far exceeds replacement) confirms this positive outlook.

Less methodically, TheTravel.com in late September 2023 deemed Tel Aviv "the happiest city in the world," commending its "rich cultural heritage, kind people, and abundance of food, shopping, and learning," as well as its "progressive ideologies."[1] In another confirmation, U.S. Secretary of State John F. Kerry noted that, "People in Israel aren't waking up every day and wondering if tomorrow there will be peace because there is a sense of security and a sense of accomplishment and of prosperity."

Yet, this happiness is surprising, even odd. Reports about the Muslims who make up nearly 20 percent of Israel's population invariably portray them as permanently alienated from the Jewish state; they alone should

1 After October 7, TheTravel.com reduced Tel Aviv to the third-happiest city.

sink the rankings. Then, the Jewish majority of nearly 75 percent faces a genocidal enemy, the Palestinians, which poses two enduring and distinct threats: murderous assault and international condemnation.

Palestinians attack violently and ceaselessly. The Palestinian Authority (PA) that rules most of the West Bank sponsors and endorses low-intensity attacks, such as knife-stabbings, car-rammings, gun onslaughts, and suicide bombings. Hamas and Palestinian Islamic Jihad (PIJ), the dominant forces in Gaza, dispatch kites and balloons carrying explosives, launch rockets and missiles, and assault with a massive air-water-land-and-tunnel operation.[2] Israelis face a uniquely persistent violence that not only maims and kills citizens but also puts them on edge and requires a huge, expensive, intrusive, and unavoidable security apparatus.

Second, the Palestinian spread a slander of Israel as the world's most horrid and bellicose country, one that finds wide acceptance, especially among Muslims, the Left, the far-Right, and dictators. This message even finds political heft in democratic countries, including among U.S. members of Congress, the British Labour Party, the first minister of Scotland, and several presidents in Latin America. Should it continue to grow, this form of anti-Zionism poses an existential threat to Israel no less than Iran's nuclear weapons. Indeed, just as lawful Islamism poses greater dangers than Muslim violence, so the Palestinians' delegitimization threatens Israel more than their violence.

Israelis' usual serenity, seemingly unperturbed by such tensions and dangers, implies an acceptance of a perilous status quo, a disinclination to take problems seriously, a resignation to persistent violence, and an indifference to venom. That may not be healthy.

This book. In the pages ahead, I hope to achieve three favorable results. First, to convince Israelis that hostility toward their country, orchestrated by Palestinians and growing especially on the Left, needs to be addressed, then to offer ideas on effecting this, so that they can live fully normal lives. Second, to ameliorate the Palestinian condition by unburdening them of their extremism, thereby addressing the source of their ninety-ninth-ranked happiness. Third, to offer a way for Israel's Muslim citizens to address their unsettled circumstances and to find a new way forward.

---

2 The following analysis focuses on Hamas because it makes the key decisions in Gaza.

No small order, this, especially when set against a long record of failed diplomacy by famed statesmen. Actually, that dismal record justifies a re-thinking of the Palestinian-Israeli conflict.

I call my effort Israel Victory. Its goal is to bring about fundamental shifts in long-standing and distinctive Palestinian and Israeli mentalities, leading to a change of heart among Palestinians so that they abandon their campaign to destroy the Jewish state. It's time to end the habit of Israeli concessions to appease insatiable Palestinian demands; now, Israel makes the demands. Israel Victory means Palestinians accepting the Jewish state for both its sake and theirs. Thus, the subtitle, "How Zionists Win Acceptance and Palestinians Get Liberated." There is no short-cut and no alternative.

Israel Victory raises many, and complex, questions. How did those two mentalities originate? Why the long record of diplomatic failure? What role does Islam play? What constitutes victory? How does one recognize a Palestinian change of heart? Which policies should Israel adopt?

The following analysis explains how we got here and how to remedy the problem by taking on five tasks in six parts. Parts I and II explain the nearly one-and-a-half-century-long Palestinian and Israeli mentalities of, respectively, rejectionism and conciliation. Part III draws lessons from past diplomatic failures. Part IV leaves the Middle East to consider defeat and victory in general. Part V provides background to Israel attaining victory. Building on these preliminaries, Part VI offers specifics and lays out the benefits for all involved. Divided differently, the first half explains how we got into the current mess; the second offers ideas how to escape it.

My analysis contains several key arguments: (1) Despite massively changed circumstances, Palestinians and Israelis have acted with great consistency since their first nationalistic encounter 140 years ago. (2) Their actions are extreme in their opposite ways and unique in all the world. (3) A supersessionist Islamic form of Zionism sustains Palestinian rejectionism. (4) Israelis tend to over-focus on Palestinian violence while underestimating the danger of Palestinian slander. (5) Israelis need to engage in introspection to understand their mistakes. (6) Palestinians are more open to accepting Israel than is generally realized. (7) Ending rejectionism lies less in violence (which has a long record of not working) than in messaging (which has barely been tried).

Two persistent themes dominate: Palestinian evil and Israeli folly. The former is succinctly covered in Chapters 1 and 2, but the latter requires

Chapters 3, 4, 5, 6, and 11. Words like "failure," "errors," and "incompetence" characterize this analysis.

I wish to stress that although Chapter 12 contains two specific ideas on how Israel can attain victory, I offer those ideas under gentle duress. My priority is not to advocate any particular policies but to convince Israelis to return to the classic goal of victory. How to achieve it is secondary for me. I hope that possible disagreement over those two ideas does not impede agreement on the goal of victory.

In preparing this book, I have drawn on my writings. This being an essay, not a research study, I have generally omitted sources because, with few exceptions, the facts and quotes are well known and easily confirmed.

I focus on residents of Israel, the West Bank, Gaza, and eastern Jerusalem because they are the main actors in this drama. I devote less attention to Palestinian-origin persons living elsewhere and to the non-Palestinian Arabs and their governments.

I thank my colleagues at the Middle East Forum for their assistance, comments, and critiques: Nave Dromi, Gary Gambill, Efraim Karsh, Ashley Perry, Gregg Roman, and Alex Selsky. The Middle East Forum has generously supported this work. In addition, Joseph Braude, Michael C. Davies, Martin Kramer, Beila Rabinowitz, and Ruth Wisse offered wise counsel. Michael Bohnen asked a question that led to a change in the sub-title. Don Dubin hosted me at the event that prompted this book. I am grateful to Adam Bellow for the idea of this book, then commissioning it.

APOLOGIA[3]

Before plunging into the Palestinian-Israeli conflict, I wish to address five personal matters: my credentials, my support for Israel, my preference for strategy over apologetics, my emphasis of ideas over material factors, and my justification for discussing this topic.

Credentials. I have intensely followed the Arab-Israeli conflict since the Six-Day War in 1967. I wrote my first public analysis of it in 1970, and published my first newspaper article on it in 1979. Since those beginnings, I have written about 800 times on the topic and spoken publicly on it at least as often. I first visited Israel in 1966, eastern Jerusalem and the West Bank in 1969, and Gaza in 1976. I resided in the Middle East for four

3 Meaning not *apology* but a *defense of one's opinions.*

years. I met Yasir Arafat and every Israeli prime minister of the past forty years except one (Yair Lapid).

I began studying the Middle East in 1969 and received two degrees in it. I taught Middle Eastern history at Harvard and co-taught "Policy and Strategy" at the U.S. Naval War College. The latter looked at ten historic wars and asked students to assess the competence of leadership through the filter of *On War* by Carl von Clausewitz. As the course description explains, it aims to equip mid-career U.S. government officials with the means "to grapple with the complex interrelationship among policy, strategy, and grand strategy that spans the peace-war continuum." Translated: One needs to figure out the destination before choosing a path. This may sound obvious, but most warfare finds this counsel not followed. Its spirit permeates this study.

I experienced America's first-ever major military defeat in 1975 not as a soldier in Vietnam but as an active, engaged supporter of the war. As such, I witnessed first-hand how a powerful country loses the will to keep fighting. That personal familiarity with political defeat shapes my views in two ways pertinent to this study: appreciating the vital role of demoralization, and the means by which it is effected. In brief, if a weak North Vietnam could defeat the mighty United States, surely mighty Israel can defeat the weak Palestinians.

Ideas, not money. I subscribe to the primacy of ideas. Therefore, this book emphasizes the role of beliefs, good and bad alike, rather than economics or other material factors. Ideas run the world: Good ones create freedom and wealth; bad ones, oppression and poverty. Materialists, in contrast, tend to reduce causation to money. But poverty itself does not lead to political action; ideas do. Of course, money matters, but it is a means to an end; ideas are the end. You are not what you eat; you are what you think.

Anyone involved in public affairs falls under the sway of ideas. As the British economist John Maynard Keynes put it, "Practical men who believe themselves to be quite exempt from any intellectual influence, are usually the slaves of some defunct economist. Madmen in authority, who hear voices in the air, are distilling their frenzy from some academic scribbler of a few years back…it is ideas, not vested interests, which are dangerous for good or evil."

Bad ideas have always existed; but they acquired new importance with the advent of liberalism in the late seventeenth century. Before then, conservatism—respecting tradition while adapting it to new circumstances—had prevailed. An individual king's or religious leader's besotted vision could only go so far before convention rolled it back. Liberalism rendered tradition optional by optimistically deeming each person on his own capable to think through the great issues from first principles.

We know how that turned out: Radical ideas proliferated, starting with the Enlightenment. The floodgates opened for theories unmoored from experience and common sense, including conspiracy theories. These ideas incubated through the nineteenth century came to terrible fruition after World War I with fascism, Nazism, socialism, and communism. As British historian Paul Johnson notes, "The worst of all despotisms is the heartless tyranny of ideas."

Support for Israel. The Palestinian-Israeli conflict ranks as perhaps humanity's most impassioned dispute, with opinion irreconcilably bifurcated between pro-Israel and anti-Israel partisans. This analysis is no exception; I unequivocally back Israel. Here is why:

Outsiders to the conflict face a clear and stark choice: Endorse the Palestinian goal (implicit in the case of the PA, explicit in that of Hamas) of destroying Israel; or endorse Israel's goal of winning its neighbors' acceptance. Either Palestinians give up on anti-Zionism or Israelis give up on Zionism; either Israel disappears or it wins acceptance. The Palestinians want to destroy Israel; Israel wants its neighbors to leave it alone.

Thus, to state the choice makes clear that there is no choice—the first is barbaric, the second civilized. Of course, every decent person wants Israel to be accepted by its neighbors. How can I endorse the goal of destroying any country, much less a flourishing one? With rare exceptions, every democratic leader and parliament supports Israel's drive to win acceptance (even if they disagree, sometimes strenuously, on the details). Further, as I argue in this analysis, a pro-Israel stance is also genuinely pro-Palestinian. Indeed, Palestinians will gain the most when Israel unequivocally wins, thus liberating them from their furies.

Therefore, I stand with Israel.

Strategy not advocacy. I offer strategic counsel to Israel, not advocacy on its behalf. Advocates offer passionate statements of justification and condemnation. Their work involves morality: Who is right and wrong? Which combatant acts with justice, which is evil? Advocates who win this vital argument shape public opinion, which in turn directs government policies.

But morality and justice are not the only debate; another one, more specialized, concerns strategy—not who is right or wrong, but how to achieve one's goals. This discussion focuses on an assessment of forces and figures out how to win. The strategist takes the goal for granted (here, Palestinian acceptance of defeat by Israel) and focuses on achieving it.

Advocacy and strategy each have their role. The advocate speaks of right and wrong; the strategist deals with success and failure. Passion marks the former; ice runs through the latter's veins. The advocate would choke on presenting his adversary's viewpoint, but the strategist routinely puts himself in his opponent's place (as in war games).

I focus on strategy, that is, figuring out how to win. This is, I believe, the best use of my skills. Apologetics, debates, defenses, polemics, public diplomacy, refutations, and responses have a crucial role; but I am engaged in finding the path to victory.

Justification. What business have I, an American citizen living in the United States, neither Palestinian nor Israeli, publicly making policy recommendations to Israel vis-à-vis the Palestinians? This issue arises for two reasons.

First, external busybodies have long made the Arab-Israeli conflict a favorite arena, whether because religiously engaged, intellectually challenged by its complexities, militarily fearful of its dangers, or diplomatically ambitious for accolades. As a result, outside powers regularly try to impose their own schemes. Although both Israelis and Palestinians occasionally go along with these, they often resent the interference. Israeli leaders ask outsiders, in effect, "Who assigned you to solve our problems?" As Danny Danon, a leading Likud politician, showed in *Israel: The Will to Prevail*,[4] Jerusalem historically has done best when it made policy independently, based on its own interests, not following the American lead. PA leader Mahmoud Abbas has similarly "called for the Palestinians and Israelis to be allowed to reach peace on their own, rather than it be imposed from the outside." Acquiescing to this consensus, I advocate no resolution but seek to guide Israelis better to understand their national interests and suggest a strategy.

Second, Israelis who dispute my analysis have told me off, instructing me to keep my opinions to myself. When, for example, I criticized the Israeli government for releasing a notorious murderer to Hezbollah, a counterterrorism analyst at Tel Aviv University challenged the legitimacy of my opining on this topic. Yoram Schweitzer found my "contents and

4 Danny Danon, *Israel: The Will to Prevail* (New York: St. Martin's Press, 2012).

tone...patronizing and insulting, overlooking as they do the fact that the government and public have the right to decide for themselves...and to shoulder the resulting price." He lashed out at me for offering an opinion on Israeli issues from my "secure haven thousands of miles away" in the United States.

Schweitzer is hardly alone. Prime Minister Yitzhak Rabin addressed American Jews in 1995, admonishing them that they

> have no right to patronize Israel. They have no right to intervene in the way the people of Israel have decided, in a very democratic way, on which direction to go when it comes to war and peace. They have the right to speak to us, but by no means to act, as Americans, against the policy of the government of Israel.... Whoever does not have daughters or sons who serve in the [Israeli] army has no right to intervene or act on issues of war and peace.

(Note the paradox of an Israeli telling Americans they have no right to disagree with Israelis—even as he disagrees with Americans.) In like spirit, as Ariel Sharon prepared his arch-controversial decision to pull all soldiers and citizens from Gaza, Israeli diplomats in the United States instructed Americans opposed to this move, "Please do not second-guess the government of Israel or the Israeli citizens."

I respect this position without accepting its discipline. Distance from a topic can offer a useful perspective. As a non-Israeli, I have very often criticized Israeli policy and, if I do say so myself, have a pretty good record opposing the entire Oslo process, unilateral withdrawals from Lebanon and Gaza, and the proposed West Bank annexation. Specifically, the following analysis emphasizes the Palestinians' international impact more than Israelis usually do. In this spirit, Israeli historian Moshe Dann finds that Israel Victory coming from the outside is just what his country needs. "We Israelis have been beaten down and brainwashed," he writes to me. "Now you appear from far away to heal us, to lead us back to sanity and life."

Daniel Pipes
Philadelphia
December 31, 2023

ABBREVIATIONS

BCE: before the common era
BDS: boycott, divestment, and sanctions
CBM: confidence-building measure
CE: common era
COGAT: Coordinator of Government Activities in the Territories
EU: European Union
IDF: Israel Defense Forces
ISIS: Islamic State of Iraq and Syria
NGO: Non-governmental organization
October 7: October 7, 2023
PA: Palestinian Authority
PIJ: Palestinian Islamic Jihad
PLO: Palestine Liberation Organization
UN: United Nations
UNRWA: United Nations Relief and Works Agency

PART I

Palestinian Rejectionism

Revolution Until Victory
—Fatah slogan, ca. 1967

We don't want peace. We want war, victory.
—Yasir Arafat, Palestinian leader, 1972

Palestinians "have never missed a chance of losing an opportunity."
—Abba Eban, Israeli politician, 1983

WORLD WAR II ENDED IN 1945, but Second Lt. Hiroo Onoda of the Imperial Japanese Army rejected many attempts in the following years to inform him of Japan's surrender. Instead, he continued to fight a guerilla campaign for Emperor Hirohito from hiding places in the jungles on the Philippine island of Lubang until 1974. During that twenty-nine-year period, he senselessly murdered about one Filipino and injured three others per year, plus he damaged and stole property. Only when his former commander traveled to Lubang and ordered Onoda to give up did the aging soldier accept that his emperor had acknowledged defeat and therefore he, too, must lay down arms, which he finally did.

The Palestinians of the West Bank, Gaza, and eastern Jerusalem are Onoda writ large, emulating the grizzled, vicious soldier. They, too, battle on for a failed cause, destroying property, murdering senselessly, and ignoring repeated calls to end hostilities. Just as Onoda attacked on behalf of a supposed divine emperor, they inhabit a fantasy world that promises an awe-inspiring new order through acts of wholesale destruction, one in which Jesus was a Palestinian, Jerusalem was always exclusively Islamic, and Israel is on the verge of collapse.[1]

Expressing this ambition, every year or two, Palestinian leaders initiate a spasm of unprovoked violence against Israelis, usually invoking a conspiracy theory (the favorite: "Al-Aqsa [Mosque] is in danger"). The violence, initiated in the spirit of Hiroo Onoda, might involve stone-throwing in the West Bank, knife stabbings in Jerusalem, car-rammings in Tel Aviv, or massacring hordes streaming out of Gaza. With time, the paroxysm peters out, only to start up again at a later time.

Whence comes this inexhaustible passion for destruction? What sustains it? And what weakens it? Answers require going back nearly one-and-a-half centuries.

---

1 Iranian dictator Ali Khamenei has helpfully provided the precise date when Israel will vaporize: September 9, 2040. His acolytes built a large doomsday clock to count down the days—which unfortunately, due to a power outage, has stopped running on at least one occasion.

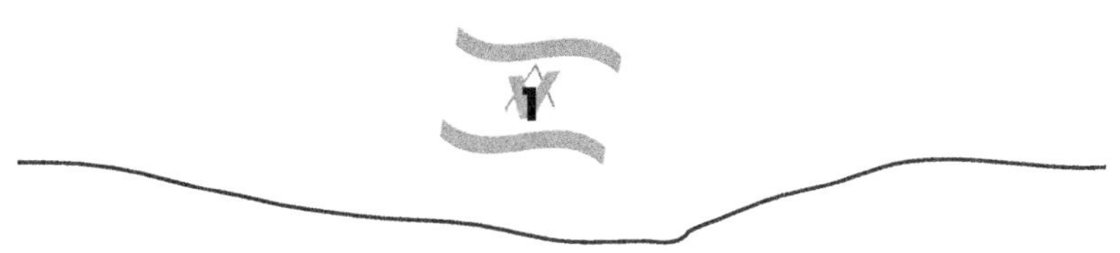

EXPLAINING THE VIRULENCE

PALESTINIAN POLITICAL CULTURE IS UNIQUE in its undying genocidal radicalism. In all the world and in all of history, nothing resembles the fanaticism of the campaign by Palestinians against Jews near and far. The Middle East Forum's Hussein Aboubakr Mansour correctly sees "the absolute and final negation of Zionism, by any means necessary" as "the most central problem of the Palestinian-Israeli conflict." I call this *rejectionism*: an unconditional refusal to accept any aspect of Jewish presence in Palestine. Rejectionism denies Jewish ties to the Land of Israel, fights Jewish ownership of that land, rejects Jewish political power, refuses to trade with Zionists, murders them where possible, and allies with any foreign power, including Nazi Germany, Soviet Russia, Saddam Hussein's Iraq, and Khomeinist Iran, to destroy them.[1]

That a Palestinian leader helped to convince Hitler not to expel Jews but murder them in the Final Solution offers one indication of its uniqueness; the attempt to strangle Israel at birth offers another; its century-plus-long endurance a third.

What has rejectionism achieved for the welfare of Palestinians? Not much, with most of them living under PA or Hamas dictatorships. The happy few live in eastern Jerusalem under Israel's democracy. Despite this bleak record, rejectionism remains strong. And that determination demands explanation.

---

1 Rejectionism has two variants. The hard approach works explicitly for the destruction of Israel. The soft approach calls for a bi-national state that strips Israel of its Jewish identity, encourages Muslim immigration, and eventually turns "Israel" into "Palestine." The latter variant tends to pop up only during "peace process" negotiations. This study focuses on the former variant.

HISTORY

Early hostility to Zionism. Local opposition to modern Zionism emerged immediately but had limited form, with disputes in the 1870s limited to issues such as rights to grazing and water. It took about thirty years for both sides to begin to realize that those disputes had a larger nature. Zionists denied this reality while Palestinians were slow to see Zionism as something distinct from broader European incursions.

The very first modern Jewish settlement in Palestine began in 1870, when the Paris-based Alliance Israélite Universelle purchased land for Mikveh Yisrael, a Jewish agricultural school, on the authority of no less than a decree (*firman*) of the Ottoman sultan. But the peasants of a neighboring village, having long farmed the land, viewed it as their own property. They accosted the Ottoman governor of Damascus, demanding that he annul the sale. In this early clash lay the seeds of what followed.

Many more battles over rights to farming, grazing, trespassing, water, and building repeated in the following years, setting off rounds of violence that turned fiercer over time. The first large-scale Palestinian attack on Zionists took place at Petah Tikva in 1886, leading to "widespread destruction, vandalism, and looting, including the loss of all its animals and the uprooting of newly planted trees," as described by Alan Dowty of Notre Dame University. The first Zionist was shot and killed in 1890 and the first Palestinian fell dead in 1896. But these remained strictly local problems.

Opposition to Zionism began to coalesce over time. The first declaration of pan-Arabism (or Arab nationalism), Negib Azoury's pathbreaking 1905 book, *The Awakening of the Arab Nation*, informed readers that "Our movement comes just at the moment when Israel [i.e., Jewry] is so close to succeeding in its plans for universal domination." Anti-Zionism was expressed through the dual phenomenon of intense romanticism about the land ("This is Palestine; transformed into a sacred shrine/So kiss its soil, wet with dew) and dehumanizing slogans about Zionists ("Palestine is our land and the Jews are our dogs"). Restricting immigration and retaining control of land topped the issues, followed by countering the official use of Hebrew and limiting Zionist power on municipal councils.

Then the larger picture became clear. As Slovak scholar Emanuel Beška writes, "the months at the end of 1910 and the first half of 1911 represent the turning point in the attitudes of the educated Arab public toward Jewish land purchases in Palestine, Jewish immigration, and the

Zionist movement." That turning point had a decidedly negative quality: "a number of Arab journalists, notables, and officers became involved in anti-Zionist activities and campaigns; and the quantity of articles critical of Zionism published in the Arabic press markedly increased."

Such views jelled in World War I and its aftermath. As a gesture to win Jewish support in World War I, the British government in 1917 issued the Balfour Declaration designating Palestine as the "national home for the Jewish people." In March 1920, the first major, fatal communal violence took place when Arabs attacked a Jewish village, leading to thirteen deaths. In April 1920, London received the League of Nations' Mandate for Palestine with the goal of establishing the "national home for the Jewish people" promised in the Balfour Declaration. By the end of 1920, Muslim Arabic-speaking peoples living in the mandate hesitantly and for the first time began to see themselves as *Palestinians* rather than Syrians, Arabic speakers, or Muslims.

• • •

Amin al-Husseini. In May 1921, the British authorities appointed a young and unqualified Amin al-Husseini (ca. 1895–1974) as mufti (Islamic legal authority) of Jerusalem, and inadvertently crowned him as the first Palestinian leader. As German scholar Klaus Gensicke explains, Husseini's "hatred of Jews knew no mercy and he always intervened with particular zeal whenever he feared that some of the Jews could escape annihilation." The effects of that appointment reverberate to this day.

Husseini's rejectionist ideas had three probable sources. First, he lived in the context of a Bedouin tradition of annihilation. The long-serving British consul James Finn, who lived in Jerusalem from 1845 to 1872, captured this Bedouin rapaciousness, especially vis-à-vis settled peoples:

> None but those who have seen it can appreciate the devastation wrought in a few hours by these wild hordes. Like locusts they spread over the land, and their camels, only too glad to revel upon the luxury of green food, strip every leaf off the vines, and devour, while they trample down, all corn or vegetable crops, leaving bare brown desolation where years of toil had made smiling fields and vineyards. Nor is this all, for the cattle and flocks are swept off to the desert by the marauders

> who leave behind, for the unfortunate peasant, nothing that they can carry away.

And what nomads did not finish off, the villagers did themselves. Israeli scholar Arieh Avneri recounts instances "when the defeated themselves destroyed their property, uprooted their vineyards and their olive groves, burned and destroyed anything they could not take with them, and went into exile. They left behind scorched earth."

Rejectionism's second source derived from a half-century of growing Palestinian versus Zionist strife, noted above. Third, Husseini served as a politically aware officer in the Ottoman army during World War I, geographically not far from what the U.S. House of Representatives later called the Turks' "campaign of genocide against Armenians, Greeks, Assyrians, Chaldeans, Syriacs, Arameans, Maronites, and other Christians."

Bedouin, peasants, and Turks: Through them and perhaps other sources, Husseini developed a monstrous hostility toward Jews. Soon after World War I ended, he told a Jewish colleague of Syrian descent, Isaac Abraham Abbady, "This was and will remain Arab land. We do not mind you [Jewish] natives of the country, but those alien invaders, the Zionists, will be massacred to the last man.... Nothing but the sword will decide the future of this country." That phrase, "massacred to the last man," serves well as Husseini's slogan. He frequently reiterated this point in the following decades, asserting that Palestinians would "continue to fight until the Zionists are eliminated and the whole of Palestine is a purely Arab state."

In this uncompromising campaign, Husseini used any and all tactics. He organized and encouraged unprovoked violence against the British and the Jews, including a three-year long *intifada* (uprising), known as the Arab Revolt, from 1936 to 1939. He promoted the antisemitic blood libel and the *Protocols of the Elders of Zion* forgery, made Jerusalem into a flashpoint, and was probably the first Muslim leader to call for *jihad* (religious war of Muslims against unbelievers in accordance with Islamic law) against Zionists. Husseini lived in Germany during the war years, 1941 to 1945, and proved so useful that he earned an audience with Hitler. Nor was that a courtesy visit; as Israel's Prime Minister Binyamin Netanyahu pointed out, based on the study by Barry Rubin and Wolfgang G. Schwanitz, *Nazis, Islamists, and the Making of the Modern Middle East*,[2] Husseini had a central

2 New Haven, Conn.: Yale University Press, 2014.

role in formulating the Final Solution that led to the murder of six million Jews. Thus did he and the Nazis mutually radicalize each other.

• • •

Husseini's legacy. Husseini mentored the young Yasir Arafat (1929–2004), perhaps his relative, who for forty-five years from 1959 faithfully carried out the mufti's genocidal program as head of many institutions, including Fatah, the Palestine Liberation Organization (PLO), and the Palestinian Authority. Arafat flaunted rejectionism throughout his career, even after ostensibly accepting Israel in the Oslo Accords: "We plan to eliminate the State of Israel and establish a purely Palestinian state. We will make life unbearable for Jews by psychological warfare and population explosion," he announced in 1996. "We Palestinians will take over everything, including all of Jerusalem." The PLO spin-off, the PA, announced: "We'll liberate our land from [Israel]. It won't remain at all. Not a single settler, Israeli, or Jew will remain in our land."

Husseini spent the post-war years in Egypt, where he influenced the Muslim Brotherhood. Its founder, Hassan al-Banna, declared that "Israel will exist and will continue to exist until Islam will obliterate it, just as it obliterated others before it." Hamas, the Brotherhood's 1987 spin-off in Gaza, also continues with Husseini's hallmark genocidal rejectionism. In a typical statement, Fathi Hammad, a member of the Hamas political bureau, threatened in 2019:

> There are Jews everywhere! We must attack every Jew on planet Earth—we must slaughter and kill them, with Allah's help.... I say to those in the West Bank: How long will you sit in silence? You can buy knives for five shekels! How much is the neck of a Jew worth to us—isn't it worth five shekels, or even less?... We will die while exploding and cutting the necks and legs of the Jews! We will lacerate them and tear them to pieces, Allah willing.

The PLO and Hamas, both Husseini derivatives, competed to win Palestinian allegiance, with the former an ideological chameleon and the latter determinedly Islamist (seeking to apply Islamic law under a caliph). Their differences widened in 1993, when Arafat formally recognized Israel in the Oslo Accords; the 1988 Hamas Charter had stated that "so-called peaceful solutions and international conferences" contradict its principles. That disagreement over tactics henceforth bifurcated rejectionism. The PA argues for negotiating with Israel, lowering the Zionists' guard, winning concessions, then pounding Israel through violence and international delegitimization. Hamas sticks to consistent, old-style violent rejectionism.

All six of the major Palestinian leaders so far—Amin al-Husseini, Ahmad al-Shukeiri (the first PLO leader), Yasir Arafat, Mahmoud Abbas, Ahmed Yassin (the founder of Hamas), and Yahya Sinwar (the architect of October 7)—made destroying the Zionist presence their only goal. Whatever their differences in outlook, personnel, and tactics, nearly all major Palestinian organizations—Fatah, the Popular Front for the Liberation of Palestine, the Palestine Liberation Organization, the Palestinian Authority, Hamas, and Palestinian Islamic Jihad—are lineal descendants of Amin al-Husseini. "Massacred to the last man" remains their slogan.

Husseini's efforts played a large part in the Arab states' decision to go to war with Israel. Of particular importance was the General Islamic Congress he hosted in Jerusalem in 1931, which launched the Palestinian issue as a pan-Islamic concern and helped to imbue the Arab states with their own form of rejectionism. Abdul Rahman Azzam (1893–1976) provides one example of this transmission. He participated in the congress, was elected to its executive committee, and in 1945 became the first secretary-general of the Arab League. In that capacity, he was the one to reject any compromise with the Zionists in 1947, asserting instead that the Arab states were hungry for war with the budding Jewish state: "The Arab world regards you as invaders and is ready to fight you. The conflict of interests among nations is, for the most part, not amenable to any settlement except armed clash." Azzam became notorious for calling on the eve of Israel's independence for "a war of extermination and a momentous massacre which will be spoken of like the Mongolian massacres and the Crusades."

Nor was Azzam alone. In response to the UN vote creating Israel, Amin al-Husseini's relative Jamal promised that "blood will flow like rivers" as Palestinians and their allies abort the nascent Jewish state. Ismail Safwat, the coordinator of Arab state forces attacking Israel in 1948– 1949, defined the war aim: "to eliminate the Jews of Palestine and to completely cleanse the country of them."

True to their word, Palestinians and their Arab state allies ethnically cleansed every Jew from the mandatory territories they controlled—

including villages, Jerusalem's outskirts, and the ancient Jewish Quarter of Jerusalem's Old City. (About a million more Jews were subsequently expelled from or forced to flee their homes in Arabic-speaking countries from Morocco to Iraq.)

How important was Husseini? His influence over Palestinians and Islamists means that his legacy still dominates the Palestinian-Israeli arena a half-century after his death. Zvi Elpeleg, a biographer of Husseini, finds that "his influence on the refusal to accept the existence of a Jewish state was greater than that of any other leader." *Middle East Quarterly* editor Efraim Karsh concludes: "Just as the Holocaust might have well not happened without Hitler, just as tens of millions of Russians and Chinese might not have perished without Stalin and Mao, so Palestinian Arabs might not have followed a course of anti-Jewish hatred and incessant conflict without Husseini."

REJECTIONISM'S ABIDING POWER

Even as the small and vulnerable Yishuv (the pre-state Jewish community in Palestine) grew into the affluent and powerful country of Israel, Palestinian attitudes stayed remarkably stationary, ever refusing to accept Jews, Judaism, Zionists, and Israelis, fantasizing about destroying the state and terminating the Jewish presence. Palestinian identity became inextricably tied to rejectionism, which survived the Balfour Declaration, the establishment of the State of Israel, the retreat of Arab states, the Soviet collapse, and much else. Wars and treaties came and went, personnel changed, ideologies, objectives, tactics, and strategies evolved, all leaving little impact on the core goal. This remarkable constancy does not get the attention it deserves.

• • •

Expressions. Rejectionism manifests itself via its drive to kill Israelis and eliminate Israel.

Killing Israelis. The assault on individual Israelis has wide popular support, with the "street" probably yet more enthusiastic than its leadership. Instructional videos on social media teach Palestinians on how best to murder Israelis, whether by knife or gun. The killing of Israelis meets with rapture. To cite one example, after a bomb went off at the Hebrew University in Jerusalem in 2002, killing nine and wounding eighty-seven, thousands of Gazans celebrated by marching in the streets, shouting slogans, and brandishing firearms to express their delight.

This phenomenon reaches its apex when parents express joy—to all appearance sincere—on learning of their children's demise while attacking Israelis. Ibrahim Al-Nabulsi, eighteen, engaged in drive-by shootings of Israeli soldiers and civilians, and helped to found the violent anti-Israel West Bank gang called the Lion's Den; when the Israel Defense Forces (IDF) came for him in 2022, he fought a gun battle and ended up dead. Thousands then attended his funeral and an informal shrine emerged at his place of death, complete with the moldy remnants of his last meal. His father Alaa, fifty-three, a "colonel" in the PA "security services," was tasked with catching criminals precisely such as his son; despite this role, Alaa approved of his son's actions. "As a father, it was hard for me to tell him not to get involved in this. What else could I tell him? That it's OK to live a life of humiliation?" More ebulliently, he added, "Ibrahim was hunting them, not the other way around. Whenever he heard about an Israeli army raid, he was the first to go out and confront them. This was his fate. We praise God." Ibrahim's mother spoke enthusiastically of her son's death while making the V-for-victory sign: "Ibrahim triumphed. My son, who is dearer to me than my own soul, has returned to his lord." She added elegiacally about his message to Palestinian children:

> Ibrahim wanted to send a message to a specific group—to the children, who will be brought up on jihad, Allah willing. When these children see the *mujahid* [fighter of jihad] as a humble, loving, and truthful person who does not eat anything that is *haram* [forbidden], they are going to love jihad, thanks to Allah, and jihad will become their way of life. Even if they do not learn it at school, they are going to learn it from their role model—people who are wanted [by Israel]. Thanks to Allah, Ibrahim got his message across.

In another case, the mother of Hassan al-Qatanani, who murdered an Israeli mother and her two daughters, boasted of his actions:

> He loved martyrdom. He would say to me, day and night, "Mom, I want to be martyred." He would kiss my hand and say, "Pray to Allah that I will be martyred." I would say: "May

> Allah give you what you want, *inshallah* [if it please God]." Praise be to Allah for granting him what he wanted.... Anyone with courage in his heart cannot accept what the Jews did to us. We should fight them with our children, with our money, with our families, with our fingernails. We should devour the Jews with our teeth.

As a Gaza Islamic scholar and the father of dead child put it, "Our children...are dear to us, but Palestine and Islam are dearer and more important." Such perversity staggers.

Murderers of Israelis have a sacred status in Abbas' PA. Referring to them as martyrs, Abbas declared that, "Even if we have only a penny left, we will give it to the martyrs, the prisoners, and their families. We view the prisoners and the martyrs as planets and stars in the skies of the Palestinian struggle, and they have priority in everything."

Destruction of Israel. Palestinians are not shy about their intent not just to eliminate the State of Israel but to destroy it, a legacy of Bedouin, peasant, and Turkish annihilationism. The never-amended 1968 charter of the PLO states that "the liberation of Palestine will destroy the Zionist and imperialist presence." Yasir Arafat said in 1972, "Peace for us means the destruction of Israel and nothing else," and repeated this sentiment in 1980: "Peace for us means the destruction of Israel." Yahya Sinwar announced in 2021 that "God has decreed that we must attack Tel Aviv," and promised that Hamas with its allies can "destroy" the city.

The plans can get more specific. In May 2023, the PA endorsed PIJ's Khalil al-Bahtini speaking of an intent "to blow up all of the Zionist entity's cities." Just ahead of October 7, Hamas leader Saleh al-Arouri explained how, in the next war, Hamas will close Israel's air and sea spaces, shut down its electricity, water, and communication services, and close the economy.

As a well-known rhyming Palestinian slogan in Arabic puts it: "Our struggle with the Jews/Is a struggle of existence, not of borders." When an American in mid-2019 asked Mohammad Shtayyeh, the PA "prime minister," for his proposal to remedy relations with Israel, Shtayyeh went silent. In other words, Israel cannot ever satisfy the PA. Consistent with this, Hassan al-Kashef, director-general of the Palestinian "information ministry," has argued for the only contact with Israelis being to demoralize them through violence.

Nor are these empty threats. In 1948, on taking the Jewish Quarter of Jerusalem, Jordanian forces engaged in what Israel later termed "the wanton destruction of all but one of the thirty-five Jewish houses of worship that... had graced the Old City for centuries." In the early 1950s, Palestinian leader Musa al-Alami built a large experimental farm that employed thousands of "Palestine refugees" near Jericho boasting 10,000 banana trees, 12,000 other trees, 16,000 vines, 400 dunams of cotton, 400 dunams of vegetables, fields of grain, and 80,000 fowl. The farm also included a clinic, a school, and a swimming pool. But because this farm contradicted the rejectionist imperative that refugees not be settled outside Israel, many Palestinians saw its efforts at economic self-sufficiency as a plot to accommodate Israel's existence. The anger exploded in 1955, when thousands of Palestinians attacked the farm, burnt it to the ground, brutalized its residents, and tried to murder Alami. A half-century later, in 2005, a group of American Jewish donors purchased the intact high-tech greenhouses that the Israelis had left behind following their retreat from Gaza, and donated this infrastructure to Gazans; in the old spirit, the Gazans looted and destroyed it. *Vae victis.*

Palestinians widely express support for destroying the Jewish state. Surveying 400 Palestinian opinion polls over 12 years, Israeli historian Daniel Polisar found that, "Since 2005, regardless of the methodology and the precise wording of the questions, the maximalist option has won every time, usually by large margins," where the maximalist option means "a Palestinian or Islamic state from the Jordan River to the Mediterranean Sea," that is, a Palestine replacing Israel. Indeed, a steady 80 percent of Palestinians have believed over the past century that they can destroy the Jewish state. David Pollock of the Washington Institute for Near East Policy further finds that Palestinian attitudes toward Israel have become more ambitious over time. Whereas in 2015, 56 percent of West Bank residents and 44 percent of Gazans endorsed the two-state solution, that is, accepted Israel at least temporarily, those numbers declined in 2020 to 9 percent and 21 percent, respectively, a massive reduction.

• • •

Tactics. Novel tactics, such as creating a permanent refugee population and a supersessionist ideology, go far to keep rejectionism vibrant.

Refugees. Rejectionism has spawned a population of "Palestine refugees" unwilling to accept loss in war and go on to reconstruct their lives. Instead, and against their own interests, they blindly insist on getting back to their own or their ancestors' properties. Starting a new, normal life outside Israel equals betraying the cause. Only the permanent refugee status is valid, with its culture of dependency and rage. This pattern was set as soon as Israel came into existence. Reflecting on the Alami experimental farm destruction cited above, Israeli authors Adi Schwartz and Einat Wilf conclude:

> Faced with a choice between humiliation from a life of poverty and adversity in the refugee camps and the perceived humiliation of accepting Israel as a fait accompli, the refugees chose to remain in the camps.... The refugees were fully conscious in the choice they made: no to the state of Israel, even at the cost of staying in the camps forever.

That rejectionist spirit inspired Palestinians to transform the United Nations agency dedicated to refugee welfare, the UN Relief and Works Agency for Palestine Refugees (UNRWA), into a large and permanent bureaucracy that purposefully keeps them mired in the refugee status. In contrast to all other refugee populations, which diminish in number as people settle or die, UNRWA expands the number of refugees over time.[3] Thus, an infant born in Syria in 2024—if of the right parentage—may carry refugee status. UNRWA itself proudly acknowledges this bizarre phenomenon: "When the Agency started working in 1950, it was responding to the needs of about 750,000 Palestine refugees. Today, some 5.9 million Palestine refugees are eligible for UNRWA services."

By normal counting, the number of genuine refugees, who were born the latest in 1949, decreases by the day. My actuarial estimate puts their number in 2024 at about 10,000—0.2 percent of those holding this status. When the last genuine refugee from Mandatory Palestine dies, presumably in the 2050s, the pseudo-refugees will continue to proliferate and the

3 This magic happens via four major steps that expand the definition of a "Palestine refugee." First, UNRWA allows those who become citizens of a state (Jordan in particular) to remain refugees. Second, it extends the definition to "descendants of Palestine refugee males, including legally adopted children." Third, it adds refugees from the Six-Day War; today they constitute about a fifth of the total. Finally, it treats many residents of the West Bank and Gaza as refugees, even though the two-state-solution implies that they are already home.

"Palestine refugee" status will, at current rates, swell indefinitely. Steven J. Rosen of the Middle East Forum has sardonically noted that, "given UNRWA's standards, eventually all humans will be Palestine refugees."

Alone among the masses of dislocated peoples in the years surrounding World War II, Palestinians are frozen in the status of refugee—in some cases, unto the fifth generation. The other estimated one hundred million refugees from that era, including my parents, settled in their new homes many decades ago, making it unimaginable that I, much less my children, should consider ourselves refugees. Only "Palestine refugees" stew in "refugee camps" in a self-perpetrated and willful descent into poverty, indignity, futility, stagnancy, grievance, and nihilism, suffering from the ravages of lives truncated and distorted by an impossible and ugly "right of return" intended to destroy the Jewish state. This anomaly of ever-proliferating phony refugees has a plain purpose: to sustain rejectionism through the fantasy of a mass "return" while sharpening an ever-larger dagger at Israel's throat.

Paradoxically, Palestinians' attitudes became more extreme as they weakened relative to their enemy. It started as a dispute over land and water rights. It turned into a nationalist rivalry. It became a rejectionist ideology. It acquired a genocidal dimension. Finally, it acquired a supersessionist ideology, that of Islamic Zionism.

ISLAMIC ZIONISM

The creation of a counter-narrative to Zionism sustains rejectionism and helps to explain its growing extremism.

• • •

The uniqueness of Jewish Zionism. Many millions of modern Westerners emigrated to settle in the Americas, in Africa, in Australia, and parts beyond. But no emigration resembled that of Jews to Zion. Those others involved setting out to new, mostly unfamiliar places. Only Jews had maintained a remnant in their ancient, indigenous homeland despite millennia of imperial conquests and colonial settlements. Only Jews continuously immigrated to their homeland, even acquiring temporary autonomy (in Tiberias in the mid-sixteenth century) within it. Only Jews saw their destination as a land endowed with sacred attributes. Only Jews longed for the land of immigration in daily prayers, annual religious occasions ("Next year in Jerusalem"), and life-cycle events. Only Jews revived their ancient spoken language used in that land and made it the new lingua franca. Only Jews re-established national sovereignty over their ancestral home.

When one party longs for an object, others naturally also come to value it more. Thus did Jewish nationalism inspire Palestinian nationalism. Were it not for another people who saw Palestine as their "national home," its residents would have continued to view this area as a province of something larger, whether Greater Syria, the Arab nation, or the Muslim community. If not for Jewish aspirations, Muslim attitudes toward Palestine would no doubt have resembled their indifference toward the territory of Transjordan, a coolness only slowly eroded by many years of governmental effort by Amman. Palestinian nationalism promised the most direct way to deal with the challenge presented by Zionist immigrants—a challenge not felt on the East Bank.

Starting around 1900, Muslims living in Palestine responded by following suit, by developing their own version of a love for Zion—a phenomenon I call *Islamic Zionism*.[4] As Zionists articulated a vision of Palestine becoming the Jewish national home, Islamic Zionists turned Palestine into a lost Islamic idyll. As Jews returned to the land of milk and honey, Palestinians devised an intense longing for the land of orange groves and olive trees. As Jews established the State of Israel, Palestinians demanded to replace it with a State of Palestine.

This newfound Muslim passion for Jerusalem and Palestine, scholar of Islam Khalid Durán notes, amounts to an "attempt to Islamize Zionism… in the sense that the importance of Jerusalem to Jews and their attachment to it is now usurped by Palestinian Muslims." As Islamic Zionism ascended among Palestinians, this ultimate act of cultural and national appropriation acquired a surreal intensity that spewed a toxic loathing for the original Zionism, denying its history and seeking its destruction, as expressed through genocidal rejectionism.

Just as Israel is no mere plot of land for Jews, Palestine acquired a paramount meaning for Palestinians. Zionists and their supporters see the establishment of Israel as a quasi-messianic event of epic importance, as Winston

4 Alternatively, it might be called *Muslim Zionism* or *Palestinian Zionism*. Unlike Christian Zionism, which supports the Jewish return to Zion, Islamic Zionism competes with and refutes it.

Churchill articulated in 1948: "The coming into being of the Jewish state in Palestine is an event in world history to be viewed in the perspective not of a generation, or a century, but in the perspective of 1,000, 2,000, or even 3,000 years." In opposition, naturally, Palestinians see Israel's destruction as no less quasi-messianic, turning that conflagration into the resurgence of Palestinian pride, Arab identity, Muslim power, and the defeat of Western (that is, Christian) imperialism.

For Mahmoud Darwish, called the Palestinian national poet, the territory's loss to Israel represents the fall from grace, the bitterness of exile, and the loss of power. George Habash, leader of the Popular Front for the Liberation of Palestine, stated that, "The Palestinian revolution is a stage in the world revolution." Similarly, Yasir Arafat claimed his PLO to be "part of the world revolution which aims at establishing social justice and liberating mankind." Iran's Supreme Leader Ali Khamenei called Israel's destruction "the most important cause of the [Iranian] revolution" while its President Ebrahim Raisi described it as "the most important issue of the World of Islam today." Important eschatological Muslim writers connect the seizure of Jerusalem from Jewish control and the destruction of Israel to the End Times.

• • •

Denying Jewish history. The logic of Islamic Zionism requires that Palestinians deny Jerusalem's sacred and historical importance to Jews and erase all Jewish connections to the Land of Israel, replacing them with a Palestinian heritage. Toward this end, the nationalist Palestinian establishment of scholars, clerics, and politicians has constructed a revisionist edifice made up in equal parts of fabrication, falsehood, fiction, and fraud.[5] It draws on two main sources: pre-Israelite history, and the Zionist storehouse of longing for the Land of Israel. Its confused account includes inconsistent and even contradictory elements, all deployed in the supreme effort to deny a Jewish connection.

Some components of this brew include: The ancient Hebrews were Bedouin tribesmen. The Bible came from Arabia. Instead of Moses taking the Israelites to the Promised Land, Musa (a common name in Arabic)

5 For greater detail, see Yitzhak Reiter, *Jerusalem and Its Role in Islamic Solidarity* (New York: Palgrave Macmillan, 2008), especially Chapter 4.

led Arabic-speaking Muslims to Palestine. Biblical figures are turned into Muslims. Any Jewish presence in Palestine ended in 70 CE. Today's Ashkenazi Jews descend from the Khazar Turks.

Amin al-Husseini called the Western Wall a "purely Muslim place" to which Jews have no "connection or right or claim." Mahmoud Abbas says the Israelis have "been digging for 30 years to find any evidence or proof of the existence" of Jewish ties to the Temple Mount but "they haven't found anything. [It] belongs exclusively to the Muslims." The political implication is clear: Jews lack any rights to Jerusalem. As a street banner puts it: "Jerusalem is Arab." Jews are unwelcome intruders.

Palestinians claim to predate the Jews by invoking an imaginary lineage to the Canaanites, thereby predating the Israelites; thus, Saeb Erekat of the PLO claimed to be "a son of Jericho, aged 10,000 years.... I am the proud son of Canaanites, and I existed 5,000 years ago." Arafat invoked an imaginary Canaanite king, Salem, and spoke movingly about this Palestinian "forefather" after whom "the monumental city" of Jerusalem was supposedly named.

The Jebusites, a Canaanite people whom the Bible indicate controlled Jerusalem before King David's conquest of the city for the Jews, play a special role in Islamic Zionism. Claiming Jebusite heritage allows Palestinians to argue that they preceded Jews in Palestine and that therefore the area belongs to them alone. Arafat asserted that "Our forefathers, the Canaanites and Jebusites, built the cities and planted the land; they built the monumental city of Bir Salim [Jerusalem]." PLO leader Faisal Husseini insisted, "I am a Palestinian. I am a descendant of the Jebusites, the ones who came before King David."

Palestinian leaders also stress continuity from ancient times. The PA mufti, Muhammad Hussein, claimed that Palestinians "have been firmly established upon this land [of Palestine] since the Canaanite era." Mahmoud al-Habash, the PA's supreme Shariah judge focused on Jerusalem:

> Our forefathers and historical lineage, the Jebusite Canaanites, built Jebus, Jerusalem, the City of Peace—the Canaanites called it the City of Peace—5,000 years ago. Our presence in Jerusalem has not ceased for 5,000 years. Nations and occupations have passed through, and colonialism, whether brief or long. It came and left, but the people of Jerusalem stayed. These transients will move on, while the people of Jerusalem

> will stay. They have no place in Jerusalem. Jerusalem is ours, not theirs.

Responding to a quote attributed to Benjamin Netanyahu that Jews have historical rights to the Land of Israel dating back to 3000 BCE, an Abbas representative, Abdullah al-Ifranji, retorted that "the people of Palestine have a history in the land of Canaan going back to 7000 BCE."

According to this account, Canaanites built Solomon's Temple in Jerusalem. If a Jewish Temple existed, it was elsewhere. Sometime in the early 1950s, the Temple Mount's Islamic authorities deleted the references to Solomon's Temple that had appeared in its earlier guide books. The PA mufti, Ikrama Sabri, told an Israeli reporter in 1998, "I heard that your Temple was in Nablus or perhaps Bethlehem." Two years later, Arafat more assertively told Bill Clinton, "Solomon's Temple was not in Jerusalem, but Nablus." At other times, even Nablus is excluded; a PA spokesman stated that "There is no historical proof—despite all the excavations—that [the Jews] had any kind of presence in this land" of Palestine.

The emphasis on Canaan leads to curious results, such as the PA's "Ministry of Culture" staging a historical drama in the West Bank town of Sabastia in 1996 concerning the polytheistic god Ba'al, lord of fertility and weather. It dressed up young Palestinians in costumes to enact a passion play in which Ba'al emerged supreme, defeating the Israelites. Israeli journalist Ehud Ya'ari witnessed and described the event:

> Young people—in flowing robes tailored especially for the event, decorated with Canaanite motifs, on light wooden chariots built according to specifications from drawings found in the Megiddo excavations—made their way through Sabastia's narrow alleyways to a stone stage in the center of the village. There, they recreated the legend of Ba'al, the supreme Canaanite god, and his struggle with his brother Mut, god of the underworld. In the end, Ba'al emerged victorious with the help of his sister Anat, the goddess of war. The narrator of the text put special emphasis on the warning against the "Habiru" tribes (the Hebrews), who were moving into the land.

To top it off, Bakr Abu Bakr, a member of Fatah's Revolutionary Council, calls the historic "Children of Israel" an "Arab tribe that became extinct." Present-day Israelis, in contrast, "have no connection to them," but are European colonialists who justify stealing land from Palestinians by pretending to be descendants of the ancient Israelites. One children's textbook explains that Israelis are "foreigners who came from all ends of the earth, foreigners who did not know Palestine and did not live in it—neither them nor their fathers and forefathers." In an audacious act of cultural arrogation, another PA schoolbook asserts that the "Zionist occupation" appropriated Canaanite names and thereby "has stolen the Palestinian national heritage and history." Tell es-Sultan consists of archeological ruins dating back to 2600 BCE near Jericho and considered the world's oldest town; when a United Nations organization listed it as a "World Heritage Site in Palestine," Mahmoud Abbas approvingly commented that this action "testifies to the authenticity and history of the Palestinian people."

Denial of Jewish history goes beyond words to the destruction of archeological evidence that ties Jews to the Land of Israel. For example, the PA in May 2023 initiated construction work at El-Unuk, an Early Iron Age site connected to the Israelite entry into Palestine, deleting its information about the Jewish presence.

Given that this cocktail of claims relies on biblical history, it depends for authentication (ironically) on the Jewish Bible. When an assertive Brazilian journalist said to Arafat in 1991, "You are struggling for an entity—the Palestine state—that, from a historic and geographical viewpoint, has never existed," Arafat gave a weirdly Zionist-like reply: "You must read the Bible because it contains abundant historic references that demonstrate the existence of a cultural and geopolitical Palestinian identity for many thousands of years."

Dependence on the Bible implies that Islamic Zionism contradicts the mainstream Muslim understanding of history, which looks to the Koran for validation. Issam Amira, a prominent Palestinian Islamist associated with the Hizb ut-Tahrir movement, ridicules the "Canaanite roots" claim:

> The people of Palestine have no historical right to Palestine. They have no right that dates back 2,000, 3,000, or 4,000 years...our history is simple and it is not ancient. Our history dates back only 1,440 [lunar] years [to the Battle of Yarmouk in 636 CE when Muslims conquered Palestine]. 1,440 years ago we had no rights of any kind. Absolutely none.

Amira condemns Arafat, saying that he "cursed his own people" by making Canaanite claims and instructing Palestinians that Islam is their only identity. This criticism points to the limitations and vulnerability of Islamic Zionism.

Nonetheless, it prevails today. Palestinian Media Watch, an Israeli organization, sums up the procedure: The PA "takes authentic Jewish history, documented by thousands of years of continuous literature, and crosses out the word 'Jewish' and replaces it with the word 'Arab.'" Just as Islam makes a supersessionist claim to replace Judaism, so Islamic Zionism makes a supersessionist claim to replace Jewish Zionism. Just as Muslims scorn Judaism as riddled with distortion (*tahrif*), Palestinians scorn Jewish Zionism as fraudulent.

This concoction then drives Palestinian emotions and politics.

• • •

Eternal Jerusalem. The Koran mentions neither Jerusalem nor Palestine by name but Muslims widely understand both to be included in scripture, making both regions Islamically significant—and further boosting Islamic Zionism.

Jerusalem served as the first *qibla*, the direction toward which Muslims pray, before Mecca replaced it. Verse 17:1 of the Koran refers to the Further Mosque (*al-masjid al-aqsa*) without indicating its location. A caliph subsequently built a mosque in Jerusalem with this name and forevermore Muslims have widely connected these two unrelated facts to associate Jerusalem with their prophet's life, creating a permanent Koranic connection to Jerusalem.

Verse 5:21 quotes Moses calling on the Israelites, "O my people, enter the Holy Land (*al-ard al-muqaddasa*) which God has assigned to you." While the land is presented as holy to Jews, the specialness carries over to Muslims. Haim Gerber of the Hebrew University observes that "a sense of uniqueness and difference from other regions, even from Syria, was no doubt imparted to the inhabitants of Palestine by the basic fact that, following Judaism and Christianity, Islam too considered Palestine a holy land."

When it comes to Jerusalem, Islamic Zionism leads to exact copies of the Jewish prototype:

- *Continuity.* Donniel Hartman of the Shalom Hartman Institute called Jerusalem "one of the few remaining unifying concepts in our deeply divided Jewish world." Arafat waxed poetic about Jerusalem as "the capital of our children and our children's children. If not for this belief and conviction of the Palestinian nation, this people would have been erased from the face of the earth, as were so many other nations."
- *Emotional significance.* Mayor of Jerusalem Ehud Olmert said in 1997 that Jerusalem represents "the purest expression of all that Jews prayed for, dreamed of, cried for, and died for in the 2,000 years since the destruction of the Second Temple." Arafat in 2000 declared that Jerusalem "is in the innermost of our feeling, the feeling of our people and the feeling of all Arabs, Muslims, and Christians."
- *Eternal capital.* Olmert greeted Pope John Paul II on arrival in 2000 with "Welcome to the eternal capital of Jerusalem." Likewise, Israel's President Ezer Weizman welcomed him to "the eternal and indivisible capital of the State of Israel." A day later, Arafat called the pontiff an "esteemed guest of Palestine and its eternal capital, Jerusalem." Hamas also describes Jerusalem as the "eternal capital of the State of Palestine."

When Palestinians appropriate Jerusalem's unique role in Jewish history, religion, politics, and emotions, they retroactively transform the city's minor and transactional place in Islam. In fact, Jerusalem rose and fell as a religious or political focal point of Muslim interest depending on utilitarian needs. When it fulfilled Muslim purposes, the city grew in Muslim esteem and emotions. When those purposes diminished, usually upon Muslims securely controlling it, Muslim interest in it promptly waned. This cyclical pattern repeated six times over fourteen centuries, during the time of Islam's prophet Muhammad, the Umayyads, the early Crusades, the Ayyubids, the British, and the Israelis.

Focusing just on modern times, Ottoman neglect prompted scathing Western responses. For example, French novelist Gustav Flaubert in 1850 described Jerusalem as "Ruins everywhere, and everywhere the odor of graves.... The Holy City of three religions is rotting away from boredom, desertion, and neglect." In 1876, American novelist Herman Melville described the Holy Land as a "caked, depopulated hell." Western visitors to Jerusalem described it as "ruined," "contemptible," "debris-filled," "desolate and miserable," "rotting away from boredom, desertion, and neglect," and "a pauper village" (that last comes from Mark Twain).

This lack of interest ended only with the British conquest in 1917, when Palestinians rediscovered Jerusalem and used it instrumentally to rouse Muslim sentiments against the British and the Zionists. Most notably, Amin al-Husseini convened the Jerusalem General Islamic Congress in 1931 to turn a Palestinian fight into an Islamic issue; as Basheer M. Nafi of the University of Reading explains, the congress' purpose "was to place Palestine on the political agenda of many Islamic nations and forces." Husseini succeeded: "it was an important achievement of the Congress to help transform Palestine into a pan-Arab and pan-Islamic problem."

When Jordanian troops seized the Old City in 1948, however, interest plummeted. Jerusalem became an isolated provincial town, less important than Nablus. The economy stagnated and many thousands of Muslims abandoned the city. Taking out a bank loan, for example, required going to Amman, the capital. The decline in Jerusalem's religious standing was perhaps most insulting to the city. Mosques lacked sufficient funds. Jordanian radio broadcast the Friday prayers not from Al-Aqsa Mosque but from an upstart mosque in Amman.

Jerusalem's importance only revived when the whole city came under Israeli control in 1967, again becoming a focal point of Muslim politics. The PLO's original covenant of 1964, revealingly, made no mention of Jerusalem; the amended version of 1968, after the city fell under Israeli control, called Jerusalem "the seat of the Palestine Liberation Organization." The city's Islamic stature soared. King Faisal of Saudi Arabia had not bothered to visit Jerusalem when he could but now that he could not, he spoke movingly of his yearning to pray there. More surprisingly, he declared it religiously "just like" Mecca—a novel, if not a blasphemous, idea.

Since then, many others—notably Iran's Ayatollah Ruhollah Khomeini, Jordan's King Abdullah II, and Türkiye's President Recep Tayyip Erdoğan—have cried for Jerusalem. A 2017 incident showed the continued international passion for Jerusalem among Muslims. Palestinians smuggled weapons into the Temple Mount and used them to kill two Israeli policemen and wound two others, prompting the Israelis to install metal detectors. The ensuing Palestinian outrage then echoed with loud, unthinking support from Muslim Brotherhood chief theorist Yusuf al-Qaradawi, Jordan's monarch, the Arab League, the Organization of Islamic Cooperation, and beyond.

Indeed, as rival Jerusalem Days suggest, Islamic Zionism can exceed Jewish Zionism. Israel's version commemorates the city's unification under its control in 1967. But, as Israel Harel writes in *Haaretz,* this tribute has declined from a national holiday to just "the holiday of the religious communities." In contrast, the Muslim version of Jerusalem Day—instituted by Khomeini in 1979—attracts crowds of as many as 300,000 people in distant Tehran, is celebrated by Muslims across the United States, and serves as a global platform for rousing anti-Zionist harangues (though it, too, appears to be losing attendance).

Palestinian claims to Jerusalem lead some, especially in the Western media, to pretend that Tel Aviv, not Jerusalem, serves as Israel's capital.[6] The style guide of *The Guardian,* a British newspaper, for years stated that "Jerusalem is not the capital of Israel; Tel Aviv is." Under threat of legal action, the newspaper later corrected this with "it is wrong to state that Tel Aviv—the country's financial and diplomatic centre—is the capital" while still not acknowledging Jerusalem to be the capital, insisting that "Israel's designation of Jerusalem as its capital is not recognised by the international community." The BBC called Tel Aviv the "Israeli capital," as did Canadian television network CTV. Agence France-Presse, *The New York Times,* and *The Washington Post* used "Tel Aviv" as a synonym for Israel's capital. The confusion also reaches into political circles; when questioned about the identity of Israel's capital, Barack Obama's spokesman Jay Carney tied himself into knots as he avoided the self-evident reply.

• • •

Holy Palestine. Islamic Zionism has transformed Palestine even more dramatically than Jerusalem.

Jews have *Eretz Yisrael* ("the Land of Israel") and Christians have *Terra Sancta* ("Holy Land"). Although the Koran also refers to this territory as the Holy Land (*al-ard al-muqaddasa*), Palestine historically had no special status in Islamic tradition and Muslims did not cherish it. Palestine existed neither as a political nor cultural unit during the centuries of Muslim rule over the area. It was not a fixed cartographic entity but a concept without

6 Tel Aviv does host the headquarters of the Ministry of Defense.

formal boundaries like Scandinavia or New England. It usually included territory on both sides of the Jordan River. The only time Palestine existed as a polity was either under the rule of Jews (Judea, Israel) or Christians (Crusader kingdoms, the British empire).

As Princeton scholar Bernard Lewis writes, for Muslims the name *Filastin* "had never meant more than an administrative sub-district and it had been forgotten [after the Crusades] even in that limited sense." Muhammad Y. Muslih of Long Island University notes that, "Under the Ottoman regime (1517–1918), there was no political unit known as Palestine." Long-time British resident Elizabeth Anne Finn explained in 1873 that the peasants of Palestine "speak Arabic, and call themselves Arabs, but they feel no patriotic attachment to Palestine as a *whole*.... This want of national coherency is the strongest feature in character of the population of Palestine."

Despite having little political and no religious import among Muslims, the name Palestine continued in use, gaining currency over time. Indeed, the territory "had slowly taken shape in the course of the nineteenth and early twentieth centuries in the consciousness of both its inhabitants and its central government," according to German historian Alexander Schölch.

From these inauspicious beginnings, the romance of Palestine grew into what it is today, an extremely powerful nationalist force rivaling the Jewish original. Already, Amin al-Husseini referred to it as "Arab holy land" and Arafat called it "the promised land." With the foundation of the Palestine Liberation Organization in 1964, Palestine acquired political expression, quickly becoming a household word. The PLO proclaimed the "State of Palestine" in 1988 and the territory acquired official status in 1994 with the creation of the Palestinian Authority.

The PA pressured governments, international organizations, corporations, reference works, and others to recognize it as a state. This campaign has had considerable success, as institutions around the world, public and private, pretend that a "State of Palestine" actually exists. The PA maintains diplomatic missions in ninety-five countries—while Israel maintains diplomatic missions in just seventy-eight countries. Athletes have represented the fictitious "State of Palestine" at the Olympics since 1996.

Islamic Zionism also demands replacing the name *Israel* with *Palestine*. Israel may be an actual state, but it sometimes disappears from view. The U.S. merchandising giant Target sold globes showing Palestine but not Israel. Verizon, the largest U.S. mobile telephone provider, has texted customers arriving at Ben-Gurion Airport in Lod, Israel, with a "Welcome to

PALESTINE" message. The Dutch airline Transavia listed Palestine as a destination, though it does not fly there; and it did not list Israel, though it does go there. A Ryanair flight attendant informed passengers en route to Tel Aviv of their destination as "Palestine." Qatar, host of the World Cup, offered online tickets for sale to residents of "Palestine" but not to those of Israel. *Palestine: A Guide* by Mariam Shahin fantasizes that Israel does not exist; the small town of Jaffa fills up a chapter of twenty pages while the vastly larger city of Tel Aviv is barely mentioned. Even on Israeli television, an Arabic news show called the Galilee "Occupied Northern Palestine."

• • •

Emulating Zionism. Celebrating Jerusalem and Palestine is just the start of Islamic Zionism, for Palestinians have modeled ideas, institutions, and practices—nearly everything—on the Jewish model.

Given that the post-World War I delineation of a territory called "Palestine" was a Zionist achievement, the very existence of a Palestinian Arab identity stemmed from Zionism. So, too, with the growth of that identity. As UCLA professor James Gelvin notes, "Palestinian nationalism emerged during the interwar period in response to Zionist immigration and settlement."

The PLO (founded in 1964) can be understood only with reference to its Zionist inspiration, the World Zionist Organization (founded in 1897). The globe-trotting unofficial ambassador Chaim Weizmann provided a close prototype for Yasir Arafat. Israel's 1948 Proclamation of Independence inspired the PLO's 1988 Declaration of Independence in subject matter, organization, and even in specific phrasing.

The Yishuv created a unique non-sovereign, quasi-governmental apparatus that included the nuts and bolts of administration (such as educational institutions, labor unions, political parties, militia, and an intelligence service). Palestinians made a first attempt at copying this structure in Jordan (1968–1970) and a second in Lebanon (1970–1982), before finally succeeding with the Palestinian Authority (since 1994) and Hamas (since 2007).[7]

---

7 The main difference lies in the Yishuv not pretending to be a sovereign government and the PA strenuously trying to assert just this.

Emulating the Jewish diaspora, Palestinians sometimes call themselves the "Jews of the Middle East." They correctly point to being more educated and mobile than the majority populations among whom they live, just as they suffer prejudice, dispossession, and repeated expulsions. Israel's 1950 "Law of Return" automatically grants Israeli citizenship to any Jew making *aliyah* (emigrating to the Land of Israel); Palestinians claim a "right of return" entitling every "Palestine refugee" and his descendants to move to Israel.

Palestinians even, outrageously, claim to suffer a holocaust at Israeli hands paralleling the Holocaust Jews suffered at Nazi hands. In that spirit, just as Zionists tried to land the *Exodus 1947*, a worn-out freighter with 4,500 Holocaust survivors on the beaches of British-controlled Palestine, the PLO in 1988 staged a repeat with an old Greek car ferry, renamed *Al-'Awda*, or "The Return." (Neither succeeded in landing passengers.)

These and many more parallels point to the Palestinians' profound ties to their mortal enemy, their inability to separate themselves from it, and their ferocious hatred of it. Palestinians have become what the Germans call a *Doppelgänger*—an evil twin and nemesis—of the Zionists. As Ruth Wisse of Harvard University points out, "The national consciousness of Palestinian Arabs is so politically focused on what belongs to the Jews that they cannot concentrate on what is theirs to enjoy."

REJECTIONISM'S MIXED RECORD

Rejectionism involves two sorts of tactics to weaken Israel: local violence and international delegitimization. The former has failed as spectacularly as the latter has succeeded.

• • •

Violence. Palestinian stoning, knife stabbing, lynching, arson, car-ramming, weaponized kites and condoms, shooting, bombing, rockets, missile barrages, intifadas, and massacres have a deliberate brutality and heartlessness, purposefully imposing personal and familial anguish on enemies. But the viciousness also has larger purposes: to discourage Israelis, cause an exodus, frighten away visitors, reduce capital inflows, heighten security expenses, and induce government repression. Already in 1968, Arafat spoke of "Creating and maintaining an atmosphere of strain and anxiety that will force the Zionists to realize that it is impossible for them to live in Israel." He and others subsequently repeated that hope many times.

But the effort failed. Israelis are not dispirited and have not fled the country. Tourists and capital have flowed in. The repressive crackdown never occurred. Israelis score high on happiness indices. Instead, rounds of violence invariably end with Palestinians taking more casualties, their houses demolished, their buildings flattened, and their economy battered.

Worse, violence counterproductively hardens Israeli opinion, reduces Israeli good will, and diminishes—if not extinguishes—their readiness to make concessions. The extraordinarily generous offers during the Oslo Era (1993–2008), and especially those of Ehud Barak in 2000 and Ehud Olmert in 2008, are ancient history. Israelis will need many years of Palestinian good behavior, including truth, moderation, propriety, and non-violence, ever again to view them as positively as they did back then. The "Palestine" that once seemed imminent now looks like a mirage. Anger now reigns.

Violence against Israel's airplanes, pizzerias, kibbutzim, and bedrooms has also carried an international price. "Palestinian terrorism" has become a byword, with the Bing search engine recording more than seven million entries in English alone. Taking this violence to the West—with Sirhan Sirhan assassinating Robert F. Kennedy, Mohammed Saleh participating in the New York City landmarks plot, and Nidal Malik Hasan mass-murdering Fort Hood soldiers—further damaged the Palestinian reputation. Overall, then, savagery against Israel has completely failed.

• • •

Delegitimization. But that failure pales beside the success of the Palestinians' narrative which, arguably, has an unparalleled reach in the media, education, religion, and politics. Palestinians freely resort to brazenly antisemitic motifs, as when Mahmoud Abbas stated that "certain rabbis in Israel have said very clearly to their government that our water should be poisoned in order to have Palestinians killed." Drawing on the perverse genius of the *Protocols of the Elders of Zion*, they present Zionism differently according to their audience: an "Islamophobic" movement repressing Muslim victims; an imperialist movement of whites subjugating an indigenous people; Jews oppressing, exploiting, and massacring a Christ-like population; or Nazis turning Gaza into an open-air concentration camp.

Falling back on the classic tactic of accusing the enemy of one's own intentions, Palestinians developed a theory of Israeli rejectionism. Here journalist Ramzy Baroud proclaims that "the pro-Israel camp is fighting for the complete erasure of everything Palestinian," neatly ignoring decades of Israeli efforts to live harmoniously next to a Palestinian polity. There he states that, "For Palestinians, victory means freedom for the Palestinian people and equality for all. For Israel, victory can only be achieved through the erasure of Palestinians," cleverly reversing reality. The PA's official paper, *Al-Hayat Al-Jadida*, makes such views look mild:

> As is its custom, [Israel] insists on committing a new crime while realizing its craving for murder.... Bloody hands pull the trigger on a hunch, as long as the target is Palestinian.... The occupation...spread out its snipers everywhere and began to shoot live gunfire—not randomly, but rather in order to wound and kill.

The passage concludes by calling Israel "an expert in the language of sadism."

Such calumnies resonate in the wider world. As the aftermath of October 7 showed, Palestinians can uniquely call on the sympathies and resources of an immense support network that includes Muslims, leftists, dictators, journalists, activists, educators, students, artists, priests, and assorted do-gooders. That the academy has broadly adopted this view, as have significant elements in the world of arts and the media, renders anti-Zionism self-perpetuating.

Palestinians especially dominate international institutions. Not counting the "State of Palestine," the Arab League has twenty-one member states and the Organization of Islamic Cooperation has fifty-six, giving their membership enormous weight in international organizations to horse-trade and discredit Israel. Some examples: Founded in 1961, the "United Nations Special Committee on the Situation with regard to the Implementation of the Declaration on the Granting of Independence of Colonial Countries and Peoples" (for short, the "Special Committee on Decolonization") has long been uniquely focused on criticizing Israel. In 1968, the UN General Assembly created the "Special Committee to Investigate Israeli Practices Affecting the Human Rights of the Palestinian People and Other Arabs of the Occupied Territories" that adds more calumnies. In 1975, the UN General Assembly voted by a two-to-one ratio on a resolution to declare

Zionism, or Jewish nationalism, "a form of racism and racial discrimination" (but revoked it in 1991). With a single 2013 exception, every UNESCO country-specific critical resolution in recent years has focused on Israel. In 2022, the UN General Assembly condemned Israel fifteen times and all other countries thirteen times. In one of its typical actions, the UN's World Health Organization (WHO) singled Israel out for severe condemnation with the support of many democracies (Belgium, France, India, Ireland, Japan, Luxembourg, New Zealand, Spain, and Switzerland), even as it elected North Korea to the WHO executive board.

Palestinian-origin persons living in the West have reached influential positions in many fields from which they spread rejectionism. Think of the academic Edward Said, his Columbia University colleague Rashid Khalidi, University of California-Berkeley's Hatem Bazian, U.S. Congresswoman Rashida Tlaib, New York City activist Linda Sarsour, Islamist functionary Nihad Awad (real name: Nehad Hammad), self-styled comedian Dean Obeidallah, Imam Omar Suleiman, the glamorous sisters Bella and Gigi Hadid, British Islamist Azzam Tamimi, and German politician Sawsan Chebli.

As for the Left, the section on "The Left Turns Anti-Zionist" (pp. 33-45) documents its shift in outlook.

• • •

Rejectionism shackles Palestinians to a fraudulent history, political repression, and a death cult. But all evidence points to a majority accepting this situation and not being willing to change, determined to destroy Israel almost regardless of cost to themselves. What explains this tenacity?

EXPLAINING THE TENACITY

WHY DO PALESTINIANS, DESPITE CONSTANT hardship and loss, persist in rejectionism? How do they, uniquely, sustain a genocidal program for more than a century? Why don't they moderate, put more emphasis on the good life, accept the overpowering reality of Israel? A mix of Islamic doctrines, historical legacies, alliances, and specific Palestinian features account for this exceptionally enduring radicalism.

RELIGIOUS FACTORS

Islam sustains rejectionism among Palestinians, a predominantly observant Muslim population, in several ways.

Jihad. The Koran and other scriptures contain a great number of instructions that Muslim jurisprudents stitched into a cohesive body of laws, called the *Shariah*. For a Muslim to live a fully pious life means obeying it in its entirety. Because some of the Shariah requires governmental implementation (for example, concerning warfare, justice, and taxes), Islam impels Muslims to make sure that their leaders are pious Muslims. Depending on conditions, then, Islamic political action takes two basic forms. Where Muslims rule and non-Muslims do not threaten that rule (such as Iran under the shah and Türkiye under the secularists), implementing the Shariah means replacing existing leaders with new ones who act and rule in accord with the Shariah. Where non-Muslims rule, implementing the Shariah means putting Muslims in power, which is the work of jihad (religious war of Muslims against unbelievers in accordance with Islamic law).

Israel fits this latter circumstance, creating the context for a Koranic imperative to wage jihad against it; that is, rejectionism. Amin al-Husseini articulated this program: "We pray that the jihad of Palestine...for liberty and independence will achieve full success and a complete victory," as have all subsequent Palestinian leaders. Their constituency sees Israel as usurping Muslim sovereignty, so this appeal resonates widely.

Martyrdom. Based on the Islamic celebration of martyrdom (*istish'had*) in the pursuit of jihad, Palestinians have cultivated a martyrs' ethos that motivates aggression against Jews, Israelis, and others. Their institutions, both PA and Hamas, have developed ideas and established mechanisms to convince normal men and women to want to die. As Hamas puts it, "being killed in battle in the way of Allah is the highest thing that every Palestinian aspires to." The process begins by inculcating two things into its children: a hatred of Jews and a love of death.

Hatred of Jews is inculcated through unconstrained, vile, and blatant antisemitism. School curricula, camp activities, television programming, and religious indoctrination relentlessly portray Israelis in the Nazi spirit, as sub-human creatures to be exterminated: sharks, crocodiles, scorpions, and snakes. Conspiracy theories accuse Jews of harming and exploiting Muslims.

The oft-repeated Hamas assertion "we love death more than you love life" sums up the second attitude. This indoctrination negates the instinct for self-preservation, convincing impressionable young people that sacrificing their lives by killing Jews represents the most noble act possible. When asked what he feels when he prays for the souls of "martyrs," Ikrama Sabri, the PA mufti replied, "I feel the martyr is lucky because the angels usher him to his wedding in heaven." And if the martyr is a child? "The younger the martyr, the greater, and the more I respect him." Sabri cited a young man who told of wanting to marry "the black-eyed women of heaven," referring to the houris promised to jihad warriors in heaven, and a day later he "became a martyr." The young man's mother, the mufti went on, must have been "filled with joy about his heavenly marriage." Along the same lines, a story about a boy narrated by a young girl on Fatah's official Facebook page recounts how

> his mother promised him a gift if he finished his food. The boy wondered in excitement: "Is it a toy?" His mother approached him with a glowing look while carrying the gift. He looked, and it was a rifle! He shouted loudly: "O Mommy! Mommy! What is this? Is this the gift?" She picked him up, hugged him, and said: "My son, we were not created for happiness. In my eyes you are meant for Martyrdom!.... Jerusalem is ours, our

> weapon is our Islam, and our ammunition is our children. And you, O my son, are meant for Martyrdom."

We were not created for happiness. Well, not the usual definition of happiness: In a farewell note, a suicide attacker instructed his family, "Do not cry over me, rather make sounds of joy, as this is the wedding of your martyr son.... My last will is that no one cry at my funeral procession that leads to paradise, rather hand out dates and make sounds of joy at the wedding of martyrdom."

The system works. "Our biggest problem is the hordes of young men who beat on our doors, clamoring to be sent [on suicide missions]," explained a Hamas leader. "It is difficult to select only a few. Those whom we turn away return again and again, pestering us, pleading to be accepted." A Hamas operative concurred, noting that when one recruit is selected,

> countless others are disappointed. They must learn patience and wait until Allah calls them. After every massacre, every massive violation of our rights and defilement of our holy places, it is easy for us to sweep the streets for boys who want to do a martyrdom operation. Fending off the crowds who demand revenge and retaliation and insist on a human bombing operation—that becomes our biggest problem!

With such recruiting, it is no wonder Hamas' military setbacks have limited impact.

Palestine as waqf. Islamic doctrine holds that once a land has been conquered by Muslims, it becomes part of the lands of Islam (*Dar al-Islam*) and an inalienable Islamic patrimony (a *waqf*). Accordingly, its loss constitutes a robbery, and Muslims must exert to bring it back under their rule. Muslims historically responded to the loss of territories in Europe, Bernard Lewis notes, with the expectation that these were "Islamic lands, wrongfully taken from Islam and destined ultimately to be restored." Three centuries after the whole of Spain fell to Christians in 1492, for example, Muslims continued actively to dream of a restoration. This assumption of righteousness and inevitability has an abiding hold on Muslim imaginations, as shown by such aggressions as that of Türkiye in Cyprus or Syria in Lebanon.

Palestine became a part of Dar al-Islam after its conquest by Muslims in 638 CE, six years after the Islamic account records the death of

Muhammad.[1] Muslims then ruled it until 1917, with the exception of two centuries, from 1097 to 1291, when Crusaders controlled parts of it. The British ruled all of it from 1917 to 1948 and Israel, most or all of it thereafter. This history has created a deep sense of entitlement: Palestine belongs under Muslim control.

Jews. Jews have the misfortune of being both a major presence in Muhammad's life and in the Koran. And while positive elements exist (the Koran is arguably a Zionist text; see verses 5:20–21 and 7:137), Jews' overwhelming presence in both is adverse, whether because they challenge the prophet of Islam or are condemned by him. In all, according to Hebrew University's Meir M. Bar-Asher, an "overarchingly negative vision of the Jews supplied a basis for de-legitimating and belittling them."

Subsequent Muslim interactions with Jews found the latter almost always a powerless people; for Muslims, this became assumed, making Jewish sovereign power from 1948 forward the more intolerable, insufferable, and even ominous. Bad enough that Christians, the historic enemy, had become so much stronger in the modern era, but Jews, too? Add to this the (Christian-originated) conspiracy theories circulating about Jews and they could convincingly be presented as an existential threat, perhaps even more so than Christians, a more obvious opponent. The result? Palestinians are the most antisemitic population in the world, with an Anti-Defamation League survey in 2014 finding 93 percent of them holding anti-Jewish views.

THE LEFT TURNS ANTI-ZIONIST

These days, leftist politicians, academics, students, NGOs, editorialists, and assorted do-gooders routinely criticize Israel. This marks a shift from the Left's earlier years and sometimes renders it more hostile than Muslims. That switch, which dates back to a series of events in the early 1990s, helps to sustain rejectionism.

• • •

1 I use this round-about phrasing because modern historians question the accuracy of the Arabic literary sources that inform the Islamic traditional. For a summary of that research, see Robert Spencer, *Did Muhammad Exist? An Inquiry into Islam's Obscure Origins*, rev. and expanded (New York: Bombardier Books, 2021).

Switching sides. In Israel's early years, the Left showed pro-Israel sympathies. Joseph Stalin provided so much political support and armaments to Israel's coming into existence between 1947 and 1949 that Abba Eban, Israel's first UN ambassador, observed that "we couldn't have made it, either diplomatically or militarily," without Soviet help. Broadly speaking, until the 1970s, American liberals sympathized more with Israel than did conservatives. Symbolic of these inclinations, Democrats Harry Truman and John F. Kennedy rank among the most pro-Israel of U.S. presidents, Republicans Dwight Eisenhower and Gerald Ford among the most antagonistic.

Then things changed, in some part due to the non-socialist Likud party taking power in 1977, but in larger part due to the Soviet Union's unrelenting propaganda against Israel from 1967 to 1989, from the Six-Day War to the cusp of its own collapse. Although undertaken to forward parochial Soviet foreign relations, the anti-Zionist campaign had a global impact, turning progressives against Israel. Then, when the Soviet Union disappeared, the global Left replaced it, partnering with Islamists to spread an anti-Zionist message in non-Muslim countries, with a significant impact on educational institutions, philanthropies, the media, legal systems, and politicians. The United Nations' 2001 Durban conference against "Racism, Racial Discrimination, Xenophobia and Related Intolerance" marked the full-blown emergence of this phenomenon. It has since continued to grow, with Israel ever-more criticized and ostracized.

The Left's turn away from Israel instinctively made the Right ardently pro-Israel, finding in it a religious, spiritual, cultural, scientific, and security beacon. The reasons vary from "Those who bless Israel, God will bless; Those who curse her, He will curse" (a paraphrase of Numbers 24:9) to celebrating the "Start-up nation."

By now, attitudes toward Israel follow an almost linear progression of growing negativity as one goes from right to left. Opinion surveys in the United States between 2000 and 2023 show that liberal Democrats are consistently the least pro-Israel, followed by conservative Democrats, independents, liberal Republicans, and conservative Republicans. For example, a 2015 Pew Research Center poll asked, "In the dispute between Israel and the Palestinians," do you sympathize "a lot with Israel?" To this 19 percent of liberal Democrats assented, 22 percent of conservative Democrats, 27 percent of independents, 33 percent of liberal Republicans, and 63 percent of conservative Republicans. In 2016, a major U.S. survey for the first time showed liberal Democrats to be more anti-Israel than pro-Israel.

The same phenomenon exists, for example, in Brazil where leftist president Luiz Inácio Lula da Silva (2003–2010, and since 2023) and rightist president Jair Bolsonaro (2019–2022) each reversed the other's Israel policy. An early 2023 incident in Spain neatly illustrated the point. As soon as the leftwing mayor of Barcelona terminated a sister-city relationship with Tel Aviv due to what she called "the systematic violation of human rights of the Palestinian population," the rightwing mayor of Madrid accused her of antisemitism and offered to strengthen relations with the "democratic, law-abiding and rights-abiding" State of Israel.

• • •

Focus on Palestinians. Liberal and leftist opposition to Israel tends to accept the state's existence and focuses its anger narrowly on Israeli policies toward the roughly three and a half million Palestinians living in the West Bank, in Gaza, and in eastern Jerusalem. This is the Left's almost exclusive issue vis-à-vis Israel. It barely notes or cares about Israel's domestic issues, such as Ashkenazi-Mizrahi relations, the price of cottage cheese, or even the status of its Muslim citizens. Nor does it care much about such foreign issues as Israel's relations with China or Egypt, a possible attack on Iran's nuclear infrastructure, or Israel's own possession of nuclear weapons. Finally, it conspicuously ignores the far more severe plight of Palestinians living in Jordan, Syria, or Lebanon, not to speak of oppressed Muslim populations in places like Myanmar and China's Xinjiang province.

This narrow focus is the more striking when one recalls that Israel withdrew from Areas A and B of the West Bank where 90 percent of Palestinians live, and every inch Gaza, terminating any control of the latter territory and severing any responsibility for its population. Despite this unilateral and total retreat, plus massive provisioning of supplies thereafter, Israel's critics continue to hold it accountable for Gaza, entirely ignoring the repression of Gazans by Hamas. Pre-October 7, Human Rights Watch called Gaza an "open-air prison" run by Israel. Western academics went further and called it a "concentration camp."

Through masterful marketing, the perceived victimization of a small and powerless population has catapulted it into becoming a premier global issue of human rights, absorbing infinitely more attention than, say, the far larger civil wars in Cameroon, Democratic Republic of the Congo, Sudan, Ethiopia, and Myanmar. Leftist support helps to explain why the

PA and Hamas engage in violence against Israel even when they know in advance they will lose every military contest: Because they also know that the fighting further enhances their status on the Left; academics tout their cause, students get enraged, apparatchiks send them money, and politicians celebrate their extremism. While Palestinians invariably initiate the violence, Israeli get slammed for responding. Thus, Palestinian attacks have the double benefit of both killing Israelis and fueling the Left's anger against Israel. Israeli protestations and justifications meet with cold responses.

• • •

Examples. A wide range of NGOs from Amnesty International to the World Council of Churches have jumped on the bandwagon. Other examples include the Black Lives Matter platform, which accuses Israel of "apartheid" and "genocide"; North America's nominally academic Middle East Studies Association; and a communist labor union in India representing sixteen million farmers, which apparently joined the Boycott, Divestment, and Sanctions (BDS) movement calling for a cut in economic ties with Israel. Hard-left politicians almost everywhere represent the most anti-Zionist views in their countries; in one example, they opposed the U.S. House of Representatives' resolution congratulating Israel on its 75th anniversary.

New York City, the metropolitan area with the largest Jewish population in the world, and for one and a half centuries a global center of Jewish life, exemplifies the change. As political consultant E.J. Hare documents, the rise of hard-left and anti-Zionist politicians is underway, to the point that they abstain or even vote against "a resolution establishing April 29 as 'End Jew Hatred Day,' a perfunctory, procedural gesture of support for a community alarmed by an uptick in antisemitic violence." And this is just the beginning:

> Today's leftist city council and state assembly members are tomorrow's mayors, governors and members of Congress. And there are strong indications that the Democratic Party's foot soldiers—staffers, campaign workers, and activists—who will eventually run for lower-level positions are even further left than their bosses.

Here, "even further left" equates to "even more hostile to Israel."

Leftist hostility toward Israel takes extreme verbal forms, as several examples from pre-October 7 reveal. Slogans shouted out in a demonstration in New York's Grand Central Station, one of the city's most prominent spaces, included: "Free them all, Zionism must fall! Settler, settler, go back home! Palestine is ours alone! We don't want no two states, we want all of it! Five, six, seven, eight, crush the settler Zionist State!" English musician Roger Waters of Pink Floyd fame compared Israel to Nazi Germany. Rafiki Morris of the All-African People's Revolutionary Party stated at a rally in Washington, D.C., that "The only good Zionist is a dead Zionist."

Some leftists go beyond words: American student Rachel Corrie made the ultimate sacrifice in 2003 by purposefully placing herself in the path of an armored bulldozer operated by the IDF, getting herself crushed, killed, and turned into another sort of Palestinian "martyr."[2]

The hostility to Israel extends to democratic governments. For example, as Middle Eastern scholar Bassam Tawil notes, "The EU does not interfere anyplace else on the planet other than [the West Bank]—not for the Kurds, the Assyrians, the Yazidis, the Uyghurs, the Kashmiris, the Tibetans or the Greek Cypriots. The Palestinians continue to be the *only* group on the EU's list of people with whom to interfere." And interfere the EU did, spending hundreds of millions of dollars to promote illegal Palestinian building activities. Further, Israel's response to attacks almost inevitably led to EU criticism for its perpetuating a "cycle of violence" and using "disproportionate force."

Anti-Zionism has become so central for the Left that support for Israel now tarnishes one's progressive credentials, as the experience of American liberals is illustrated by feminist Phyllis Chesler, jurist Alan Dershowitz, historian Richard Landes, television commentator Bill Maher, and politicians Ritchie Torres and John Fetterman.

"Woke" corporations have joined the battle. Airbnb, an online marketplace for short-term homestays, banned Israelis living in the West Bank from renting out their homes on the platform, while permitting Palestinians to do so. Then, facing discrimination lawsuits, Airbnb reversed course and

---

2 Corrie became a leftist heroine. In contrast, the many anti-Israel activists killed by Palestinians, including Ziva Goldovsky, Ian Sean Feinberg, Angelo Frammartino, Juliano Mer-Khamis, and Vittorio Arrigoni, have been forgotten. On them, see my blog, DanielPipes.org, "Palestinians Attack Their Supporters," April 15, 2011, and subsequent updates.

stated it "will not move forward with implementing the removal of listings in the West Bank from the platform." To accommodate anti-Israel sentiments, however, Airbnb also announced that it "will take no profits from this activity in the region." In a similar spirit, premium ice cream maker Ben & Jerry's did not renew its contract with its Israeli manufacturer as a way to pull out from sales in the West Bank. Facing opposition, Ben & Jerry's parent company, Unilever, sold the rights to its Israeli manufacturer.

Not all divestitures were reversed, however, just those that adopted an overtly discriminatory tack. When General Mills sold its 60 percent stake in an Israeli joint venture that principally markets dough products, it innocuously presented the sale as just "another step in General Mills' Accelerate strategy, which is centered on strategic choices about where to prioritize our resources to drive superior returns." Smartly, it made no mention of a high-powered multi-year campaign pressuring for the divestiture, or the political cheering that surrounded the sale. Presumably, future corporate actions will follow the General Mills word-salad model.

Leftist anti-Zionists include educators, students, journalists, artists, and bureaucrats. Leftwing priests, pastors, and rabbis spew vitriol. Among politicians, it is true, Bernie Sanders did not become president of the United States, nor did Jeremy Corbyn become British prime minister, but rabid anti-Zionists have a foothold in both country's legislatures. Anti-Zionist forces are globally on the ascent, as witnessed by Gabriel Boric ("Israel is a genocidal and murderous state") and Luiz Inácio Lula da Silva, elected the presidents of Chile and Brazil, respectively, in 2022, while anti-Zionist Humza Yousaf was elected Scotland's first minister in March 2023. Current trends suggest that the Élysée Palace, 10 Downing Street, and the White House are within eventual reach.

Leftist anti-Zionism is growing. It faces legal restrictions and business interests, but the movement has momentum and moral energy.

• • •

Replacing the Arab states. A tectonic shift in attitudes toward Israel has taken place. Since the creation of Israel, Palestinians, Arabs, and Muslims provided the mainstay of anti-Zionism, with non-Muslims merely their auxiliary. But then, as Arab states quietly reconciled themselves to Israel's existence, the global Left noisily took up their slack. By now, the global Left often acts more stridently anti-Zionist than the Arabs. Arab leaders, for example, show near-indifference to the absence of Palestinian Israeli diplomacy, while leftists express anger over it.

Top: In late October 2018, Israel's Minister of Culture and Sport Miri Regev cried with joy when Israel's anthem played at an International Judo Federation event in Abu Dhabi.

Bottom: In early November 2018, a BDS campaign succeeded in removing a Water Polo World League match from Molins de Rei, Spain, forcing it to be played elsewhere.

Sports offer an example. Miri Regev, Israel's minister of culture and sports, attended the Abu Dhabi Grand Slam competition in the United Arab Emirates in late October 2018 when an Israeli judoka won a gold medal. She burst into tears of joy as Israel's flag waved and the national anthem played. After the ceremony, she called the event "a dream come true," adding that, "For two years we had talks in order to reach this moment and it was hard to stop the tears."

Just over a week later, Israel's women's water polo team had a qualification match for the Water Polo World League tournament in the historic town of Molins de Rei, Catalonia, Spain's most leftwing region. Acquiescing to pressure from the BDS movement, Molins de Rei banned the Israeli team, so it played the game elsewhere. In reaction, the president of the Israeli Water Polo Association wryly noted: "If an Israeli team can perform in Abu Dhabi with the Israeli flag and anthem, we should also be able to play" in Spain.[3] But that was not the case.

On a larger scale, while the Emirati government has significant security relations with Israel, U.K. Labour leader Jeremy Corbyn promised that his government would "immediately suspend the sale of arms...to Israel." Jewish U.S. presidential candidate Bernie Sanders declared that "to the degree that [Israelis] want us to have a positive relationship, I think they're going to have to improve their relationship with the Palestinians," while Egypt's President Abdel Fattah al-Sisi signed a major natural gas deal with Israel. The (Muslim) president of Chad turned up in Israel but a (non-Muslim) singer from New Zealand did not. Even as the UAE sovereign wealth fund looked to invest $10 billion in Israel, its Norwegian counterpart considered ending all investments in Israel.

This pattern even extends to warfare, as exemplified by the Hamas-Israel fighting in May 2021. "While many in the West denounced Israel for its military strikes in the Gaza Strip over the past week," noted Khaled Abu Toameh of the Gatestone Institute in 2021, "prominent Arab writers and political analysts held the Iranian-backed Hamas responsible for the violence and bloodshed." Contrarily, Salman el Herfi, the PA's "ambassador" in Paris, said that in stopping Israeli annexation of parts of the West Bank,

3 At the game, the Israeli association president gave the team a Zionist pep talk, the local Jewish community came out to cheer, and "The girls started to play like I never saw them playing. They told me afterwards that they were lifted up [because] all these people came to support them."

"the European Union played a much more important role here than did the United Arab Emirates."

October 7 again highlighted this difference. The global Left showed intense antipathy to Israel. In South America, for example, Belize suspended diplomatic relations due to "unceasing indiscriminate bombing"; Bolivia accused Israel of "crimes against humanity" and broke diplomatic relations; Chile recalled its ambassador in response to "the unacceptable violations of international humanitarian law committed by Israel"; Colombia's President Gustavo Petro repeatedly compared Israel to the Nazis and recalled his ambassador; and Honduras recalled its ambassador in protest against "the serious humanitarian situation." In contrast, the Arab states generally issued low-key condemnations and even the two (Bahrain and Jordan) that withdrew ambassadors did so quietly. For example, Bahrain mildly explained the decision to suspend economic ties due to its "historic position in support of the Palestinian cause."

These trends appear likely to continue, with Arab states increasingly impatient with the Palestinians and leftists ever-more inclined to see Israel as an "Islamophobic," imperialist, apartheid, or neo-Nazi state.

This support from the Left hugely encourages Palestinians to stick to rejectionism.

• • •

Explaining Leftist Anti-Zionism. But why did the Left turn against Israel, a liberal, democratic state engaged in self-defense which has made repeated concessions?

Exceptional public relations prowess transmogrified the tiny, weak, and relatively prosperous Palestinian population into the world's most prominent leftist issue, one which benefits from immeasurably more solicitude than far more wretched peoples anywhere, from next-door Syria to nearby Sudan to distant Myanmar. The ever-present backdrop of antisemitism also plays a role. Together, these two factors morphed antisemitism into anti-Zionism, and Israel into the Jew of nations. Then, a sequence of five developments in the 1990s specifically turned the non-Muslim Left against Israel: the 1990 Iraqi conquest of Kuwait, the 1991 collapse of the Soviet Union, the 1992 Maastricht Treaty, the 1993 Oslo Accords, and the 1994 ending of South Africa's apartheid regime.

1990. Saddam Hussein's conquest of Kuwait prompted a massive, American-led expeditionary force that expelled Iraqi forces from Kuwait. Along the way, in a futile hope to bring other Arab states to his side, Saddam launched a missile attack on Israel that turned out to be the final, hopeless Arab state aggression on Israel. His failure permitted Palestinians to emerge definitively as Israel's main enemy.

As they did, the Left's perception of Israel fully shifted from underdog to overdog. It previously saw Israel as a small, heroic, democratic country valiantly battling for its existence against a vast body of Arabic states stretching from the Atlantic Ocean to the Indian Ocean. Now, it became the great power despotically looming over a much smaller "Palestine." David had become Goliath. Israelis now lost the battle to win the sympathy that goes to the victim. They might recall the Holocaust and quote Arab threats to "throw the Jews into the sea," but they possessed the high-rise buildings and the air force. Palestinians helped the process by conjuring up every injustice from a (non-existent) massacre at Deir Yassin in 1948 to recent controls on movement, redolently termed "Christ at the Checkpoint." Israelis pointed to the potential destruction of their country, the only Jewish state, but Palestinians trumped this with their vast, decayed "refugee" camps.

A 2007 study established the underdog advantage. Researchers showed two maps to American college students. One showed Israel as a near-microscopic presence surrounded by a sea of Arab territory from Morocco to Oman, the other showed a large Israel in contrast to a diminutive West Bank and Gaza. Asked which side they sympathized with more, a stunning 30 percent more respondents (76.7 percent vs. 46.7 percent) sympathized with small Israel over big Israel. After the Kuwait War, Palestinians succeeded in making big-Israel the default map, with a consequent jump in support for them. The big-Israel map even prevailed in Israel itself, rendering the small-Israel map a museum piece.

1991. The Soviet Union collapsed, bringing the Cold War superpower rivalry to a shuddering halt. As Lenin's creation vaporized, a weak, confused Russia replaced it, along with a clutch of lesser countries fleeing Moscow's grip. This collapse liberated the Left from its stale, decades-long apologetics for the USSR, rendering it free to express its anti-Americanism in more creative ways. Israel's uniquely warm, strong, emotional, high-profile, and most special of special relationships with the United States made it an especially ripe target. In 1991, Jerusalem voted far more often with Washington than any other government in the UN General Assembly, 87.5 percent of the time, followed by the United Kingdom with just 79.6 percent. (In contrast, Iraq had the lowest ranking, at 7.6 percent.) Typically, when only one or two states voted with Washington, Israel was one of them. The two states formally entered into "strategic cooperation" in 1981. The U.S. government signed its first free-trade agreement with any country in 1985 with Israel, opening the entire American market to Israel by gradually eliminating tariffs. This thick relationship also made Israel a unique American proxy for leftists.

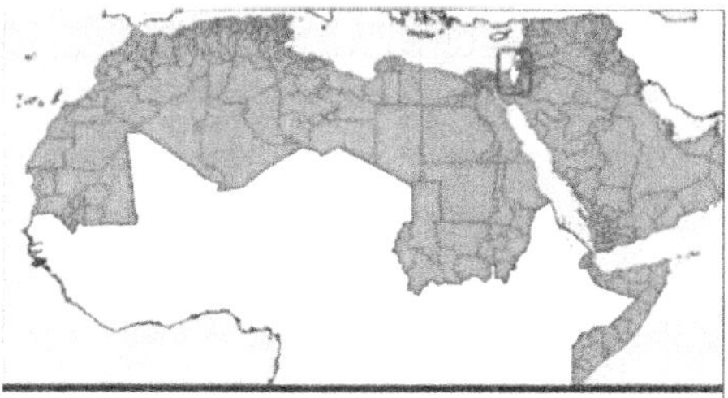

Pro-Israel advocates show a tiny Israel in a huge Arabic-speaking region. Anti-Israel advocates show a large Israel increasingly looming over a tiny Palestinian presence.

1992. When the twelve member states making up the European Community signed the Maastricht Treaty (formal name: the Treaty on European Union), they created the European Union (EU) and the goal of an eventual "federal Europe." This "new stage in the process of European integration" included, for starters, a European citizenship, a European currency, and other Europe-wide institutions.

As the Israeli philosopher Yoram Hazony points out, this evolution fit a new thinking about the international order. The old approach, dating back to the 1648 Treaty of Westphalia, saw the nation-state as a legitimate and positive institution, the best way to protect peoples and allow them to flourish. Figures as varied as the English philosopher John Stuart Mill and U.S. President Woodrow Wilson celebrated the nation-state ideal.

But that paradigm, Hazony argues, "pretty much collapsed" as European intellectuals and politicians blamed Nazi Germany on the nation-state, which they characterized "as a source of incalculable evil." Their new approach, ultimately based on German philosopher Immanuel

Kant's 1795 treatise on *Perpetual Peace*, advocates the abolition of nation-states in favor of an international government. Supranational institutions such as the United Nations and the European Union represent that ideal and model. Hazony notes that "the multinational empire—the form of government which John Stuart Mill had singled out as the very epitome of despotism—is now being mentioned time and again with fondness as a model for a post-national humanity."

Jews, the Holocaust, and Israel play a surprisingly central role in the shift from nation-state to multinational empire. The old paradigm endowed Israel with legitimacy to fight the millennial persecution of Jews that culminated in Nazi genocide; "Never Again" implied a strong Israel protecting Jews. The new paradigm, however, falsely ascribes the Holocaust to a nation-state, Germany, having gone mad. (Falsely, because the German Reich, an aspiring multinational empire, not a nation-state, carried out the Nazi atrocities.) "Never Again" now translates into opposition to any nation-state gaining the power to replicate the Nazi outrages. Seen thus, Israel is not the answer to Auschwitz; the European Union is.

Worse, that Israel pursues the Western world's most militant policy of self-defense makes it the foremost represent of an old, discredited world order and its actions particularly appalling (with the United States running second). Thus, arose a syllogism popular on the Left: (1) Nationalism caused Nazism; (2) Israel is the West's most nationalist country; therefore, (3) Israel is the most Nazi-like Western country. Israel's standing on the Left has deteriorated, Hazony concludes, "not because of this or that set of facts, but because the paradigm through which educated Westerners are looking at Israel has shifted."

The new paradigm applies exclusively to Western states; North Korea, China, and Iran, to take some prominent examples, get a free pass. They may bellicosely pursue national or multinational interests without invoking the Left's wrath. Such logic accounts for the otherwise inexplicable 2003 Eurobarometer poll that found Israel judged as by far the world's greatest threat to peace. (The United States tied for second place with North Korea and Iran.)

The emergence of the European Union solidified this way of thinking.

1993. The Oslo Accords, ironically, contributed to the heightened criticism of Israel by bringing far more international attention to the Palestinians, thereby exacerbating the volume and reach of their complaints. The pre-Oslo stand-off remained seemingly immovable in its boring rut; post Oslo, the conflict became dynamic and inflamed, with Israel the object of incessant Palestinian grievances, broadcast far and wide.

1994. Apartheid, the overtly racist system in South Africa that from 1948 favored those of European stock over Africans, collapsed between 1990 and 1994, culminating in the election of Nelson Mandela as president. Apartheid had garnered intense international opprobrium against South Africa; when that system dissolved, leftist critics of Israel proclaimed it—the foremost remaining bastion of supposed European colonialism—the new apartheid state. This was not an entirely new criticism; already in 1967, Maxime Rodinson, a high-profile Middle East specialist of French nationality and Marxist persuasion, published a book titled *Israël, fait colonial?* ("Israel, a colonial fact?"), but the argument achieved new prominence and power when the self-acknowledged apartheid state disbanded. This view reached a vast international audience with the United Nations' anti-racism conference held, not coincidentally, in Durban, South Africa, in 2001. Jimmy Carter gave it new respectability in his 2006 book *Palestine: Peace Not Apartheid.*

Together, these five developments over five consecutive years go far to explain the Left's turn against Israel, which it increasingly portrayed as perpetrator, colonizer, occupier, invader, and oppressor.

OTHER FACTORS

A host of other factors also contribute to the uniqueness of Palestinian tenacity: external support, the Crusader inspiration, the Middle Eastern readiness to eliminate states, the Palestinian claim to a "right of return," political leaders' skill at avoiding the consequences of defeat, ideological maps, careerism, conspiracy theories, and Israeli timidity.

Allies. Through their entire 150 years of confrontation with Zionists, Palestinians have continuously benefited from powerful external patrons. First, the Ottoman Empire all-out supported them. The British from 1917 were nuanced, but they appointed Amin al-Husseini, and, contrary to the Mandate's terms, severely limited Jewish immigration. Nazi Germany gave intense backing, symbolized by a Hitler-Husseini meeting. Independent Arab states then fully entered the fray. When those states suffered catastrophic defeat in 1967, the Soviet Union moved in. Islamists generally and Iran specifically also replaced the Arab states after 1973. The global Left replaced the Soviet Union after its 1991 collapse. Türkiye joined a decade later. Other allies—international organizations and dictators especially—further encourage the Palestinian reverie.

Israel has allies, too, foremost the U.S. government, other democracies, conservatives, traditional Christians, Hindus, and Jews. However impressive the quality of these groups, they do not match the Palestinians in continuity, partisanship, or quantity. Little wonder that Israel finds itself in a uniquely unfavorable position, as symbolized by its lopsided losses in international organizations.

The Crusader analogy. Especially during Israel's early years, Palestinians portrayed the country as the reincarnation of the medieval Crusader kingdoms which their ancestors had defeated. Taking inspiration from this analogy, they felt optimistic about repeating that success. Israeli historian Emmanuel Sivan wrote in 1973 that, "The struggle waged today by the leaders of the Arab movement of liberation [against Israel] is the very same conducted by the Ayyubids and the Mamelukes [two medieval Muslim dynasties] in order to beat off the Crusaders." Although this theme lost persuasiveness as Israel gained in strength, the Crusader analogy still reverberates. A huge banner in a West Bank street some years ago portrayed Arafat as Saladin, the Muslim leader who expelled the Crusaders from Jerusalem, riding a white horse bearing a sword. In 2000, the PA-appointed mufti of Jerusalem declared that, like Saladin, Muslims today must fight for the whole of Palestine "from the [Jordan] River to the [Mediterranean] Sea." The PA daily *Al-Hayat al-Jadida* scorned Zionism in 2013 as "no more than a new Crusade against the region."

Politicide. The idea of annihilating a state and scattering or killing its people ("politicide") is a pattern nearly unique to the Middle East; thus do Palestinian ideas about destroying Israel fit into a surprisingly commonplace mentality. During Iraq's six-month occupation of Kuwait in 1990 and 1991, Saddam Hussein accomplished precisely this; Kuwait's name disappeared along with its institutions, flag, and currency, while many of its people fled into exile. Syria's Hafez al-Assad emasculated Lebanon and extruded much of its population during the 1976 to 2005 occupation. Other states stand in danger of the same fate: Bahrain could be invaded at any time and transformed into the fourteenth province of Iran. Jordan could fall into the maw of Syria, Iraq, or Saudi Arabia. Armenia could be eliminated by Azerbaijan. Cyprus, 37 percent occupied by Türkiye, could fall entirely to it. How can Palestinians not be encouraged by these examples?

Right of return The demand that "Palestine refugees" whether genuine refugees or not—be allowed move to Israel stands at the crux of the Palestinian demand of Israel. Not winning this all-important "right of return" explains why PA leaders twice, in 2000 and 2008, turned down lavish Israeli offers of territory. As Schwartz and Wilf explain, "Palestinians have constantly rejected any formulation, agreement, or settlement that might foreclose this option of return, even at the price of statehood." The demand lives on, enshrined in organizations like "Al-Awda: The Palestinian Right to Return Coalition" that advocates turning back the clock and implement the refugees' "natural right to return to their towns and villages."

Finessing defeat. Palestinian leaders uncannily avoid the consequences of failure on the battlefield. Military loss hardly damages them and can even be politically helpful. This pattern began in 1968 with the Battle of Karama, the first major armed confrontation of Arafat's Fatah with Israel; Arafat so convincingly claimed victory that Israel's Major General Aharon Yariv conceded that "although it was a military defeat for them, it was a moral victory." In 1982, Arafat transformed a humiliating retreat from Beirut into a political victory through verbal magic, emphasizing how long it took for the Israelis (eighty-eight days) to defeat him, much longer than they needed to defeat conventional Arab armies (nine days in 1956, six in 1967, and twenty in 1973). Rashid Khalidi, then a PLO flack and now a chaired Columbia University professor, went so far as to compare the minuscule Beirut operation (and its few hundred Israeli deaths) with the Nazi two-and-a-half-years-long siege of Leningrad (with its approximately two million deaths). The passage of time further transformed this rout into a glorious success; in the Hamas retelling some years later, "our people… humiliated [Israel]…and broke its resolve." A year later, Arafat transmuted Syria's expulsion of PLO forces from Tripoli into another moral success.

Similar reinterpretations turned battlefield defeats of Hezbollah in 2006 and of Hamas in 2008–2009, 2012, 2014, 2021, and 2023 into glorious victories. Every time, Hamas and PIJ leaders proclaimed themselves victorious. PA leader Mahmoud Abbas called his Hamas counterpart, Ismail Haniyeh, after eight days of fighting with Israel that left Gaza badly battered in 2012, to "congratulate him on the victory and extend condolences to the families of martyrs." The conclusion of eleven days of Hamas-Israel fighting in 2021 inspired euphoric claims of victory by Hamas, though it had nearly been destroyed. Following the devastation of Gaza in late 2023, Yahya Sinwar surfaced after two and a half months on the run to proclaim wildly inflated enemy casualties and to insist that Hamas forces are "smashing the Israeli army and will continue to do so." One wonders whether Hamas will survive this self-proclaimed "glorious victory." [4]

Inaccurate maps. Arabic-language maps produced by both the PA and Hamas contain three curious anachronisms. First, they represent the Mandate for Palestine, which disappeared with the British withdrawal in 1948, as reality. Stretching from the Jordan River to the Mediterranean Sea and from Lebanon to the Red Sea, this map endlessly appears in every form of Palestinian communication—in books and media, at children's summer camps, on posters, T-shirts, and high school matriculation exams—ever pretending it is early 1948 and Israel has never existed.

Second, the maps wish away cities founded by Zionists (such as Petah Tikva, Tel Aviv, Netanya, Eilat, and Ashdod), thereby presenting Palestine as it was over one and a half centuries ago, before the modern Zionist movement began.

Third, Palestinian maps hardly ever show the contours of the West Bank and Gaza. Accordingly, monolingual Palestinians know neither the region's boundaries, nor where Israel actually exists, nor the very existence of many of its cities. Unhinging the Jewish state from the realities of geography turns it into an abstraction. These anachronisms combine to perpetuate the illusion of Israel's hypothetical and transient nature. How easy, then, to take the next step and imagine it gone.

---

4 This Palestinian pattern fits into a larger context; a study of twenty-one military losses by Arab states and the Palestinians since 1956 finds that none of these severely harmed the leaders and sometimes benefited them. See Daniel Pipes, "Give War a Chance: Arab Leaders Finesse Military Defeat," *Middle East Quarterly,* Vol. 28, No. 3 (Summer 2021).

Pro- and anti-Israel businesses sell similar pendants in the shape of Mandatory Palestine.

Careerist revolutionism. Palestinian leaders have turned rejectionism into a business; lacking other marketable skills, they need permanent conflict with Israel to earn a living. Nearly all PA and Hamas functionaries make excellent money in the pursuit of Israel's extinction; the Israeli government estimates that Hamas' top three leaders (Ismail Haniyeh, Moussa Abu Marzook, and Khaled Mashal) combined are worth $11 billion.

Further, leading a revolutionary movement with global stature holds greater allure than administering a country, with its attendant worries about potholes, education, and medical care. Unwilling to become the mundane leader of a minor state, Arafat made sure to keep himself a global figure. As Bill Clinton wrote about him,

> Perhaps he simply couldn't make the final jump from revolutionary to statesman. He had grown used to flying from place to place, giving mother-of-pearl gifts made by Palestinian craftsmen to world leaders and appearing on television with them. It would be different if the end of violence took Palestine out of the headlines and instead he had to worry about providing jobs, schools, and basic services.

Agreeing, former Kuwait minister Sami Al-Nesf observed that, "The victory of the Palestinian cause means defeat of the Palestinian leaders, because they only care to keep the 'cause' intact." A Gazan named Othman ascribes mercenary motives to Hamas: "Back in the days of the first and second intifadas, we used to believe in something called resistance. But today, the 'resistance' has become a business." Every tobacco stand and coffee shop is forced to pay Hamas protection money, he says, and when war breaks out, Hamas leaders "sit in their bunkers while we have to bear the brunt. And at the end they tell us it's a victory."

Conspiracy theories. Palestinians live in a mental world largely defined by fear of the hidden hand. To give a flavor of the paranoia, consider three proofs provided by Arafat that Israel plans to grab most of the Middle East:

Addressing the UN Security Council in 1990, he flaunted an Israeli coin and interpreted a design on it to signal Jerusalem's plans to conquer "all of Palestine, all of Lebanon, all of Jordan, half of Syria, two-thirds of Iraq, one-third of Saudi Arabia as far as holy Medina, and half of Sinai." (In fact, the design outlines the remnants of a coin issued in 37 BCE by Mattathias Antigonus II, the last Hasmonaean king.)

In a *Playboy* interview, Arafat revealed the Israeli flag's hidden symbolism: its two horizontal blue lines represent the Nile and Euphrates rivers "and in between is Israel." (In fact, the blue lines derive from the design of a Jewish prayer shawl.)

Speaking to a Yemeni audience, he announced that Israel's parliament contains an inscription, "This is your land Israel, from the Nile to the Euphrates." (In fact, none of the millions of visitors to the building has laid eyes on such an inscription.)

Israeli timidity. As noted in Chapter 4, "Placating the Enemy," Israel's security establishment, which often has the last word on policy, resists the tough steps that might cause the Palestinians to rethink rejectionism. As is, Palestinians who aggress hardly pay a price. At worst, they spend a few years in the resorts the Israelis call prisons. And with this pivot, we change focus from Palestinians to Israelis.

PART II

Israeli Conciliation

We do not rejoice in victories. We rejoice when a new kind of cotton is grown or when strawberries bloom.

—Golda Meir, Israeli prime minister, ca. 1970

The Oslo Accords made Israel the first country in history ever to arm its enemy with the expectation of gaining security.

—Ruth Wisse, Harvard professor, 2009

IMAGINE A FUTURE U.S. PRESIDENT saying to a future Israeli prime minister: "The Palestinian war on Israel damages American interests. I ask you, our ally, to do whatever it takes, within legal, ethical, and practical boundaries, to end this threat."

How might the prime minister respond? Would he seize the moment to bring down the Palestinian Authority? Would he take steps to shape a new Palestinian mentality? Or would he decline the offer?

My prediction: After intense consultations with Israel's security services and heated cabinet meetings, the prime minister would reply to the president with, "No thanks, we prefer to continue with our existing approach."

Why such a reluctance? The answer lies in the historic Israeli policy of conciliation. Conciliation is to Zionists as rejectionism is to Palestinians, a constant and unique mentality that goes back to the Ottoman period. It represents the polar opposite of rejectionism but has lasted equally long and has a no less futile record. As with rejectionism, conciliation once had a certain logic; today, it lacks any.

Conciliation has two components, enrichment and placation, one economic, the other about security. Both are highly unconventional, if not unique, methods of engaging in warfare; the usual ones are economic deprivation and security toughness. Both Israeli policies rest on the hope that being nice will win reciprocal gestures. Each has spectacularly failed.

Both are entrenched in Israel, but enrichment more deeply so than placation. Enrichment emerged at the dawn of modern Zionism, advocated by some of its greatest figures. Placation dates back only to the Oslo Accords of 1993.

When a U.S. president gives the green light, Israel's prime minister should put aside conciliation and take advantage of the opportunity.

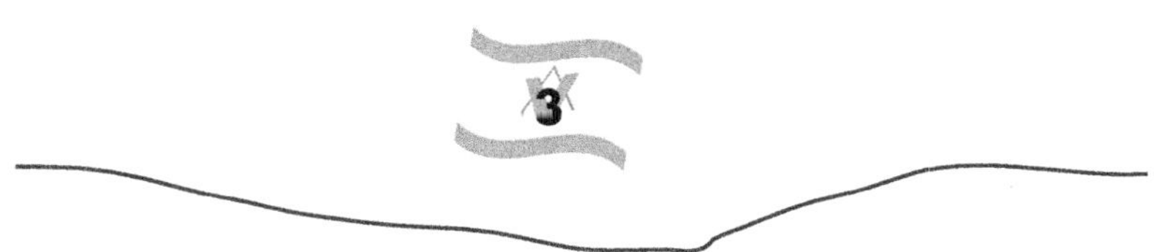

ENRICHING THE ENEMY

ZIONISTS HAVE BEEN DEBATING HOW to approach the Palestinians since the 1880s. Seduce them through economic benefits or break their will through military strength? Woo them or overpower them? The parties now represented by Labor and Likud approximately represent these two historic approaches, which can be characterized as conciliatory versus confrontational, build-hope versus end-hope, be-nice versus be-scary, buy-quiet versus impose-defeat, kind versus tough.

Overwhelmingly, the policy of enrichment has prevailed. The Zionist leadership then and now wants Palestinians to become prosperous, adopt middle-class values, settle into bourgeois good citizenry, and perhaps even thank their Jewish neighbors for their well-being.

HISTORY

Enrichment policy deserves close attention for two reasons: First, it has dominated policy toward the Palestinians,[1] even among Likud members; second, it is highly unusual, if not unique, and therefore demands elucidation in a way that the quite ordinary confrontational approach would not.

• • •

Economic warfare. Conflict has an inherently economic dimension. Armed forces cut supply routes, impede navigation, establish blockades,

1 Also toward the Arab states. In an act of conciliation unique among modern states, Israel agreed three times to return part or all of the Sinai Peninsula to Egypt: under British pressure in 1949, under U.S. pressure in 1957, and of its own volition in 1979–1982. Conciliation also led to gas fields handed over to Lebanon, medical help to Syrians, water to Jordan, and agricultural aid to Egypt.

impose sanctions, apply embargoes, and starve enemies. Medieval forces pillaged enemy territory through the *chevauchée* or the *cabalgada*, the *ghazw* (or razzia), and they besieged fortresses into submission. During the Napoleonic wars, the British Navy established a naval blockade to cut France off from supplies and France responded in kind. World Wars I and II witnessed extensive use of economic deprivation. In 2023, Azerbaijan cut off Armenians living in Nagorno-Karabakh. The U.S. government uses this tactic: Generations-old embargoes remain in place on Cuba and North Korea, newer ones on Iran, Syria, and Venezuela. When the UN had problems with Rhodesia, South Africa, Libya, Iraq, and Afghanistan, it imposed economic embargoes to cripple those countries. After its invasion of Ukraine in 2022, the West instantly minimized trade with Russia.

The goals of economic warfare are multiple and intuitive: weaken the military machine, demoralize the enemy, punish the leadership, turn the population against its rulers, incite a palace revolt. In earlier times, such methods were absolute, affecting everyone and everything; now, they have loopholes for food and medicines, making them more humane but less effective. The economic growth of despotisms (China) has further diminished their efficacy.

Were Israel to engage in economic warfare, in other words, its actions would fit a universal norm. Indeed, when it responded to six months of sustained violence in 2001 by withholding tax money from the PA, denying entry to laborers into Israel, restricting movement in PA territories, ending sales of water, food, medicine, and electricity, these had the intended impact. "University graduates, architects and engineers, men who once wore suits," reported the *Chicago Tribune*, "now hawk flavored water, fruit, paper napkins and chewing gum alongside street children with their hands for alms." Palestinians complained about their plight. "I've been confined to my home for more than a month. I have eight children, we've eaten all we have," lamented a falafel seller in Nablus. "Today is my wedding day, and I want to die," exclaimed a bride who had few guests at her marriage, no food to serve them, and received minimal presents from them. Per-capita income fell about one-third, from $2,000 to $1,400. The population living below the poverty line went up by 50 percent. Unemployment went up four-fold, from 11 percent to 45 percent. Recipients of United Nations aid increased tenfold, from 8.5 percent to 85 percent. As evidence that these steps took their intended toll, the U.S. ambassador to Israel, Martin Indyk, estimated the Palestinian economy to be "on the brink of collapse." A United Nations source predicted that, if nothing were done, the PA "could collapse by the end of March [2001]."

Rather than congratulate Israel for an effective non-violent response to violence, however, Jerusalem found itself pressured from all sides, in U.S. Secretary of State Colin Powell's words, to "lift the siege." London's *Independent* helpfully explained the logic behind this pressure: Economic problems caused a slide into an anarchy that undercut the PA's ability to negotiate with Israel "over restoring calm." In other words, Jerusalem's sanctions hurt its own interests. This fit a larger assumption that resolution with Israel requires Palestinian economic well-being. Caio Koch-Weser, a vice president of the World Bank, explained that for diplomacy to succeed, "the Palestinians need to see improvements in their living conditions very quickly." Republican U.S. Representative Henry Hyde added an immortal insight: "To have peace, there has to be some benefit to the parties that are fighting each other."

Twenty-plus years later, those pressures and assumptions remain in place. In a May 2023 assessment, the World Bank assumed that Israel has a responsibility to improve the economy of its enemies in the West Bank and Gaza.

Those calling on Israel to ease the economic pressure implicitly believe that no matter what the Palestinians' actions—break their word, incite hatred, engage in violence, spread global odium—Israel's enlightened self-interest requires it to assure that Palestinians prosper economically. Therefore, Israel may never, under any circumstance, deploy the standard economic weapon. Why not? Whence the strange idea that Israel alone should enrich its enemy?

It originates neither in the U.S. government nor the World Bank but in Israel itself, and specifically from the country's long tradition of conciliation. With the rare exception, such as the 2001 episode, Israeli leaders seek to improve Palestinian economic welfare; I call this the policy of *enrichment*.

Enrichment represents the deepest, most powerful, and most enduring of Israeli approaches to its Palestinian foe. It developed at the very outset of Zionism, founded in the naïve assumption that Palestinian economic self-interest would push other concerns aside, that gains from advances in welfare would reconcile Palestinians to Jewish immigration and the creation of a Jewish homeland. From this emerged the Zionist hallmark, the unique idea that the movement's progress depended not on the universal tactic of depriving an enemy of resources, but on the opposite one of helping Palestinians to develop economically.

Four figures had key roles in the evolution of enrichment: Theodor Herzl (1860–1904), David Ben-Gurion (1886–1973), Moshe Dayan (1915–1981), and Shimon Peres (1923–2016).

• • •

Theodor Herzl, dreamer. The first modern Zionist manifesto, published in 1882 by the BILU group of immigrants to Palestine, included a promise "to help our brother Ishmael [the Palestinians] in the time of his need." In these simple words, it established the pattern of wanting to help the Palestinians economically, one to be greatly elaborated over time.

In the same spirit, Zionism's philosopher and advocate of manual labor, A.D. Gordon (1856–1922) argued that Jews' attitude toward Palestinians "must be one of humanity, of moral courage which remains on the highest plane, even if the other side is not all that is desired. Indeed, their hostility is all the more reason for our humanity." Isaac Epstein (1862–1943), a leading Zionist educator, observed that the Arab people "must, for its own good let the Jews into the country, for it is powerless to improve its situation and to extricate itself from its poverty and ignorance by its own efforts; only our people can provide for their needs." Such cooperation would enable "the renaissance of two ancient and gifted Semitic people with great potentialities, who complement each other."

Theodor Herzl, the Viennese journalist who both wrote the key tracts of modern Zionism and convened the main Zionist organization, further developed this idea in *Altneuland* ("Old-New Land"), his 1902 novel setting out a vision of the Jewish homeland. That vision includes a single Muslim Palestinian, one Reschid Bey (Rashid Bey in English spelling), a merchant expressing the happy appreciation that Herzl imagined and hoped Palestinians would direct to what Reschid Bey called "the beneficent character of the Jewish immigration."

Zionism's economic benefits drove that appreciation: "Our profits have grown considerably," Reschid Bey tells a Zionist. "Our orange transport has multiplied tenfold since we have had good transportation facilities to connect us with the whole world. Everything here has increased in value since your immigration..... It was a great blessing for all of us." Pressed whether poor Palestinians gained as much as landowners like himself, Reschid Bey enthuses:

> Those who had nothing stood to lose nothing and could only gain. And they did gain: Opportunities to work, means of livelihood, prosperity.... When the swamps were drained, the canals built, and the eucalyptus trees planted to drain and "cure" the marshy soil, the natives (who, naturally, were well acclimatized) were the first to be employed, and were paid well for their work!

Pressed further—aren't Zionists intruders?—Reschid Bey holds firm: "The Jews have enriched us. Why should we be angry with them? They dwell among us like brothers. Why should we not love them?" He even declares: "We Moslems have always had better relations with the Jews than you Christians." That love implies no need for a Jewish military force in Old-New Land.

The imaginary figure of Reschid Bey represents the permanent symbol of what Zionists hoped to find: a reasonable, sated Palestinian grateful for economic benefits and indifferent to Zionism's political implications.

• • •

David Ben-Gurion, optimist. The period of British occupation, from 1917 to 1948, proved the great testing time for enrichment. From about 1915,[2] the Zionist leader Ben-Gurion tried to win the Palestinians' trust by offering them benefits: "Our renewal in this land will come through renewal of the land itself, and that means the renewal of its Arab inhabitants." He offered Palestinian farmers, who relied on "outmoded and primitive" agricultural methods," to learn from their Zionist counterparts. He hoped the Palestinian working class would emulate Zionist workers to organize a labor movement for confronting the *effendi* class of landowners and other notables. Ben-Gurion expected that Palestinians, grateful for the many benefits Jews had brought them, will "welcome us with open arms, or at least will reconcile themselves to our growth and independence." Implied

2 I rely here on Shabtai Teveth, *Ben-Gurion and the Palestinian Arabs: From Peace to War* (Oxford: Oxford University Press, 1985).

in this approach was the belief that Palestinian and Zionist workers had no conflict of interests.

In his grander flights of imagination, Ben-Gurion looked beyond the Palestinians and offered that Zionists would "extend political and economic help to the Arabs," by which he meant helping Syrians against France and also assisting Arabs with "investments in Iraq, Saudi Arabia, and Yemen."

By 1947, this outlook turned into a hope that Arabs prospering in the Jewish state would serve as its ambassadors: "If the Arab citizen will feel at home in our state...[and] if the state will help him in a truthful and dedicated way to reach the economic, social, and cultural level of the Jewish community, then Arab distrust will accordingly subside and a bridge will be built to a Semitic, Jewish-Arab alliance."

Ben-Gurion had multiple and somewhat contradictory reasons for forwarding this hopeful approach. Some had a pragmatic basis. Palestinians many times outnumbered Zionists, so a more aggressive attitude would likely backfire. To prevent Jewish workers' wages from being undercut, Palestinian wages need to rise; in this sense, as Ben-Gurion put it, "the fate of the Jewish worker is linked to the fate of the Arab worker. We will rise together or sink together." To encourage diaspora Jews to immigrate to Palestine, the Zionist movement needed a "moral and humanitarian basis"; plus, they would not likely move to a war zone. Winning the British authorities' favor, especially increasing Palestinian employment, brought benefits.

Other reasons derived from Ben-Gurion's socialism. Comradely relations with a less-advanced people and freeing them from capitalist oppression stood central in his program. Socialist blinders inclined him to excuse Palestinian enmity by blaming it on British imperialists and Palestinian effendis. He also indulged the conceit, in the words of his biographer, that "socialism would eradicate Arab hatred by liberating the Arab worker from his servitude and the grip of the clergy." Interpreting Palestinian violence as the work of criminals and "human scum" avoided having to confront the unpleasant reality of growing Palestinian nationalism.

• • •

Moshe Dayan, "Jewish mother." Enrichment burst out anew in 1967, following Israel's almost effortless seizure of the Golan Heights, the West Bank, eastern Jerusalem, Gaza, and the Sinai Peninsula. Jerusalem could have seized the opportunity to impress on the conquered populations their weakness and the immutability of the Jewish state. Instead, led by Defense Minister Moshe Dayan, who had nearly complete control over the crucial initial post-war decisions, it had another priority entirely: to soften hostility by improving the Palestinians' quality of life.

The policy bore important similarities to that of Ben-Gurion's forty years earlier, although circumstances differed profoundly, with Israel now a powerful state, socialism largely discredited, Palestinian rejectionism firmly entrenched, and no British overlords to please. Ben-Gurion and other Yishuv leaders devised a conciliatory policy in the face of mortal danger; in contrast, Dayan's policies came at Israel's moment of supreme power.[3] They therefore carry special interest.

Dayan used his power to impose as light, undemanding, benevolent, and helpful a regime as possible. He minimized the disruption of Israel's conquest, hoping (in the words of Shabtai Teveth, a contemporary observer) that "establishing mutual co-existence between Jews and Arabs" would create "a relationship of good-neighbourliness" and with that, a reduction in hostility.

Dayan admonished the soldiers under his command, speaking of West Bank residents: "Give them the feeling that the war is over and that nothing has changed." In this spirit, he ordered troops out of inhabited areas and into camps separate from towns, provided loans to keep city administrations functioning, returned requisitioned equipment and vehicles, and, most famously, handed control of the Temple Mount to the waqf, the Islamic authority. Shlomo Gazit, appointed by Dayan as Israel's first coordinator of policy for the West Bank and Gaza, saw his role to be "to take care of the needs of the local population." Investments included improving and extending the electricity and water grids as well as the health system.

Dayan personally implemented what came to be informally known as the "Dayan Policy." He told the Palestinians, "If you keep the peace, we won't bother you with security matters" and "You have the option of either rebelling or of acquiescing in the situation." In other words, he cared not at all what West Bankers thought, said, wrote, or did so long as they abstained from violence and rebellion. He permitted non-violent demonstrations and petitions, however hostile, seeing these as acceptable ways

3 I rely here primarily on Shabtai Teveth, *The Cursed Blessing: The Story of Israel's Occupation of the West Bank* (London: Weidenfeld & Nicolson, 1970).

to vent frustrations. Indeed, the policy went further; Middle East Media Research Institute (MEMRI) president Yigal Carmon explains that it

> included a ban on political activity of any kind, as well as an instruction to avoid any preferential treatment of moderate elements.... In practice, however, implementation of the policy went much further: extremist PLO supporters were treated sympathetically by the Israeli authorities.

School textbooks revealed the military government censors' relaxed attitude. The censors decided, in Teveth's description,

> to examine the textbooks according to three principles they set up for themselves: not to censor historical facts, even if their symbolic significance was not palatable; nor to censor anti-Jewish sentiments extant since ancient Islam; and not to censor general slogans about homeland and nation, which were the essence of nationalistic education.... Generalizations about Jews as treacherous and liars were again eliminated from history books, but a single statement like "Haled said: 'Jews always engage in deceit and fraud and are always conspiring'" was not censored.

Agriculture invoked the Israelis' generous, even amorous, side:

> West Bank farmers had discovered a new world of modern agriculture and the Israeli agricultural experts were enthusiastically embarking on a challenge they had never dreamed of: to advance the backward agriculture in one fell swoop. The farmers on either side of the barricade could be likened to a pair of lovers.... In this affair, it seemed that the Israeli experts were the more active of the partners. Instructors of the Israeli Ministry of Agriculture spread out in teams throughout the West Bank.

These arch-conciliatory steps met with surprise and resistance among many of Dayan's subordinates. When the Israeli military governor of Jenin saw how the war had disrupted the grain harvest, he commandeered five modern combines from Israeli farms. One of the combine drivers recalled: "I was among those who conquered the place. We are incapable of being conquerors. A month before I was risking my life, and now here I was helping them harvest their grain." *We are incapable of being conquerors.*

Teveth reproduces a conversation between two Israeli administrators, one (Zvi Ofer) skeptical about assisting West Bank farmers, the other (Eytan Israeli) eager to provide such services:

> Zvi: "What I don't understand is why you have to improve their agriculture more than they are asking for. Leave them alone."
>
> Eytan: "What do you mean, leave them alone?"
>
> Zvi: "Don't give them experimental fields. Don't introduce new varieties of wheat. Don't develop them."
>
> Eytan: "Should we help them to spray the fields with insecticides or should we let diseases spread?"
>
> Zvi: "Help them in their way of doing things and just as they have been doing them all these years, but don't be a Jewish mother to them."
>
> Eytan: "In other words you don't want agriculture in the Nablus Region improved?... Sixty per cent of West Bank residents live off farming and its services. If we want to live in peace with them, like good neighbours, we'll have to trade with them. It would be to our benefit if we traded with a rich rather than with a poor, backward neighbour."

Note the classic statement of enrichment: "If we want to live in peace with them...we'll have to trade with them." Not surprisingly, more West Bankers gained materially from the Israeli occupation than lost by it.

Palestinians expressed confusion and skeptical gratefulness about this treatment. On two extraordinary occasions, after offering grants and long-term, low-interest credit to residents of Qalqilya whose houses had been destroyed, Dayan was feted by them with *'Ash Dayan* ("Long live Dayan"), a no doubt heady experience that further encouraged his benign policy. The mayor of Hebron, Muhammad Ali Ja'bari, gratefully stated: "Neither I nor the citizens of Hebron expected to be treated so well." His Nablus counterpart, Hamdi Kanaan, explained to Dayan: "We have never experienced the tactics you are employing in Nablus, not under the Turks, not under the British and not under the Jordanians." Ja'bari hosted "a magnificent reception" in honor of Dayan in his grand house, after which Dayan complemented him as one of the Palestinians' sagest leaders. Returning the compliment, Kanaan publicly called Dayan "a wise man and an outspoken statesman."

But this policy came across as feeble. A West Bank notable explained, as paraphrased by Teveth, how

> the Nablus people had been expecting a slaughter. Suddenly not only were neither they nor their property harmed, but Dayan had removed movement restrictions and made every effort to get things back to normal. Since the Arabs were accustomed to being ruled by force, both by their own kinsfolk and by foreigners, the Turks and the British, they interpreted Dayan's policy as weakness.

British journalist David Pryce-Jones reported at the time how West Bankers expected death, rape, religious intolerance, and expulsion:

> But what was to be made of the military government's officials who kept on coming to insist that the Arabs would be left alone and unharmed if they left the Israelis alone and unharmed? And that being the case, they returned with experts who liked to drink coffee and offer their services, making suggestions for mundane improvements to do with crop-yields per dunam, irrigation, marketing and credit facilities. They were conquerors no doubt but they were also worried little men in open-necked shirts and the cheapest of machine-sewn trousers, men who looked as if they were perpetually about to make a gaffe, or might bite their finger-nails. Their goodwill was something like an unsolicited gift on a doorstep, difficult to accept or reject.

The Dayan Policy also had a dark side, favoring rejectionists, as explained by Yigal Carmon, a former officer in Israel's military intelligence:

> It included a ban on political activity of any kind, as well as an instruction to avoid any preferential treatment of moderate elements. This applied equally to supporters of Jordan

> and to the handful of individuals who strove for Palestinian autonomy under the aegis of Israel, whose most notable representative was the renowned attorney from Ramallah, Aziz Shehadeh. In practice, however, implementation of the policy went much further: extremist PLO supporters were treated sympathetically by the Israeli authorities and extremist newspapers such as *Al-Fajr* and *Al-Shaab* were granted licenses on direct instructions from Minister of Defense Moshe Dayan. The official explanation given for this was that Israel did not intervene in the public conduct and freedom of speech of residents of the territories so long as they refrained from terrorist activities.

Thus did a stunning victory on the battlefield translate into enfranchising Israel's worst enemies. With the retrospective of nearly sixty years, the deficiency of Dayan's approach is apparent, for what a population thinks, says, writes, and non-violently does ultimately drives its politics. By ignoring rejectionism, the Dayan Policy missed the opportunity to push Palestinians toward accepting Israel's existence. In this, Israelis anticipated the American "war on terror" in 2001, which pretended not to notice the Islamist ideology that inspired 9/11.

Imagine how Israelis would have been treated had they been the ones conquered; that perhaps best points to the extreme nature of their conciliation and the vast gap between it and rejectionism.

• • •

Shimon Peres, epigramist. Although Menachem Begin, an opponent of enrichment, became prime minister in 1977, breaking the Labor monopoly on power, this only made faith in enrichment grow stronger in a Labor party recoiling from Begin's policies, reaching new extremes. Foreign Minister Shimon Peres, a protégé of Ben-Gurion and Israel's perennial politician, made it the centerpiece of government policy during the Oslo Era (1993–2008). Hoping to turn Palestinians into a society of Reschid Beys, he refreshed the old idea and put it into service via his government positions and an influential book, *The New Middle East*.[4] Peres argued for the

4 Shimon Peres and Arye Naor, *The New Middle East* (New York: Henry Holt, 1993).

PLO to take control of the Palestinian territories, helping it to become economically successful, and expecting that newly bourgeois Palestinians would end the violence.

Peres announced that "any war entered into now will be an unnecessary one...with no victor," somehow overlooking the fact that his country was already at war with the Palestinians. He doubled down on this misconception with the statement that, "In the past, the central issue of the Arab-Israeli conflict was the Palestinian problem. This is no longer true; now it is the nuclear threat," a reference to Iran.

Having waved the conflict with Palestinians away, Peres set about building friendships with them through economic ties. He lobbied Europeans and Americans to invest heavily in the West Bank and Gaza. He revived—and took to new heights—the plan to win Israel's acceptance through bestowing economic, medical, legal, and other benefits on them. He envisioned "a Jordanian-Palestinian-Israeli 'Benelux' arrangement for economic affairs...allowing each to live in peace and prosperity." He predicted the whole Middle East inevitably uniting "in a common market."

Ninety years and much bitter experience after *Altneuland*, Peres reverted to Herzl's gauzy fantasy of a Zionist utopia; more surprisingly, he brought much of Israel's population with him in the form of the Oslo Accords.

Palestinians, living in a conspiracy theory–mad region, naturally suspected the worst, responding to Peres' vision with uncomprehending disbelief, seeing it as a plot for Israel to gain hegemony over the Middle East and eventually the world. Ibrahim Ghawsha, a spokesman for Hamas (as reported by the Dutch correspondent Solomon Bouman) predicted shortly after the Oslo Accords' signing that

> Israel would misuse what he saw as the predominantly economics-based agreement with the PLO economically to dominate the Middle East from the Nile to the Euphrates, as a variant to military dominance. "We know the Jews well," he said. "They are hard workers. With their modern industry, they make the best products at low prices. We are afraid of economic domination."

Peres' slogan about a "New Middle East" came across as code for economic domination and his grandiose statements ("Our real aim is to change the Middle East") further confirmed such fears.

Given the uniqueness and illogic of enriching an enemy, one cannot entirely fault this skepticism.

THE CURRENT SCENE

By now, most Israeli Jews execrate the Oslo Accords and reject the concept of enriching Palestinians. Voting patterns and polling data suggest that they have become steadily tougher-minded since about 2003.[5] Israeli youth have especially soured on enrichment, making Israel the rare democratic country where the young vote more conservatively than the old.

Yet, no matter what the election results, helping Palestinians to prosper remains policy. The Israeli electorate having changed its mind about enriching Palestinians means that politicians no longer openly proclaim this goal. Public disenchantment translates into enrichment becoming quieter, almost surreptitious, even as it also became consensual in elite circles. Most notably, Israeli leaders now offer non-monetary benefits and want others to pay the cash.

• • •

Elite consensus. Enrichment has become more widespread among elites in recent years, coming to include the Left, the security establishment, and the mainstream Right.

The Left. Unsurprisingly, the Left holds to its traditional policy of enrichment. Two examples: Gershon Baskin, a private Israeli citizen engaged in negotiating with Palestinians, wrote in 2011 that, "Economic growth has created a kind of deterrence against a return to violence.... Even with Hamas in power in Gaza...it is better for our neighbors to be gainfully employed than hungry, frustrated, and angry." Foreign Minister Yair Lapid in 2021 outlined a two-part plan, "Economy for Security," that offered Hamas "reconstruction in exchange for disarmament." Part one exchanged a calibrated improvement of Gaza's electricity, health, and transportation systems in return for Hamas stopping its military build-up. Part two exchanged major infrastructure projects, including a seaport and a connector to the West Bank, in return for the Palestinian Authority regaining

5 Unlike diaspora Jewry, especially in the United States, which generally still looks to enrichment.

control of Gaza. Of course, Hamas scorned the offer, reminding Lapid that it (unlike the PA) does not play these games.

The security establishment. Major General Kamil Abu Rukun, head of the Israeli Defense Ministry's Coordinator of Government Activities in the Territories (known as COGAT), justifies humanitarian aid to Gaza because it "helps our security. The protests at the border fence started because of the distress in Gaza, and our role is also to keep southern Israel calm." COGAT approved thousands of work permits for Gazans to work in Israel to promote Gaza's economy. An unnamed Israeli security official observed in early 2022 that "Gaza without an economy is less stable than Gaza with an economy." IDF Chief of Staff Gadi Eisenkot argued for Israel helping Gaza in five areas: electricity, water, sewage, food, and healthcare. One IDF official had bigger plans: "We'd like to see a Gazan economy with its own manufacturing. Developments in agriculture and fishing, and future development of industry, of bigger projects."

As for the West Bank, the IDF in 2022 produced a video to promote Jenin—a town it would militarily invade a year later—as an economically dynamic tourist attraction. COGAT partnered with Israel's Agriculture Ministry to set up aquaculture farms in Jenin and Tulkarem to raise bass fish for human consumption. The aim of the project, in the words of a *Times of Israel* article, "is to allow West Bank residents to grow their own food and strengthen food security for Palestinians." Although the security barrier separating Israel from the West Bank cost $4.2 billion, Palestinians find it easy to go through it, over it, or under it. "Military officials for years turned a blind eye to the thousands going through the fence for work in Israel," the *Times of Israel* explains, because they believe that "the relatively higher wages workers earned on the Israeli informal labor market and then brought back with them to the West Bank served to ease the pressure on the economically depressed territory." This laxity remained in place despite the open road it provided for attacks on Israeli citizens; 90 percent of the roughly 21,000 Palestinians arrested for terror-related offenses between 2018 and 2022 had entered illegally.

The mainstream Right. The Israeli drive to end Palestinian enmity by treating Palestinians well has found wide support among rightist leaders, something nearly unknown during earlier eras.

Avigdor Liberman, head of the Yisrael Beiteinu party, wanted "to help Gaza succeed" and "replace jihad with prosperity," by which he meant helping with economic growth to offer hope and visions of a better tomorrow to Gazans. When defense minister in 2017, he offered Gazans: "The moment Hamas gives up its tunnels and rockets, we'll be the first to invest." Eerily echoing both Shimon Peres and Yasir Arafat, he hoped that Gaza will become "the Singapore of the Middle East." Likud ministers joined the effort. Economy Minister Nir Barkat sought to triple Palestinian incomes because "eventually, if it's good for them, it's good for us." Minister of Intelligence Yisrael Katz hoped to raise $5 billion in Chinese or Saudi funding for a mega-project of his own devising, namely an artificial island off the Gaza coast complete with seaport, airport, electricity generator desalination plant, and resort.

Benjamin Netanyahu, Israel's longest-lasting prime minister (in three separate terms, so far: 1996–1999, 2009–2021, and since 2022) does not speak of winning Palestinian good will through prosperity. To the contrary, as he explains in his autobiography, he grew up in a household inspired by Revisionist Zionism that stressed Jewish power. He tells how his father Benzion "was greatly influenced by [Ze'ev] Jabotinsky's 1923 essay, 'The Iron Wall,' which argued that Arab reconciliation with Zionism would occur only when the Jewish state became so strong that the Arabs would abandon any hope of destroying it." Through his long political career, Benjamin has always spoken in ways that uphold that tradition, giving him a reputation for toughness among friend and foe alike.

His actual record shows him to be a matter-of-fact conservative who dowses brushfires as they occur while downplaying principles and consistency on the one hand or grand ambitions on the other. Highly cautious, he places a priority on maintaining calm and stability, often through a program of semi-clandestine enrichment, whether by Israel itself or by others.

• • •

Enriching the PA and Hamas. Fearing the impact on Israel of the PA's collapse and hoping to render Hamas less aggressive, the Netanyahu government has directly and indirectly turned large sums over to these two enemies.

Directly. In the West Bank, it increased economic benefits to residents in early 2023, hoping that this gesture would reduce the possibility of violence (and also to appease American pressure). A week before October 7, Jerusalem effectively gifted the PA $92 million. First, it halved the gasoline tax it is entitled to take by terms of the 1994 Protocol on Economic

Relations from 3 percent to 1.5 percent, saving the PA $21 million on an annual basis. Second, it transferred $71 million extra in taxes funds to the PA. This amount came on top of another $90 million earlier in the year.

As befits a government shy about enriching its enemies, Netanyahu's Israel sought indirect methods to boost the Palestinians, primarily by providing non-monetary benefits or finding funds from outside sources.

Israel subsidized water; a spokesman for the Water Authority noted that "water prices for the Palestinian Authority are...lower than the water rates for Israeli communities and companies." In other cases, Israel turned a blind eye to the theft of water and electricity in the West Bank. Jerusalem approved development of the Hamas Marine gas field in June 2023 with the goal of earning the Palestinians billions of dollars, thereby enhancing "Palestinian economic development and maintaining security stability in the region." Additionally, it provided half of Gaza's electricity pre-October 7 effectively at no cost, explains Elai Rettig of Bar-Ilan University:

> Although technically, the Palestinian Authority (PA) is responsible for paying for the electricity supply to Gaza, it instead accumulates the debt until it is periodically forgiven and erased...attempts to claim Gaza's electricity debt or threaten to disconnect it were aborted, mainly due to the legal consensus that Israel is responsible for supplying necessities to the Gaza Strip despite no longer occupying it de facto.

Medical permits offer another non-monetary form of enrichment; in 2022, Israel issued 110,000 of them to West Bankers and 17,000 to Gazans. Tourism offers a lesser but still meaningful vehicle of making nice. In 2011, the authorities issued more than 60,000 tourist permits, mainly to West Bank schools and summer camps to take children visiting beaches, the zoo, and mixed Jewish-Arab cities. A security source explained the rationale: "We want Palestinians, especially young ones, to see another kind of Israeli, not only soldiers and settlers. Anything that can help them blow off steam and relax. Perhaps instead of demonstrating...they'll go to the beach." *Perhaps...they'll go to the beach*: That sums up the enrichment fantasy.

The Netanyahu government even provisioned Gaza during warfare. During the Hamas attack on Israel in 2012, when Hamas launched 1,506 rockets and missiles from Gaza, Israel sent 124 trucks with food and medicines to Gaza, kept the water and electricity supplies flowing, and continued to provide funds. During the Hamas Israel war of 2014, the Israeli Electric Company sent technicians to repair electricity wires going into Gaza destroyed by a Hamas rocket, risking the lives of its employees for the welfare of an enemy population. As Guy Bechor of the Interdisciplinary Center in Herzliya wryly observed, "We represent the first instance in history of one side feeding and financing its enemy, even during a time of war between the two."

Private Israeli citizens offered another indirect method of support. Members of an Israeli volunteer organization, Road to Recovery, drove 2,700 of the most indigent patients gratis from the border to their medical appointments, sometimes hours away. Learning in 2020 about the dire water situation in Gaza, Georgian-Israeli philanthropist Michael Mirilashvili donated or heavily discounted seven Watergen machines that, like dehumidifiers, extract clean water from the air, plus the solar panels that permit them to function off the grid. Asked about his motives, Mirilashvili explained that "they are our neighbors and it's a great pity to look at them suffering from such severe water shortages." These robust machines continued to work even after Israel's post-October 7 attack on Gaza.

Indirectly. An Israeli consensus urges outside aid to the PA. President Shimon Peres applauded John Kerry's offer of $4 billion. Netanyahu supported Donald Trump's plan to hand "more than $50 billion in new investment over ten years." His government specifically campaigned in 2011 for outside funding to the PA: "Israel calls for ongoing international support for the PA budget and development projects," on the basis that this "will contribute to the growth of a vibrant private sector, which will provide the PA an expanded base for generating internal revenue." A 2011 Israeli government document, *Measures Taken by Israel in Support of Developing the Palestinian Economy and Socio-Economic Structure*, detailed its "calls for ongoing international support for the PA budget and development projects that will contribute to the growth of a vibrant private sector." Prime Minister Naftali Bennett's government, according to a 2021 report, was "set to ask donor countries to restore their financial contributions to the Palestinian Authority."

As for Gaza, that second 2011 document explained Israel's "Civilian Policy" in Gaza, which is "aimed at improving the quality of life in Gaza [and] has enabled an economic and humanitarian recovery in the area." In this spirit, Netanyahu ignored an intelligence report on Hamas' multi-million-dollar investment portfolio that included about forty Middle Eastern companies. Israel also pleaded with international donors to help Gaza, for example, by supplying water desalination plants, while what the daily *Yediot Ahronot* mysteriously called "private Israeli and foreign elements" paid for a solar field to increase the electricity supply to Gaza—a nice little present to help to manufacture and launch rockets, missiles, and other weapons.

• • •

Getting Qatar to pay. Qatar, an ally of Iran and Türkiye, deserves special attention. To a small extent, Qatar funded the PA but Hamas received the great bulk of its donations.

Qatari funding began under Prime Minister Ehud Olmert, whose office in 2008 acknowledged enabling the transfer of hard currency to Hamas, conceding that this "takes place with the knowledge of the Israeli government, for diplomatic reasons," having decided that this "was an Israeli interest." To which, Nitsana Darshan-Leitner, director of the Shurat HaDin Israel Law Center, retorted that Israel "cannot fight against the Hamas terrorist organization with one hand and continue to secretly finance it with the other." She revealed that trucks from Arab banks in the West Bank "bring new banknotes and shekels issued by the Bank of Israel to the Gaza crossings, where the money is exchanged for dollars and euros smuggled to Hamas.... This means that Israel is essentially laundering Hamas's smuggled money."

Not just that, but each month for years, *The New York Times* reports, "Israeli security officials met Mohammed al-Emadi, a Qatari diplomat, at the border between Israel and Jordan. From there, they drove him to the Kerem Shalom border crossing and into Gaza." *Al Jazeera*, Qatar's television channel, reported that "some $30m in cash was delivered in suitcases to Gaza each month."[6] Eventually, under Qatari pressure, UN agencies took over Emadi's function. According to *Al-Monitor*, that monthly payment of $30 million divided into three projects of $10 million each: $100 to each of 100,000 destitute families, fuel for the power plant, and paying for both Hamas employee salaries and projects for the unemployed.

Qatari funding continued and even increased during Netanyahu's prime ministry. In 2012, the emir of Qatar celebrated his visit to Gaza with

---

6 In addition, starting in late 2021, Qatar began funding Hamas by sending free fuel via Egypt.

a pledge of $400 million to Hamas. In 2013, he pledged $250 million on the occasion of the Arab League summit in Doha. News dribbled out of further grants: $31 million approved by Defense Minister Liberman in 2016, $20 million in 2019, $50 million in 2020. Qatari sources report a pledge of $500 million to Gaza in 2021 and total aid to Gaza as of September 24, 2023, of "more than $2.1 billion."

Jerusalem was closely involved with these transfers.

- In 2019, the Netanyahu government (according to Reuters) "initially blocked the latest Qatari transfer, but relented...after the Israeli military recommended that it be allowed in."
- In 2020, Qatar threatened to cut its financial donations to Gaza unless Israel desisted from a policy (annexation of parts of the West Bank) it disapproved of.
- In 2021, an Israeli Foreign Ministry spokesman announced that Qatar's grant "will be sent and distributed in close coordination with the Israeli government."
- In 2023, days before October 7, Qatari officials met with Mossad chief David Barnea and quizzed him on whether Israel wanted payments to Hamas to continue; of course, it did.

Netanyahu blinded himself to the obvious reality that Hamas kept a share of Qatar's funds for itself, though everyone else knew this. Western governments for years had drawn this conclusion. Defense Minister Liberman resigned his position and brought down the government in protest: "I did not agree to allow Qatari money to enter" Gaza. Another defense minister, Benny Gantz, accused Netanyahu of paying "protection money" to Hamas with Qatar's money. On retiring as the head of Mossad, Yossi Cohen mentioned the hope that Qatari money "would lead us to a settlement with Hamas," adding, "but things got a little out of control." Major General (res.) Amos Gilad recalled the illusion that "if you fed [Hamas] with money, they would be tamed." Permitting the cash flow was a "dramatic, tragic mistake," he added. *Ha'aretz* military correspondent Amos Harel knew that "Qatar had given Hamas billions of dollars, most of which it used to expand militarily." MEMRI's Yigal Carmon knew that Hamas used most of Qatar's money "to build tunnels, develop its rocket array, and construct the 'metro,' the underground city," while "only a minuscule portion" of it went to civilians. Israeli intelligence even cracked the code of Hamas' sources of income—but sat on this information and did nothing with it.

Arguably, Netanyahu's record of conciliation is more insidious than his predecessors'; they acknowledged their views and methods, whereas he said one thing and did another, confusing the electorate.

EXPLANATION AND ASSESSMENT

How has the enrichment of Palestinians worked out? Did it have positive economic results? Did it soften Palestinian attitudes?

• • •

More prosperity, more rejectionism. Enrichment did indeed enrich. It also, ironically, boosted rejectionism.

Improved living standards. The British Foreign Office reportedly had a saying, "Keep the Persians hungry and the Arabs fat" and enrichment perfectly fit this outlook. The first British high commissioner in Palestine, Herbert Samuel, endorsed enrichment: "It is essential to make the Arabs feel in their hearts that they are better through the British Mandate." Secretary of State for the Colonies Winston Churchill counted on the Zionists, informing Palestinians in 1921 that a Jewish national home

> will be good for the world, good for the Jews and good for the British Empire. But we also think it will be good for the Arabs who dwell in Palestine.... You can see with your own eyes in many parts of this country the work which has already been done by Jewish colonies, how sandy wastes have been reclaimed and thriving farms and orangeries planted in their stead.

Churchill encouraged his audience "to take a wise and tolerant view of the Zionist movement" and admonished it: "If instead of sharing miseries through quarrels you will share blessings through cooperation, a bright and tranquil future lies before your country." He cheerfully predicted that the success of Zionism would be "accompanied by a general diffusion of wealth and well being...and by an advance in the social, scientific and cultural life of the people as a whole."

British authorities subsequently noted the economic results of enrichment. In 1930, the Shaw Commission reported that "Jewish immigration and enterprise have been of great advantage to Palestine." In 1937, former prime minister David Lloyd-George, declared: "There can be no doubt that the Arab population of Palestine has profited enormously by the Zionist enterprise." That same year, the Peel Commission concluded that "the Arabs have benefited by the development of the country owing to Jewish immigration." The commission also framed the mandate's obligations "to be mutually compatible owing to the conciliatory effect on the Palestinian Arabs of the material prosperity which Jewish immigration would bring to Palestine as a whole."

Scholars Baruch Kimmerling and Joel S. Migdal report that Zionist spokesmen took pride in this success, noting "how Jewish agriculture had helped enable peasants to free themselves from debilitating 'feudal' relations, which had ground them down in poverty and debt. The Zionists also pointed to their introduction of new practical techniques—irrigation, growing fodder for animals, new seed varieties—for the improvement of peasant farming." Palestinians, too, acknowledged an improvement, with Yusuf Hanna of the *Filastin* newspaper stating that, "Any Arab would openly admit in private how much plenty and progress the Jews have brought him and his country in the course of their building up a national home."

More rejectionism. Did an economic boom translate into political acceptance and "Thank you, let us live in harmony together"? Hardly. Human nature being what it is, enrichment increased hostility.

Husseini himself did not mince words: "We want no progress, no prosperity" deriving from Jewish immigration." When Ben-Gurion told the Palestinian politician Musa al-Alami in 1934, "We bring a blessing to the Arabs of Palestine and they have no good cause to oppose us," Alami retorted, "I would prefer that the country remain impoverished and barren for another hundred years, until we ourselves are able to develop it on our own." A Palestinian informed the Peel Commission: "You say my house has been enriched by the strangers who have entered it. But it is *my* house, and I did not invite the strangers in, or ask them to enrich it, and I do not care how poor or bare it is, if only I am master in it." (Note the verb *enrich.*)

The Peel Commission correctly concluded that enrichment had failed politically. Palestinian prosperity, it asserted, "has had no conciliatory effect. On the contrary, improvement in the economic situation in Palestine has meant the deterioration of the political situation." Almost a century later, Zionists have still not quite figured this out.

Later enrichment and hostility. After 1967, the Dayan Policy greatly improved living standards, when an approximately 120,000 Palestinians working in Israel before 1993 provided an economic engine. Efraim Karsh recounts the massive changes:

> During the 1970's, the West Bank and Gaza constituted the fourth fastest-growing economy *in the world*—ahead of such "wonders" as Singapore, Hong Kong, and Korea, and substantially ahead of Israel itself...mortality rates in the West Bank and Gaza fell by more than two-thirds between 1970 and 1990, while life expectancy rose from 48 years in 1967 to 72 in 2000 (compared with an average of 68 years for all the countries of the Middle East and North Africa). Israeli medical programs reduced the infant-mortality rate of 60 per 1,000 live births in 1968 to 15 per 1,000 in 2000 (in Iraq the rate is 64, in Egypt 40, in Jordan 23, in Syria 22).... By 1986, 92.8 percent of the population in the West Bank and Gaza had electricity around the clock, as compared to 20.5 percent in 1967; 85 percent had running water in dwellings, as compared to 16 percent in 1967; 83.5 percent had electric or gas ranges for cooking, as compared to 4 percent in 1967; and so on for refrigerators, televisions, and cars...the number of schoolchildren in the territories grew by 102 percent, and the number of classes by 99 percent, though the population itself had grown by only 28 percent. Even more dramatic was the progress in higher education. At the time of the Israeli occupation of Gaza and the West Bank, not a single university existed in these territories. By the early 1990's, there were seven such institutions, boasting some 16,500 students. Illiteracy rates dropped to 14 percent of adults over age 15, compared with 69 percent in Morocco, 61 percent in Egypt, 45 percent in Tunisia, and 44 percent in Syria.

Such was the record. But spokeswoman Hanan Ashrawi spoke for the PA leadership in 2001 when she summarized Israeli rule as "a unique combination of military occupation, settler colonization, and systematic oppression. Rarely has the human mind devised such varied, diverse, and comprehensive means of wholesale brutalization and persecution." (One suspects she projected, characterizing a hypothetical Palestinian rule over Jews.)

Palestinian leaders spurn Israeli offers of economic help. Political analyst Ibrahim Al-Madhoun called thems "silly" and explained that Hamas rejects such bribes because it "does not wish to turn the case of liberating the land and Palestinians into an economic issue." Top Hamas official Mahmoud Zahar added: "If we wanted to turn the Gaza Strip into Singapore, we could have achieved that with our own hands." Khalil al-Hayya, a Hamas politburo member explained that "Hamas' goal is not to run Gaza and to bring it water and electricity and such." The attack on October 7, he noted, "was not because we wanted fuel or laborers. It did not seek to improve the situation in Gaza."

The pattern of Palestinians treated in Israeli hospitals, usually at no cost, offers one spectacular proof of enrichment's failure. They show ingratitude on two levels. On the lesser level, the patients attempt to murder their benefactors.

- In 2005, a twenty-one-year-old Gaza woman successfully treated in Beersheba for burns from a gas-tank explosion returned to the hospital for follow-up treatment, but this time she carried explosives with the intent to become a suicide bomber killing as many young people as she could.
- In 2011, a Gazan mother whose infant lacked an immune system and who was saved at an Israeli hospital announced on camera that she wanted him to grow up to be a suicide bomber.
- In 2017, two sisters entered Israel from Gaza so one of them could receive cancer treatment; they used the opportunity to smuggle explosives for Hamas.
- In 2022, a Hamas operative from Gaza entered Israel for unspecified medical treatment, which he then exploited to remain in the country illegally and to pass intelligence to his commanders in Hamas and also recruit for Hamas.

On the greater level, Palestinian leaders exhibit their gratitude for excellent medical care given to their close relatives through large-scale murder. Hamas leader Ismail Haniyeh's mother in-law, niece, daughter, and granddaughter all won permission to leave Gaza and enter Israel for medical treatment, which they received. Israeli doctors saved the life of Hamas leader and October 7 architect Yahya Sinwar by removing a brain tumor when he was a prisoner in Israel. To complete the irony, the nephew of one of Sinwar's medical team members, Yuval Bitton, was abducted on October 7.

• • •

Explaining Palestinian rage. So abysmal a failure raises two questions: Why did enrichment fuel hatred and violence? Why did Zionists nonetheless persist with this failed policy?

Three main explanations account for the heightening in Palestinian bellicosity. First, offering economic aid before a war ends strengthens the enemy's position and builds its morale. The PA and Hamas use additional funds not to enable consumer spending, much less to encourage democratic values, but to stoke aggression by funding the infrastructure of combat, building military forces, rallying the population, and lobbying more effectively against Israel. Sending resources to Arafat, Abbas, Haniyeh, and Sinwar does not help with "restoring calm," per *The Independent*, but encourages their aggressive goals through extra resources.

Economic assistance should *follow* defeat, when the enemy has given up its war aims. Hitler, Mussolini, and Tojo did not benefit from enrichment. American aid packages flowed to Germany, Italy, and Japan only after their forces lost on the battlefield, their enemy regimes had fallen, their populations acknowledged defeat, and friendly governments had come to office. Similarly, the French-German partnership only followed on the ending of Nazism.

Second, in autocracies, enhanced economic power usually fuels aggression, as seen the cases of the United Kingdom, Germany, Japan, China, and Türkiye. Wealth made possible the British Empire that ruled over about one-fourth of the world's population and land mass. As late as 1892, the typical German was described as an "obscure and impractical dreamer"; industrialization made him into a hyper-aggressive imperialist (World War I) and racist (World War II). Japanese economic success in the 1920s fueled ambitions to rule all of East Asia. As China has become the workshop of the world, it also became more bellicose. Impressive growth under Erdoğan went hand in hand with a new Turkish aggressiveness. Thus does economic advancement fuel belligerence. Why should Palestinian autocrats be different?

Third, rejectionism builds on Islamism, which disdains economic welfare. The PLO charter states that, "Doctrines whether political social or economic, shall not occupy the people of Palestine from the primary duty of liberating their homeland." The Hamas slogan stresses not full employment or rising income levels but "God is its target, the Prophet is its model, the Koran its constitution: Jihad is its path and death for the sake of God is the loftiest of its wishes." Khomeini captured this sentiment with his usual pithiness: "We did not create a revolution to lower the price of melon." To be sure, economic strength is important, for it strengthens Muslims in their battle against non-Muslims, but Islamists see wealth as a means, not as an end. Money serves to train cadres and buy weapons, not to enjoy a good life.

• • •

Explaining Zionist persistence. If enrichment augments rejectionism, it makes no sense for Israel to keep pushing it, ever counting on clean water and late-model cars to work their elusive magic. A number of historical and psychological factors, plus the "something to lose" theory explain this improbable stubbornness and surprising endurance.

Jewish history. Jews, with their millennial experience of oppression, religious persecution, racism, pogroms, and the Holocaust, have developed a unique sense of empathy and morality. The last thing they wish to do is oppress another people. Most Zionists and their diaspora supporters prefer to induce rather than coerce Palestinians, deploy carrots rather than sticks, coax not compel, conciliate not confront.

Prestige. Conciliation has a venerable legacy, being the original Zionist outlook and espoused by many of the movement's greatest leaders. Who are you or I to gainsay Herzl, Ben-Gurion, Dayan, and Peres?

Humanitarian concern. While the Israeli desire to enrich Palestinians originated in pragmatism, it has grown into a genuine sense of support and concern. This comes out with special clarity in times of crisis. When the economic situation in Gaza worsened in early 2018, one might imagine Jewish Israelis, the object of Hamas' murderous intentions, to be unconcerned or even pleased about their enemies' problems. But no: A headline explained that "As Gaza approaches 'famine,' Israel, rather than world, appears most concerned." In part, this was for practical reasons—worrying about the cost to Israel for collapse in Gaza—but it also had a moral dimension: Prosperous Jews cannot sit by as their neighbors, however hostile, sink into the mire.[7]

Contrast in wealth. Many Israelis feel discomfort at the gap between their economic well-being and the visibly lower standard of living in the West Bank, Gaza, and eastern Jerusalem. Western political circles, notes Yifa Segal of the Jerusalem Institute for Strategy and Security, then built on this sensitivity, insisting that "the wide gap between Israeli and Palestinian economic well-being aggravates the conflict."

Materialism. Assuming with Marxists that money matters more than ideas, enrichment sees handsome apartments, excellent medical care, and fine schools as the antidote to nationalist, Islamist, or other aspirations. Like the residents of Atlanta, prosperous Palestinians should be too busy to hate. Or, better reflecting the Israeli view: Sated villains do not bother to attack. They go to the beach.

Projection. When Israelis lure Palestinians with enrichment, they assume their own proclivity, ignoring the Palestinians' determination not to let the prospect of prosperity influence their goals. Hazem Qassem of Hamas noted this in 2021: "Israel, expecting that economic solutions would cause the people to abandon their goals of liberation and return, does not understand the Palestinian people." Precisely.

"Something to lose." Enrichment policy assumes that richer people aggress less because they have more at stake. It aims to diminish violence, Segal writes, "by reducing frustration and grievance on the one hand and raising the cost of terror attacks on the other."

Meir Ben Shabbat, the national security advisor, explains that "Israel wants to improve Gazans' well-being and address their humanitarian concerns, in part because this would make it clear that they would have a lot to lose if they engage in conflict." A member of Kibbutz Nir Am near the border with Gaza agrees: "If the economy in Gaza gets worse, there will be a lot of Palestinians who, in the deep, deep sense of the word, have nothing to lose." Former ambassador to the United States Michael Oren concludes that "Israel was spared many thousands of rockets thanks largely

---

7 The same applied to Syrians during their civil war; beyond the favorable publicity of treating wounded civilians, Israelis showed a genuine concern for their neighbors.

to its decision to admit the Gazan workers.... The idea was to give Hamas the one thing it lacked: something to lose, thereby raising the price it would pay for aggression."[8] The "something to lose" doctrine sees well-being as a sedative.

The same logic explains Israel's boosting a hostile UNRWA. Security officials worry, writes Ariel Kahane of *Israel Hayom* that "cutting UNRWA's budget could be extremely problematic, saying that while Israel had no objection to cutting the agency's budget in the West Bank because other organizations would fill the void, no such organizations could do the same in Gaza." His *Israel Hayom* colleague Nadav Shragai adds that the security establishment "wants quiet and is afraid that if UNRWA is unable to help hundreds of thousands of needy Palestinians due to budget cuts, Israel will see rioting, an escalation in violence, and terrorist attacks."

For self-interested reasons, Palestinians sometimes encourage this belief. The CEO of a major bank in Ramallah observed that "You're not going to join an intifada when you have to make mortgage payments." A leader of the PA's Preventive Security Service recounted that many violent Hamas and PIJ members have "no food to eat" and "nothing to live for." Even Abu Toameh expects contented Palestinians to abandon rejectionism: "The PA and Hamas leaders are apparently worried that the Palestinians would forget about the jihad against Israel once they have jobs and a strong economy."

• • •

Opposition to enrichment. Enrichment may be an ensconced Israeli policy, but it has critics.

Ze'ev Jabotinsky (1880–1940), the Revisionist Zionist leader, is enrichment's most authoritative opponent. He argued in his famous 1923 essay "The Iron Wall" for the futility of trying to win Palestinian good will. "That the Arabs of the Land of Israel should willingly come to an agreement with us is beyond all hopes and dreams at present, and in the foreseeable future." They will accept Zionists "only when there is no hope left. Only when not a single breach is visible in the iron wall." At that point,

---

8 The Project Raven revelation that Qatar gave Benjamin Netanyahu $65 million for his election campaigns in 2012 and 2018 could also have influenced Israeli acceptance of that country's largess to Hamas.

finally, "both peoples, like good neighbors, can then live in peace." He also observed that the Arabs' "instinctive patriotism is just as pure and noble as our own; it cannot be bought, it can only be curbed...by *force majeure*." Peace will follow only when Palestinians internalize the impossibility of destroying the Jewish presence.

Refuting Ben-Gurion and enrichment, Jabotinsky derides the hope that "the Arabs will voluntarily consent to the realization of Zionism in return for the cultural and economic benefits we can bestow on them."

> The Compromisers in our midst attempt to convince us that the Arabs are some kind of fools who can be tricked by a softened formulation of our goals, or a tribe of money grubbers who will abandon their birth right to Palestine for cultural and economic gains.... This childish fantasy...comes from some kind of contempt for the Arab people, of some kind of unfounded view of this race as a rabble ready to be bribed in order to sell out their homeland for a railroad network.

Nor was Jabotinsky alone. The writer Israel Zangwill (1864–1926) warned Jews against the delusion of believing in "settlement through good will and mutual agreement." Provoking alarm among fellow Zionists, he went further and called for expelling the Palestinians.

Even Ben-Gurion, the avatar of enrichment, changed his mind as persistent Palestinian unwillingness forced him to acknowledge the inutility of enrichment. By 1936, he came to sound like Jabotinsky:

> Arab leaders see no value in the economic dimension of the country's development, and while they will concede that our immigration has brought material blessing to Palestine, they nonetheless contend—and from the Arab point of view, they are right—that they want neither the honey nor the bee sting.

He went on, bitterly: "Do you think that, by extending economic favors to the Arabs, you can make them forget their political rights in Palestine?" No, "Let's not deceive ourselves and think that when we approach the Arabs and tell them 'We'll build schools and better your economic conditions,' that we've succeeded." They will not accept to see themselves "as complete strangers in the land which is theirs." He acknowledged that he had been "naïve then to imagine...that the Arabs think like us."

Ben-Gurion drew policy conclusions. He rejected "simply doing favors for the Arabs" and dismissed selfless aid to the Palestinians as no less than "moral corruption." Ben-Gurion so completely gave up on alliance with Palestinians, he now saw (as his biographer Shabtai Teveth explains) that "the growing strength of the Yishuv was the only thing that could bring the Arabs around to agreement and peace." He even used the phrase "iron wall" in reference to protecting Zionist settlements from Palestinians.

Reviewing this drastic change, his biographer wonders about the sincerity of Ben-Gurion's earlier promotion of enrichment. Yet his later reversal faded from memory and Ben-Gurion's legacy remains one of conciliation. Enrichment remained the norm, blossoming with the Oslo Accords. Israelis daring to disagree with it became marginalized along with Meir Kahane, the American-born rabbi evicted from the Knesset, Israel's parliament, who stated: "Because I respect the Arab...I understand that we cannot buy their logic and national pride with syrupy words, with indoor toilets and with 'better living conditions.'"

Only with the tarnishing of the Oslo Accords did criticism of enrichment become acceptable. For example, former Israeli MP Einat Wilf blasts the security establishment for thinking that funds to Gaza are buying it calm, and so doing "anything possible to ensure that the funds keep flowing, even if that means that the calm is purchased at the cost of a war that will go on for decades."

Today, some in Israel's security establishment accept the failure of enrichment. Segal explains that, "On the one hand, certain parties in the government and the IDF continue to claim that more work permits and more economic aid will reduce terror, while on the other hand Israel Security Agency [Shin Bet] experts insist that such conclusions are in error." In that vein, Doron Matza, a former Israeli intelligence agent, argues: "It's time for Israel to sober up and recognize that economic [enrichment] carries no promise whatsoever of a secure peace."

Israel's ambassador to Germany Ron Prosor adds a rare critique from the inside:

> The security system has automatically supported UNRWA for all these years out of short-range vision. No one wants the change to take place on his watch. Everyone is afraid of the ramifications, and no one considers the strategic angle. If I was Coordinator of Government Activities in the Territories, I also

> wouldn't want to rock an already leaking boat. I'd be happy that someone else would continue to feed and take care of this enormous elephant sitting in the middle of our living room.

Only in the Israeli government that came to office in late 2022 does one hear such criticism from ministers. When Netanyahu agreed to help the PA's finances, Finance Minister Bezalel Smotrich prevented this by not signing off on the measures, although eventually his resistance was circumvented. In response to the PA going to the International Court of Justice for an opinion on what it called Israel's "occupation" of Palestinian land, Israel in January 2023 called this an act of "political and legal war" and imposed a series of sanctions, including a threat to withhold $39 million from the PA and pay that amount to the families of victims of Palestinian attacks. Orit Strock, Israel's minister of Settlements and National Missions, responded to a Political-Security Cabinet meeting to discuss ways to strengthen the PA: "Strengthen the Palestinian Authority? The one that pays salaries to those who murder us? The one that educates for war against us? The one that persecutes our soldiers in The Hague and conducts an international attack against us? The one that robs our land in a systematic plan and with huge budgets?"

Such dissident views, however, have had a vanishingly small impact on Israeli policy. Enrichment rules.

PLACATING THE ENEMY

CONCILIATION CONTAINS TWO COMPONENTS, CONCERNING economics and security. *Placation* refers to excessive Israeli caution and timidity vis-à-vis the Palestinians.[1]

THE PROBLEM

Whereas enrichment reaches back to the misty earliest days of Zionism, placation has a more recent origin, dating specifically to the evening of September 13, 1993, hours after the Oslo Accords' signing. Earlier that day, Yasir Arafat had so-sincerely announced to the world on the South Lawn of the White House: "The PLO recognizes the right of the State of Israel to exist in peace and security." That evening, however, he went on Jordanian television to assure a narrowly Palestinian audience that the Oslo Accords he had just signed were but a step toward the PLO's 1974 ten-point "Plan of Phases," according to which it would acquire territory by any means possible, establish an "independent combatant national authority" on it, and use this base to expand. He also privately assured unhappy colleagues that the Palestinian Authority served only as a transitory step toward Israel's destruction.

Clearly, the Israelis should have showcased Arafat's public remarks and stopped the whole diplomatic process right there till he made full amends by retracting his statement and promising henceforth to stick to his White House assurances. Instead, they ignored this transgression and the innumerable ones that followed, including incitement, illegal construction,

1 While this study emphasizes Israel's strategic policy of placation, it is also true, as the country's many critics publicize, that it deploys harsh and even unjust tactics (such as those portrayed in the television series *Fauda*) in its attempt to protect itself from Palestinian violence. While deployed in self-defense, these are never justified.

and murders, hoping these were transitional bumps on the path to a successful outcome. But placation failed, bringing instead more violence and delegitimization.

• • •

The phenomenon. Placation began on the Left, which ended up discredited by its failure. Surprisingly, this did not end the mentality, which then spread to the security establishment and to the Right.

Personnel. Having accepted Yasir Arafat as their "partner for peace," Israel's leftist leaders excused his transgressions, appeased his aggressions, averted their eyes from his crimes, and hoped their own positive outlook would be infectious. But—shock—placation failed, and linking their electoral fate to Arafat proved ruinous; together, the Labor and Meretz parties won fifty-six seats in the 1992 parliamentary elections and four in 2022.

Beyond losing votes, the Oslo Accords debacle contributed to undermining the center-Left's confidence and its intellectual decline. As Israeli journalist Haviv Rettig Gur explains, rather than respond to the Right's policies with ideas of its own, it prefers to frame them "as a nefarious, foreign-inflected conspiracy.... On judicial or constitutional reform, economic policy, natural gas, Palestinians, Iran, and countless other questions, the center-left sometimes knows what it opposes, but can rarely articulate what it supports."

The Left still encourages overt placation, though now most loudly from the margins. HaMoked for the Protection of Individuals defends Palestinian murderers of Jews. Ta'ayush betrays Palestinians who sell land to Jews. (One member said of them: "Straight away I give their pictures and phone numbers to the [PA's] Preventive Security Force. The Palestinian Authority catches them and kills them. But before it kills them, they get beat up a lot.")

With the Left's electoral and intellectual decay, an entirely different and perhaps unexpected element of Israeli life took up its banner of deference to the Palestinians: the country's esteemed security establishment made up of the IDF, Shin Bet (or Shabak), Mossad, Aman, the police, the border police, the transport police, the prison service, the antiquities authority, the Knesset guard, the national guard, the civil guard, and others.

It can seem like two Israeli security establishments exist side by side: an offensive fight-to-win establishment dealing with states, and a defensive police-style counterpart dealing with Palestinians and other non-state actors.[2] The former enjoys a deserved reputation for creativity, ingenuity and daring, winning admiration for its remarkable military and espionage successes against the Arab states and more recently in its confrontation with Iran. The latter represents an uncelebrated, dull, and reticent counterpart; not the Israel Defense Forces but, as a wag puts it, the Israel Defen*sive* Forces. The former seeks victory, the latter seeks quiet. It took six days of war against three states vs. eighty-eight days against the PLO and ninety-six days and counting against Hamas by the end of 2023; Entebbe in 1976 vs. Jenin in 2002; stealing Iran's nuclear archive vs. the botched execution attempt by inserting poison into a Hamas leader's ear; battlefield prowess vs. gentle concern for Palestinian sensitivities; knocking out the Iraqi and Syrian nuclear reactors vs. the ineptitude that led to October 7.

Examples. The unwillingness to prevent the purposeful Palestinian destruction of Jewish heritage presents an exceptional example of timidity. An almost-routine news item from 2021 reports that "Palestinian roadwork destroyed portions of a 3,200-year-old wall on the biblical site of Joshua's altar on Mount Ebal, near Nablus…under the civilian control of the PA…. Palestinian workers had ground ancient stone from the site's exterior wall into gravel to pave the road as well as made use of stones from within the site itself." Notoriously, Israeli authorities permit the destruction of Temple Mount archeological treasures. In one example, a letter to the prime minister provided "horrifying" details concerning riots on the Temple Mount on April 15 and 16, 2022: "The rioters pulled out ancient stones, including sections of columns, and threw them around the Temple Mount." In all, hundreds of antiquities were disturbed.

The IDF repeatedly displays an unwonted delicacy vis-à-vis Palestinians.

- In 2018, as part of a study tour of Rawabi, a West Bank Palestinian town, IDF personnel had to disarm and "disguise or…shed any Jewish and Israeli symbols and refrain from speaking Hebrew."
- In May 2021, out of concern for the safety of the soldiers' friends and families visiting the Old City of Jerusalem, the IDF moved a swearing-in ceremony from the Western Wall to northern Israel.

2 Israel allowed Hezbollah to acquire 130,000 rockets and missiles, then evacuated a quarter-million Israelis in 2023.

- In June 2021, "due to professional and safety considerations"—a discreet reference to Bedouin violence—it moved a course for squad commanders from an open area in the Negev desert to within a military base.
- In 2022, the elite Golani Brigade's visit to Jerusalem was canceled because headquarters was "afraid we would attract the attention of Arabs during Ramadan and then some incident could happen."

The IDF leadership shies away from psychological warfare against Palestinians and punishes individual soldiers who spontaneously engage in it. In May 2023, a sergeant and a corporal received prison sentences of fourteen days and fifteen days respectively for burning the PLO flag and posting the video on social media: "This behavior is inconsistent with the IDF code of ethics" thundered the verdict. Such incidents multiplied in Gaza after October 7 and included:

- Graffiti with *Am Yisrael Chai* ("The people of Israel live") or the names of October 7 victims.
- Reciting *Shema Yisrael* ("Hear, O Israel") over a mosque public address system in Jenin.
- Publicly celebrating Hanukkah, the holiday that recalls a much earlier Jewish military victory.
- Plans to hold a Nova Festival in Gaza or to refound former Israeli towns in Gaza.
- Distributing pictures of enemy combatants in their underwear and blindfolded.

Far from being appreciated, these actions got the soldiers reprimanded, suspended, punished, or even court-martialed.

Influence. The security establishment's timid views matter greatly. When the public and politicians take a robust stand against the Palestinians, placatory security forces often oppose them and usually prevail. Most broadly, this meant sticking with the framework of the Oslo Accords, no matter how discredited that had become. Maurice Hirsch of the Jerusalem Center for Public Affairs explains that "the Israeli security establishment...managed to convince Israel's government that maintaining the semblance and pretense of the existence of the 'Palestinian Authority'...is in Israel's best strategic interest."

Some examples:

After Palestinian jihadis (fighters of jihad) killed two Israeli policemen with weapons hidden on the Temple Mount in 2017, Israel's government placed metal detectors at the entrance to the sacred esplanade. Palestinians responded to this seemingly uncontroversial step (plenty of other mosques have such protection) by insisting on their removal. Israel's populace and politicians both overwhelmingly wanted the devices to remain, but the security establishment warned that leaving them in place would prompt violence, chaos, and possibly the PA's collapse. They quickly disappeared.

In October 2018, Defense Minister Avigdor Liberman disagreed with his bureaucracy over provisioning Gaza, as summarized in two *Times of Israel* headlines: "Liberman: No fuel or gas will enter Gaza until all violence stops" and "Defense establishment opposed cutting off Gaza fuel—report." As the second article explained, in a comment straight out of *Yes, Minister*, officials complained that "they were blindsided by Liberman's decision." Naturally, the establishment prevailed, which contributed to Liberman's resignation as minister a month later.

In 2019, Defense Minister Naftali Bennett ordered the IDF not to turn over bodies of Palestinian murderers to their families. Intense opposition from the security establishment followed, with former deputy chief of the Shin Bet Yitzhak Ilan stating that, "Failure to return the bodies... doesn't help and may even cause harm.... It is simply wrong that we fall to the level of terrorist organizations." That view prevailed and the security cabinet promptly reversed Bennett's order.

In 2022, after a murderous axe and knife attack killing four in the town of Elad, now-Prime Minister Bennett wanted to assassinate the attack's organizer, Yahya Sinwar. He ordered IDF Chief of Staff Aviv Kochavi to do so immediately, to which the latter reportedly replied, "If you want to eliminate Sinwar, you have to convince me that it is justified." Not being convinced, Kochavi refused the order. Sinwar went on to organize October 7.

In July 2023, Defense Minister Yoav Gallant quashed broadly popular legislation requiring the burial of Palestinian murderers' corpses in special cemeteries while prohibiting their transfer to families or sponsoring organizations, who routinely use such funerals to glorify the murderers and incite vengeance. He did so on the grounds that the measure would exacerbate tensions.

The security establishment has another power: frustrating politicians' will by ignoring their orders. The government in July 2023 cracked down on the illegal construction of Palestinian buildings in the West Bank only to find that the IDF head of Central Command, Major General Yehuda Fuchs on his own prerogative chose not to carry out its directives. In frustration, Likud Knesset member Dan Illouz tweeted: "The political echelon sets the strategic agenda while the military echelon is the operator. This is how things must be conducted, otherwise, we will have anarchy. The general's actions are beyond the pale." His protest did not reverse the general's ukase.

Politicians across the Israeli political spectrum resent the security establishment's power, as symbolized by the views of two former ministers of justice. Leftist Yossi Beilin observed that Israel's civilian leaders "don't really know how to criticize the army, even when they work up the nerve to do so. As a result, they tend to give in to its demands." Rightist Gideon Sa'ar concurred, finding that the security agencies have "no advantage" when it comes to strategic issues. "Politicians must be assertive and smart enough to decide on these and then instruct the security heads on their objective."

I shall focus on five major themes of placation. Two concern Palestinian security prisoners (their perquisites and redemptions) and three concern weak responses to Hamas (policy, defense, and offense).

• • •

Security prisoners. The Israel Prison Service distinguishes between criminal and security prisoners; the latter category break the law for political reasons and are the exclusive concern here.

Prisoner perquisites. Two Israeli organizations jointly point out that no other government "allows murderous terrorists to make announcements to the media and incite the region from prison." The prisons have also become literal graduate schools in what are euphemistically called "Israel Studies," that is, M.A. and Ph.D. degree-giving programs at Al-Quds University that hone prisoners' skills, including their knowledge of Hebrew, which they find useful on their almost inevitable release. Hamas leader Yahya Sinwar boasted: "We turned [Israeli] prisons into sanctuaries of worship and academies for study."

Then there are the personal comforts. The prisons have aspects of what future National Security Minister Itamar Ben-Gvir called a "summer camp" or a "five-star hotel," including mutton and freshly baked pita bread, kitchens to prepare their meals, long, wasteful, hot showers, electronic devices (including mobile telephones), free dental care, and smuggling sperm to impregnate wives. (One estimate finds a child a month born in this way over the past decade.) Inmates also enjoy a wide choice of shampoo and television channels. A 2019 report found, according to a Jewish News Syndicate (JNS) summary, that Palestinian murderers "received millions of shekels' worth of special food for holidays, an expensive TV in every cell, a ping-pong table and games, workout machines, unlimited newspapers and lavish family visits."

Ben-Gvir implemented reforms to reduce those perquisites; he also stopped the PA from funding the canteen accounts of some 6,000 security prisoners, amounting to more than $7 million a year. In response, Shin Bet accused him of "violating the status quo" and about 40 percent of the security prisoners threatened bloodshed and a hunger strike during Ramadan, a show of strength that prompted the Israel Prison Service to reverse most, if not all, of his reforms. Hamas aptly called this retreat "a new victory."

Regulations permit security prisoners one family visit every two months but prison authorities over time allowed monthly visits. When Ben-Gvir insisted on applying the regulations, the prisoners threatened a hunger strike and he met opposition within the government (especially from the prison service and Shin Bet). Prime Minister Netanyahu ended up overruling him.

Nasser Abu Hamid had a role in the murder of at least seven Israelis. However, the Israeli taxpayer paid more than $40,000 to treat his cancer over the course of a year, funding not just chemotherapy but the most expensive and advanced immunotherapy protocols. When Iham Kamamji, convicted of murder, lost his Sony PlayStation 2 video game privileges, he sued the prison authority.

A scandal erupted in 2022 when news emerged that the prison service pimped out its women guards. According to one report, "female soldiers who were guards at the prison had been pressed into serving as eye candy or worse for some inmates, as a means of keeping prisoners from getting out of hand." The administration also made them available in exchange for intelligence information. According to another report, the harassment took place on a near-daily basis and included "sex crimes, indecent acts, verbal abuse, and attempts at sexual assault." One former prison guard referred to herself as a "sex slave" and reported: "My commanders handed me over to that terrorist...and made sure that I was left alone with him." In early

2023, the state attorney indicted the former commander and the former intelligence officer of Gilboa Prison for failing in their duties and breach of trust. Not a five-star hotel; a five-star bordello.

Or, as one former prison commissioner put it, "They are getting better conditions than any other terrorists in the world."

Prisoner exchanges. Over a thirty-five-year period, from 1978 to 2013, Israel engaged in many exchanges of security prisoners with non-state groups. Some of them:

- 1978: Israel exchanged 76 prisoners for 1 Israeli.
- 1983: Israel exchanged 4,830 prisoners for 6 Israelis.
- 1984: Israel exchanged 291 prisoners and 72 bodies for 6 Israelis and 5 Israeli bodies.
- May 1985: Israel exchanged 1,150 prisoners (including Ahmad Yassin) for 3 Israelis (the "Jibril Agreement").
- July 1985: Israel exchanged 331 prisoners for 39 foreign passengers seized on a TWA flight to Beirut. (Israel denies the two events were connected.)
- 1996: Israel exchanged 123 Hezbollah bodies for 2 Israeli bodies.
- 1998: Israel exchanged 65 prisoners and 40 bodies for 1 Israeli body.
- 2004: Israel exchanged 429 prisoners and 59 bodies for 1 Israeli (Elhanan Tannenbaum, who admitted he went to Lebanon to pursue a drug deal) and 3 Israeli bodies.
- 2007: Israel exchanged 1 prisoner and 2 bodies for 1 Israeli body.
- June 2008: Israel exchanged 1 prisoner for 20 Israeli bodies.
- July 2008: Israel exchanged 5 prisoners (including Samir Kuntar), plus 199 bodies, for 2 Israeli bodies.
- 2011: Israel exchanged for 1,027 prisoners (280 of them murderers responsible for killing 569 Israelis; their number included Yahya Sinwar, who went on to lead Hamas), for 1 Israeli (Gilad Shalit).
- 2013: Israel exchanged 78 prisoners for good will.

Totting up these numbers, and excluding corpses, Israel exchanged 8,284 prisoners for 18 Israelis over thirty-five years, a ratio of 461 to one. A 2014 Israeli law effectively ended this extraordinary trade, though Israel continued to turn over the corpses of murderers on the grounds that this had no significance.

A study by the Almagor Terror Victims Association of the 6,912 Palestinian security prisoners arrested between 1993 and 1999 and then prematurely released, found that 80 percent returned to violence, "whether commanding, instructing, or killing directly." A 2006 Almagor study counted more than 180 Israeli civilians murdered by prematurely released security prisoners, plus many more wounded.

The trade resumed after October 7. It differed in two ways from the pre-2014 version. First, the numbers were less disproportionate: 240 prisoners for 105 hostages. Second, popular pressure for Israeli hostages to be returned drove the process, not the wishes of the security establishment.

Conclusion: The treatment of enemy prisoners has been and remains the single most humiliating aspect of Israeli placation.

• • •

Gaza. Weakness characterizes Israel's overall policy as well as its defensive and offensive responses to Hamas attacks.

Policy. Ariel Sharon (1928–2014) was a renowned military commander from the 1950s forward who entered politics on the nationalist Right in 1973 and served in many ministerial positions, including defense and foreign affairs. He built an extremist reputation as summed up by his 1998 admonition to Israelis to "Move, run, grab more hills, expand the territory. Everything that's grabbed will be in our hands. Everything we don't grab will be in their hands." He became prime minister in 2001 and won re-election by a landslide in January 2003, defeating a Labor opponent, Amram Mitzna, who had made "evacuating the [Jewish] settlements from Gaza" the centerpiece of his campaign. Sharon ridiculed such a unilateral withdrawal on the grounds that it "would bring the terrorism centers closer to [Israel's] population centers."

By December 2003, however, Sharon suddenly and without explanation had reversed course and adopted Mitzna's policy, announcing that "Israel will initiate the unilateral security step of disengagement" from Gaza. Against passionate objections and cries of treachery, he doggedly pursued withdrawal, which took place in 2005. Intense speculation accompanied this move, with rumors swirling about Sharon hoping to avoid corruption charges, securing his legacy, and much more. *The Wall Street Journal*, for example, speculated that the lure was being feted at the Élysée Palace in Paris with "the full French treatment: honor guards with their plumed helmets, the military defile and the three-star state banquets held in Louis XV-style settings." Whatever his motivation, Sharon's radical switch signaled Hamas that even the toughest-seeming Israeli politician would buckle under sustained pressure.

Weak defenses. Israelis living near Gaza came under constant attack in 2018 from kites, balloons, inflated condoms, and helium-filled children's toys carrying explosives and incendiary devices, leading to substantial damage to houses, property, roads, farmland, and parks, exhausting the country's firefighting capabilities. The IDF declined to target those sending off such devices, condescendingly informing the public: "The alternative to kite terror is war. If we respond too strongly it could lead to an escalation of hostilities. You would be in your bomb shelters, and you don't want that." On one occasion, when Hamas' kites ignited thirty fires, the IDF responded by destroying the ringleader's empty car.

Hamas-sponsored riots in 2018 caused what the IDF called "extensive damage" to the gas lines, electricity infrastructure, and a conveyor belt at the Kerem Shalom border crossing between Israel and Gaza, which then closed for repairs. Israeli officials who toured the area were "astonished by the devastation and destruction Palestinians left in their wake," then charged the Israeli taxpayer $9 million in repairs to get the gas, electricity, and imports back on their way to Gaza.

Responding to two rockets from Gaza aimed at Tel Aviv in 2019, the IDF urged the offer of several inducements—an expanded fishing zone, fewer restrictions on the export of agricultural products, and increased monthly cash deliveries from Qatar—to avoid further attacks on the city.

Weak punishments. Alternatively, Israel resorted to punishments, such as economic deprivation or military damage, to influence Hamas behavior. But the brevity of these retributions signaled Hamas that it need only hunker down for some days or weeks for Jerusalem again to permit trade, hand over tax monies, and allow in foreign funds to fix the damage—in other words, for a return to normal.

To get a sense of Israel's almost comical ineffectiveness, note the repeated punishments of Hamas aggression by reducing the amount of fuel available to it, always briefly and partially. Some examples, all concerning attacks from Gaza:

- January 2008: Prime Minister Ehud Olmert responded to rocket attacks with tough talk: "As far as I'm concerned, Gaza residents will walk, without gas for their cars, because they have a murderous, terrorist regime that doesn't let people in southern Israel live in peace." Fuel deliveries to Gaza were cut for just five days.
- November 2008: Israel responded to rocket attacks by partially halting fuel deliveries for a week.
- July 2018: Israel responded to incendiary devices by suspending fuel deliveries for four days, pointing out that this step "will not affect the delivery of food and medicine into Gaza."
- August 2018: Israel responded to incendiary devices and violence along the Israel-Gaza border by briefly freezing all fuel deliveries.
- October 2018: Defense Minister Liberman responded to incendiary devices by stating that, "Until violence in the Gaza Strip stops entirely, including the launching of incendiary balloons and the burning of tires near Israeli communities, the supply of fuel and gas to the Gaza Strip will not be renewed." In response, senior defense officials argued for Israel continuing to deliver fuel to prevent an economic collapse in Gaza, even if incendiary balloon attacks continue. Compromising, Liberman blocked only some fuel deliveries. These resumed after about ten days.
- June 2019: Israel responded to incendiary devices by temporarily ending fuel deliveries.
- August 2019: Israel responded to rocket attacks by temporarily halving fuel deliveries.
- October 2019: Israel responded to rocket attacks and an attack on an Israeli fuel depot, killing two civilian workers, by reducing food and fuel deliveries for two weeks. Government spokesman Arieh Mekel explained that Israel wanted to avoid

further suffering: "We want to continue and provide supplies to Gaza because we…do not want a humanitarian crisis."

- August 2020: Israel responded to incendiary balloons and rocket attacks by reducing fuel deliveries. This cut electricity in Gaza from about twelve hours to four a day.
- September 2023: An attempt by Hamas to smuggle explosives into the West Bank led to halting exports from Gaza for a week.
- October 2023: The total, immediate cut-off of supplies after October 7 lasted longer than usual: twenty days.

These eleven episodic and failed displays of reprisal and pressure point to Israel's unserious approach to Hamas, resembling summer squalls more than effective policy.

Further, Israel's Gaza policy has a larger problem than ineffectual punishments, namely the self-evidently insufficient ritual of "mowing the grass," or occasionally smashing Hamas and Gaza in the hopes of winning a period of calm before Hamas initiates the next round of fighting. Thus, when asked what Israel hoped for from its 2021 "mowing the grass" operation in Gaza, IDF Head of Operations Major General Aharon Haliva replied: "A minimal quiet period of five years after the operation would be considered a success." Not even an underfunded police force would accept such a limited ambition. Nor did the IDF win five years of quiet, for large-scale attacks resumed in 2023. The strategist Avigdor Haselkorn counts fifteen mow-the-grass operations between 2005 and September 2023, nearly one a year. Former Mossad and military officer Sima Shine describes grass mowing as "no policy." Zvi Yehezkeli of Israel's Channel 13 deems the IDF "afraid of Gaza," which gets to the heart of the matter.

• • •

Pretending to win. Deputy Knesset Speaker Zvi Hauser characterizes Israel as being content with the "appearance of victory in the eyes of its enemies," arguing that in the difficult neighborhood of the Middle East, the country needs "actual victory in order to ensure our survival." Former minister Yuval Steinitz observes that Israel went to war to achieve a "decisive victory" to destroy its enemies in the period before the Oslo Accords; after that, it merely sought an "appearance of victory." As an illustration of pretend-victory, he reviewed Israeli operations in Gaza and how Israel declared that each operation had achieved its goals.

For example, after a round of war in 2021, Netanyahu announced that the IDF managed "to inflict a severe blow on terrorist organizations, to undermine their capabilities, and to restore calm while establishing deterrence." After fighting with PIJ in May 2023, Netanyahu claimed that Israel dealt it "the hardest blow in its history," creating "a new equation." He warned Israel's enemies, "We see you everywhere. You cannot hide. We will choose the time and place to attack you." Netanyahu boastfully continued:

> The performance was indeed perfect. With complete surprise and continuous initiative, we eliminated Islamic Jihad's entire top brass in Gaza, destroyed 17 Islamic Jihad command centers, eliminated dozens of terrorists, struck missile storage sites, took out anti-tank squads and more.... Whoever hurts us—whether successful or not—will pay with their life. Today Israel's enemies—in Gaza and beyond—know that even if they try to hide, we can and are willing to reach them at any time.... We flipped the script.

A review of operations in Israel's six wars with Hamas and PIJ since 2008 reveals the hollowness of such boasting.

- 2008–2009: Hamas sent around 600 rockets and 200 mortar shells to Israeli territory reaching as far as the Israeli cities of Ashdod and Beersheba.
- 2012: 1,500 rockets reaching as far as Tel Aviv and Jerusalem.
- 2014: 4,600 rockets in ninety days.
- 2021: 4,400 rockets in twelve days, threatening the parliament building itself, "sending people down to shelters."
- May 2023: 1,000 rockets in five days.
- October 2023: 1,200 Israeli residents murdered, 240 captured, more than 12,000 rockets between October 7 and December 31, 2023.

In short, despite repeated claimed Israeli victories, the Hamas-PIJ combination has greatly grown in numbers and fatalities. Paraphrasing King Pyrrhus: One more such victory and Israel is finished.

Conclusion: Inconstancy in dealing with Hamas, from the lure of economic prosperity to occasional destruction of Gaza's infrastructure, predictably failed.

EXPLAINING PLACATION

Three main factors account for the phenomenon of placation: the IDF's problems, awe of the Palestinians, and outside pressure.

• • •

Problems in the IDF. The Israel Defense Forces has a superb reputation. A closer look finds many serious limitations.

Loss of fighting spirit. Major General (res.) Yitzhak Brik has perhaps the most negative views of any former IDF flag officer, arguing that the military has lost its fighting spirit. He has the credentials to make this criticism, being the recipient of the Medal of Courage for his service in the Yom Kippur War of 1973, a former commander of the IDF's academies, and former Ombudsman for Soldiers' Complaints in the IDF. Fear of taking casualties, he finds, has spawned "a weak army that hides behind separation barriers and fences, and only activates the Air Force." In fact, "The IDF is looking for every possible way to maintain peace." Brik finds that "discussion on whether to go to battle focuses on a war's potential costs and casualties, rather than a campaign's intrinsic value or its necessity for Israel's national security." Consequently, "The leaders of Hamas and Islamic Jihad realize that the IDF has no intention of defeating them" either on the battlefield or in the overall conflict. He predicates the IDF's rebuilding on two foundations: "reviving the ethos of self-sacrifice and sanctifying the value of victory."

Like a police force. The security establishment tends to see Palestinians, due to their military weakness, more like criminals than soldiers; in response, it has morphed into a law enforcement–like force. Like the police, the IDF aspires to quietude, to no destruction of property nor harm to people. Generals seek victory, police chiefs seek tranquility. Armies disrupt, law enforcement stabilizes. Armies kill, police save lives. Generals do not enter battle with the goal of saving lives and avoiding legal complications; but police chiefs insist that the struggle with criminals must cause no collateral damage and break no laws.

Short-termism. The Israeli security establishment tends to have a short, even myopic, horizon vis-à-vis Palestinians. It takes pride in preventing short-term violence while tending not to worry about the further future. In the apocryphal order of an Israeli officer to his troops: "Secure the area until the end of your shift." Prime Minister Yitzhak Rabin's wife Leah explained his mentality: "He was very pragmatic, hated to deal with something that would happen years down the road. He only thought of what would happen now, in the very near future." Note that "pragmatic" here does not imply ending the conflict.

Politicians also suffer from short-termism. Because no single party has ever on its own formed a government in Israel, policy emerges from a partisan battleground of unwieldly coalitions which impedes the formation of coherent and long-term planning. Ungainly, contentious partnerships tend, in the view of the Middle East Forum's Jonathan Spyer, "to avoid focus on long-term strategic issues, in preference for addressing immediate threats." Why try to address a distant problem when it can be kicked down the road? Short of drastic changes to Israel's political system, this limitation will continue to hobble planning.

Moral superiority. From its early days, Zionism contained within it a pride in behaving better than the enemy. Let Palestinians engage in vengeance, attack civilians, believe in conspiracy theories, and ally with dictators; Zionists will work for the welfare of all, self-restrain their use of force (*havlagah*), never use violence wantonly ("purity of arms"), and ally with democracies. This has both moral and practical goals: to maintain Jewish ethics and to be seen as a worthy ally of the United Kingdom or United States. In 1921, for example, the essayist Ahad Ha'am (1856–1927), responded to a reported act of vengeance by Jews against a Palestinian boy with:

> Is this the dream of a return to Zion about which our people have dreamt for centuries? That we now come to Zion to stain its soil with innocent blood?... Are we really doing it only to add in an Oriental corner a small Levantine people who vie with other Levantines in shedding blood, in a desire for vengeance and in angry violence?

This pride can impede Israeli responses. Note IDF Chief of Staff Gadi Eisenkot's reasons in 2018 why the IDF did not stop Hamas incendiary balloons and kites that set fire to Israeli agricultural fields, as expressed in a cabinet meeting exchange with Education Minister Naftali Bennett.

> *Bennett*: Why not shoot anyone using aerial weapons [balloons and kites] against our communities? There are no legal constraints. Why not shoot at them instead of firing warning shots? We are talking about terrorists in every regard.
>
> *Eisenkot*: I don't think that shooting at children and youth who sometimes fly balloons and kites is the right thing to do.
>
> *Bennett*: And what about those clearly identified as adults?
>
> *Eisenkot*: Are you suggesting dropping a bomb on people flying balloons and kites?
>
> *Bennett*: Yes.
>
> *Eisenkot*: This goes against my operative and moral position.

This "moral position," stirred a furor but was not repudiated.

Deference to diplomacy. The "peace process" so dominated during the Oslo Era that the security establishment learned to defer to it. Brigadier General (res.) Yehuda Wagman finds "confusion in the upper ranks of the IDF. It has no concept towards reaching victory but rather sees itself as part of the diplomatic process." However, as Wagman points out, "Diplomatic processes and reaching understandings are not how you end conflicts." The Middle East Forum's Naveh Dromi notes that victory had been the IDF's goal until that was replaced by a reliance "on diplomacy, negotiations and compromise. Even Israel's constant battles on its northern and southern borders, against Hezbollah and Hamas respectively, were fought more in line with the diplomatic clock than any military strategy." Fighting by the clock became especially evident after October 7, when the U.S. government demanded a timetable for the ending of hostilities.

Reluctance to rule Palestinians. Emphatically not wanting again directly to rule the West Bank or Gaza, the security establishment views with suspicion any policy that might lead to this outcome. (Such attitudes remain in place vis-à-vis the PA and the West Bank; after October 7, policy toward Hamas and Gaza is in flux.) It treats the PA deferentially, wanting it to fulfill vital functions, fearing its collapse, seeking ways to strengthen it. "Things now are about as good as possible," they imply about the West Bank, "so please stay away with any hare-brained ideas about our getting tougher." This attitude leads to skepticism of a more ambitious approach, and severe reluctance about any initiative that might provoke Palestinian ire. The PA, of course, full well understands this and gets away with literal murder.

Contentment. Security leaders generally find current circumstances in the West Bank broadly acceptable. They appreciate the PA under Mahmoud Abbas, for all its hostility, as a useful security partner. True, Ramallah incites murder domestically and delegitimizes the State of Israel internationally, but better to endure these aggressions than to lose its partnership.

Inertia. Israel's renowned security establishment naturally prefers to stick to known practices, avoiding new concepts and the experimentation they entail. Why fix what's not broken? Best to keep doing things in the time-hallowed way. As Hillel Frisch of Bar-Ilan University notes, "Much of the IDF brass and former brass pine for the tried and true." This induces a reluctance to embark on an unproven policy. In the devastating assessment of Brigadier General (res.) Yossi Kuperwasser, "The IDF defines victory as achieving its mission." (Ponder that one.)

The temptation of passivity. The addition of many-layered missile defenses—Arrow, David's Sling, Iron Beam, Iron Dome—Elliot Chodoff of Israel Strategic Solutions explains, "led to a shift in Israeli civil defense strategy from a critical adjunct of protecting civilians while the military defeated the enemy to an end in itself. The IDF is thus no longer required to defeat the enemy. It is considered sufficient that civilian casualties be minimized." He deems this "a serious strategic error" because it turns the tactic of protecting civilians into a strategy. First, a non-response to attacks "emboldens the attacker and erodes deterrence." Second, "An attack on a state's territory erodes its sovereignty." Third, the outside world becomes "accustomed to Israel's toleration of attacks on its civilians" and gets upset when Israel does react.

Future careers in politics. Some senior commanders go on to political careers, in which case they do better with uncontroversial records, unsullied by national or international opprobrium. The stiff competition among political parties to win the favor of Eisenkot, a bland and undistinguished former IDF chief of staff, confirms the utility of staying away from controversy.

Leftism. Contrary to expectations, a leftwing outlook helps with promotions in the IDF. Defense Minister Liberman once sardonically said to the top IDF brass, "I sometimes feel here like I'm in consultations with… Peace Now" (a leftist anti-military group). Caroline Glick, a *Jerusalem Post* columnist, went so far as to state that, due to the political views of two of its leaders, "the IDF General Staff is in open rebellion against the government and the citizens of Israel."

In conclusion, the IDF largely lives off its legacy, with its glory years ending in 1967. To put it differently, the more the underdog, the greater the Zionist skill: Think the Haganah militia from 1920 to 1948, the War of Independence, the Six-Day War, and the shadow war with Iran. Conversely, the more the overdog, the worse the performance: in particular, the incessant Palestinian skirmishes, culminating in October 7.

• • •

Awe of Palestinian resolve. Palestinian determination tends to dispirit Israelis.

Palestinian boastfulness. Palestinian leaders often brag of their unique *sumud* (steadfastness, tenacity). Yasir Arafat vowed: "We will never surrender," Mahmoud Abbas proclaimed that Palestinians "will never give up their right to Jerusalem as the capital of their state," Mahmoud al-Zahar, a senior Hamas figure, insisted that Palestinians will never "give up one inch of Palestine even after 70—700—7,000 years." Others repeated these boasts. A prominent medical doctor, Said ElHaj, echoed that "Palestinians will never give up their lands." A teacher participating in a demonstration in the West Bank town of Kfar Qaddum swore, "We'll never give up."

Hanan Ashrawi, a prominent anti-Israel critic, announced with apparent sincerity that Palestinians will battle unto the end of time to destroy the Jewish state: "There is an erroneous assumption that the Palestinians are defeated, and they have to accept the fact of their defeat." No, she asserted, "The Palestinians are willing, generation after generation, to continue their struggle." More soberly, Palestinian academic Hussein Agha assessed that "Palestinian defeat is not complete and Jewish victory is also not complete," concluding that "the desperate acts of stabbings and rammings are unprompted Palestinian reminders to Israel that we are here; we have not given up; your project is incomplete."

Israelis despair of winning. Observing Palestinian tenacity, Israel's security establishment finds the boasts convincing; which other people have sustained a comparable genocidal rejectionism? Just as the police everywhere tend to see criminals as incorrigible troublemakers, so wizened Israeli security chiefs view Palestinians as feral adversaries. In a private conversation leaked to the public, Israel's Police Commissioner Kobi Shabtai was caught saying about Israeli Arabs: "They kill each other. That is their nature. That is the mentality of the Arabs." Unable to imagine the Palestinians doing anything but attack Israelis, the latter pre-emptively give up the possibility of resolution; can hyenas stop attacking lions?

If the Palestinians endured a century's worth of blows, this line of thinking holds, they can absorb anything Israel throws at them now. Historian Martin Kramer explains:

> In 1948, half the Palestinian population (700,000) fled. Every inch of Palestine was lost in 1967, when another 250,000 fled. Their "liberation" movement was subsequently driven with crushing force from Jordan and Lebanon. According to Palestinians, the Israelis killed their hero-leader, Arafat. Yet, none of this persuaded them that their defeat was final.

This pessimism makes the security leaders adopt leftist-like positions. Long and bitter experience, not misty idealism, better explains their despair. Such thinking has caused the IDF, Israeli journalist Lazar Berman notes, to "become stuck in a paradigmatic rut that has placed long-term security—let alone victory—out of reach." Whatever their politics, such reasoning leads to placation.

Policy implications. Commanders for Israel's Security, a group of nearly 300 reserve IDF officers who reached the rank of general, representing 80 percent of those in that category, agrees to a two-state solution, or a separation from the Palestinians, at nearly twice the rate of the general Jewish Israeli population. Efraim Inbar of Bar-Ilan University dismisses the goal of victory over Hamas as "naïve" on the grounds that Israel "cannot eradicate a well-rooted Hamas." Instead, he advocates "mowing the grass," an occasional reminder to Hamas' rulers and other Gazans of Israel's overwhelming power, as "Israel's strategy for protracted intractable conflict." This approach dismally implies that Israel accepts aggression from Gaza, with its attendant damage to property and persons, as a permanent fact of life.

Inbar continued to advocate this policy after October 7, arguing that "Israel's deterrence failed partly because the IDF did not mow the grass often enough. Even if it attains its goals in Gaza—the destruction of Hamas' military capabilities—the IDF will still have to mow the grass afterwards." Only endless mowing can limit any Palestinian entity to "a marginal security risk."

Such pessimism ignores the fact that placation strengthens sumud. Note the trajectory of the Oslo Accords. In 1993, a combination of three factors—the exit of the Arab states, the Soviet Union's collapse, and Saddam Hussein's defeat—shook Palestinian resolve and compelled Arafat to take the unthinkable step of shaking hands with Israel's prime minister and publicly recognizing his country. But then a series of Israeli withdrawals confused the Palestinians: Jericho and parts of Gaza in 1994, Areas A and B of the West Bank in 1995, Lebanon in 2000, and all of Gaza in 2005. Compounding this pattern, two Israeli prime ministers made bizarrely generous offers in 2000 and 2008. Little wonder that Palestinian leaders thought they were winning. Little wonder that they arrogantly turned these offers down as insufficient—reasonably expecting to do even better in the future.

Israelis have long been resigned to Palestinian violence. Of course, they want it to end, but not enough to take effective steps. Just as motorists prefer to absorb traffic fatalities rather than stop driving or drive tank-like vehicles at slow speeds, so Israelis stick with placation rather than seek victory.

• • •

Western criticism. As a small state constantly an international cynosure, Israel must gauge how others see it, especially as it attracts unparalleled condemnation. The government of Israel worries incessantly about outside disapproval, especially from the democratic West, a major source of legitimacy, trade, and immigration.

The liberal temper of the times demands that Western states use great caution in deploying superior power when fighting a non-Western insurgency. Within this general outlook, the IDF comes under special (and often unfair) inspection, making its leadership all the more cautious and restrained. While the morality and legality of its actions have repeatedly been vindicated by international panels (for example, by the Friends of Israel Initiative's High Level Military Group report), the sting remains. This hurts especially when it carries an imminent threat of arrest due to an International Criminal Court warrant, such as happened to Major General (res.) Doron Almog; facing detention on arrival in Great Britain, he did not disembark from the El Al plane he arrived on but remained on it and returned straight to Israel.

Placation offers the great benefit of avoiding crises, something Israel's security leaders understandably cherish. Preferring to keep things quiet on their watch, they naturally shy away from provocative steps. Placation avoids the spike in anti-Zionism—UN Security Council resolutions, Arab state chills, big-city rallies, attacks on synagogues—that follows when Israel takes action against Palestinians. However beneficial a more robust policy in the long run may be, its implementation creates too many short-term headaches. In the author's meeting with Prime Minister Netanyahu in 2017, he responded positively in the abstract to the idea of victory, but made clear that he was not about to bring the extra problems on himself that it entails.

Israel's use of force brings an immediate international cost, as it often finds itself condemned. Op-eds being as important as bullets, Israel shies away from taking tough steps. The tiny, illegal Palestinian settlement of Khan Al Ahmar epitomizes this hesitation. Never containing more than 200 residents, it sprung up at a key location in 2010, initially with a school, due to the efforts of an anti-Israel NGO largely funded by Italian taxpayers, *Vento Di Terra*. The Israeli authorities immediately served a demolition and relocation order which met with legal challenges, culminating in the Supreme Court ruling in favor of the order in 2018. International opposition to such a step then came from many sides—United Nations agencies, the International Criminal Court, the United Kingdom, the European Parliament, Human Rights Watch, Amnesty International, and American Jewish leaders, among others. In January 2023, the EU office to the Palestinians announced that "Representatives of Belgium, Brazil, Denmark, the EU, France, Germany, Ireland, Italy, Japan, Mexico, the Netherlands, Norway, Spain, Sweden, Switzerland, the UK, and like-minded missions today visited the Palestinian community of Khan Al Ahmar to express their concern at the threat of demolition facing the village." Some of these claimed that demolition would not only be a violation of international law but possibly also a war crime. This large and very public outcry pressured the Israeli government to punt; at the time of writing, it had nine times asked the Supreme Court to permit it to postpone taking action.

Nor is this the only case, just the best known. In parallel, National Security Minister Itamar Ben-Gvir in February 2023 pushed to raze a twelve-apartment, four-story illegal apartment building in the Wadi Kadum neighborhood of eastern Jerusalem. But, even facing a much lower level of international pressure (just some Western embassies), Prime Minister Netanyahu ordered repeated stays.

Such is the power of "world opinion," especially on the Left and among Muslims, where it almost always opposes Israeli actions. How much easier, then, to continue with the status quo and defer taking even such small steps as demolishing Khan Al Ahmar. The high cost of deploying force has prompted many Israelis to assume that diplomacy—the so-called peace process—offers the only path forward.

PART III

Diplomacy Fails

Just because the Middle East peace process failed does not mean it should be abandoned.

—Martin Indyk, U.S. diplomat, 2001

There's nothing new under the sun when it comes to Middle East peace.

—Philip Gordon, U.S. diplomat, 2017

SOON AFTER THE CREATION OF Israel, a tradition emerged of relentless U.S. efforts to remedy relations between the Arabs and Israel. Most presidents floated at least one major initiative, including the Johnston water plan of 1953, the Dulles "Operation Alpha" plan of 1955, the Johnson refugee plan of 1962, the Rogers plan of 1969, the Carter plan of 1977, the Reagan plan of 1982, the Madrid conference of 1991, the Camp David summit of 2000, the Annapolis conference of 2008, the Kerry plan of 2013, and the Trump plan of 2020.

Hubristic statements accompanied many of these initiatives, along the lines of George H.W. Bush announcing that "the time has come to put an end to Arab-Israeli conflict." Inspired by American views and priorities—rather than Middle Eastern ones—they all failed. Noting this pattern, the American intellectual Irving Kristol memorably turned the Latin proverb "Whom Jupiter wishes to destroy, he first renders mad" (*Quem Iuppiter vult perdere, dementat prius*) into "Whom the gods would destroy, they first tempt to resolve the Arab-Israeli conflict."

The term "peace process" dates to Henry Kissinger's Arab-Israeli diplomacy in the 1970s. Harold Saunders, the American diplomat who coined it, defined it as "a series of mediated agreements imbedded in a larger political process." Until 1979, the focus of the inaccurately named "Middle East Peace Process" (implying that the region contained no other conflicts) concerned Israel and the Arab states, culminating that year in an Egypt-Israel peace treaty. After that, diplomatic engagement shifted primarily to the Palestinians. U.S.-sponsored "peace processing" vis-à-vis the Palestinians began full tilt in 1988 and continued relentlessly until 2008, then revived episodically.

This meant moving beyond the relatively easy Arab states, for Palestinians had imbibed anti-Zionism more deeply, were fractured into many grouplets, and the issues proved more intractable. Accordingly, resolution, decision-making, and follow-through all became more difficult. But it took years for that to become evident.

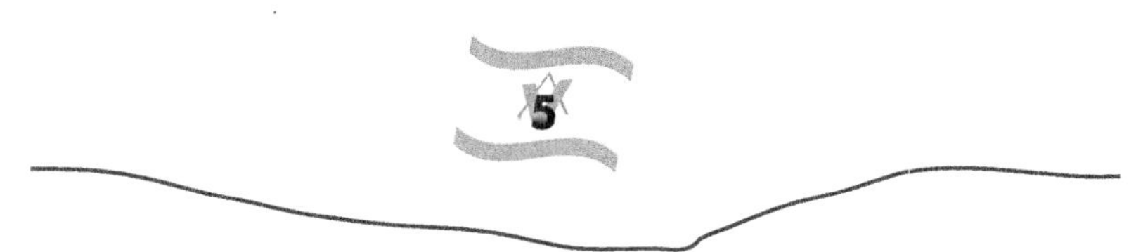

THE OSLO ACCORDS: ISRAEL'S NAKBA

THE OSLO ACCORDS ARE, ALONG with the war of independence in 1948–1949 and the Six-Day War of 1967, a critical event in Israel's history. With them, simple warfare between Israelis and Palestinians became a more subtle, intricate dance of cooperation and conflict. An issue that previously had largely united Israelis now bitterly divided them. Vapors of the "Oslo spirit" dispelled any notion of Israel defeating the Palestinians, even as the reverse remained very much in place. The Oslo Accords began a new era, the one we still live in, characterized by Palestinian perfidy, Israeli folly, and foreign ineptitude.

PALESTINIAN PERFIDY

The White House hosted a glamorous lawn ceremony on the beautiful late summer morning of September 13, 1993. This event culminated secret negotiations over many months and featured the very unlikely duo of Israeli's Prime Minister Yitzhak Rabin and long-time Palestinian genocidal leader Yasir Arafat. "The Handshake" (as it was then capitalized) between them sealed the agreement formally called the "Declaration of Principles on Interim Self-Government Arrangements." Many years later, Yossi Beilin, an Israeli politician involved with the accords, acknowledged that "the elating ceremony created exaggerated expectations."

• • •

Exaggerated expectations. Called the Oslo Accords in tribute to the city where negotiations were centered, the agreement laid the basis for the two parties' mutual recognition and the end of their hostilities. Each committed to what the other most wanted: recognition and security for Israelis, dignity and autonomy for Palestinians. Arafat not only formally accepted

Israel ("The PLO recognizes the right of the State of Israel to exist in peace and security") but he spoke movingly of the occasion: "Our two peoples are awaiting today this historic hope, and they want to give peace a real chance." The Palestinian Authority, a five-year interim governing body, came into existence with the expectation that it would lead to eventual sovereignty.

Premised on rewarding the Palestinians for good behavior, the accords aspired to create a vague "New Middle East" in which economic cooperation would serve as the basis to reconcile historically hostile peoples. It attempted to reach this goal via such mundane efforts as a Housing and Construction Program, a Small and Medium Business Development Plan, a Human Resources Plan, and an Infrastructure Development Program for water, electricity, transportation, and communications.

Other than a small band of skeptics (and Palestinian opponents of Arafat), the world at large saw in the Oslo Accords a brilliant solution to a hitherto unsolvable conundrum. President Bill Clinton, the event's sponsor, lauded it as a "great occasion of history and hope." Secretary of State Warren Christopher ruminated on how "the impossible is within our reach." Arafat called it an "historic event, inaugurating a new epoch." Foreign Minister Shimon Peres of Israel discerned in it "the outline of peace in the Middle East." Days after the ceremony, Peres recalled his euphoria:

> While signing the documents on the lawn of the White House, I could almost sense the breeze of a fresh spring and my imagination began to wander to the skies of our land that may have become brighter to the eyes of all people agreeing and opposing. On the lawn you could almost hear the heavy tread of boots leaving the stage after a hundred years of hostility. You could have listened to the gentle tiptoeing of new steps making a debut in the awaiting world for peace.

The press agreed and provided saturation coverage, with American television devoting hours of uninterrupted programming and newspapers devoting as many as six full pages. Pundits like Anthony Lewis of *The New York Times* called it "ingeniously built" and "stunning." *Time* magazine made Arafat and Rabin two of its "men of the year" for 1993. Arafat, Rabin, and Peres jointly won the Nobel Peace Prize, which cited the trio for "substantial contributions to a historic process through which peace and cooperation can replace war and hate."

The optimistic statements by the great and good turned out to be wrong; that small band of skeptics was right. Accords expected to lead to calm and reconciliation had the opposite effect, spawning more violence and toxic attitudes. That lovely 1993 scene amounted to farce.[1] Both sides ended grievously disappointed, the war continued, and the "State of Palestine" looks ever-further away.

In the long history of diplomacy, has another victorious power ever turned over two contiguous territories to a fanatic, murderous, and unbowed enemy? The Oslo Accords amounted to Israel's *nakba* (Arabic: catastrophe). Natan Sharansky, the civil rights hero, snarkily observed that, "If there is one crime against the Palestinians to which Israel should plead guilty, it is the Oslo Agreement." Three decades of subsequent incompetence (Exhibit A: the 2005 unilateral withdrawal from Gaza) have further confirmed its erroneous premises.

• • •

Disappointment. Palestinians and Israelis agree on little, but they near-unanimously concur on Oslo having been a disaster.

Palestinians. The PLO suffered a double whammy in 1991 due to siding closely with the defeated Saddam Hussein during the Kuwait crisis and the collapsed Soviet Union. These developments left Arafat much weakened, compelling fundamental adjustments. Doing what he had to do, he sweet-talked the Zionists. It worked, and the homicidal leader acquired legitimacy and territories.

During the prior decades under direct Israeli control, from 1967 to 1993, Palestinians had flourished. Political violence diminished. Residents of the West Bank and Gaza could travel locally without checkpoints and access work sites within Israel. They benefited from the rule of law and an economy that more than quadrupled without depending on international aid. Functioning schools and hospitals emerged, as did several universities.

---

1 Many years later, a subsequent Israeli foreign minister, Shlomo Ben-Ami, commented: "I can't guarantee that Arafat even read the Oslo Accords. All he wanted was to be allowed back into the [Palestinian] territories, and to attain this goal he was willing to sign onto Oslo."

On arriving in Gaza in 1994, Arafat grandly promised to turn it into "the Singapore of the Middle East." In fact, his rule ended the prior progress. Internal despotism and external aggression combined to turn Gaza, then his areas of rule in the West Bank, not into Singapore but into Somalia. For Arafat's subjects, this meant economic dependence, failed institutions, corruption, inhumanity, tyranny, loathing, Islamism, a death cult, and suicide factories.

The town of Mawasi provides an example. Before the unilateral Israeli withdrawal from Gaza, Rafael D. Frankel reported in 2008 in *The Christian Science Monitor*, Mawasi "was a town of fertile corn crops and greenhouses" in which "grew cherry tomatoes, sweet peppers, and strawberries." But now, "nearly half the land lies barren. Only shells remain of many of the greenhouses that were stripped of valuable materials. A city that fed itself with its produce and the money its men made from working with the [Israeli] settlers, Mawasi is now dependent on food handouts from the United Nations." No wonder Gazans look back bitterly on the Oslo Accords.

Israelis. Honeyed Palestinian promises about the end of conflict vaporized, replaced by Palestinian anger and violence more febrile than ever. An Arafat-inspired rage led to the murder of more Israelis in the five years post-Oslo than in the fifteen years preceding it. If the two hands in the Rabin-Arafat handshake symbolized Oslo's early hopes, the raised two hands of a young Palestinian male dripping with the blood of the Israelis he had just lynched in Ramallah in 2000 represented its dismal demise.

Before the Oslo Accords, the Jordanian-appointed Islamic authorities running the Temple Mount (the waqf) routinely coordinated with the government of Israel. Oslo then transferred control of the waqf to the PA and Arafat appointed hostile figures intent on provoking not just Israelis but Jews worldwide by their blatant disregard of Jewish sensibilities, turning the Temple Mount into a heightened flashpoint, hoping thereby to inflame Muslim opinion against Israel.

The lies, insults, and assaults caused increasing numbers of Israelis to view the Oslo Accords as a travesty. Separation, not cooperation, became the preferred way forward, with security fences springing up to express this shift. The arrival of a million and more Jews from the ex-Soviet Union made Israel a distinctly more hardheaded society. And if Israel's elderly held on to their Oslo hopes, the youth took on much tougher attitudes.

What went wrong? Yasir Arafat, his successor Mahmoud Abbas, the rest of the PA, Hamas, PIJ, and the Palestinian population that abetted them bear full moral responsibility for Oslo's failure. From the moment of signature, they had malign intent, only pretending to acknowledge their defeat by Israel. In fact, Arafat offered his act of surrender insincerely and a sizeable majority of Palestinians spurned it. He and his aides unleashed a torrent of verbal calumnies and distortions against Israel, threatened jihad, and organized murderous attacks.

The Oslo Accords marked a change in tactics, utilizing new, more sophisticated methods while keeping the same goal. Gone was the futile reliance on violence alone, replaced by a mix of violence and negotiations. Arafat hoped the violence would batter Israelis' morale, cause them to emigrate, and dry up foreign investment even as he hoped the negotiations would win Western pressure on Jerusalem to make more concessions. As he put it in 1996, "We plan to eliminate the State of Israel and establish a purely Palestinian state.... We will make life unbearable for Jews by psychological warfare and population explosion.... They will give up their dwelling and leave for the U.S. We Palestinians will take over everything." On taking over from Arafat in 2004, Abbas continued the violence but shifted the focus to delegitimizing Israel internationally; thus, his claim, in Germany no less, about the Palestinians suffering "fifty holocausts."

ISRAELI FOLLY

The Israeli side, while morally virtuous, made a bewildering array of mistakes that beg for close analysis.

Years later, it is a challenge to convey the flavor of the Oslo Era, which ended in 2008, when Israelis shut their collective eyes and persisted, no matter what, with conciliation toward Palestinians, their supposed "partner for peace." A surge in murders, intensified delegitimization, breaking of promises—it all had minimal or no impact. Voters elected Benjamin Netanyahu, an Oslo critic, as prime minister in the 1996 election, but he barely slowed down or changed the direction of Israeli policy.

Israel's mistakes begin with the fundamental ones covered in Chapters 3 and 4, those of enrichment and placation. Adding to those, its errors specifically in response to the Oslo Accords fell into three broad categories: a shift in strategic thinking, misunderstanding the Palestinians, and poor negotiating tactics.

***

A new strategy. The Oslo Accords divide the strategic history of Israel into two periods. Purposefulness defined the first forty-five years and drift, the thirty years since. A novel approach to Israel's security concerns emerged during the 1980s[2] and crystalized with the collapse of the Soviet Union in 1991. Israel no longer faced a great power enemy, so lowered its guard. On becoming prime minister in 1992, Yitzhak Rabin commemorated this revolution with the mild but momentous announcement that Israel had reached a point at which "the threat to the very existence of Israel has been reduced." That relaxation opened the floodgates to a slew of changes. Two in particular deserve mention:

Denigrating military power. Rabin spoke mystically about security not only residing in tanks, airplanes, and ships, but even more in "the human being: the Israeli citizen…his education, his home, his school, his street, his neighborhood, the society in which he grows." He also believed that the solution to the rising tide of Islamism lay only in "economic development and an improved standard of living." Foreign Minister Shimon Peres stated that a country's scientific and technological prowess matters more than the size and strength of its armed forces, adding that the expense of the arms race and maintaining a modern army destroy the economy. The chief of staff, Lieutenant General Amnon Shahak, deemed a Syrian embassy in Israel more important than an early warning station. Major General Zeev Livneh announced that "peace is the best security."

Reluctance to take casualties. The large loss of life in the 1973 war and the poor results of the 1982 war soured many Israelis on deploying troops and losing soldiers. The Four Mothers Movement of 1997 to 2000 traumatized the IDF by managing to spark an emotional backlash against the IDF's presence in southern Lebanon, becoming partially responsible for convincing Jerusalem to accept a unilateral retreat from Lebanon. Among young people, draft evasion, hitherto all but unknown, became a problem, as did a drop in volunteers for combat units.

To reduce casualties, Rabin limited some IDF activities at the expense of achieving military goals. Politicians preferred to pursue diplomacy. Peres deemed cooperation among Middle Easterners "essential," while arms control must "become the call of the day." Deputy Defense Minister Mordechai Gur promised that "Israel will use all available political ave-

2 The following analysis relies on Efraim Inbar, "Contours of Israel's New Strategic Thinking," *Political Science Quarterly* (Spring 1996), pp. 41–64.

nues before taking military action in order not to harm the peace process." Communication Minister Shulamit Aloni wanted Israel to stop policing the West Bank and Gaza, worried that this obstructed diplomacy with Palestinians. One member of the ruling Labor party, Uzi Baram, went so far as to suggest removing rifles from Israeli soldiers who entered Palestine refugee camps.

In combination, these two factors fundamentally changed how the Rabin-led government approached the Palestinians. It jettisoned the old, tough outlook and adopted a softer attitude. Longing for resolution, Israeli citizens and leaders glibly assumed that their opponents—in Tehran, Damascus, Gaza, and Haifa—wanted likewise, cheerfully ignoring the fact that those opponents had a very different mentality, one of destruction, not resolution.

More than anyone, Shimon Peres embodied the Oslo Era due to his longevity (a member of parliament for nearly the entire time), his many powerful positions (minister of foreign affairs, minister of defense, prime minister, president), and his exceptional gift of articulation in many languages. When Yasir Arafat declared "We don't want peace, we want victory," Peres retorted with his usual epigrammatic flair, "You have to fight terrorism with wisdom." He dismissed the goal of victory with "War has solved nothing" and "We cannot solve anything with force." Hippy-like, Peres declared that the Middle East had entered a new zone of consciousness: "Instead of visions of blood and tears, there will rise visions of happiness and beauty, life and peace."[3]

Peres took pride in speaking in paradoxes and hyperbole. A favorite theme compared peace to love: "Peace is very much like love. It is a romantic process—you have to be living it, you have to invest in it, you have to trust it. As you cannot impose love, so you cannot impose peace." And: "In order to make peace, you have to close your eyes. You cannot make love or peace with open eyes." He made logic-defying pronouncements with panache, hailing the PLO's pretend-decision of April 1996 to annul its charter calling for Israel's destruction as "the greatest revolution that the

3 When asked by a member of an American Jewish Committee group on September 20, 2002, if I was not right in my negative assessment of Yasir Arafat, Foreign Minister Peres replied, "Tell Mr. Pipes that you should always sacrifice for peace."

Middle East had known in the last hundred years." In fact, this non-event had a non-impact.

As these comments from on high suggest, Israelis acted like naïfs in the bazaar, making strangely primitive errors and not learning from them. As one Israeli confided to me, his country had become the Inspector Clouseau of nations, chaotic, clumsy, and clueless. Or, in Inbar's more forgiving formulation, "Exhaustion in a protracted conflict leads the protagonists to redefine their goals."

• • •

Getting the Palestinians wrong. Israelis paid little attention to the nature of their enemy, making errors concerning the PA's dictatorial nature and its radicalism.

Unelected rulers. Israelis gullibly assumed that an unelected leader represented and brought along his population. In fact, on signing the Oslo Accords, Arafat faced massive opposition from within his own constituency: Islamists, who predominated in Gaza; radical leftist organizations based in Damascus; and rebellious elements within Arafat's own group, Fatah.

This oversight was the more surprising given Israel's prior experience with the same problem. Jerusalem signed a "Framework for Peace in the Middle East" with the Egyptian government in 1979, only quickly to be disappointed by it. The dictatorial Anwar al-Sadat neither gauged the sentiments of his population nor brought it along with him. Even if sincerely meant, the high-flying words in that treaty about "full recognition, diplomatic, economic and cultural relations, termination of economic boycotts and discriminatory barriers to the free movement of people and goods" almost immediately devolved into the minimal relationship Israelis dubbed a "cold peace." A 2017 retrospective by Moomen Sallam and Ofir Winter of Civic Egypt and Israel's Institute for National Security Studies, respectively, explained this relationship:

> Israel and Egypt have limited themselves to tactical security coordination between their armies, correct diplomatic relations, and specific cooperative economic endeavors, while the cultivation of civic relationships between the two peoples, such as large-scale economic interactions and the exchange of cultures, remains a far-off vision.

Given its Egyptian disappointment as a precedent, how could the Israeli government fall for the same trick twice? At least the Egyptian case involved a reduction in hostilities, however meager; in contrast, the Palestinian one led to increased violence.

Further, even if the Oslo Accords had miraculously turned Palestinians into sedate, law-abiding bourgeois citizens with no aggressive intentions, that likely would have mattered little to Israel, for dictators count much more than their subjects, and Palestinian leaders remained unreconstructed revolutionaries. In 1993, the Middle East boasted plenty of non-genocidal peoples ruled by extremely bellicose regimes, such as in Libya, Syria, Iraq, and Iran. Palestine would surely have been just an addition to that list.

Palestinian radicalism. Palestinian leaders before 1993 displayed a self-acknowledged and highly visible radicalism, one verging on the anti-rational. Palestinians thrilled to the soaring rhetoric and brutal vision of leaders like Egypt's Gamal Abdel Nasser or Iraq's Saddam Hussein. "When you believe in what you are doing, you don't think about the consequences," explained one Palestinian activist during the Kuwait War. As'ad Abdul Rahman, a member of the Palestine National Council, put the matter even more explicitly: "We [Palestinians] are desperate. We are not in the mood for rational discussion." It beggars the imagination that responsible, serious, experienced Israelis ignored such warning signs.

• • •

Poor negotiating tactics. Israelis made a litany of procedural mistakes. They got too friendly, willingly offered "painful concessions," talked too much about their own weakness, indulged in wishful thinking, expected too much from formal agreements, ignored continued Palestinian enmity, and granted the Palestinians' an undeserved diplomatic stature.

Too buddy-buddy. Those Israelis (and Americans) who personally negotiated with Palestinian leaders came to respect them. "Oslo Israelis" who broke bread and discovered PA representatives to be civilized, even sophisticated, dinner companions, no longer saw them as the enemy but as "partners for peace" completely serious about accepting Israel. President Shimon Peres symbolized this attitude when he addressed the PA leader as "my dear friend" in 2013, adding: "President Abbas, you are our partner, and we are yours. You share our hopes and efforts for peace, and we share yours." In 2018, former prime minister Ehud Olmert variously praised Abbas as "a partner," "a great political leader," and "a friend," adding "I liked him when we were working together as a person, as a human being."[4] So chummy had relations become that false rumors in 2013 of a sexual liaison between a top female Israeli negotiator and a top male Palestinian negotiator found believers.

Painful concessions. One prime minister of Israel after another displayed a masochistic eagerness to make "painful concessions" (meaning unilateral surrenders):

- Shimon Peres: "Israel recognizes the Palestinians' right to an independent state and is prepared to make painful concessions to make that happen."
- Ehud Barak: Israel must be prepared to make "painful concessions" for peace.
- Ariel Sharon: "I am ready to make painful concessions for peace."
- Ehud Olmert: Israel is prepared to make "far-reaching compromises" and "very painful concessions."
- Benjamin Netanyahu: "My predecessors were prepared to make painful concessions. So am I."

(Perhaps willfully parodying his Israeli counterparts, Yasir Arafat once declared that, "We have made a strategic decision committing ourselves to the peace process, offering significant and painful concessions.")

Nor were these empty promises. Notable "painful concessions" included the Oslo Accords and their aftermath (1993–1997), the withdrawal from Lebanon (2000), the withdrawal from Gaza (2003–2005), plus permitting a Palestinian militia. Perhaps most remarkable of all were the two offers of unilateral retreat that Palestinian leaders turned down. According to documents and press reports:

- *2000*: Ehud Barak offered the PA about 95 percent of the West Bank and 98 percent of Gaza; in return for keeping about 5 percent of the West Bank and 2 percent of Gaza, the PA would get about 2 percent of pre-1967 Israeli territory. In addition,

4 "Oslo Americans" made similar mistakes. For example, leading peace-processor Martin Indyk called Mahmoud Abbas a "personal friend for three decades."

Barak offered a "Permanent Safe Passage" between the West Bank and Gaza, plus a de facto division of Jerusalem, including most of the Old City and nearly all of the Temple Mount.

- *2008*: Ehud Olmert offered (in the course of thirty-six meetings with Abbas) 94 percent of the West Bank, 6 percent of pre-1967 Israeli territory, the Temple Mount placed under a five-party committee (Saudi Arabia, Jordan, the PA, the United States, Israel), a land bridge between the West Bank and Gaza (which by now was now under Hamas rule), and the return of 5,000 Palestine refugees. In return, Israel would annex 6 percent of the West Bank that include the major Israeli towns.

Bill Clinton said of Arafat's refusal in 2000, "the deal was so good I couldn't believe anyone would be foolish enough to let it go." In contrast, the PA complained that, "The United States proposal seems to respond to Israeli demands while neglecting the basic Palestinian need: a viable state." Arafat and Abbas turned down these offers presumably expecting yet better deals ahead. One shudders to think of Israel's woes had the 2000 and 2008 offers been accepted.

Signaling weakness. In a bizarre and probably unique display of vulnerability, Israeli leaders openly, even proudly, sent out moans of fatigue, discouragement, and feebleness. Prime Minister Yitzhak Rabin said of Israelis, "The people are weak.... The people will have difficulties withstanding an additional war...this is why we have to make concessions." A most extraordinary expression came in 2005 from Vice Prime Minister Ehud Olmert, a former hard-liner vis-à-vis the Palestinians turned dreamy weakling. "We are tired of fighting, we are tired of being courageous, we are tired of winning, we are tired of defeating our enemies, we want that we will be able to live in an entirely different environment of relations with our enemies." Oblivious to how such words came across, blind to their impact, Israelis managed not to notice that each concession amplified hostility while further radicalizing, exhilarating, and mobilizing the Palestinian body politic to more ambition and violence.

Magical thinking. Israeli flattery of the Palestinians became a parody of itself. Prime Minister Yitzhak Rabin actually stated in a formal speech that "the Palestinians were not in the past, and are not today, a threat to the existence of the State of Israel." Of course, Peres joined in, saying of Israel's most determined enemy, "We want to help the Palestinians. The stronger they will be, the better partner they will be." Ehud Olmert predicted that, once the Palestinians become for Israel "friends, our partners, our good neighbors," then "the Middle East will indeed become what it was destined to be from the outset, a paradise for all the world." Olmert also made the astonishing declaration that "Peace is achieved through concessions. We all know that."

Magical thinking also extended outside the Palestinian arena. In March 2000, the Israeli cabinet voted unanimously to withdraw all IDF troops from southern Lebanon by July, where they had been stationed for two decades. Against any semblance of logic, politicians presented this vote as a flexing of muscle and a challenge to the country's enemies. Foreign Minister David Levy declared that the pullout would weaken Syria's position; Internal Security Minister Shlomo Ben-Ami asserted that Syria leader Hafez al-Assad was very stressed by the move. Supporting this interpretation, journalist Dan Margalit suggested that the threat of a unilateral withdrawal and the sight of Israeli tanks returning home would spur Syria to return to the negotiating table.

Overestimating signatures on documents. Rabin, Peres, and the rest assumed that signatures on an official document implied a shift in outlook. When Arafat one fine day claimed to recognize Israel, they uncritically believed him and gushed with praise and benefits, not stopping to test the fine words. They prematurely made concessions on territory, water resources, armaments, Jerusalem, and more. In fact, Arafat made a tactical retreat with the Oslo Accords at a moment of weakness and—as he immediately signaled—remained intent on Israel's destruction. Now he controlled two territories adjacent to Israel and enjoyed international legitimacy, with the immense benefits that entailed. In retrospect, the credulity of the tough-guy Rabin and his successors astonishes.

Not enforcing agreements. Despite an over-emphasis on written documents, Israel permitted the Palestinians to breech all of their solemn agreements with near impunity. Major examples include the 1993 Oslo Accords, the 1994 Cairo Agreement, the 1994 Agreement on Gaza and Jericho, the 1995 Interim Agreement, the 1997 Hebron Protocol, and the 1998 Wye River Memorandum.

Active enemy. Prime Minister Yitzhak Rabin had a favorite phrase about this that he often repeated with different wordings. "You don't make peace with friends. You make it with very unsavory enemies," or "We make peace, or we negotiate meaningful steps towards peace, with enemies. Sometimes bitter enemies," or "One does not make peace with one's friends. One makes peace with one's enemy." In this spirit, his government and his successors initiated an array of concessions, hoping and expecting the Palestinians to reciprocate.

Contrary to Rabin's slogan, however, one does not end hostilities "with very unsavory enemies" but with *former* very unsavory enemies. That is, with *enemies that have been defeated.* Resolution nearly always requires one side in a conflict to be defeated and thus give up its goals. Former Speaker of the House of Representatives Newt Gingrich rightly argues that a "peace process" does not lead to resolution but only follows it. "There can be no peace until Hamas is defeated.... Then there can be a genuine peace process."

False parity. As the elected head of a democratic and sovereign government, Yitzhak Rabin erroneously granted diplomatic equivalence at the Oslo Accords signing ceremony to Yasir Arafat, leader of an unofficial, dictatorial, and murderous organization. This visual and protocol equivalence set the precedent of equating a violent thug with a democratic leader, creating a false equality between the PLO and Israel and endowing the PLO with the same stature as the State of Israel. This dysfunctional illusion of similarity quickly became assumed, ingrained, and unquestioned. Decades later, this parity continues to create a false sense of Palestinian entitlement and to haunt the negotiations by giving the PA undeserved prestige and influence.

Rather than the prime minister, the Israeli standing with Arafat at the White House should have been someone like the second secretary at the Israeli embassy in Norway. That would have delivered the necessary signal that Arafat's protocol equivalent registers stoopingly low in the diplomatic hierarchy. That, to be sure, likely would have denied the Nobel Peace Prize to Rabin; his vanity, it would seem, prevailed.

• • •

Reflections. For Israeli leaders during the Oslo negotiations, hope sprang eternal that offering compromise, concessions, conciliation, declarations of fatigue, efforts to "make peace," flexibility, generosity, goodwill, mediation, painful concessions, restraint, trust, unilateral retreats, and vulnerability would inspire the Palestinians to reciprocate. For some reason, they did not.

Indeed, the accords had the opposite effect, inflaming Palestinian hostility and inciting irredentist dreams. Palestinians unsurprisingly misinterpreted Israel's errors as signs of demoralization and weakness. They probed for signs of feebleness and thought they found these in Israel's actions, especially its two unilateral retreats (Lebanon in 2000 and Gaza in 2005) and its two unilateral offers (Barak to Arafat in 2000 and Olmert to Abbas in 2008). Understandably, they saw Israel as a country ripe for collapse and expected that a swift kick would bring the whole Zionist edifice crashing down. The result was a radicalized and mobilized Palestinian body politic. In speech and actions, the hope of destroying Israel acquired evermore traction. Claims to the entire land of Israel proliferated, as did attacks on Israelis. Exhilarated, Palestinians ramped up the violence, believing they had a fatigued Israel on the run, that pure revolutionary fervor made up for economic and military weakness, that Muslims would annihilate Jews.

In this way, Oslo made a bad situation worse. Quiet hopes to destroy Israel at its start in 1993 transformed into the venomous speech and violent actions later that year and remain still evident more than three decades later. Thus did Israel's extravagant mistakes turn a would-be "peace process" into a "war process." Or as Israeli Major General (res.) Uzi Dayan puts it, a "rest-in-peace process."

FOREIGN INEPTITUDE

Palestinian perfidy and Israeli folly start the story. Foreign ineptness completes it. Schwartz and Wilf cursorily dismiss international efforts: "decades of shuttling, strong-arming the sides, and endless hours of negotiations came to naught because none of the diplomats or negotiators truly understood and dealt with the root causes of the conflict." Oblivious to history, wrong in their assumptions, amoral in the pursuit of an agreement, over-confidant about their abilities, childishly delighted by their high status, and paying no price for repeated failures, foreigners bigfooted, swaggered, and bungled.

• • •

The new "Eastern Question." The war on Israel has inspired the most intense and longest diplomacy since World War II, involving far more actors than any other issue, from great powers to religious institutions to murderous gangs. No other contemporary issue has so consumed statesmen, international organizations, reporters, or senior common rooms; whole forests have fallen to produce libraries full of books. The conflict has only one comparable precedent, Europe's Eastern Question of the long nineteenth century (1789–1914), the competition for influence over the Ottoman Empire and its former territories.

The Arab states' war on Israel featured major events—rounds of war, Sadat visiting Jerusalem, shuttle diplomacy—with supremely high profiles. The conflict transformed some negotiators (Henry Kissinger) and journalists (Thomas L. Friedman) into superstars while defining the legacy of a U.S. president (Jimmy Carter).

As Arab states withdrew from the arena, the Palestinian war on Israel came to dominate. It, too, had headline events—the Sabra and Shatila massacre, the Oslo Accords, October 7—and created superstars, especially Yasir Arafat. Although smaller geographically, its complexity draws in great powers, international organizations, regional governments, and sub-state actors. Its many meetings include bilaterals, multilaterals, international conferences, and summits. Its mechanisms include confidence-building measures, mediation, negotiations, peace plans, peace processes, road maps, rural retreats, special negotiators, summit meetings, track-two diplomacy, and trial balloons.

This attention starkly contrasts with the decidedly modest stakes involved. The territory at issue is miniscule, oil and gas have almost no direct role, weapons of mass destruction are absent, the number of fatalities viewed from a global perspective has been negligible.

On this last point: Counting the number of human deaths incurred in conflicts between 1950 and 2007, the Arab-Israeli conflict as a whole (including the Arab states) ranked forty-ninth, with some 51,000 deaths, according to research by German scholar Gunner Heinsohn. Of these deaths, about one-tenth, or 5,100, occurred in fighting between Palestinians and Israelis, making it something like the 200th most fatal conflict of that time period. Turned around, this means that hundreds of other conflicts since 1950 led to more deaths. In contrast, the little-known Congolese civil wars have taken the lives of 3.8 million persons, almost a thousand times more fatalities. Of a grand total of approximately eighty-five million persons killed in conflicts since 1950, roughly one of every 17,000 persons thus killed was a Palestinian or Israeli in conflict with each other.

Outsiders have plenty of ideas about bringing Palestinians and Israelis together and are not shy about expressing these, funding them, and pressing for them. Intense foreign involvement translates into influence; foreign do-gooders have, via opinions, weapons, money, and diplomacy, substantially shaped the Palestinian-Israeli conflict. Yet, their record has been undistinguished and inspires little confidence; meddling seems a fair description, even for the most involved and most competent of the lot—the U.S. government.

• • •

U.S. engagement. A sense of urgency long hovered over the conflict. As Barack Obama took office in 2009, for example, energized foreign policy Solons insisted on his immediate involvement. Richard N. Haass and Martin Indyk, both of the Council on Foreign Relations, demanded that Obama make it "a personal priority" while assigning the secretary of state "to take the lead" and stressing the need to appoint a special envoy "reporting to the president through the secretary of state." Thomas L. Friedman of *The New York Times* instructed the new president that because "We're at a hinge of history…half of U.S. diplomacy is going to be about how to make peace between Palestinians." He concluded that, "It's five to midnight and before the clock strikes 12 all we need to do is rebuild Fatah, merge it with Hamas, elect an Israeli government that can freeze settlements," among other steps.

On cue, Obama did as instructed. On his first full day as president, he appointed former senator George Mitchell as special envoy for the Middle East and telephoned the leaders of Israel, Egypt, Jordan, and the PA. The White House press secretary justified this eccentricity by saying that Obama used his initial moments in office "to communicate his commitment to active engagement in pursuit of Arab-Israeli peace from the beginning of his term." A few days later, Obama granted his first formal interview as president not to an American station but to Al-Arabiya television channel.

Obama later vowed "to personally pursue this outcome [a Palestinian-Israeli resolution] with all the patience and dedication that the task requires." He also announced that, "The moment is now for us to act" to ease tensions between Israel and its neighbors and declared: "I want to have a sense of movement and progress." He went on to predict success: "I'm confident that if we stick with it, having started early, that we can make some serious progress this year." In the face of immobility, he later announced impatience with Palestinian-Israeli diplomacy: "We can't afford to wait another decade, or another two decades, or another three decades to achieve peace."

Such expressions fit a pattern, as other presidents also disproportionately and personally immersed themselves in the Palestinian-Israeli issue. Clinton hosted Yasir Arafat more often in the Oval Office than any other foreign figure. He spoke glowingly at the Oslo Accords signing of that being the moment "when we dare to pledge what for so long seemed difficult even to imagine: that the security of the Israeli people will be reconciled with the hopes of the Palestinian people." George W. Bush spoke of the day approaching "when Palestinians will enjoy the blessings that freedom brings and all Israelis will enjoy the security they deserve." Donald Trump expressed characteristic optimism in his own abilities: "I'm working very, very hard on trying to finally create peace between the Palestinians and Israel, and I think we'll be successful." He announced his view that brokering a Palestinian-Israeli deal "is, frankly, maybe not as difficult as people have thought over the years" and "I think there is a great possibility that we will make a deal."

U.S. secretaries of state also submerged themselves in this issue. After only a few months as top American diplomat in 1982, George Shultz observed, "unless you do something about it, in the job of secretary of state you will spend 100 percent of your time on the Middle East. The subject consumes you and it's coming at you all the time." In one example of this consumption, Shultz stopped off fourteen times in Middle Eastern cities in fourteen days in April and May 1983 in pursuit of a Lebanese-Israeli agreement. Shultz's successor, James Baker, devoted nearly half his memoir as secretary of state to the Middle East. Baker's successor, Warren Christopher, was virtually secretary of state for the Middle East. Palestinian-Israeli diplomacy had particular personal importance to Condoleezza Rice, who devoted most of her last two years as secretary of state to it. She recounts in her autobiography a conversation with George W. Bush when he offered her that position, saying that they needed to talk "as directly as we ever had" to raise "the one substantive issue" on her mind. "Mr. President," she said, "we need to get an agreement and establish a Palestinian state." Bush replied, "We'll get it done." John Kerry made his first official phone calls as secretary of state to the Israeli and Palestinian leaders, then visited the PA twelve times and Israel thirteen times.

Historian Max Boot in 2007 summed up the meager results of this exertion:

> Pretty much every Secretary of State since the Truman administration has devoted considerable energy to brokering peace between Israelis and Palestinians. None succeeded.... But there seems to be something about the Secretary of State's job that forces its occupants to keep on undertaking this Sisyphean labor regardless of whether or not it makes sense.

At the working level, diplomats who immersed themselves in Palestinian-Israeli relations acquired the ironic name of *peace processors*, as though a variation of the kitchen utensil. Though mostly American (Martin Indyk, Daniel Kurtzer, Aaron David Miller, Dennis Ross, Harold Saunders), they also include Europeans, including a Briton (Tony Blair), a Bulgarian (Nickolay Mladenov), a Norwegian (Terje Rød-Larsen), and a Spaniard (Josep Borrell).

• • •

Assuming Palestinian acceptance of Israel. Amid this flurry of activity, politicians, diplomats, journalists, and scholars miss the stubborn fact of genocidal Palestinian rejectionism. First-hand experience accumulated over decades by intelligent, well-informed, and personally committed foreigners does not break the static and entirely specious view of Palestinians as a normal belligerent with normal priorities. A priori assumptions permit them to ignore, outflank, overlook, or finesse the facts in front of them and instead believe the fine words enunciated on the White House lawn about accepting the existence of Israel. This fundamental error then inspires many bad policies, including:

Please the Palestinians. Diplomacy invariably requires the Israelis to sacrifice their own security. Outside powers revel in pressuring Jerusalem to be more forthcoming, with one president and prime minister after another vowing to pursue this approach and thereby resolve the Palestinian-Israeli conflict. Once Arafat said the magic words in 1988 ("we totally and absolutely renounce all forms of terrorism, including individual, group and state terrorism")[5] a diplomatic process began that placed nearly the entire

5 Arafat's heavily accented English prompted some listeners to debate whether he in fact "announced all forms of terrorism" or "renounced all forms of tourism."

burden of concessions on Israel. Satisfying Palestinian grievances became key to ending the conflict. Jerusalem having a conciliatory mentality, duly made concessions large (handing over territory) and small (permission for Gazans to fish in the Mediterranean Sea), in the perpetual hope of satisfying outside mediators and Palestinians alike. Those concessions may all have crashed on the hard rock of Palestinian intransigence but, thirty-plus years after Oslo, true believers still demand that Israel make yet one more concession.

"Partners for peace." The U.S. government sees its enemies—Saddam Hussein, Osama Bin Laden, Vladimir Putin—as opponents to be defeated; but Yasir Arafat and Mahmoud Abbas having uttered some pretty words wondrously transformed them into Israel's peace partners—though this term has, happily, fallen by the side in recent years.

Land for peace. This formulation, which initially emerged in the context of negotiations between the Arab states and Israel, swaps Israeli-held land for assurances of non-belligerence—or hard assets for airy promises. That the Palestinian parties making those promises are dictatorships not obligated by their predecessors' commitments and prone whimsically to change policies renders this fundamentally uneven proposition yet more unbalanced. That Palestinians seek to destroy Israel compounds its absurdity.

A quick two-state solution. While the idea of a Palestinian state alongside the Jewish state is reasonable in the abstract, it is untenable so long as Palestinians refuse to accept Israel. For one, as some enemies of Israel explicitly point out, it will be only temporary, until they manage to conquer all of Palestine, "from the river to the sea." For another, its very consideration encourages continued rejection of Israel. Even the lunatic Libyan dictator Muammar al-Qaddafi lucidly understood this: "The establishment of a Palestinian state in the West Bank is not a final answer, but just a beginning that was put forward to liberate the rest of Palestine; that is why the Israelis reject the creation of a Palestinian state."

Discuss "final-status" issues. How will things look when the conflict is over? Speculation about a future Palestinian state, including the nature of its sovereignty, its borders, its privileges, and its governance, encourages Palestinians to expect they can achieve statehood without first accepting Israel. To be sure, policy planners in a remote sub-basement should be thinking through the contours of a final-status agreement, but those in positions of power should not broach the topic, as it encourages continued Palestinian rejection of Israel.

Rely on good will. Outsiders tend to see such efforts as the Seeds of Peace program, the Neve Shalom experiment, and other track-two diplomatic encounters as crucial to improving relations, though they have had no visible impact beyond a handful of individuals. Nor should this come as a surprise, for when have good-will measures resolved a conflict? Widespread Palestinian refusal to accept Israel means that protracted and close contact tends to lead to deepened hostility, as manifested by opinion polls and violence. Both sides prefer divorce to marriage.

• • •

Other errors. In addition, outsiders make a medley of other mistakes.

Encourage enrichment and placation. Outsiders support these twin failed Israeli policies, explained in Part II, for they exactly fit the American and other agendas.

Unchanging demands. The persistent, unchanging nature of the Palestinians' position, always denying Israel's existence, from 1948 to the present, no matter what, has transformed them into something like a perceived force of nature. Negotiators see them as unresponsive as an ice storm or an earthquake. Instead, they invariably turn to Israel, ever the reasonable party, for concessions.

Double standard. Should Israelis act badly, peace processors come down heavily on them, while hardly caring about Palestinian misbehavior. When Finance Minister Bezalel Smotrich in March 2023 said that a Palestinian village "needs to be wiped out" in revenge for an unprovoked double murder of Israelis, his repeated apologies did not stem the relentless criticism nor the calls for his dismissal. In contrast, when Moshir al-Masri, a top Hamas official in Gaza, two days later threatened Israelis with "O Zionists, your blood is free to take and killing you is an act of closeness to Allah, may God be exalted," no one paid attention to such a routine statement, much less pressured the speaker to apologize or be dismissed.

Nor is it just rhetoric. Even a faked Palestinian killing, such as that of Mohammed al-Dura by the IDF in 2000, gets enormous and sustained global attention.[6] In contrast, the PA signed multiple, solemn international

6 On its being faked, see Nidra Poller, "Myth, Fact, and the al-Dura Affair," *Commentary*, September 2005.

treaties protecting children and prohibiting their involvement in warfare[7] but then brazenly incited and recruited children ages fourteen and younger to carry out attacks on Israelis; no one noticed. Alan Baker, the Israeli legal analyst who publicized these facts, plaintively asked why the West chooses "to ignore Palestinian violations of international laws and norms." In the U.S. context, this is known as the "soft bigotry of low expectations."

Worse, Western states *encourage* the PA not to fulfill treaty obligations to Israel. For example, a confidential June 2022 document obtained by JNS reveals how the European Union brushed the Oslo Accords aside in pursuit of a commitment "to contribute to building a Palestinian State within 1967 borders." Toward this end, it worked actively to help the PA take over parts of the West Bank (Area C) that Oslo assigned to complete Israeli control. Due to such EU support, the Israeli organization Regavim concludes, "Israel is quantifiably losing the construction battle to the Palestinians in Area C."

Linkage. The concept of "linkage," a mistaken belief that Palestinian-Israeli relations drive Middle Eastern politics, bestows an outsized importance on the West Bank and Gaza. Barack Obama offered a classic expression of this view: "To the extent that we can make peace...between the Palestinians and the Israelis, then I actually think it strengthens our hand in the international community in dealing with a potential Iranian threat." Not just that; Obama also saw a Palestinian-Israeli deal reducing the threat of jihadis, easing problems in Iraq and Afghanistan, and "peeling Syria out of the Iranian orbit." A great number of top political and military figures, mostly American, endorsed linkage, including Lloyd Austin, Hillary Clinton, David Petraeus, Martin Schulz, and Donald Trump.

Assume mutual exhaustion. The Palestinian dedication to destroy Israel remains strong, as does the Israeli determination to fend off an existential threat. Not understanding this basic fact, clueless negotiators intrude with the assumption that the combatants are spent. George Mitchell articulated this error in 2002: "Life is unbearable for ordinary Israeli citizens because

7 Including t he 1989 Convention on the Rights of the Child, the 2000 Optional Protocol on the Involvement of Children in Armed Conflict, the Protocol Additional to the Geneva Conventions of August 12, 1949, and relating to the Protection of Victims of International Armed Conflicts (Protocol I) June 8, 1977, the Rome Statute of the International Criminal Court, and the Paris Principles on the Involvement of Children in Armed Conflict.

of the fear of the suicide bombings and other threats. Life is unbearable for ordinary Palestinians: their economy has been destroyed. So I think they're [both] soon reaching the exhaustion factor when they'll recognize that there is no military solution." This assumption drastically underestimates both parties' staying power.

Hamas benefits from civilian misery. Through history, dictators have viewed the lives of their troops as expendable, as cannon fodder. Battlefield gains justify any loss of life, from ancient Greece to Wagner prison recruits in the Battle of Bakhmut. Hamas has done something probably unprecedented, however. Since seizing control of Gaza in 2007, it has purposefully tormented its subject population for public relations purposes. It bases troops and missiles in mosques, churches, schools, hospitals, and private homes because it *wants* Gazans to be bombed, hungry, suffering, homeless, injured, and dead. The more misery endured by Gazans, the more convincingly Hamas can accuse Israel of aggression and the wider and more vehement the support it wins from antisemites of all persuasions—Islamists, Palestinian nationalists, far-leftists, and far-rightists. This unique form of barbarism, predictably, baffles observers.

• • •

Given this host of errors and a curiously narrow perspective, it hardly surprises that the outside world's myriad initiatives, missions, plans, and schemes tend to vaporize, forgotten and unmourned.

6

PLANS GALORE

THROUGH DECADES OF DIPLOMACY, GOVERNMENTS (especially the American) and international organizations (especially the United Nations and the European Union) willfully overlooked the unpleasant reality that Palestinians seek to destroy Israel. Instead, in genteel fashion, they understood the Palestinian-Israeli conflict as limited to secondary issues, such as borders, resources, and sanctities. Accordingly, all their efforts ended in failure and rendered a bad situation worse.

This also applies to the newest entrant in the "peace processing" derby—the People's Republic of China, which has offered its own plan and indicated an eagerness to join the diplomatic dance. Its June 2023 iteration, as summarized in *The New York Times*, has three parts: "the creation of a fully sovereign Palestinian state, based on 1967 borders, with East Jerusalem as its capital; a call for increased international aid to a Palestinian state; and the convening of a 'larger, more authoritative, more influential international peace conference' to promote talks." These three elements quintessentially repeat errors of past decades.

In striking exception to its predecessors, the Biden administration (as of this writing, at the close of 2023) has not launched its own "peace plan," nor has it come under much pressure to do so. Have the do-gooders become disillusioned? Are other issues—the climate, China, Ukraine—deemed more urgent? Possibly. Or, this could be but a pause, with the "peace process" resuming at any time, especially with a new U.S. presidential administration taking office in January 2025.

If the incessant record of failure since 1993 should give pause to would-be peacemakers, new degree holders in peace studies lurk out there, eager to try their hand. Plus, assorted busybodies cannot stay away from the excitement, while idle foreign ministers dream of a Nobel Prize. Thus, the great do-gooder effort could come roaring back at any time, with the powers again joining forces to impose their collective wisdom on Israel, compelling it again to make concessions imperiling its security, with predictably doleful results. In anticipation of this eventuality, it pays to sift through the jumble of existing plans, many of which retain supporters and could be resuscitated at any time.

THE PLANS

A colorful array of proponents has promoted a wide range of mutually exclusive plans to end the Palestinian-Israeli conflict.

Oslo's failure spurred a host of new plans to remedy the situation. They issued primarily from the United States and Israel, with an echo or two from Europe and the Arab states. They emphatically did not emerge from the Palestinian side—hardly surprising, given that Yasir Arafat and Mahmoud Abbas perfected the art of waiting for a next round of concessions.

Diplomat after diplomat trotted to Jerusalem and Ramallah, the informal PA capital, carrying plan after plan. Simply enumerating the names of these twenty-seven obscure and deservedly forgotten efforts exhibits their futility. They include: the

- Beilin-Abu Mazen Document of 1995
- Wye River Memorandum of 1998
- Sharm El Sheikh Memorandum of 1999
- Camp David Summit of 2000
- Clinton Parameters of 2000
- Taba Summit of 2001
- Mitchell Plan of 2001
- Tenet Plan of 2001
- Zinni Plan of 2002
- George W. Bush's June 2002 speech
- Arab Peace Initiative of 2002
- London Conference of 2003
- Road Map of 2003
- Geneva Initiative of 2003
- Wolfensohn Mission of 2005
- Ward Mission of 2006
- Benchmarks for Peace of 2007
- Jones Mission of 2007
- Annapolis Process of 2007–2008
- Fraser Mission of 2008
- Mitchell Mission of 2009–2011
- Dayton Mission of 2010
- Amman Talks of 2012
- Kerry Initiative of 2013–2014
- Peace Initiative in the Middle East of 2016
- Initiative for the Middle East Peace Process of 2017
- Trump Peace Plan of 2020

Curiously, despite multiple efforts by the George W. Bush administration (note the fifteen plans listed above between 2001 and 2008, almost two a year), Haass and Indyk complained in 2009 about Bush's "neglect of this issue." Such disdain points to excessive expectations.

Plans fall into three main types: discarding Oslo, improving Oslo, and ignoring Oslo. The following explanations go from toughest on the Palestinians to softest on them:

• • •

I. Discarding the Oslo Accords. The very harshest idea, associated with rabbi, activist, and politician Meir Kahane, calls for an involuntary "transfer" of Palestinians, expelling them, against their will, if necessary, from Eretz Yisrael (including the West Bank, Gaza, and Israel itself), to parts unknown. Once a common view,[1] and even briefly British policy, it moved to the political fringe until protracted Palestinian violence won it meaningful support in Israel. A February 2002 poll showed 35 percent of respondents wanting to "transfer the residents of the territories to Arab states." A March 2002 poll, asking more specifically about "annexing the territories and carrying out transfer," found 31 percent in favor. The rising popularity in 2022 of Itamar Ben-Gvir, a politician who in the past espoused these views, and his appointment as minister of National Security, indicates their renewed prominence.

A milder version of expulsion encourages the voluntary exodus of Palestinians. Under this plan, associated with Israeli academic Martin Sherman, who calls it the "Humanitarian Paradigm," Israel cuts off all trade and services (water, electricity, fuel, postal services, electronic communications, port facilities, tax collection, remittances, etc.) to the West Bank and Gaza, then offers Palestinians sufficient money to convince them voluntarily to leave for "a better, safer life elsewhere" in the world. An October 2001 poll reported 66 percent of Israelis supporting this scheme. It found renewed support after October 7, when politicians publicly discussed ways to encourage Gazans to emigrate.

---

1 The expulsion of Palestinians was a persistently recessive theme among both Zionists and Westerners, as well as some Arabic speakers, in the half-century before Israel's creation. For documentation, see Chaim Simons, *A Historical Survey of Proposals to Transfer Arabs from Palestine 1895–1947* (London Grosvenor House Publishing Limited, 2021).

Annexation of parts of the West Bank became a live prospect in mid-2020, when Israeli leaders thought President Donald Trump would accept this step. He did not, so the plan was not fully fleshed out, but it involved the unilateral adding of new lands to the State of Israel, with no Palestinian gains. Polling found that a mere 9 percent of Israeli Jews saw annexation as the preferred option.

Israelis also developed a reciprocal version of annexation, swapping Jewish-majority land in the West Bank for Muslim-majority land within Israel proper, what Avigdor Liberman calls a populated-territory exchange. For example, Labor's Ephraim Sneh suggested that: "About 5 percent of the West Bank territory with the largest concentration of Israeli settlement blocks, especially those close to the Israeli border, would be annexed to Israel. Israel, in return, would give up lands on its side of the border," presumably areas with high Muslim concentrations.

Caroline Glick's One-State Solution calls for Israel to annex the whole West Bank, extend Israeli sovereignty over it, and apply Israeli civil law throughout. As in eastern Jerusalem since 1967, Palestinians would enjoy permanent residency and have the opportunity to apply for citizenship. Extrapolating from the history of Muslim eastern Jerusalemites, Glick argues that few West Bankers would become Israelis. A 2015 poll found 36 percent of Israeli Jews agreeing with this approach.

The Jordan-is-Palestine plan redirects Palestinian aspirations away from Israel and toward Jordan, a country already hosting a very substantial Palestinian population. Advocates expect this shift of focus to cause Palestinians to lose interest in Israel and leave Israelis alone. Major figures on Israel's Right, including Yitzhak Shamir and Ariel Sharon, endorsed this project.

The New State Solution promoted by Sergeant (res.) Benjamin Anthony parallels Jordan-is-Palestine except that it redirects Palestinian attention to a 1,600-square-kilometer parcel of Sinai land in Egypt.

The Palestinian Emirates scheme of Bar-Ilan University's Mordechai Kedar turns the West Bank population into "citizens of seven independent city-states," namely Jenin, Nablus, Ramallah, Jericho, Tukaram, Qalqilya, and the Arab part of Hebron. These independent states would replace the Palestinian affiliation, which Kedar considers artificial, allowing their populations to deradicalize and prosper.

Most simply, some advocate building a physical wall between the two populations. "A Protective Fence: The Only Way" was a popular bumper sticker in Israel in early 2002.

• • •

II. Improving the Oslo Accords. Other efforts, now mostly defunct, focus on repairing faults in the Oslo Accords.

In a major June 2002 speech, President George W. Bush offered enhanced benefits on the condition that the Palestinians practice good governance, an idea originally proposed by the Israeli politician Natan Sharansky. Proclaiming it "untenable for Palestinians to live in squalor and occupation," the president outlined a vision whereby, as a means toward ending hostilities with Israel, the Palestinians would develop "entirely new political and economic institutions based on democracy, market economics, and action against terrorism." He specifically mentioned transparent financial institutions, objective auditing, and an independent judiciary.

The State Department retorted to Bush in September 2002 with its "Road Map," the product of consultations with the "Quartet" made up the U.S. and Russian governments, the European Union, and the United Nations. Its formal name, the "Concrete, Three-Phase Implementation Road Map," suggests its incremental quality. The complex plan called for a first phase in early 2003, in which Palestinians hold "free, fair, and credible elections" and Israel withdraws to its positions of September 28, 2000, "as the security situation improves." The second phase, starting later in 2003, would "focus on the option of creating a Palestinian state with provisional borders based upon a new constitution." The final phase, in 2004 and 2005, would see Israeli-Palestinian negotiations "aimed at a permanent-status solution" with the goal of Israel pulling back "to secure and recognized borders" from the territories it conquered in 1967. Like all such plans, the Road Map is vague about conditions to be imposed on the Palestinians and specifically what, if any, penalties they would pay for noncompliance.

Others wanted to speed up the Road Map. The Israel Policy Forum, a leftist American advocacy group, offered an even more detailed four-step "On Ramp" to the Road Map.

No less impatiently, British Prime Minister Tony Blair announced a London Conference to include the Quartet, the Palestinians, and officials from Egypt, Saudi Arabia, and Jordan. (Blair conveniently left out the Israelis, a clever way to facilitate agreement.)

In later years, Americans focused more on dangling vast sums of money before the Palestinians while making minimal demands on them: John Kerry's "Breaking the Impasse" initiative of 2014 offered them a relatively stingy $4 billion while Donald Trump's "Peace to Prosperity: A Vision to Improve the Lives of the Palestinian and Israeli People" conjured up a far more munificent $50 billion.

Some would-be peacemakers drop all conditions on the Palestinians, preferring only to shower them with benefits. Representative Henry Hyde, chairman of the House International Relations Committee, proposed a "Middle East Marshall Plan" that promised the Palestinians (and others) a comprehensive economic development program. Hyde argued in 2002 for aid to the Palestinians on the basis that "people who had hope of a better life in economic terms would not resort to violence." Likewise, former head of the World Bank James Wolfensohn and the Quartet's special envoy charged with fixing the beleaguered Palestinian economy, decided that, in the words of *The Wall Street Journal*, "the Middle East conflict needs not only a political settlement but also an economic one. Prosperity, Wolfensohn believes, will blunt the appeal of extremism and give Palestinians a stake in building a new state after years of nearly continuous violence." American journalist Dan Perry suggested in 2021 that Israel send $100 billion in a "unilateral and generous [step] aimed at improving the lot of individual Palestinians." In June 2023, the World Jewish Congress' Ronald S. Lauder repeated the call for a Middle East Marshall Plan.

Then came a miscellany of plans. Martin Indyk, a sometime-U.S. official, called for international troops to replace the IDF and establish a "trusteeship" over the West Bank and Gaza, thereby laying the basis for "credible, representative, accountable, and transparent institutions." Thomas Friedman proposed a scheme whereby "a joint American-Palestinian security force" would replace Israeli control over the territories, followed by American troops who would stay on "indefinitely." Israel's Labor party in 2005 called for an arrangement whereby Israeli towns in the West Bank are turned over to the PA, then leased back on a long-term basis.

Due to its religious significance to both Judaism and Islam, the Temple Mount in Jerusalem had witnessed major clashes after 1929, and also served as a tool of Palestinian incitement ("Al-Aqsa is in danger"). Several plans, including those of the Geneva Initiative and Israeli politician Yossi Beilin, sought to deal with this flashpoint by dividing the holy esplanade into sovereign districts.

Some wanted a change in the Palestinian leadership by pushing out Arafat or Abbas and their cronies. These further divided between those (like Benjamin ben Eliezer of Labor) who favored a policy of waiting until a new Palestinian leadership emerged on its own and others (like Benjamin Netanyahu of Likud) who urged that Israel actively remove Arafat and replace him with a more pragmatic and flexible leadership that Netanyahu believed to be "waiting in the wings."

Micah Goodman of Israel's Shalom Hartman Institute proposed "shrinking the conflict" based on an "invisible consensus" having emerged in Israel about the Palestinians. He called for "an effort to create territorial contiguity between Palestinian autonomous islands in the West Bank, connect this Palestinian autonomy to the wider world, and promote Palestinian economic prosperity and independence." David Makovsky of the Washington Institute for Near East Policy proposed mutual "gradualism on the Palestinian issue" by "encouraging a range of trust-building exercises" or confidence-building measures (CBMs).

• • •

III. Israeli withdrawal. Simplest of all, this approach entails no wall, no pesky conditions, no road map, no ramp, no monies, no foreign troops, no change in leadership, and no shrinkage. Rather, Israel immediately pulls all its forces from all the territories, dismantles all Israeli towns and outposts there, transfers out all Israeli citizens, and closes down its entire machinery of control. The hope is to inspire a reciprocal mood of accommodation by the Palestinians or, failing that, a de facto separation benefiting both sides.

The leftwing Israeli organization Peace Now promoted this notion with the slogan "Leave the Settlements, Return to Ourselves." Many others put forward variants of this idea: Saudi Crown Prince Abdullah in 2002 ("The Arab Peace Initiative"); Amram Mitzna, the Labor candidate for prime minister in 2003; the Geneva Initiative of 2003; ex-U.K. prime minister Tony Blair in 2015; virtually every government; and the overwhelming majority of leftists, academics, journalists, and diplomats around the world, not to speak of religious and business leaders.

THE PLANS' DEFICIENCIES

These many plans differ in spirit, running the gamut from too-tough to appeasing, and they contradict each other in specifics (expel the Palestinians vs. unilateral Israeli withdrawal). But they share important qualities. All give up on Oslo's optimistic assumption of Palestinian-Israeli comity as the basis for negotiation. All manage the conflict without resolving it. All seek to finesse war rather than win it. All ignore the need to address Palestinian rejectionism.

As a result, each plan has major deficiencies. So long as Palestinians reject Israel, debates about one-, two-, and three-state solutions, about carving up the Temple Mount, or about electricity grids and water supplies, are for naught.

• • •

I. Discarding the Oslo Accords. Kahane's plan forcefully to "transfer" Palestinians ranks as the very worst of many bad plans, solving nothing while creating insurmountable problems. It would prompt internal Israeli divisions, exacerbate Palestinian hostility, and inflate the ranks of Israel's enemies. Expulsion would also disgust and outrage many Israelis, leading to their alienation and emigration, possibly threatening the state; in comparison, the battle over judicial reform through the first three quarters of 2023 was but a walk in the park. Palestinians would be more aggressively hostile than ever. Expulsion would spur an international alliance to isolate Israel, with profound costs to it in every sphere of life, impoverishing and imperiling the country; the isolation of apartheid South Africa would look mild in comparison.

Plus, the intended "transfer" would never occur, as no state would receive the expelled Palestinians, who would instead heroically return to Israeli-controlled territories. Two dress rehearsals provide evidence for this outcome.

After the murder of a border policeman in 1992, Israel deported 417 members of Hamas and PIJ to Lebanon. Lebanese authorities refused to let them in, so what became known as the "400" spent up to a full year, including a harsh winter, camped out in tents in a desolate no-man's land between the two countries, warmed by intense and sympathetic media coverage (*The New York Times*: "400 Arabs Ousted by Israel Are Mired in

Frozen Limbo" and "Ousted Arabs Shiver and Wait in Lebanese Limbo"). Then, inevitably, Israel repatriated them. Benefiting from vast and sympathetic media coverage, many (including Ismail Haniyeh) went on to leadership positions in Hamas, which gained handsomely from this incident. In all, Hebron journalist Khaled Suleiman commented, the deportations "succeeded in strengthening Hamas among the Palestinians."

A lesser version of this same drama took place a decade later. About 200 Palestinian gunmen in 2002 violently took over Bethlehem's Church of the Nativity, which Christians hold to be the birthplace of Jesus. Reluctant to attack so holy a site, the Israelis instituted a siege that lasted five weeks, punctuated by occasional shootings. Finally, Israel agreed to release about fifty-five gunmen to Gaza or to be flown out to exile in various countries. In 2005, Israel permitted them all to come back, with the prime minister's spokesman assuring, "We promise that they won't be arrested upon their return."

Were Israel actually to attempt deporting millions of ordinary men, women, and children, they would be refused entry, and the same boomerang would take place, though on a vastly larger scale. The expellees would respond with renewed dedication to harm Israel, whether through violence or political action, encouraged by Israel's isolation and their own worldwide support. "Transfer" might satisfy emotionally, but an *Arabrein* Israel is infeasible, perilous, and doomed.

Sherman's voluntary departure scheme of Palestinians from the West Bank avoids these perils but is also unrealistic. Nationalism, social pressure, and threats of violence will abort the scheme. And, were it to find any takers, who would let them immigrate? Egypt has vehemently rejected such an option and built barriers adjoining Gaza, which Hamas calls the "Wall of Death," to prevent it. Jordan has also made clear its unconditional opposition.

Annexing Jewish-majority areas in the West Bank also provokes hostile international responses; and for what? No government has recognized Israel's 1967 annexation of Jerusalem and presumably none will do so vis-à-vis parts of the West Bank. This step amounts to a symbolic act that brings no tangible benefits, only drawbacks. In short, one does not end a war by expelling or annexing enemies.

Territorial swaps sound good in theory but run up against practical problems. Israel's Muslim citizens have repeatedly indicated that, in their great majority, they do not want to be subjected to the tender mercies of the

Palestinian Authority; they may not like Israel, but they do appreciate its rule of law, insurance plans, standard of living, and much else. Therefore, they would likely oppose such a step; were it to go through, they would move from their homes to other parts of Israel not designated to be traded.

Caroline Glick's One-State Solution turns the fraught situation of Jerusalem's non-citizen Muslim population into a model for its much larger West Bank counterpart. It endangers Israel in either of two ways. Should West Bankers decide to remain as permanent residents who lack the full rights of citizens, a two-tier body politic emerges that would likely provoke a massive international campaign, one credibly accusing Israel of apartheid. Alternatively, Palestinian leaders might change tactics and instruct West Bankers to apply for Israeli citizenship, something the PA's Ahmed Qurei already signaled in 2008: "If Israel continues to reject our propositions regarding the borders [of a future Palestinian state], we might demand Israeli citizenship." Should this occur, it potentially increases Israel's Muslim citizenry from about one-fifth of the population to about one-third, a possibility that looks the more likely given the increasingly favorable attitude of Jerusalem's permanent residents toward Israeli citizenship. Further, many of those new Muslim citizens would be extremely hostile to their Jewish co-nationals. Such an outcome would only please those wanting to undo the Jewish nature of Israel.

Jordan-is-Palestine meets near-total opposition among both Palestinians and Jordanians. And were it forced through, it would fail, as Jordan could never substitute for Palestine, while the prospect of Amman replacing Jerusalem amounts to an absurdity. Palestinian nationalism being a copy of Zionism, Muslims are no more likely to accept Amman as their holy city than would Jews. Further, were such a policy implemented, it would add Jordan as a base from which to launch a Palestinian conquest of Israel.

The New State Solution of Benjamin Anthony is based on a misunderstanding. A September 2014 *Times of Israel* news item reported that an unnamed senior Egyptian official (namely, President Abdel Fattah al-Sisi) "suggested settling Palestinians in an area 1,600 square kilometers large adjacent to Gaza" as a way to "end the [Palestine] refugee story." This turned out to be an inaccurate translation, and Sisi's office vehemently denied the report.

The Palestinian Emirates echoes Sherman's voluntary departure scheme in that it is harmless to attempt but also infeasible. After a full century of the Palestinian identity, the chance of it being replaced by a Jenin or Qalqilya identity hovers at about nil.

As for physical separation, the Sharon government built a security barrier along much of a line approximately dividing Israel from the West Bank by 2004. It included a fence, a wall, and a buffer zone. Arguing that this combination "will contribute to the security of all Israeli citizens," it did reduce attacks coming from the West Bank. While operationally useful, hunkering down behind a fence and buffer zone sends the Palestinians the message of Israel as a cowering and passive society, spurring further ambitions. Thus, a fence or wall serves as a useful tool to save lives but cannot end the conflict.

• • •

II. Improving the Oslo Accords. Premised on the false assumption that Palestinians accepted Israel's existence on that sunny morning at the White House in 1993, these plans blithely build on that erroneous foundation by seeking further Israeli concessions to satisfy the never-satisfied Palestinians.

While good governance is certainly welcome in principle, its charm fades so long as Palestinians seek Israel's destruction. One usually does not wish to enhance an aggressor dictatorship's competence and economic reach. While Russia makes war on Ukraine, who hopes that Vladimir Putin (quoting George W. Bush about the Palestinians) will develop "entirely new political and economic institutions"? Is the West not glad to see the Chinese Communist Party stumble over demographic problems, zero-COVID-19 lockdowns, real-estate debt crises, and Belt and Road Initiative excesses?

The same criticism applies to the Middle East Marshall Plan. To the extent the original Marshall Plan worked (and the British development economist Peter T. Bauer has trenchantly deflated the notion that it deserves its high reputation), it filled a need for capital. That, to put it mildly, is hardly the Palestinian economy's main challenge; the PA's terminally corrupt leadership would pocket much of the aid; and the Palestinian war against Israel has very little to do with poverty or any other economic issue. Fundamentally, though, the promise of money suffers from the same conceptual mistake as good governance: It rewards Palestinians even as they continue to make war on Israel. Is it too banal to note that the original Marshall Plan began only three years after World War II ended? Conversely, when aid flowed prematurely to Afghanistan and Iraq, before a sense of defeat or an acknowledgment of errors, it went spectacularly to waste.

Anyway, there has been a functional equivalent of a Middle East Marshall Plan, for the Palestinian Authority alone has received close to $30 billion, beyond which other projects (such as UNRWA) have received much more. A lot of good that did, either economically or in terms of conflict resolution.

Then comes the U.S.-Russian-EU-UN. brainstorm, the Road Map. It leads in the wrong direction by politely asking the Palestinians temporarily to reduce their violence against Israelis, in return for which they gain a state. It imposes even fewer demands on the Palestinians than the Oslo Accords it would replace, and it makes even less pretense of expecting them to comply with its conditions; plus, Moscow's inclusion permanently discredits this initiative. The "On Ramp" and other such plans share precisely the same errors, just to a greater extent.

Various proposals to use foreign soldiers and intermediaries in a war zone are plainly unworkable; can anyone imagine Americans, Canadians, or Europeans accepting fatalities to prevent Palestinians from attacking Israelis? To ask the question is to answer it. Were further proof needed, the ignoble story of the European Union Border Assistance Mission, which literally ran away from its duties on the Gaza-Egypt border, provides it.

Schemes to divide the Temple Mount fit into a common Middle Eastern pattern of splitting control in contested areas. A review by Hillel Frisch finds that "they have led to only one outcome: failure." Among those: Syrian-Israeli demilitarized zones; Palestinian-Israeli cohabitation in eastern Jerusalem; and power-sharing arrangements between Palestinians and Jordan, Palestinians and Lebanon, and Greeks and Turks on Cyprus. The same unsatisfactory pattern holds on the Temple Mount, where Islamic institutions within the context of Israeli sovereignty and laws lead to constant tensions. Clear lines of authority work better than such divisions.

Looking for improvement in Palestinian leadership by waiting for new faces blithely assumes that the next round of leaders will be less hardline than the current one, for which there is no evidence. For Israel to select new PA leaders merely perpetuates a corrupt, genocidal regime.

Goodman's "shrinking the conflict" is just another in a long line of attempts to finesse the heart of the conflict, Palestinian refusal to acknowledge Israel, and instead focus on tangential issues, such as electricity supplies, sewage disposal, and import-export inefficiencies. Were it so easy, the conflict would long ago have ended. Makovsky's CBMs are unobjectionable but premature and of dubious value; when one party seeks the other's demise, where can confidence be found?

• • •

III. Israeli withdrawal. The prospect of a unilateral Israeli pullback from the West Bank and Gaza in return for precisely nothing enjoys immense international popularity. Unfortunately, Israeli pullbacks invariably prompt violence. Note three examples:

- *1993*: The Oslo Accords inspired many more armed attacks. As noted, more Israelis were murdered in the five years post-Oslo than in the fifteen years preceding it.
- *2000*: Israel withdrew troops from southern Lebanon in the assurance that this would purchase quiet on its northern border. Instead, Israel's enemies understood the retreat to vindicate Hezbollah-style violence. A direct line connects that retreat in May 2000 to the Palestinians' intransigence at Camp David in July 2000 and then to the "Aqsa intifada" in September 2000.
- *2005*: The withdrawal of all Israeli civilians and soldiers from Gaza cleared the way for Hamas to take control of the territory two years later, leading to five major rounds of fighting along with uncounted minor rounds. The withdrawal also encouraged Hezbollah to start the Second Lebanon War in 2006 and to amass an arsenal of more than 150,000 missiles and rockets.

The record shows unilateral Israeli retreats to be the second-worst option of all, trailing only expulsion.

• • •

Two recent plans. After decades of stagnation, two strikingly different concepts emerged in the 2020s, one from the Trump administration, the other from the Saudis.

The Trump plan. The most recent American plan came in 2020, sponsored by Donald Trump. It avoids the prior mistake of putting the onus on Israel to please the Palestinians, but "Peace to Prosperity: A Vision to Improve the Lives of the Palestinian and Israeli People" repeats some old errors and devises new ones.

Without ever demanding that Palestinians accept the Jewish state, it focuses on building up Palestinian hope. The plan not only offers a "State of Palestine," but mentions this reward 170 times in the course of the thirty-nine-page text, more than four times per page. It grants this state full-fledged independence. It bestows Israeli citizenship on 250,000 Palestinians, prompting Israeli politician Naftali Bennett to term the plan a "disaster."

Noting that Gazans "suffer from massive unemployment, widespread poverty, drastic shortages of electricity and potable water, and other problems that threaten to precipitate a wholesale humanitarian crisis," the plan promises to usher them into "a prosperous future." It promises grand economic advancement, as signaled by the plan's title and subtitle, and more than $50 billion in foreign investment over ten years. "Peace to Prosperity" estimates that its prescriptions could cause the Palestinian GDP to "double in 10 years, create over 1 million new jobs, reduce the unemployment rate below 10 percent, and reduce the poverty rate by 50 percent."

Toward this end, the plan goes into excruciating detail (shades of the Oslo Accords). For example, the word *electricity* occurs 116 times. The call for a "Dead Sea Resort Area," requires that Israel allow Palestine to develop this project to the north of the Dead Sea along with a road allowing Palestinians "to travel from the State of Palestine to this resort area, subject to Israeli security considerations." It also foresees raising and spending $25 million over a two-year period to provide "robust technical support to the Palestinian public sector to develop a new trade regime and framework."

As for a new error, the Trump plan endorses Israel annexing half of Area C, about 30 percent of the West Bank, a provocation that only damages Israeli interests. In brief, the Trump plan heightened the old approach of enrichment while adding original errors of its own, promising misguided benefits to Israel. It should not be the basis of future American efforts.

The Saudi plan. In an echo of the Trump plan, a joint EU-Saudi plan unveiled in September 2023 called the "Peace Day Effort" offers incentives (a "Peace Supporting Package") to encourage the two sides to reach an agreement, though details about the "100 percent carrots" remain unknown at the time of writing. Its provenance makes it remarkable: a joint effort of the EU, Saudi Arabia, and the Arab League in cooperation with Jordan and Egypt. Problem is that Palestinian leaders will not be bribed by benefits; they want to destroy Israel.

• • •

Economic distortion. As a coda to the foreign plans, it bears noting that the outpouring of external financial aid has distorted the Palestinian economy and, in the words of MEMRI Senior Research Fellow Anna Mahjar-Barducci, "brought no growth to the Palestinian people." Indeed, it lowered the standard of living. Rarely has the law of unintended consequences worked so creatively.

The PA offers a textbook example of how to ruin an economy by smothering it under well-intentioned but misguided donations. In the words of Peter T. Bauer, "Foreign aid is a system of taking money from poor people in rich countries and giving it to rich people in poor countries." Foreign aid corrupts and distorts an economy; and the greater the amounts involved, the greater the damage. Nowhere are the per capita amounts involved so great as among the Palestinians.

Thanks in large part to Israeli support, the PA has received monumental amounts of foreign money; close to $30 billion between 1994 and 2020, a bit over $1 billion per year. In the years after 2008, the European Union alone supplied that amount annually. The West Bank has a Palestinian population of 1.85 million, so (ignoring Gaza the first few years), that comes out to a per capita annual donation of about $5,000, a uniquely generous amount. Other foreign funding, for example via UNRWA, added further to this amount. In 2020, the U.S. House of Representatives "approved $250 million in funding for Israeli-Palestinian dialogue programs and Palestinian business development," or $110 million for dialogue programs and $140 million for investments.

A snapshot of West Bank and Gaza statistics compiled by Ziv Hellman of Bar-Ilan University in late 2007 reveals the distortions of this aid:

- Palestinian annual per capita income contracted by about 40 percent since its $2,000 peak in 1992 (before the Oslo process began) to less than $1,200 fifteen years later.
- Per capita Israeli income, ten times greater than the Palestinians' in 1967 grew to twenty-three times greater.

- Deep poverty increased in Gaza from 22 percent of the population in 1998 to nearly 35 percent in 2006; it would be about 67 percent if not for remittances and food aid.
- Direct foreign investment barely existed, while local capital mostly got sent abroad or invested in real estate and short-term trading.
- The Palestinian economy was "largely based on monopolies in various industries granted by PA officials in exchange for kickbacks."
- The PA's payroll was so bloated that the cost of wages alone exceeded all revenues.

One telling detail: At times during Yasir Arafat's reign, a third of the PA's budget went for "expenses of the President's office," without further explanation, auditing, or accounting. The World Bank objected, but the Israeli government and the European Union endorsed this corrupt arrangement, so it remained in place.

Unsurprisingly, Hellman characterized the Palestinian economy as being "in shambles."

• • •

Reflections. The Oslo Accords, the subsequent diplomacy, and the other plans all failed, as will likely future ones. Not one squarely confronts rejectionism. Each relies on gimmicks to finesse this problem. Each sidesteps the hard and nasty work of tackling the basics in favor of the gentler task of addressing symptoms. This holds true as much for "transfer" at one end of the spectrum as it does for unilateral withdrawal at the other.

In retrospect, those many plans already wasted thirty years. They inexcusably delayed resolution by diverting attention from the core issue and instead buoyed Palestinian hopes of reward even while working to eliminate Israel. The Palestinians were on the ropes in 1993; had Israel continued with its prior tough policy, they might have given up their war on Jews and Israel after another twenty years, around 2013. But Oslo rewarded Palestinian hostility and encouraged Palestinian exhilaration, thereby extending the conflict and delaying its resolution.

Although the Oslo process is widely seen as defunct, its apologists insist it remains the only game in town: Days before October 7, Dennis Ross and David Makovsky of the Washington Institute for Near East Policy wrote that "for all of Oslo's detractors, critics were never able to put forward an alternative approach." In this spirit, sunny and unrealistic schemes continue to be hatched (note the proposals above by Perry, Goodman, and Makovsky himself) offering enrichment to Palestinians in the perpetual hope that they finally will respond positively. Thus does Oslo's premise live on.

But the time is well past to flog the same old "peace process." An alternative approach very much exists—Israel Victory—and the second half of this study develops it in detail. Accordingly, we here take leave of the stale, anomalous Palestinian-Israeli imbroglio and turn to an alternative. Part IV presents the historical record of war and peace, defeat and victory, both worldwide and Palestinian-Israeli. Part V explains the background to the conflict. Part VI offers an optimistic, non-violent, non-Oslo approach to its resolution.

PART IV

Defeat and Victory

The purpose of military science is victory.

—ARISTOTLE, ca. 350 BCE

The object [of war] is victory.... The mind must always embrace the idea of victory.

—CARL VON CLAUSEWITZ, Prussian strategist, 1832

THE EPIGRAPHS ABOVE EXPRESS THE traditional approach to war: Defeat the enemy, attain victory. Through millennia, thinkers and warriors concurred on victory as the goal of warfare. British Prime Minister Winston Churchill gave immortal expression to this outlook during his country's darkest time in World War II: "You ask, what is our aim? I can answer in one word: It is victory, victory at all costs, victory in spite of terror, victory, however long and hard the road may be; for without victory, there is no survival."

This consensus hardly comes as a surprise, for victory is instinctive. In any conflict, from schoolyard brawl to world war, each participant continues until one side gives up and the other emerges as winner. Who does not win, loses. Indeed, victory and defeat are so universal, they extend to animals; a gorilla becomes, and stays, the group's alpha male by defeating his challengers.

Technological advancement did not alter this enduring human truth as humans advanced from clubs to muskets to aircraft carriers. The advent of nuclear weaponry in 1945, however, confused this commonsensical approach, opening a new and befuddled era when victory became an uncertain goal. Only in recent years, and especially in the aftermath of Russia's invasion of Ukraine, has the traditional understanding partially begun to return.

The next two chapters delve into the concept of victory and trace its evolution, showing how a once simple, intuitive, and universal concept became muddled. This concept and its undoing explain why Israelis shy from victory.

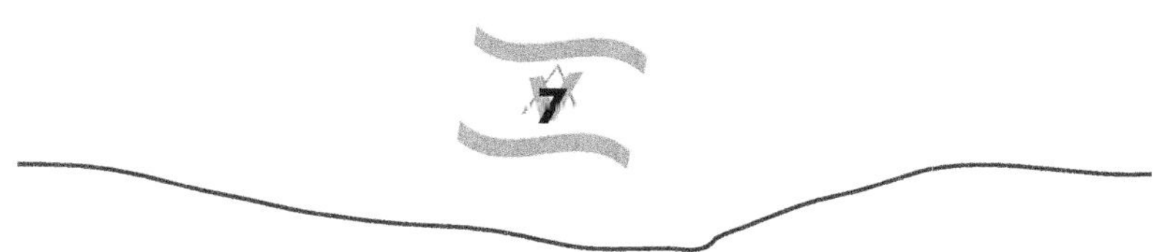

UNIVERSAL PATTERNS

WE TEMPORARILY LEAVE THE PALESTINIAN-ISRAELI conflict to look at the range of human experience in war in three parts. Victory is the goal. Defeat makes it possible. Clear resolution has its advantages over unending war.

THE NATURE OF VICTORY

Until 1945, a near unanimity existed about victory as the purpose of warfare, though what precisely *victory* means is open for debate. Willpower has a critical role in deciding wars. Ironically, the loser decides when victory occurs.

• • •

The goal of war. Chinese strategist Sun Tzu urged his readers around 350 BCE: "Let your great object be victory." His near-contemporary, the Greek philosopher Aristotle, as we have seen, agreed.

Skipping centuries ahead, Italian commander Raimondo Montecuccoli wrote around 1670: "The objective in war is victory." French essayist Montesquieu echoed him in 1748 with "The object of war is victory." Carl von Clausewitz (1780–1831), perhaps the all-time most influential thinker about war, instructed that the aim in war is "the overthrow of the enemy." He also looked beyond the military to the psychological: "Victory consists not merely in the conquest on the field of battle, but in the destruction of armed forces, physically and morally, which can in general only be effected by a pursuit after the battle is gained." Clausewitz mentions *victory* (*Sieg* and its variants in German) 380 times in the original text of *On War*.

A century later, in 1934, U.S. Army Lieutenant General Harold L. George confirmed this view, writing that "the object of war is now and always has been the overcoming of the hostile will to resist. The defeat of the enemy's armed forces is not the object of war; the occupation of his territory is not the object of war. Each of these is merely a means to an end; and the end is overcoming his will to resist."

The Allies in World War II focused on victory. In response to the surprise Japanese attack on Pearl Harbor in 1941, U.S. President Franklin Delano Roosevelt declared that "the American people in their righteous might will win through to absolute victory." (Absolute Victory became an American byword and a World War II board game still commemorates it.) Commanding general and future president Dwight D. Eisenhower wrote in 1944: "In war there is no substitute for victory." The Petroleum Industry War Council featured a picture of Eisenhower with a statement addressed to petroleum personnel: "Your work is vital to Victory."

HMS Victory, launched in 1765, Lord Nelson's flagship at the Battle of Trafalgar in 1805, and the world's oldest naval vessel still in commission.

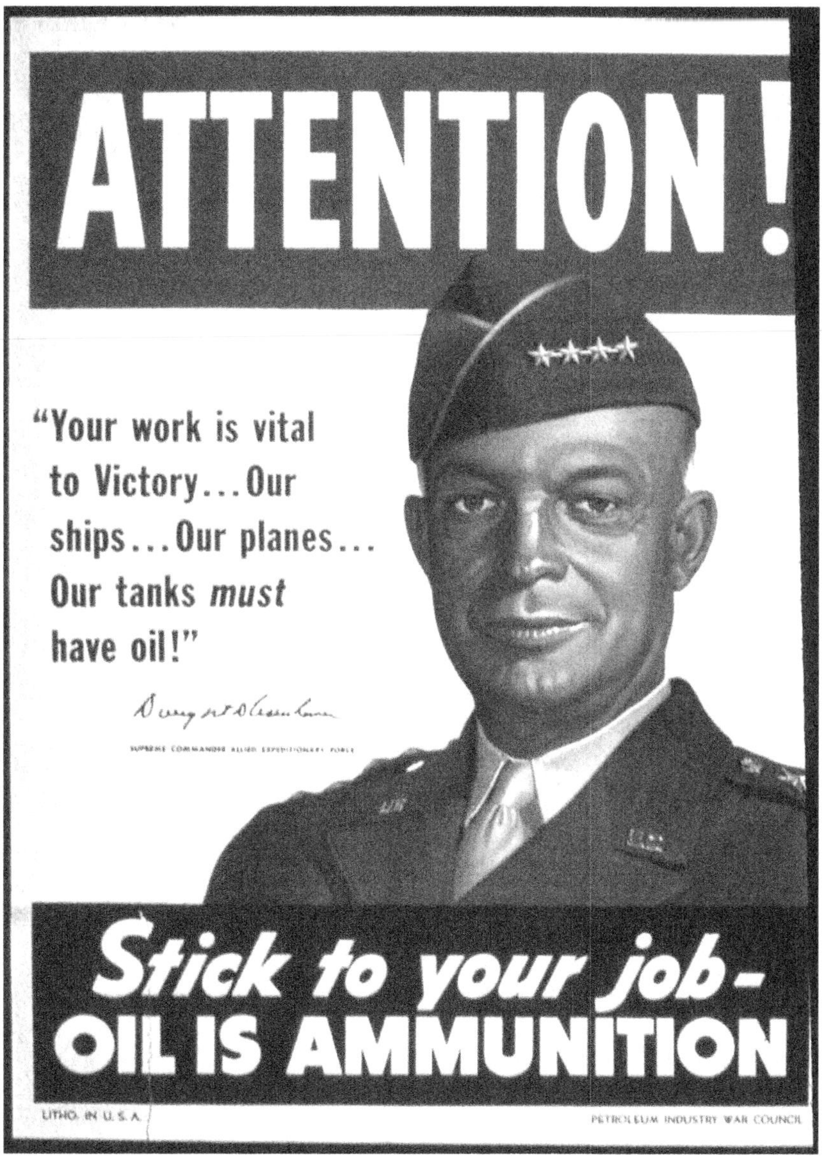

Sometime in 1943-45, the four-star general Dwight Eisenhower admonished American petroleum workers to do their part for victory.

Victory was long a part of everyday vocabulary. The British *HMS Victory*, a 104-gun ship launched in 1765, served as the flagship for several commanders, including Lord Nelson at the Battle of Trafalgar against the

French and Spanish fleets in 1805 (and, yes, he was victorious); it remains in service today, the world's oldest warship still in commission. The Victory Building opened in Philadelphia in 1873. British soldiers and sailors fighting in the world wars had a special affection for Victory cigarettes ("The cigarette that's winning the war"). Stripped-down Victory bicycles appeared in the United States soon after Pearl Harbor. The many U.S. Studebaker-US6 trucks sent to the Soviet Union during World War II under the Lend-Lease program came to be known as Victory Trucks. The Allies of World War II celebrated Victory Days. Citizens in many countries planted Victory Gardens. Victory streets, avenues, boulevards, and plazas abound.

Despite this profusion of references, the meaning of *victory* is not obvious, and specialists, admits Beatrice Heuser of Reading University, struggle "with the concept of what victory in general means."

• • •

Definition. Richard Hobbs calls victory a "mysterious and enticing shadow" in his 1980 book, *The Myth of Victory: What Is Victory in War?* In a 2006 book, *The Meaning of Military Victory*, Robert Mandel finds that "across time, circumstance, and culture, victory has had dissimilar and often unclear meanings for winners and losers." In a 2007 book, *Victory in War: Foundations of Modern Military Policy*, William C. Martel of Tufts University concludes that victory is used by policymakers and scholars "to cover an extraordinarily wide range of outcomes." But then he proposes a definition no more exact than "an all-purpose word used to describe imprecisely the concept of a success in war." Timothy W. Crawford of Boston College bemoans the fact that "in strategic discourse we have trouble defining, measuring, and arguing about victory in coherent and consistent terms." For J. Boone Bartholomees, Jr., of the Army War College, "assessments of victory are often merely gut feelings, much like the Supreme Court's definition of pornography, as something that depends on community values and you know when you see it." As these comments suggest, the scholarly debate is confusing.

Martel helpfully distinguishes between three types of victory: on the battlefield (tactical), in changing the opponent's actions (political-military), and in fully defeating the opponent (grand strategic). Our concern here centers on the grand strategic.

Clausewitz offers a way forward, defining warfare as "an act of force to compel our enemy to do our will." Patricia Sullivan of the University of North Carolina, Chapel Hill, builds on this in *Who Wins? Predicting Strategic Success and Failure in Armed Conflict* by defining strategic victory as "attaining the primary political objectives for which an actor chose the costly and risky tool of military force." Note that, in keeping with the grand strategic level of analysis, Sullivan emphasizes political, not military objectives. Similarly, Max Singer, a founder of the Hudson Institute, explains that victory "means achieving your essential goal" and that defeat "is giving up your central goal because you realize it cannot be achieved."

In this spirit, *victory* in the following analysis means forcibly and successfully attaining one's main war goals, causing the enemy to give up its main war goals and accept its loss over the long term. More simply put: Victory equals imposing one's will on an enemy and the enemy acknowledging this reality. Conversely, *defeat* means failure to attain one's main political objectives and having to give up on those war goals over the long-term.

Thus defined, victory and defeat also apply to non-military activities. For example, the leftist American theoretician Saul Alinsky extended these concepts to the political sphere in his 1971 work *Rules for Radicals*:

> This liberal cliché about reconciliation of opposing forces is a load of crap. Reconciliation means just one thing: When one side gets enough power, then the other side gets reconciled to it.... If you're too delicate to exert the necessary pressures on the power structure, then you might as well get out of the ball park.

Moreover, what victory means can change with circumstances, and objectives shift in the course of warfare. Michael C. Davies of King's College London points out that the United Kingdom began fighting in World War II "to restore a free, independent Poland while simultaneously maintaining (and preferably extending) its empire, and maintaining its existing liberal-aristocratic social contract." Although it failed to attain any of these goals, that hardly diminished the British victory. Contrarily, aims can grow. Ukraine's President Volodymyr Zelensky initially defined victory as "saving as many lives as possible" and "when a person is alive." But a September 2022 Gallup Poll found that his compatriots overwhelmingly defined victory as regaining all the territory lost to Russia since 2014, including Crimea, a sentiment that led Zelensky eventually to adopt that goal, declaring that the Russians "have to leave our territory."

Victory typically, but not always, means compelling the enemy to give up its war goals by crushing its will. A combatant can give up on its war aims for other reasons, such as an accretion of economic and political pressures, reduced military capabilities, constricted ability to maneuver, demoralized fighters, or popular revolts.

Great Britain and France, long seen as "natural and necessary enemies" of each other (in the words of an eighteenth-century British ambassador in Paris, the Earl of Stair) terminated seven and a half centuries of enmity (1066–1815) and signed the Entente Cordiale in 1904 due to shared worries about a new enemy, Germany. A rogue meteorite or threatening aliens could one day prompt an all-human coalition. Such "no victor, no loser" resolutions are the exception in modern times, however.

Nor does defeat require a military thrashing or economic destruction, much less the annihilation of a population, as Americans witnessed when they lost in Vietnam in 1975. The University of Pittsburgh's William Spaniel explains that, "Very few wars end with one side's complete military defeat, where that side cannot effectively fight any further. Rather, wars tend to continue until one side decides that prolonging the battle is no longer worthwhile, as opposed to what the other side's terms of settlement look like." In other words, wars end when one side runs out of will. Military defeat is only one way to reach that conclusion.

• • •

The role of willpower. Breaking the enemy's fortitude, morale, and willpower is often more important for victory than objective factors such as downing planes, destroying tanks, exhausting munitions, seizing land, gaining economic advantage, enjoying a technological edge, deploying more advanced weaponry, suffering lower casualty rates, or winning United Nations votes. These matter, but are not decisive. Viet Minh leader Ho Chi Minh in 1946 warned the French: "You can kill ten of my men for every one I kill of yours. But even with those odds, you will lose and I will win." He was right: North Vietnam suffered many more casualties than the French, the South, or the United States, yet it prevailed. Saddam Hussein suffered a catastrophic failure in 1991 but kept fighting until he ran out of options in 2003. The Taliban never accepted their removal from Afghanistan in 2001 and returned as victors in 2021. In all these instances, initial failure did not translate into despair, so the apparently losing side soldiered on. War continues unless battlefield losses are accompanied by psychological collapse; in this sense, *willpower* (defined as the determination to achieve victory even at the cost of major sacrifices) is key.

Conversely, despite out-manning and out-gunning their foes, major powers have repeatedly lost in modern times. The French had these advantages over their foes in Algeria but gave up in 1962. They also lost in Vietnam in 1954. The U.S. defeat in South Vietnam in 1975 occurred not because the U.S. side ran out of dollars or bullets or soldiers, nor even due to battlefield failure (it was winning the ground war) but because Americans lost the will to continue the fight. The same applies to the Soviet loss in Afghanistan in 1989 and the American loss there in 2021. Most dramatically, the Soviet Union collapsed and the Cold War ended without a fatality due to a collapse of will.

In these cases, the losers maintained large arsenals, armies, and functioning economies but realized the enemy's determination was greater, so they lacked the spirit to continue. American historian Mike Duncan explains this phenomenon:

> War is a contest of wills. Weapons, armies, fleets, and fortresses are simply the means by which one breaks the will of their enemy.... Victory and defeat are subjective psychological events, not objective material conditions. If the enemy's will is broken, a million cannons will sit idle. But if their will is not broken, it does not matter if they are disarmed or occupied, it does not matter how naked and defenseless they stand. They will simply kneel down, pick up a rock and throw it.

Efraim Karsh notes that willpower involves the entire populace:

> Ever since war was transformed in the late 18th century from a contest between professional armies into a clash between whole national entities, its outcome has been decisively dependent on the vicissitudes of national morale. No nation can sustain a prolonged war unless an influential portion of its population endorses the effort and is willing to make the necessary sacrifices, and victory or defeat in such a war is often determined

> less by battlefield strength than by sheer grit, cohesion, and persistence.

Not only are wars in recent centuries national undertakings, but they tend to take place in an ideological environment, both of which combine to make morale and will more important than ever.

How to break the enemy's will? Clausewitz argues for locating its center of gravity or main focus (*Schwerpunkt*), attacking it, and destroying it: "the defeat of the enemy consists in overcoming the resistance concentrated in his center of gravity." That center can be many things, such as a tribe, an ethnic group, a capital city, an ideology, or a leadership. John David Lewis of Bowling Green State University further explains this concept:

> The "center" of a nation's strength [is] the essential source of ideological and moral strength, which, if broken, makes it impossible to continue the war. A commander's most urgent task is to identify this central point for his enemy's overall war effort and to direct his forces against that center—be it economic, social, or military—with a view to collapsing the opponent's commitment to continue the war. To break the "will to fight" is to reverse not only the political decision to continue the war by inducing a decision to surrender, but also the commitment of the population to continue (or to restart) the war.

• • •

The loser decides. Wars historically come to an end and victory is achieved not via negotiations nor through defensive measures (such as building a wall) but by one side giving up its goals and acknowledging defeat. Fleeing the battlefield epitomizes defeat as morale breaks and despair takes over. The losing side exhausts its will to fight and abandons its war aims. Only then can the winning side claim victory.

This points to a subtlety: The loser, not the winner, decides on victory. One side must acknowledge that it cannot achieve its goals and give up those goals for the other side to emerge triumphant. The gain of a province or the destruction of an army does not suffice to end a conflict. Acknowledging defeat, not declaring victory, ends a war. Capitulation is key. You win only if the other side agrees that you won.

The Roman poet Quintus Ennius pointed this out in about 200 BCE: "The victor is not victorious if the vanquished does not consider himself so." The Israeli polymath Shimon Tzabar explained in his sarcastic 1972 book, *The White Flag Principle: How to Lose a War (and Why)*, "As long as our opponent is not defeated we cannot be victorious!" U.S. General James Mattis echoed that insight: "No war is over until the enemy says it's over. We may think it over, we may declare it over, but in fact, the enemy gets a vote." John David Lewis concludes from a review of six wars that in every one of them, "the tide of war turned when one side tasted defeat and its will to continue…collapsed."

Declaring victory, in other words, has no value in itself—something that U.S. President George W. Bush learned to his chagrin after speaking under a "Mission Accomplished" sign just weeks into what would turn out to be an eight-year long war in Iraq.

Defeat means completely and permanently giving up on one's war goals, not retreating to lick one's wounds to fight another day. Modern examples include the American South, which gave up in 1865, never to mount another insurrection; the Germans, Japanese, Italians, and others, who gave up in 1945; the 1962 French loss in Algeria, the 1975 American loss in Vietnam, and the Soviet 1989 loss in Afghanistan. No one has seriously suggested reopening any of those dossiers.

But, in theory, no war is ever definitely concluded with a permanent winner or loser, for any defeated foe can change its mind. Therefore, some apparently final defeats turn out not be. Napoleon's military career appeared over in 1814 with his abdication and banishment to Elba, until he returned for a final try in 1815. Germans seemed to give up in 1918 but they developed theories of a stab in the back (*Dolchstoßlegende*) that denied defeat and set the stage for another round of even more bellicose aggression in 1939. The Soviet Union's collapse in 1991 seemed to indicate that Russians accepted their Cold War defeat and the end of their imperial ambitions, but Vladimir Putin decided to reassert Moscow's great power aspirations with the assaults on Georgia in 2008, Crimea in 2014, and Ukraine in 2022. The Taliban of Afghanistan seemed to have irrevocably lost in 2001 but bided their time and returned to power in 2021. On another scale altogether, Mussolini vaguely hoped to undo the collapse of the Roman Empire 1,500 years earlier. Zionists did successfully reverse a defeat two-millennia old.[1]

Looking ahead, one can distantly imagine Germany and Japan becoming revanchist for their World War II losses, though that would require wholesale changes to the international order. Other defunct conflicts are easier to imagine coming back to life: Iraq vs. Kuwait, Mexico vs. the United States, or Vietnam vs. China. For practical purposes, however, we shall consider a war lost when a broad consensus gives up the earlier war goals. Signatures on a formal piece of paper help to establish defeat but are not required: For example, neither the Soviet nor U.S. governments signed surrender documents in Afghanistan.

THE BENEFITS OF CLEAR RESOLUTION

War's horrors are well known; less familiar are the benefits of clear victory and defeat, of closure after one side abandons its war aims.

Conflicts that end decisively usually lead to resolution. "In every case I can think of," writes American historian Michael Ledeen, "peace has come about at the end of a war in which there was a winner and a loser. The winner imposed terms on the loser, and those terms were called 'peace.'" Or, in the terse formulation quoted by Roman historian Tacitus, "They make a desert and call it peace."

First, one side loses, then the other wins; only later come negotiations and compromise. The Congress of Vienna took place in 1814 and 1815, after Napoleon's long rampage through Europe had effectively ended. The Paris Peace Conference of 1919 and 1920 followed the termination of World War I. Iranians, American historian Harold Rhode explains, "negotiate only after defeating their enemies. During these negotiations, the victor magnanimously dictates to the vanquished how things will be conducted thereafter."

Undisputed loss can lead to long periods of quiet. Isabelle Duyvesteyn of Leiden University observes that "the most stable form of peace is achieved after a clear-cut military victory." Systematically reviewing all civil war terminations since 1940, Harvard's Monica Duffy Toft found in 2009 that

1 These revivals recall the famous 1972 remark by China's Premier Zhou Enlai that it was "too early" to assess the impact of the French Revolution of 1789. In fact, he was referring to the French student disturbances of 1968, but the comment contains an important insight.

"civil wars ended by military victory are much more likely to stay ended" than those ended by negotiated settlements. American strategist Edward N. Luttwak explains the benefits that follow the clear resolution of a war:

> Although war is a great evil, it does have a great virtue: it can resolve political conflicts and lead to peace. This can happen when all belligerents become exhausted or when one wins decisively. Either way, the key is that the fighting must continue until a resolution is reached. War brings peace only after passing a culminating phase of violence. Hopes of military success must fade for accommodation to become more attractive than further combat.... Peace takes hold only when war is truly over.

The U.S. Civil War, which led to one and a half centuries (and counting) of quiet, offers a test case. Historian Victor Davis Hanson of the Hoover Institution notes that "there was not another American Civil War, because after the invasions of Grant, Sherman, and Sheridan between 1864 and 1865, the Confederacy lost the ability to resist, and Union armies forced an unconditional surrender and a mandated reentry into the Union." Historian Ron Chernow points to the ironic long-lasting benefits of Major General William Sherman's ferocious campaigns against the Confederacy:

> As his men trooped south, Sherman took note of enemy resilience. "No amount of poverty or adversity seems to shake their faith; niggers gone, wealth and luxury gone, money worthless...yet I see no sign of let up." Only violence on a massive scale, he believed, could subdue such a hardy and refractory breed. "I begin to regard the death and mangling of a couple thousand men as a small affair, a kind of morning dash," he wrote. "The worst of the war is not yet begun." Sherman wanted to implant in his men a fighting spirit that would alter the whole balance of the war. He also wished to inflict psychological damage on the southern people because the North was "not only fighting hostile armies but a hostile people, and must make old and young, rich and poor, feel the hard hand of war, as well as the organized armies." Better to bring the war to a speedy conclusion by hard fighting, he thought, than prolong the suffering of the conflict.... Aware of being the

> South's bête noire, Sherman hoped to take advantage of this terrifying image and foresaw the psychological effect a march would have in demoralizing the enemy. He wanted southerners to "feel the hard hand of war" and realize that, contrary to southern propaganda, the North was winning.

The decisive defeat of Napoleon led to a century's absence of general warfare in Europe, as the defeat of the Axis in World War II led to seventy-five years. Other twentieth-century examples that led to prolonged periods of quiet include Algeria defeating France; North Vietnam defeating France, the United States, and South Vietnam; Israel defeating the Arab states (especially Egypt, Jordan, and Syria); and the Sri Lankan government defeating the Tamil Tiger insurgency.

In addition to long stretches of quiet, great gains can follow from a trouncing. Israeli analyst Daniel Krygler points this out with reference to World War II:

> Humiliating defeat is never pleasant, especially for aggressors who got intoxicated with hubris and victories. Post-1945 Germany and Japan can attest to it. However, in the end, accepting defeat was the best thing that could have happened to the Germans and the Japanese. Their genocidal despotic regimes were replaced with genuine democracy and progress.

The same holds true today, historian Anne Applebaum argues, for Russia in Ukraine:

> Military loss could create a real opening for national self-examination or for a major change, as it so often has done in Russia's past. Only failure can persuade the Russians themselves to question the sense and purpose of a colonial ideology that has repeatedly impoverished and ruined their own economy and society, as well as those of their neighbors, for decades.

As a T-shirt slogan wisely asserts: "War never solved anything. Except slavery, genocide, Nazism, and fascism."

STALEMATE MEANS MORE WAR

Contrarily, this analysis implies, would-be peacemakers may in fact prolong wars. Inconclusive results mean that fighting either continues or the resumption of warfare remains possible. When victory is not achieved, when neither side has its hopes dashed and experiences the agony of defeat, war goes on or might renew. Stalemate keeps conflict alive by permitting both sides to hope to win another day. So long as the losing side preserves its war goals and continues to fight, victory is denied. Quietude follows not on defeat but on acknowledgment of defeat; lack of that acknowledge means the war continues. Ending wars without clear defeat "may simply fix the conditions under which the fighting will be resumed, at a later time and with a new intensity," warns American political theorist Michael Walzer.

According to Hanson, "Conflicts throughout history become serial when an enemy is not utterly defeated and is not forced to submit to the political conditions of the victor." He observes that "From the Punic Wars (264 BCE–146 BCE) and the Hundred Years War (1337–1453) to the Arab-Israeli wars (1947–) and the so-called War on Terror (2001–), some wars never seem to end."

World Wars I and II show how to end a war the wrong way and the right way. When World War I ended, Germany's armies remained intact, its cities standing, and its lands unoccupied. Furthermore, the Treaty of Versailles that followed World War I was not, as long believed, too harsh, but too soft, because it demanded much less of the defeated Germans than they demanded from their victims. Ferdinand Foch, the Supreme Allied Commander in World War I, disparaged it with uncanny precision: "This is not peace. It is an armistice for twenty years." Together, these factors indulged the Germans' fantasy that they had not militarily lost, but had been stabbed in the back by leftists who forced a German defeat as it was on the verge of victory. This false belief, in turn, inspired an attempt, now led by Hitler, again to try to dominate Europe. In World War II, the Allies did not repeat the same mistake but aimed for "absolute victory" to preempt the Germans trying for a third time. Accordingly, Germans emerged from the war shorn of comforting illusions, what with their cities turned to rubble, their armies ruined, and their people near starvation. Giving up, understanding the need for a fresh start, the Germans turned to Konrad Adenauer and built a successful country.

Many unresolved conflicts loom in today's world. The Korean War of 1950 to 1953 ended inconclusively, with both sides holding on to their war goals. More than seventy years later, the conflict could resume at any moment. The two countries share the world's most heavily armed border, with heavy costs for them and potential dangers for the entire world. Wars between India and both Pakistan and China ended inconclusively, with the losing side in each case interpreting its defeats as only partial and temporary. The Sino-Vietnamese War of 1979 ended with each side claiming victory and then decades of repairing relations; but its unresolved conclusion suggests that fighting could restart. Although Iraq and Iran ended their 1980 to 1988 war in a state of mutual exhaustion, the tie did not resolve their differences; only the American-led invasion of Iraq fifteen years later ended their conflict. The same applies to Russia in Ukraine, as Applebaum writes: "Yet another frozen conflict, yet another temporary holding pattern, yet another face-saving compromise will not end the pattern of Russian aggression or bring permanent peace."

Hanson offers two main reasons for stalemate. First, belligerents "are roughly equally matched," so neither side has "enough of a material or spiritual edge (or sometimes the desire) to defeat, humiliate, and dictate terms to the beaten enemy." The Anglo-French wars offer an outstanding example of this, lasting about 750 years because neither side could achieve a decisive, ultimate victory. Second, "the apparently stronger side *chose* not to win, or for a variety of circumstances was prevented from victory." For example, the United States since 1945 "chooses to fight to prevent defeat rather than to achieve lasting victory." And that is our next topic.

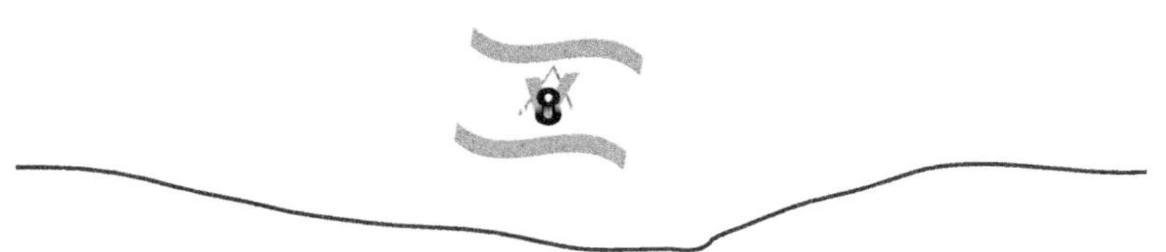

VICTORY AFTER 1945

SHUNNING VICTORY

"Before 1945, there was something like a formula for how wars were fought and ended," Katie Paul of *Newsweek* explains. "When groups disagreed, usually over a piece of land, and failed to reconcile their differences amicably, they duked it out until one surrendered and the other carried off the prize. When they ended, wars had clear winners and losers." Columbia University's Virginia Page Fortna confirms this generalization, relying on the Correlates of War research project database: Only 0.5 percent (one of 196) of wars before 1946 ended without a clear victor. (Other databases show somewhat higher percentages.)

Then, something strange happened. From 1946 forward, 44 percent of wars (thirty-five of seventy-nine) ended indecisively. After World War II, a crushing battlefield failure rarely translated into giving up. Planes shot down, tanks destroyed, munitions exhausted, soldiers deserting, treasury wasted, lives extinguished, and land conquered are rarely decisive. Consider North Korea's loss in 1953, Saddam Hussein's in 1991, and the Iraqi Sunnis' in 2003; in all three cases, battlefield defeat did not translate into giving up.

What happened to victory and what are the implications?

• • •

No more victory. In 1944, Eisenhower could still state that, "In war there is no substitute for victory," but just five years later U.S. Admiral Arthur W. Radford announced: "Victory in war is not an end in itself." That, indeed, became the new mantra. Likewise, Paul G. Hoffman, the Marshall Plan administrator, announced that the United States "should wage war not to win a war, but to win a peace." British strategist B.H. Liddell Hart was even more negative, arguing in 1952 that overly focusing on victory can start the next war: "Gaining military victory is not in itself equivalent to gaining the object of policy.... If you concentrate exclusively on victory, with no thought for the after-effect, you may be too exhausted to profit by the peace, while it is almost certain that the peace will be a bad one, containing the germs of another war."

American military doctrine after World War II changed with "astonishing speed," observes John David Lewis:

> In 1939 American military planners still chose their objectives on the basis of the following understanding: "Decisive defeat in battle breaks the enemy's will to war and forces him to sue for peace which is the national aim." But U.S. military doctrine since World War II has progressively devalued victory as the object of war. "Victory alone as an aim of war cannot be justified, since in itself victory does not always assure the realization of national objectives," is the claim in a Korean War–era manual.

It took longer in the larger culture; American leftist Tom Engelhardt argues that, "Between 1945 and 1975, victory culture ended in America." When asked in 2009 to define a U.S. victory in Afghanistan, President Barack Obama expressed his unease with the very concept of victory:

> I'm always worried about using the word "victory" because, you know, it invokes this notion of Emperor Hirohito coming down and signing a surrender to [Douglas] MacArthur... when you have a non-state actor, a shadowy operation like al-Qaeda, our goal is to make sure they can't attack the United States.... What that means is that they cannot set up permanent bases and train people from which to launch attacks.

Putting aside Obama's flawed grammar and erroneous history (Emperor Hirohito did not sign Japan's surrender document), he understood victory as no more than restricting the enemy's capabilities, as though intentions and will count not at all. In 2021, Mario Loyola of Florida International University concluded that victory is now out of reach: "Wars usually end when one side loses the will to continue fighting. That usually happens when one side faces such overwhelming force that it loses hope for ultimate victory and accepts defeat. The modern developments in the law of war make such a scenario hard to imagine."

Nor was this change limited to the United States. French philosopher Raymond Aron argued that because the "spoils of victory are no longer commensurate with the cost of battle...the only road to victory is the avoidance of war." Olaf Scholz, a future chancellor of Germany, asserted in the late 1980s that "peace cannot be achieved by military means." President Jacques Chirac of France went further in 2003: "War is always the admission of defeat and is always the worst of solutions." His foreign minister, Dominique de Villepin, made the point more emphatically: "Nothing justifies envisaging military action." Beatrice Heuser of the University of Reading wrote in 2013 that, "Victory is nothing if it does not lead to [a just and durable] peace, and such justice must be seen as reasonable by both sides to make it durable." Will F. Owen, editor of *Military Strategy Magazine*, puzzlingly wrote in 2021 that *victory* is a tactical term that "cannot be applied to wars, except by poets and politicians.... Claims of victory are irrelevant if only one side is ever compelled to modify its behaviour and the other retains its freedom of action." Victory had come to seem as irrelevant to modern life as alchemy and astrology.

What happened? The advent of nuclear weapons.

• • •

Nuclear weapons. The destructiveness of nuclear weaponry prompted an unprecedented belief that war had become unwinnable. A supremely influential 1946 book, *The Absolute Weapon*, most of all conveyed this message. Its editor and lead author, Bernard Brodie, wrote in famous lines about nuclear warfare: "If the aggressor state must fear retaliation, it will know that even if it is the victor it will suffer a degree of physical destruction incomparably greater than that suffered by any defeated nation of history.... Under those circumstances no victory, even if guaranteed in advance—which it never is—would be worth the price." He thus concluded that: "Thus far the chief purpose of our military establishment has been to win wars. From now on its chief purpose must be to avert them." In brief, *no victory is worth the price.*

Attesting to the impact of *The Absolute Weapon*'s message, Angelo M. Codevilla of Boston University finds that, "It is no exaggeration [to state] that, for seventy years, the mainstream of American thought on nuclear war has been a gloss on this volume's essays." In *The Absolute Weapon*, explains Harvard historian Richard Pipes, "a group of civilian strategic theorists enunciated the principles of the mutual-deterrence theory which subsequently became the official U.S. strategic doctrine." Its contributors argued that strategy in the future "involved preventing wars rather than winning them, securing sufficiency in decisive weapons rather than superiority, and even ensuring the potential enemy's ability to strike back." These radical new principles "ran contrary to all the tenets of traditional military theory, which had always called for superiority in forces and viewed the objective of war to be victory."

This nuclear doctrine of prevention, sufficiency, and non-victory then went on to become the universal U.S. doctrine, even in the absence of nuclear arms. As the University of Texas' Mackubin Owens explains, "during the Cold War, nuclear weapons policy and strategy suffused every aspect of national security, including non-nuclear strategy." Even a non-nuclear victory is not worth the price. In other words, the reassessment of victory that began with nuclear strategy then extended to all forms of warfare, even where it made no sense. For example, the U.S. policy of massive retaliation, announced in 1954, threatened a nuclear attack in response to a conventional problem. In this, Western strategists made a huge error, assuming that all warfare would henceforth involve nuclear weapons, or at least the credible threat of their use. Focusing exclusively on "the absolute weapon," they discarded pre-1945 strategic thinking as obsolete.

To seal the matter, Martel reports, "virtually all systematic thinking about victory came to a halt with the development of nuclear weapons and the realization that wars could lead to global annihilation within hours." The University of Reading's Beatrice Hauser sums up the post-1945 consensus as victory being "increasingly seen as a nonsensical concept in the context of a nuclear war." Accordingly, Hanson explains, the U.S. government "chose not to apply its full strength to pursue the unconditional surrender of its enemies." And the shift that began in the United States then spread to the West as a whole.

Of course, not a single subsequent war involved the use of nuclear weapons. Therefore, anti-victory nuclear theorizing undermined the actual wars fought by Western forces after 1945. American strategist Walter Russell Mead observes that, "Many Western leaders seem to have forgotten what it means to win." Alex Nachumson, the CEO of Mivtachi Israel, an organization of former IDF officers, echoes the point: "In a largely unipolar world where multilateralism and endless meetings, meaningless conventions and inconsequential conferences are the norm, [the West] has forgotten how to win."

The Korean War saw the first implementation of this non-victory policy and became the moment when victory disappeared from the U.S. vocabulary, as Codevilla recounts:

> Progressivism's perversion of our ruling class's ideas about war and peace...prevailed in the winter of 1950–51 when this class, having committed the armed forces to war in Korea, decided to order them not to defeat an enemy that had already killed some 15,000 of their number, but rather to kill and die to "avoid a wider war," and to foster an international environment pleasing to itself and allied governments.

Harry Truman, in the view of Codevilla, was a rube who unexpectedly became president and "deferred to the men who had surrounded the great Roosevelt." He portrays Douglas MacArthur as a general "who could imagine neither fighting a war for any purpose other than victory, nor refusing to employ whatever weapons would bring victory most directly" and sees Truman's 1951 firing of him as the key event in the shift from victory to advancing an international order. Once instituted, this change became permanent:

> Since then, the U.S. government has won no wars. More important, it has not sought to win wars. Instead, our foreign policy establishment has spent some 100,000 American lives and trillions of dollars in Korea, Vietnam, Iraq, Afghanistan, and elsewhere in pursuit of world order, multilateralism, or collective security. It has cited as a badge of superior wisdom its trashing of Aristotle's notion that victory is war's natural objective.

No wonder, Hanson concludes, that the American effort in Afghanistan failed:

> Americans feel that the level of force and violence necessary to obliterate the Taliban and impose a lasting settlement is either too costly, or not worth any envisioned victory, or impossible

> in such absurd tribal landscapes, or would be deemed immoral and contrary to Western values. Therefore, as in most serial wars, the U.S. chooses to fight to prevent defeat rather than to achieve lasting victory.... Western nations rarely deem an enemy so purely evil that it deserves the full force of Western might or that defeating it will be worth the potentially high cost....
>
> The result is the present age of serial Punic [that is, non-terminating] conflict, perhaps intolerable to the psyche, but in amoral terms tolerable as long as casualties are kept to a minimum and defeat is redefined as acceptable strategic wisdom.

Gentle mechanisms. As victory dropped out of the vocabularies and minds of most post-1945 Westerners, which innovations took its place? Compromise, concessions, conciliation, flexibility, goodwill, restraint, and their attendant negotiating mechanisms. Trouble is, what Codevilla dubs "world order, multilateralism, or collective security" runs contrary to millennia of human experience; wars still end primarily through defeat and victory.

Negotiations need to follow, not replace, one side acknowledging defeat. Premature diplomacy rarely ends conflicts; how much weight can words alone carry? Solemnly signed pieces of paper matter only if one side has cried "uncle." Hardly a single major interstate conflict has concluded due to someone's clever schema. In Michael Ledeen's lively phrasing, "Peace cannot be accomplished simply because some visiting envoy, with or without an advanced degree in negotiating from the Harvard Business School, sits everyone down around a table so they can all reason together." With time, the rebellion against peace processing acquired a populist edge, with American talk show host Rush Limbaugh colorfully dismissing the whole idea as a "scam":

> There isn't a single instance in the world where hostilities... have been solved with words, with doctors, with nurses, with clean water, with health care, with environmental responsibility. Sorry. It's never happened.... Victors are not determined by the best negotiators. They're not determined by who has the best diplomats. They're determined by who has the best army and who's best able to kill people and break things. And

> that's how hostilities are solved, and that's the history of the world and it's always gonna be the history of the world. And after one side defeats the other militarily, that's when the words come into play. That's when the winners dictate the articles of surrender and shove them in the face of losers and say, "Sign this. This is what you're going to have to do from now on."

Diplomacy fails most spectacularly when one side seeks to eliminate the other. This characterized the negotiations to end the Vietnam war between 1968 and 1973, talks that apparently went so well that they won Henry Kissinger and his North Vietnamese counterpart, Le Duc Tho, the Nobel Peace Prize. The Vietnam War ostensibly concluded through diplomacy, but the North continued to seek its war aims until achieving victory. Less than two years after the glittering award ceremony, in other words, North Vietnam proceeded to conquer the South. The same applied to the Palestinian-Israeli conflict, where the 1993 Nobel Peace Prize similarly went to negotiators whose work failed, and for parallel reasons. It is a conceit to think that a "peace process" can replace the dirty work of war.

In the aftermath of Hiroshima, Western strategists made a major error by focusing too much on "the absolute weapon," assuming that all warfare would henceforth involve nuclear weapons, and concluding that prior strategic thinking had been rendered obsolete. That theorizing undermined the understanding of actual wars fought since 1945, where the traditional realities of victory and defeat continue to apply.

RETURNING TO VICTORY

Victory is an innate human goal that only overly sophisticated strategists could lose sight of. Accordingly, it may have disappeared from Western doctrines, but assertions of victory remain alive and have increased in recent years.

• • •

General. Victory stayed alive outside the West. Most significantly, the Soviet leadership viewed nuclear weapons as just another tool and rejected the notion of nuclear war as unwinnable. It held, as summarized by Richard Pipes, that "thermonuclear war is not suicidal, it can be fought and won, and thus resort to war must not be ruled out." As before 1945, Moscow believed in "not deterrence but victory, not sufficiency in weapons but superiority, not retaliation but offensive action." Arguably, this doctrine lives on with Vladimir Putin, born in 1952, a member of the Communist Party and the KGB, and thirty-nine years old when the Soviet Union collapsed. His references to deploying nuclear weapons during the Ukraine crisis echo Soviet doctrine. As Andrew Monaghan of the Royal United Services Institute summarizes current Russian doctrine, victory consists of "the achievement, by one of the sides, of the political and military strategic aims of the war."

Looking at every civil war fought outside the West between 1940 and 1990, Barbara F. Walter of the University of California, San Diego, found that thirty-three of forty, 82 percent, ended in decisive victories in the form of "extermination, expulsion, or capitulation of the losing side." The Iranians launched a satellite named Victory (*Zafar*) that un-victoriously failed to reach orbit.

Some Westerners, too, continued to hold on to victory. Former U.S. General Douglas MacArthur enunciated the old goal when he declared in 1952 that, "It is fatal to enter any war without the will to win it," though he had been sacked over precisely this issue a year earlier. By 1979, American strategist Colin S. Gray wrote that he "does believe that there is a role for strategy—that is, for the sensible, politically directed application of military power in thermonuclear war." That same year, presidential candidate Ronald Reagan explained his Cold War outlook as "We win, they lose." In 1995, Ideals Publications Inc. of Nashville published *Victory: Honoring the 50th Anniversary of the Allied Triumph in World War II.* The World War II memorial on the National Mall in Washington, D.C., completed in 2004, features plaques commemorating victory at air, land, and sea. A major French film about the French Revolution, *Victory or Death* (*Vaincre ou mourir*), appeared in January 2023.

Brian Mast, then a candidate for Congress, said with reference to the Islamic State of Iraq and Syria (ISIS) in 2016 that, "The only way to guarantee peace is to make the enemy surrender." The television show *Designated Survivor*, which aired in 2018, has the U.S. president state: "As a country that's just been attacked, I think we need to answer with an unwavering commitment to victory." A 2019 Facebook recruitment advertisement for the U.S. Army states: "Army Warriors live and breathe victory." Bing West, a former U.S. assistant secretary of defense and author of books about the U.S. wars in Vietnam, Iraq, and Afghanistan, argued in an article titled "Three Wars, No Victory—Why?" that in all three cases "America… failed in its mission." He ascribes this pattern mainly to "the policy hub emanating from the White House [having] grown too confident of its own quixotic infallibility, unchallenged by a divisive Congress that is supine in matters of war. When America is not determined, we lose."

Not surprisingly, Donald Trump as president often spoke of victory. For example, he stated in 2017: "[N]early 16 years after the September 11th attacks, after the extraordinary sacrifice of blood and treasure, the American people are weary of war without victory…. The men and women who serve our nation in combat deserve a plan for victory…. Our troops will fight to win. We will fight to win. From now on, victory will have a clear definition…." He promised, in a 2019 speech about Syria, to pursue a course

> that leads to victory for America…. When we commit American troops to battle, we must do so only when a vital national interest is at stake, and when we have a clear objective, a plan for victory, and a path out of conflict. That's what we have to have. We need a plan of victory. We will only win. Our whole basis has to be the right plan, and then we will only win. Nobody can beat us. Nobody can beat us.

He added in 2020: "Let our enemies be on notice: If our people are threatened, we will never, ever hesitate to act. And when we fight, from now on, we will fight only to win. As MacArthur said: 'In war, there is no substitute for victory.'"

Others in the Trump administration echoed these views. U.S. Secretary of Homeland Security Kirstjen Nielsen in 2018 mentioned victory twice in a discussion of terrorism. "This isn't petty crime. This isn't a mere public safety problem. We are at war. And we must respond accordingly. Victory in this struggle begins with moral clarity…. This will not come easy. But our path to victory begins with collective defense." CIA Director Michael Pompeo asserted: "We can't perform our mission if we're not aggressive, vicious, unforgiving, relentless. Every minute…we have to be focused on crushing our enemies."

• • •

Ukraine. Paradoxically, Vladimir Putin's invasion of Ukraine both reinforced Western fears of victory and reinstated victory as a goal. As ever, Moscow spoke boldly. On announcing the annexation of four Ukrainian provinces, Putin announced: "The truth is behind us, and in truth there is strength, which means victory!... Victory will be ours!"

Ukraine's unexpectedly strong battlefield performance prompted Putin to revert to Cold War tactics and intimidate the West by putting his nuclear force on high alert. Retired Major General Alexander Vladimirov, author of Russia's current war doctrine, predicted that nuclear weapons would "inevitably" be deployed in the Ukraine war. The Russian ambassador to Washington, according to journalist Walter Isaacson, "explicitly told [Elon Musk] that a Ukrainian attack on Crimea would lead to a nuclear response."

This saber-rattling had the desired effect, raising the specter of World War III and making some Westerners more fearful of Russia's defeat than Russia's victory. President Emmanuel Macron of France asserted that the West "must not humiliate Russia." Fearing that his company would be "explicitly complicit in a major act of war and conflict escalation," that is, nuclear escalation, Musk selectively turned off Ukrainian access to his Starlink internet service.

As American analysts David R. Shedd and Ivana Stradner observe, "Putin knows that nothing better pushes the West's buttons than threats of nuclear escalation," so he effectively used "nuclear blackmail to play on Western fears of escalating the war in Ukraine. He has repeatedly used this tactic to successfully deter the West from...fully backing Kyiv's victory over Moscow." As a result, Keir Giles of Chatham House finds, "parts of the U.S. government are absolutely petrified of the prospect of a Ukrainian victory and appear to be working against it."

Simultaneously, Ukraine's impassioned response inspired Westerners. President Volodymyr Zelensky made victory his mantra, making repeated and eloquent references to it. Shortly after fighting began, he declared in March 2022, "We believe in victory. It's impossible to believe in anything else." In June, he countered Putin with "Victory will be ours!" In August, he went further: "Ukraine is no longer interested just in peace, we're now interested in victory." His New Year's speech at the end of 2022 promised: "We fight and will continue to fight for the sake of the key word: 'victory,'" and called for 2023 to be the "year of victory." In October of that year, he declared: "Nobody believes in our victory like I do. Nobody." Other Ukrainian politicians, such as Mariia Mezentseva, a member of parliament representing the city center of Kharkiv, amplified his mantra: "We don't need peace...we need a victory," while Foreign Minister Dmytro Kuleba called for "a complete and total Ukrainian victory" over Russia.

Moved by Ukraine's boldness, Westerners who normally avoid the word *victory* started to celebrate it. Nancy Pelosi, speaker of the U.S. House of Representatives, stated that "America stands with Ukraine until victory is won." Even a leftwing Democrat, U.S. Representative Pramila Jayapal, observed that, "Every war ends with diplomacy, and this one will too, after a Ukrainian victory." U.S. Army General Ben Hodges (ret.) suggested that Putin's war caused *victory* to re-enter the American military lexicon: When Secretary of Defense Lloyd Austin used the verb *to win* in connection with Ukraine, Hodges observed that, "In twenty years in Iraq and Afghanistan, I never heard any of the U.S. administrations talk about winning." British Foreign Minister Liz Truss generalized: "Ukraine's victory is a strategic imperative for all of us."

Commentators parsed the meaning of victory like it was again 1939. A multi-authored *New York Times* news analysis noted the many political leaders who "have called for victory in Ukraine. But just beneath the surface are real divisions about what that would look like—and whether 'victory' has the same definition in the United States, in Europe and, perhaps most importantly, in Ukraine." Americans, the article goes on, tend to see in Russian military reversals an opportunity to punish Putin and dissuade any future adventurism, while Europeans fear his actions if isolated and humiliated. These differing objectives "make it all the more difficult to define what victory—or even a muddled peace—would look like." Applebaum went further: "Our goal, our endgame, should be *defeat*. In fact, the only solution that offers some hope of long-term stability in Europe is *rapid defeat*, or even, to borrow Macron's phrase, *humiliation*." Two authors in *Foreign Affairs* reinforced this point: "A better Russia can be produced only by a clear and stark Ukrainian victory...the more decisive Russia's defeat in Ukraine, the more likely it is that Russia will experience profound political change, one hopes for the better."

Intimidation notwithstanding, the war in Ukraine did help to rebuild Western faith in victory.

• • •

Implications for the Palestinian-Israeli conflict. The post-1945 fear of victory has had conspicuously little impact on Palestinians. But it strongly affects Israelis and their Western allies.

Palestinians. Remote from Western intellectual trends, the Palestinians after 1945 maintained unchanged their long-standing goal of destroying the Zionist enterprise. The anticipated victory over Israel serves as prod, boast, and celebration. The PLO Charter of 1968 mentions victory as its goal and "Revolution Until Victory" has served as a Fatah slogan since about that time. It also served as the title of an "an urgent, eye-opening" 2015 documentary at the Brooklyn Academy of Music about "the history of modern Palestinian resistance." In 2017, the PA mission in Colombia quoted Yasir Arafat, "Our goal is the end of Israel. We don't want peace. We want war, victory." Mohammad Shtayyeh, the PA "prime minister" stated in 2022 that Palestinians "defeated the Hyksos, Romans, Greeks, Persians, Tatars, Pharaohs," and they will also defeat the Israelis. That same year, a Palestinian girl sent a message to her imprisoned father over Palestinian Authority TV, dedicating a song to him calling for "victory over America and Israel."

The Palestinian organization Fatah adopted the slogan "Revolution Until Victory" in the late 1960s.

The year 2023 witnessed an outburst of such expressions. Abbas declared in late September: "Victory is ours. We will celebrate the independence of our state in Jerusalem, our eternal capital and the crown jewel, and the flower of all cities. They [Israelis] see it as impossible and we see it as inevitable." In the interests of discretion, what victory means tends not to be explained when foreigners are present, though it can be described in blood-curdling detail in their absence. Wael Al-Zard, an Islamic scholar in Gaza, reported in March 2023 that

> There are teams in Gaza that have been making plans for months now about what is going to happen after the liberation. They are thinking about big questions.... What are we going to do once we inherit [Israel's] nuclear missiles? Yes, we are going to inherit these nuclear missiles. What are we going to do with the multitudes of Jews? What are we going to do with them? Should we throw them into the sea and make them food for the fish?

Israelis. Initially, Zionists did not participate in the post-1945 Western strategic evolution, their conflict taking place at far remove from the atomic bomb or American academic circles. Instead, Israel had its own distinctive doctrine: deterrence, or avoiding war by making it too expensive and painful for an enemy. Then, several developments changed this approach: Israel integrating more in the West's intellectual development and its strategists falling under the influence of post-1945 thinking, the Arab states' withdrawal from active warfare, their replacement by Palestinians as Israel's primary focus, the Israeli public's fatigue with war, and the Soviet Union's downfall. By the early 1990s, these caused wholesale confusion in Israeli thinking. (See "A new strategy," pp. 114-16 for details.)

Further, Palestinians posed a different kind of threat from the Arab states. The entire Oslo Accords exercise fit into Brodie's dictum that "the chief purpose of our military establishment...must be to avert" wars. In this spirit, an IDF colonel told me: "For Israel to defeat the Palestinians would be like the United States defeating Cuba. Militarily, nothing could be easier. Politically, nothing could be more trouble." Such thinking removed victory as the goal.

Westerners. For about thirty years, from 1961 to 1991, the Arab states and Israel had great power patrons in the Soviet Union and the United

States, respectively. As one of the most enduring and volatile theaters of Cold War confrontation, their conflict tended to be seen as the most likely powder keg for World War III. Therefore, those patrons preferred that neither side decisively win.

Three examples: In 1967, as the Six-Day War raged, Soviet premier Alexei Kosygin threatened U.S. President Lyndon Johnson that if Israeli "military actions are not stopped in the next few hours...necessary actions will be taken, including military," by the Soviets, adding that this "may bring us into a clash, which will lead to a grave catastrophe." Second, Moscow had plans to bomb the Israeli nuclear reactor at Dimona in 1967, not carrying through with this plan due to the complete failure of the Arab armies in the Six-Day War. Third, in 1973, during Egypt's and Syria's war against Israel, and despite American support for Israel, U.S. Secretary of State Henry Kissinger confided in the Soviet government, "My nightmare is a victory for either side." Were Israel losing, Americans worried Jerusalem might escalate to nuclear weapons. Were Israel winning, they worried that an alarmed Moscow might do so.

Mediated settlement. The retreat of Arab states from the military battlefield diminished the nuclear dimension without eliminating fears of a powder keg. However small and local, Westerners viewed the Palestinian-Israeli conflict through the prism of its international implications and therefore emphasized the need for a mediated settlement, not a decisive resolution. Palestinians lost many rounds militarily (1982, 2002, 2008–2009, 2012, 2014, and 2021) but never felt defeated, so they keep coming back to try again. Roger Berkowitz of Bard College points to the costs of foregoing victory:

> The tragedy that is the Middle East would, traditionally, have been solved by a war. One side would win, the other would lose...war would decide the issue once and for all and after its hellish baptism by blood, new lives would grow. But war today is increasingly impossible, at least wars with clear victors and losers. War is being replaced by police-actions, patrols, terrors, and assassinations that go on without end. It is nearly inconceivable that Israel and Palestine would fight a war to the end in which one side was defeated—imagine the unthinkable horrors that defeating either side would require. Victory is impossible....

> And thus we are left with the condition of eternal war without end and mini-wars that corrupt political and peaceful institutions. In a world in which war has lost its power to settle disputes, we have ongoing wars that mobilize societies. The war on terror is a permanent part of our always-mobilized societies. We are left…with the hell of war as a relatively permanent part of everyday life.

Israeli economist Robert Auman adds that Israel must repeatedly fight for its existence because it "has never been allowed to end war by decisively defeating its enemy, crushing its will and forcing it forever to abandon the idea of destroying Israel."

In short, the Palestinian-Israeli conflict saw one side rely on ageless intuition, the other on sophisticated models. Palestinians, not part of the Western discussion, retained a sound understanding of war while Israelis, being part of it, lost their way. This intellectual background helps to explain the stunning range of Israeli errors that culminated in the disaster of the Oslo Accords; it also points to the way ahead, namely the return to victory, the topic of Parts V and VI.

PART V

Approaching Victory

Something bad happened
...the State of Israel stopped winning.

—Naftali Bennett, Israeli politician

For a generation, the Holy Grail of [Israel's]
General Staff has been to reject the very concept of victory.

—Caroline Glick, Israeli columnist

AS PALESTINIAN-ISRAELI DIPLOMACY RECEDED, THE drama and demons of the Oslo Era (1993-2008) largely vanished. But little subsequently changed. Rejectionism continues to dominate Palestinian life while Israelis, deep in the rut of conciliation, lack the imagination to try something else. And so, the apparently intractable conflict rumbles on, ruining lives on both sides while endangering a democratic country.

Still, bases for hope of resolution do exist and three of them will be analyzed here, one per chapter. A reinterpretation grounded in the Palestinian-Israeli conflict's unique historic mentalities of rejectionism and conciliation offers a way to move beyond those static attitudes. Trends in the Arab states and among Palestinians, ones largely unnoticed by analysts, suggest a growing acceptance of Israel. A close look at Israel finds a new readiness to win, even if significant Israeli errors continue to obstruct the country's way forward.

9

REINTERPRETING THE CONFLICT

RESOLVING THE PALESTINIAN-ISRAELI CONFLICT STARTS with an accurate understanding. Toward that end, this chapter sets out the basics, with an emphasis on the legacy of its two supremely dissimilar but constant mentalities, rejectionism and conciliation.

BASICS

A report in the journal *Innovations in Clinical Neuroscience* and reproduced by the U.S. National Institutes of Health states that "Ishmael and Isaac planted the seed of Arab and Israeli conflict"—an assertion of bewildering ignorance masquerading as scholarship. That a journal taking pride in "providing evidence-based information" should publish such pablum points to the sad fact that no matter how extensively the Palestinian-Israeli conflict is covered in books, journalism, classrooms, and sermons, received knowledge about it tends to be unreliable, if not mendacious. So, we begin with a primer.

• • •

Key facts. History and current affairs both tend to get mangled.

History. Contrary to *Innovations in Clinical Neuroscience*, today's Palestinian-Israeli conflict dates back not to biblical times but to the emergence of two competing nationalist ideologies in the late nineteenth century. Zionism built on the millennia-old religious calling of Jews to return to their ancestral home, then under Ottoman rule. Arab nationalism roused Arabic speakers to win control of their own lands, including that same piece of territory, from the same Ottoman Empire.

Palestinian nationalism hardly existed until 1920 and only became a powerful force fifty years after that. Although relatively new and a reaction to Zionism, Palestinian nationalism now exists as a potent force. Its denial amounts to wishful thinking.

Palestinians had been the main enemy of Zionism until Israel's emergence as a sovereign state in 1948, at which time the Arab states took over the main burden of enmity and retained it until 1973, when they ceded it back to the Palestinians, who have preserved it ever since.

In a remarkable achievement, Zionism evolved from the fragile community of 1882 to the vulnerable statelet of 1948 to the military dynamo of 1967 to the economic power of 2024. Along the way, Israel became a stable, modern, affluent, democratic, law-abiding, and powerful country. It boasts great technological and cultural creativity, plus by far the highest birth rate of any advanced society. Nevertheless, it lives under the curse of persistent enmity, primarily of a small but very networked group, the Palestinians of the West Bank, Gaza, and eastern Jerusalem, plus its powerful allies around the world.

The conflict continues due to Palestinian rejectionism, the ambition to eliminate every aspect of Jewish presence in the Holy Land—with the dubious exception of the Jews descended from pre-Zionist communities (a pretense necessary to differentiate anti-Zionism from antisemitism) or of value to a successor state.

The attempt to snuff Israel out began in 1947, as soon as the UN General Assembly endorsed the creation of a Jewish state. In contrast, Israel's control of the West Bank, Gaza, and all of Jerusalem began only in 1967. Therefore, Israeli control of the latter territories does not account for Palestinian rejectionism, and the termination of that control will not end the conflict.

The conflict. The Palestinians fight to destroy Israel; Israel fights to win the acceptance of the Palestinians. The first is fundamentally offensive in intent; the second defensive. Tough and aggressive Israeli tactics (such as IDF raids) do not alter this equation.

Israel cannot unilaterally end the conflict other than by giving up and closing down. To continue to exist, it has no choice but to fight. The Palestinians can quit the conflict at any time, which would permit them to prosper.

Palestinian rejectionists have two potential methods to destroy Israel: disheartening its population through violence and undermining its legitimacy through propaganda. Of these, Israelis focus more on the former, though the latter threatens them more. Oct. 7 matters less than what followed.

Many conflicts lend themselves to compromise, such as the division of territory, funds, or rights, but not this one. Rather, the Palestinian war on Israel is binary, making Israeli and Palestinian goals irreconcilable: Either the sovereign Jewish state exists or it does not. It cannot be partial or transient. That means rejection or acceptance, yes or no, with no in-betweens. Ending the conflict means one side wins, the other side loses; victory and defeat.

This black-or-white quality renders resolution especially difficult, requiring one side fully to abandon its goal: Either Palestinians give up rejectionism or Israelis give up their sovereign homeland. The Palestinians cannot sort-of accept Israel.

Anything other than one side fully giving up its goal implies an instability that serves as the basis for future conflict. This dooms compromise solutions. Efforts at mitigation only postpone a resolution.

Who wins comes down to which side first loses the will to keep on struggling.

No other conflict inspires comparable global attention or passion. Each side benefits from the support of unparalleled vast hinterlands: Palestinians look to Muslims, Arabic speakers, leftists, fascists, and assorted dictators. Israel relies mainly on Jews, conservatives, and religious Christians; Hindus have also begun to weigh in.

Subject to political, diplomatic, legal, and moral constraints, Israel has the power to do almost anything it wants vis-à-vis the Palestinians.

• • •

Dangers facing Israel. Those concerned with the security and welfare of the Jewish state ask questions like "Is Israel Doomed?" and title their book *Will Israel Survive?* (also in a separate French version, *Israël peut-il survivre?*). One author even titled a book *The Late Great State of Israel.* This gloom results from the unique barrage of threats facing the Jewish state. Going from most to least violent, those include:

1. *Weapons of mass destruction.* Iran poses the primary threat but both Iraq and Syria made earlier efforts to build nuclear bombs, while Saudi Arabia, Egypt, and Türkiye have also shown interest. Iraq, Hamas, PIJ, and Hezbollah have shot rockets at Israel, even as Hezbollah continues to build its huge arsenal.

2. *Conventional military attack.* Armies, navies, and air forces have attacked Israel on multiple occasions, especially those of Egypt, Jordan, and Syria, but also Saudi Arabia, Iraq, and Lebanon.
3. *Low-intensity warfare, aka terrorism.* Attacks have come from many sides, including the extreme Left (such as the Japanese Red Army), the extreme Right (neo-Nazis), Arab nationalists (the Arab Liberation Front), Palestinian nationalists (the Popular Front for the Liberation of Palestine), and Islamists (Hamas).
4. *Demographic assault.* Higher birth rates offer the lure of overwhelming Israel, especially if it can be induced to open its doors to a "right of return." In this spirit, Ahmed Yassin, Hamas' founder, urged Palestinian women to realize their full child-bearing potential and Arafat referred to the wombs of Palestinian women as "the best weapon of the Palestinian people."
5. *Economic boycott and blockade.* Financial and trade boycotts as well as other attempts to undermine its economy have always dogged Israel.
6. *Ideological delegitimization.* To undermine its appeal, Israel's enemies associate Zionism with imperialism, communism, Nazism, apartheid, racism, white supremacism, Jewish exclusivism, and almost every other repulsive body of ideas.

The listing prompts several observations. First, no other contemporary state faces such an array of threats; indeed, probably none in history ever has. In this sense, Israel has inherited the Jew's burden. Second, conventional military attack (No. 2) dominated the challenge to Israel from 1948 to 1973. When that proved a failure, anti-Zionists both heightened (No. 1) and lowered (Nos. 3–6) the violence. Third, Israel has effectively defeated the threats of Nos. 2–5, leaving just No. 1 and No. 6 as major challenges; weapons of mass destruction being a matter primarily for governments to deal with, we focus here on delegitimization.

A CLASH OF MENTALITIES

Conciliation and rejectionism are both weird and unique, wildly out of sync with reality, equidistant from the norm for parties to a conflict. Given their relative strengths, Israeli and Palestinian positions reverse what one expects; Israel should be demanding, Palestinians pleading. One can debate long into the night which of them is the more absurdly inappropriate.

• • •

History. At the very start of the Zionist enterprise in the 1880s, the two parties to what is now called the Palestinian-Israeli conflict developed distinctive, diametrically opposed, and enduring attitudes toward each other.

Origins. Zionists, from a position of weakness, making up a minute portion of Palestine's population, adopted *conciliation*, a wary attempt to find mutual interests with Palestinians and establish good relations with them, with an emphasis on bringing them economic benefits. Symbolic of this mentality, Israel is the world's only country created not through conquest but via the purchase of land. David Ben-Gurion eventually turned conciliation into communal policy and major Israeli figures such as Moshe Dayan and Shimon Peres continued with variants of it.

Palestinians, from a position of demographic strength and usually with great power patronage, adopted *rejectionism*, a resistance to all things Jewish and Zionist. Evoking the spirit of Muslim supremacy, under the guidance of Amin al-Husseini it became more extreme with time, indeed genocidal and even suicidal. Just as Zionism celebrated the land in which Palestinians resided as unique and sacred, rejectionism followed suit, insisting on the uniqueness and sacredness of that land to them via Islamic Zionism. Major Palestinian figures, such as Yasir Arafat and Hamas leaders, continued with variants of this ideology.

These twin mentalities took shape early and then, as is commonly the case, persisted. As American geographer Wilbur Zelinsky explains: "Whenever an empty territory undergoes settlement, or an earlier population is dislodged by invaders, the specific characteristics of the first group able to effect a viable, self-perpetuating society are of crucial significance for the later social and cultural geography of the area." In simple language: First inhabitants tend to set cultural parameters that last for very long periods.[1] Technically, Zionists did not dislodge Palestinians, for they invariably

1 For example, tiny seventeenth-century groups established distinct cultures along the east coast of North America that endure centuries later: the French in Acadia (1604), the Virginia Company in Jamestown (1607), the Pilgrims in Massachusetts (1620), the Dutch in New Amsterdam (1624), the English slavers in Charleston (1670), and the Quakers in Philadelphia (1682). On which, see Colin Woodard, *American Nations: A History of the Eleven Rival Regional Cultures of North America* (New York: Penguin, 2011).

purchased their city plots or farms, but practically they did, for traditional rural practice allowed common usage of grazing lands and water resources that their European outlook rejected, stirring resentment and leading to armed clashes.

Varying ideologies, objectives, tactics, strategies, and actors meant details varied over the next 150 years, even as fundamentals remain remarkably in place, with the two sides pursuing static and opposite goals. Much has changed over time—wars and treaties come and go, the balance of power shifts, the Arab states retreat, Israel gains vastly more power, its public moves to the right—but rejectionism and conciliation remain basically unchanged. Zionists purchase land, Palestinians make selling it a capital offense. Zionists build, Palestinians destroy. Zionists ache for acceptance, Palestinians push delegitimization.

Abnormality. That conciliatory and rejectionist mentalities have lasted so long and changed so little makes them unique anywhere in the world, ever. In other cases, a spasm occurs that ends fairly quickly as circumstances change. Only in the Palestinian-Israeli theater do they persist.

Conciliation makes obvious sense when a weaker actor fends off a stronger one. It is more surprising and rarer when the stronger conciliates the weaker, though this does happen: Richard Nixon's policy of détente with the Soviet Union and Barack Obama's Joint Comprehensive Plan of Action with Iran offer two American examples, though they were relatively brief and highly contentious. In contrast, Israel persists with conciliation with minor debate.

Likewise, rejectionism: The genocidal fusillade against Israelis has lasted so long and stayed so constant that it feels normal. A brief genocidal campaign against a weak enemy, such as that carried out by ISIS, does happen. A protracted campaign against a stronger enemy is unheard of. A look at other Middle Eastern conflicts, also pitting Muslims against non-Muslims, establishes this.

Turks fight Greeks in Cyprus. Muslims fight Christians in Lebanon. They resemble the Palestinian-Israeli conflict in that both are unresolved long-standing problems, and both could re-ignite at any moment. But how they differ: Non-Muslims in Cyprus and Lebanon do not face persistent attacks by any means from stoning to missiles. Nor do they suffer from global hate-campaigns by politicians, international organizations, media corporations, and university professors.

The same applies to Armenians, victims of a genocide at the hands of Turks and Kurds from 1915 to 1923. Tensions still persist and flare up, especially in the fighting between Muslim Azerbaijan and Christian Armenia. Again, these frictions in no way replicate those of the Palestinian-Israeli conflict. Where are the rounds of murder and global hate-campaigns? No television shows indoctrinate Turkish children to murder Armenians. Azerbaijani imams do not dilate on the glory of martyrdom. The conflicts involving these neighbors of Israel might be called normal, taking place within boundaries. They highlight the abnormality of Palestinian rejectionism.

Likewise, the Arab states' war on Israel was normal. It began in 1948 and ended with their realization of defeat after 1973. With the rarest of exceptions, almost no conventional fighting after that has taken place, much less all-out war. The economic boycott hardly exists. Arab capitals do not issue blood-curdling statements. They do not sponsor jihadis crossing international borders or summer camps convincing children to throw away their lives.

• • •

Contemporary. Positions further hardened over time, leaving the two sides ever more frustrated.

Hardening. Palestinians realize the uniqueness of their perversion, take pride in it, and even sexualize it. Palestinian Authority TV responded to violence coming from Jenin with "Jenin is our beautiful bride, which perfumes herself daily with the scent of martyrdom." Using the same metaphor, a Hamas newspaper published an article proclaiming: "The Palestinian joy has its own fragrance; it is completely different from every other kind of happiness." What might the author be alluding to? The murder of Israelis, of course. This proves, the article continues,

> that our Palestinian people is still brimming with life and that it is standing on the ladder of glory, as long as it can tear the roof off a bus, can stab a soldier, and can continue to run over a settler [with a car] and to fire point blank at a hostile vehicle in the street. Only a Palestinian can imagine the force of the happiness that these courageous acts evoke in our heart.... [The Palestinian] cannot hide his joy and delight at any brave

> operation.... The people go out into the public squares and the streets, cheer for Palestine, express their joy and delight at the operation, pass out sweets, embrace one another.

Not only has the passage of time not moderated rejectionism but, as statements like these show, it becomes more florid and extravagant than ever, celebrating the death of Israelis in a spiral of perversion.

Israel's conciliation also grows more extreme. On conquering the West Bank and Gaza in 1967, the security establishment sought to win Palestinian favor through good will and economic prosperity, a process that intensified with time, culminating in the Oslo Accords. Israel then urged funding for the PA and (until October 7) for Hamas. Nor is conciliation limited to governmental actions; when the February 2023 murder of two Israeli brothers in the West Bank town of Huwara led to violent retaliation by rightwing Israelis, 7,000 leftwing Israelis instantly responded with a donation to Huwara residents of about $300,000. The Israeli taxpayer provided more than $40,000 for the Tishreen Association to fund a celebration of Nakba Day, mourning the Arab states' failure to snuff Israel out in 1948–1949. Hebrew University invited students from the "occupied Palestinian territories" to apply for scholarships. The Herzliya Hebrew Gymnasium, a historic high school in Tel Aviv, invited Saleh Diab, an eastern Jerusalem resident convicted of attacking Jews for political reasons, to address its student body.

Frustration. The Palestinian-Israeli conflict consists of endless, wearisome rounds of violence and counter-violence, neither of which ever achieves its purpose. The Palestinians invariably begin the hostilities with an attack on Israelis or Jews, usually unarmed. Israel responds with retribution. The two sides reiterate a spiral of Palestinian aggression and Israeli punishment, going around and around, making no progress. Palestinians suffer from poverty and the pathologies of a radicalized society, including oppression by their own leaders. Israel is the only modern, democratic, and rich country that cannot protect itself from being regularly assaulted by its neighbors.

Palestinians can damage Israel through acts of violence and by spreading an anti-Zionist message, but they cannot prevent the Jewish state from ascending from one success to the next. Israel can punish Palestinians for their aggression, but it cannot quench the rejectionist spirit and its evermore depraved expressions.

• • •

Errors. The two sides share a history of mutual bafflement, contrasting circumstances, and confusion.

Cross-purposes. Already in 1937, when Western clothing fashions were more modest than today, the British diplomat George Rendel observed how "Jewish hiking-parties with stout young women from Central Europe in exiguous tight shorts made an odd contrast to the then still more numerous native Arabs, glaring suspiciously at these strange invaders." Eighty years later, an Israeli woman confides how she feels "undressed" every time she passes West Bank men or boys. Religious Muslims, author Gershom Gorenberg notes, "misread Zionism as religious messianism, just as secularist Zionists misread [Amin al-]Husseini as a secular nationalist." Palestinians stream to greater religiosity as Israelis rush toward post-modernism. One struggles to break free of autocratic rule, the other self-imposes a stifling political correctness. One strains to find enough meat for his family, the other experiments with trendy vegan diets. One foresees itself obliterating the enemy people, the other pictures two peoples flourishing side by side.

On this last point: Palestinians mostly see the conflict as win-lose, Israelis as win-win. Strikingly, each Palestinian faction seeks to destroy its rival, but Israelis want them all to prosper. For years, the PA wanted to starve Gaza of resources and compel Hamas to give up, whereas the IDF protected Gaza's civilians. In 2018, for example, the PA tried to block fuel deliveries to Gaza that senior Israeli defense officials had sought to arrange. Israeli journalist Yaakov Lappin explains the contrast in attitudes:

> The Palestinian Authority—driven by a desire to punish Hamas for splitting off from it, and for maintaining its own, separate armed force—continues to place its own sanctions on Gaza. The PA has cut salaries to its personnel in Gaza, sought to reduce the electricity flow (and was pressured by Israel to reinstate electricity payments last month), reduced medical assistance, and generally put the squeeze on the whole of Gaza.

How different Israel:

> Israel's defense establishment has been taking steps to try and keep Gaza's economy from collapsing. Israel Defense Forces

> (IDF) officers who deal with Gaza actively encourage the [Gaza] Strip's business community to grow, increasing the number of permits for them to leave Gaza, and fostering Gazan exports. They also keep a close watch over the state of Gaza's vital civilian infrastructure, in a bid to keep it running. Israel keeps a daily supply of a variety of goods, fuel, gas, medical equipment, food, and construction material flowing into the Strip.

Miscalculations. This gap leads to miscalculations. Conciliation baffles Palestinians, prompting conspiracy theories that twist something like Moshe Dayan's generous vision of mutual economic harmony into Israeli ambition for economic hegemony. Conversely, Israelis ignore the enduring power of rejectionism and fallaciously project their own desire for the good life onto Palestinians. When a Hamas leader says, "We are a people that love death for the sake of God as much as our enemies love life," and a PA religious figure echoes him with, "We love death like our enemies love life," disbelieving Israelis cannot make sense of what they hear, so they tend to ignore such sentiments. Of course, if Palestinians prioritized the good life, they long ago would have settled into a comfortable synergy with Israel's dynamic economy. Instead, they have repeatedly shown an exceptional, almost inhuman intergenerational readiness to sacrifice their welfare for the sake of damaging Israel.

This massive cross-cultural misunderstanding did much to undermine the Oslo Accords and subsequent diplomacy. Palestinians entered them with stagnant old ambitions to destroy Israel while Israelis entered with exciting new hopes for resolution. Palestinians wanted to harm Israel and assumed the converse as well; Israelis wanted close the conflict and assumed Palestinians cherished the same prospect; in fact, they wanted to end Israel itself.

Confusion. The fact that rejectionism is not temporary, does not bend to the pressure of carrots and sticks, and does not moderate over time explains the general inability to understand it or formulate a response to it. The mentality bewilders contemporaries as something hitherto unknown, a new phenomenon that prior experience cannot explain, like the French Revolution or Soviet Russia.

Shimon Peres exemplifies this incomprehension. Although a brilliant man who filled nearly all the Israeli state's highest offices, someone who had a leading role in developing Israel's nuclear capabilities, and who lived alongside rejectionism for eighty-two years, from his arrival in Mandatory

Palestine at the age of eleven in 1934 until his death at the age of ninety-three in 2016, he failed to fathom this exceptional phenomenon. He thought it could be moderated, he assumed punishments would change behavior, and he expected goodwill to inspire reciprocity—none of which happened. His lapse in understanding led to a flamboyant ineptness.

The uniqueness of the two legacies confuses observers in various ways. First, they vainly try to stuff the two peoples into known categories. Palestinians are viewed as a colonized people, though they were no more conquered by Zionists than are Europeans at present by Muslims arriving as illegal migrants in the millions and hoping to become the majority population; both are non-belligerent large-scale immigrations. Israelis are routinely compared to imperialists, even though they moved in as civilians and created history's only country through purchase, and did so in their ancestral homeland. Terms like imperialism and apartheid betray an incomprehension of two unique legacies.

Second, unusual behavior misleads observers. Rejectionism's persistence convinces some of its truth: White-hot fury and willingness to suffer imply a morally justified cause. Surely no population can be so consistent, so angry, so fanatical for so long without good reason. Israeli efforts to document atrocities have limited impact. Contrarily, Israeli conciliation implies a sense of guilt; why else would a more powerful actor behave so timidly, symbolized by such astonishing acts of placation as trading 461 prisoners for a single Israeli?

Third, would-be peacemakers attempt to resolve the Palestinian-Israeli conflict through conventional diplomatic means, which predictably fail. The Oslo Accords, for example, came between such breakthroughs as the ending of South Africa's apartheid regime between 1990 and 1994, the Soviet Union's dissolution in 1991, and Ireland's Good Friday Agreement of 1998; surely compromise would work here, too. In this spirit, U.S. Presidents Clinton and Obama each separately dispatched George Mitchell to build on his diplomatic success in Ireland; of course, his Palestinian-Israeli efforts ended in total failure.

Resolution in this case requires either Palestinian acceptance of Israel or Israel's destruction—not compromise. Martin Sherman correctly notes that, "We are talking about a clash of two collectives with competing and mutually exclusive narratives that are irreconcilable—and only one side can win." This abnormal conflict cannot be ended through compromise. One side must win, the other must lose.

10

POSITIVE DEVELOPMENTS

SEVERAL FACTORS WORK IN ISRAEL'S favor. First, as Arabic-speaking countries focus on other issues, hoary anti-Zionist taboos have lost much of their hold, especially over their political leaders, leading to a shrug and an acceptance of the Jewish state. Second, wild-eyed radicals invariably attract media attention, but growing numbers of Palestinians are fed up with permanent revolution and seek the normal life that follows on accepting Israel. Third, after the strategic vacation of the Oslo Era, many Israelis have rediscovered the virtues of winning.

ARAB STATES TIPTOE AWAY

When Arab states' militaries took up arms against the Jewish state in 1948, they confidently expected to choke it at birth; by 1973, a record of losses prompted them quietly to desert the field of battle. Israel made this remarkable progress over twenty-five years through strategic vision, tactical brilliance, technological innovation, and logistical ingenuity. Its determination and creativity overcame oil boycotts, low-intensity warfare, and the enmity of a superpower.

• • •

25 years of war, 50 of not-war. Non-Palestinian Arabic speakers responded with some favor to Zionism, as symbolized by a 1919 agreement between the Hashemite prince Feisal bin Hussein and the future first president of Israel, Chaim Weizmann. Feisal, reported Weizmann, believed that "the Jews would be of great help to the Arabs, and that the Arab world stood to gain much from a Jewish Homeland in Palestine."

Efforts by Amin al-Husseini and others, however, soon put an end to such receptivity. Direct intervention by Arab states against Zionism began in 1936, became official in 1939, and climaxed in 1948 when six of their armies attacked the newly independent State of Israel. During Israel's first twenty-five years, from 1948 to 1973, Arab states—with Egypt, Jordan, and Syria in the lead, followed by Iraq, Saudi Arabia, and Lebanon—fought it five times (1948–1949, 1956, 1967, 1969–1970, and 1973) with huge conventional armed forces and increasing Soviet-bloc support.

The Arab states lost every round, and badly. In particular, the defeats of 1948–1949 and 1967 left leaders shocked; newborn Israel seemed so vulnerable while the Six-Day War was arguably the single-most lopsided debacle in military history. Direct confrontation with Israel lost its appeal. Israel's battlefield successes eventually established its permanence and the Arab states responded by quietly bowing out. They have remained out for more than fifty years—twice as long as their era of actively making war on Israel.

The few exceptions to this pattern—notably, a Syrian aerial confrontation in 1982 and an Iraqi missile attack in 1991—confirm this point. Their brevity, limitations, and failure reinforced the wisdom of not confronting Israel. Syria lost eighty-two planes to Israel's none. And thirty-nine Iraqi missile attacks directly killed only two Israelis. The Iraqi and Syrian regimes both started nuclear programs and both gave them up after Israel destroyed them, in 1981 and 2007, respectively.

After going into battle with guns blazing in 1948, expecting an easy triumph, rulers in Cairo, Amman, Damascus, Baghdad, and elsewhere incrementally realized over the next quarter-century that the historically helpless Jews could now beat them every time, no matter who initiated the surprise attack, no matter the terrain, no matter the sophistication of weapons, no matter the great power allies. The states tiptoed away.

Israel achieved this shift by winning a deterrence capability against the Arab states, eventually convincing their enemies to come to terms. Whoever attacked Israel paid for that mistake with dead soldiers, captured equipment, stalled economies, even toppled regimes. A deep understanding of Israel's predicament, complemented by money, willpower, and dedication, enabled the state systematically to burnish its reputation for toughness. Its leadership focused on the enemy's mind and mood, adopting policies designed to degrade its morale, inducing a sense of hopelessness, and a realization that the Jewish state is permanent and cannot be undone. In short, Israel won the respect of Arab states through resolve, not conciliation.

Although most Arab states continued to assault Israel verbally and economically after 1973, they carefully withdrew from military confrontation. With minor exceptions (such as the Lebanese armed forces skirmishing with the IDF in 1985 and 2010), they acquiesced to repeated Israeli attacks on their territory, including the elimination of the two nuclear reactors, two major incursions into Lebanon in 1982 and 2006, attacks on the PLO in Tunisia in 1985 and 1988, and repeated Israeli strikes on Syria after 2013.

Granted, no Arab state signed a document of surrender or otherwise acknowledged defeat, but defeat was their experience, as some publicly recognized. For example, Ahmad Masa'deh, a Jordanian politician, admitted in 2020 that: "There is a new reality that we...Arab countries must acknowledge, whether we like it or not: We have been defeated. We have been defeated militarily, as well as politically and diplomatically."

Six Arab states have opened full diplomatic relations with Israel: Egypt in 1979, Jordan in 1994, and the United Arab Emirates, Bahrain, Morocco, and Sudan in 2020. (Two other Arab states started in this direction but aborted: Lebanon in 1983 and Syria in 2000.) Saudi Arabia might follow after the rule of eighty-eight-year-old King Salman ends, an event that would significantly enhance Arab state acceptance of Israel. Even Prime Minister Mohammed bin Abdulrahman Al-Thani of Qatar, though an ally of Tehran and Hamas, states that, "At the end of the day, we don't have a war with Israel."

These changes manifest in a variety of ways. Negatively, no Arab government today calls for the destruction of the Jewish state; all of them focus instead on the creation of "Palestine." No Arab government still issues the horrifying threats against Israel, such as routinely emit from Palestinian sources.

Positively, in September 2020 alone, the preacher at Mecca's Grand Mosque recalled Muhammad's good relations with Jews, the Arab League turned down a Palestinian-sponsored anti-Israel resolution, and the UAE government "advised" all hotels "to include Kosher food options" in all their dining offerings. In January 2023, the UAE issued a statement that

> strongly condemned the [Palestinian] terrorist attack near a synagogue in Jerusalem, which resulted in a number of deaths and multiple injuries...the UAE expresses its strong condemnation of these criminal acts, and its permanent rejection of all forms of violence and terrorism aimed at undermining security and stability in contravention of human values and principles. The Ministry also expressed its sincere condolences and sympathy to the government of Israel and its people, and to the families of the victims of this heinous crime, as well as its wishes for a speedy recovery for all the injured.

In December 2023, Dubai banned the slogan "From the river to the sea …" at a UN climate conference.

That four Arab foreign ministers attended a meeting hosted by Israel in early 2022 (the Negev Summit) symbolized this new acceptance. *Al-Majalla*, a major Saudi magazine published in London, ran a cover story in July 2022 praising Arab Israeli citizens serving in the IDF. More substantively, Israel sold advanced military equipment to the UAE, Bahrain, and Morocco totaling more than $3 billion in two years; in 2021, that accounted for 7 percent of $11.3 billion in Israeli global military sales. Obviously, one only sells matériel to governments expected to remain long-term allies.

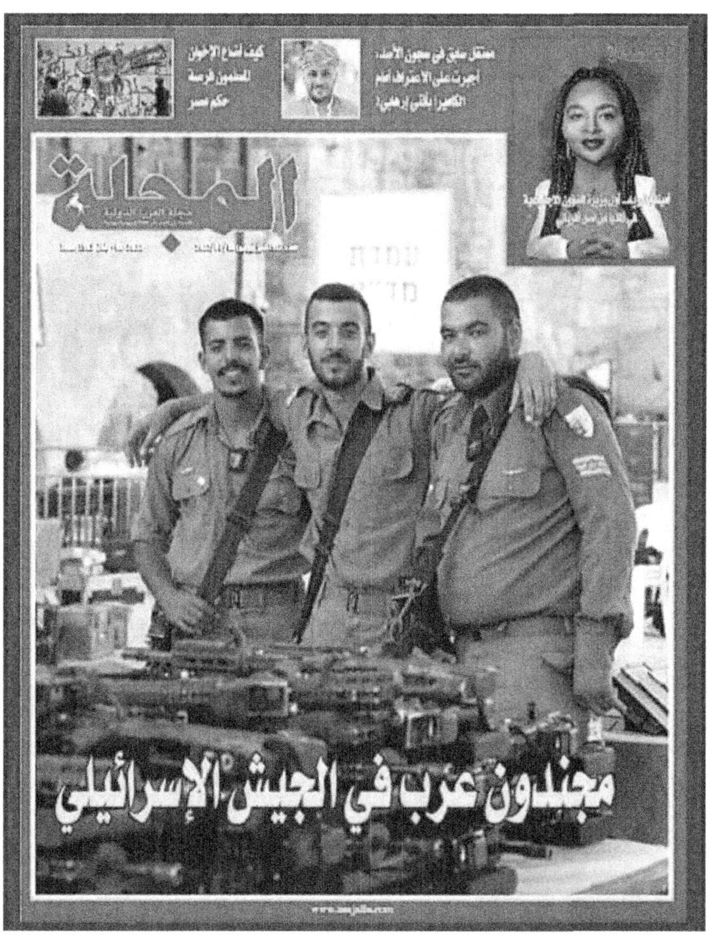

On July 8, 2022, the Saudi newsmagazine ***Al-Majalla*** featured a favorable cover story on "Arab Recruits in the Israeli Army."

The fracturing of Arab state enmity constitutes a tectonic shift. Israel's compelling the Arab states, with their far larger populations, resources, economies, and diplomatic heft, to retreat from the battlefield constitutes a signal accomplishment that deserves far more attention than it has received. While some analysts picked up early on it (American University's Amos Perlmutter in 1989: "Israel now finds the Palestine problem to be its principal threat"), many Israelis long remain unaware of this change. In 1994, for example, IDF Chief of Staff Ehud Barak argued: "In the foreseeable future, the main threat to the State of Israel is still an all-out attack by conventional armies." As late as 2022, Israeli strategist Efraim Inbar insisted that the "idea that Jewish and Arab states will coexist peacefully…ignores the reality on the ground."

Indeed, the Arab states' defeat can be undone. The Muslim Brotherhood could again take over Egypt, Jordan's monarchy could fall to radicals, Syria could become whole again, and Lebanon could become a unified state under Hezbollah rule. We can only say with confidence that, for now, they have been defeated.

• • •

Loss of interest. The retreat of Arab states and peoples has many implications for the Palestinians, spurring conspiracy theories and creating an opportunity for Israel.

A move away. Arab states started pursuing their own interests in relation to Israel, offering little more than lip-service to the Palestinians, starting most conspicuously with Anwar al-Sadat's trip to Jerusalem in 1977. This process continued apace, as the states wearied of the Palestinians never taking yes for an answer. By now, a host of other issues distract the Arab states from their earlier anti-Zionism. Internally, they face discontented subjects, economic weakness, the Islamist surge, anarchy, and a water drought. Externally, they worry about the Iranian threat, Türkiye going rogue, and civil wars in Libya, Yemen, Syria, and Iraq. By August 2023, a *Wall Street Journal* analysis found that "Saudi officials have dwindling patience for uncompromising and divided Palestinian leaders with limited popular support."

Nor is it just the governments that have lost interest in the Palestinians. Joseph Braude of the Center for Peace Communications, sees the number of pro-Israel Arabs growing due to changes arising from a number of developments: "the globalization of media, the region's shifting politics, growing awareness of local Jewish history, and the youthful impulse to rebel against authority."

A range of evidence from the non-Palestinian Middle East suggests significant cracks in the old hostility to Israel. In one striking illustration, the anti-government upheavals that began in 2010 and inaccurately called the Arab Spring, conspicuously ignored Israel and the Palestinians. The demonstrators had other, more pressing concerns, from personal freedoms to economic growth.

Already in 2010, a poll by *Al-Arabiya* television found that 71 percent of Arabic speakers do not care to know anything about Palestinian-Israeli diplomacy. At the end of 2018, an Israeli Ministry of Foreign Affairs poll based on 1,000 respondents in each country, asked about popular acceptance of formal relations with Israel. It found 21 percent of Algerians in favor, 23 percent of Saudis, 32 percent of Tunisians, 34 percent of Iranians, 41 percent of Moroccans, 42 percent of Emiratis, and 43 percent of Iraqis. The average (ignoring the difference in population sizes) comes out to slightly over one-third of respondents in the countries surveyed accepting normal relations with Israel, a far greater percentage than in earlier decades.

Leading Middle Eastern and Muslim cultural figures have publicly advocated acceptance of Israel, though many can only do so while living in the West. Their numbers include (going from west to east, listing by country of birth) British doctor Qanta Ahmed, British pro-Israel activist Kasim Hafeez, Algerian writer Boualem Sansal, Egyptian journalist Magdi Allam, Egyptian novelist Alaa Al-Aswany, Egyptian scholar Hussein Aboubakr Mansour, Egyptian singer Mohamed Ramadan, Egyptian playwright Ali Salem, Egyptian scholar and novelist Yusuf Zaydan, Egyptian author Dalia Ziada, Turkish basketball player Enes Kantor Freedom, Turkish YouTuber Ridvan Aydemir, Syrian doctor Wafa Sultan, Syrian intellectual Rawan Osman, Jordanian religious scholar Ahmad al-Adwan, Saudi social media influencer Mohammed Saud, Iraqi cultural official Sahar al-Ta'i, Iraqi beauty queen Sarah Idan, Iranian imam Mohammad Tawhidi, Iranian judo wrestler Saeid Mollaei, Pakistani activist Raheel Raza, Indian political scientist Salim Mansur, Indonesian President Abdurrahman Wahid, Guyanese professor Khaleel Mohammed, and American doctor Zuhdi Jasser.

Thus did the large Arab-Israeli conflict become the small Palestinian-Israeli conflict.

Suspicions. Palestinians routinely hold the Arab states responsible for the so-called catastrophe (*nakba*) of 1948–1949 and Israel's coming into existence, neatly absolving themselves of blame. Fatah ascribed the defeat of 1949 to "Treacherous conspiracies on the part of Arab regimes." This touched a nerve: According to a June 2023 poll by the Palestinian Center for Policy and Survey Research, 38 percent blame the defeat on the "weak and conspiratorial Arab [state] role," 36 percent blame the British Mandate, 16 percent blame Zionists, and only 7 percent blame themselves.

Subsequent wars saw similar suspicions of treachery. In 1967, Jordan's king supposedly play-acted at fighting Israel, issuing blank ammunition to his forces and Jordan's High Command allegedly sponsored an extremist Palestinian organization, the Victory Legions, to undercut Fatah. Meanwhile, the Saudi king funded Israel to defeat Egyptian forces. In 1982, Arafat claimed the Arab states had deserted the Palestinians because, "We did better in this war than all the Arab states. They therefore couldn't let us win.... So we were alone. Not just the Syrians; all of them intentionally left us on our own." During the first *intifada*, Hamas claimed, Arab rulers "pretend to support the uprising but in fact are immersed in a deep sleep." It also accused Arab states of intervening to "prevent the holy war from advancing, on the claim that Palestine would be liberated by the Arab armies, and that this was [an Arab] national problem and not a territorial problem."

Palestinians drew lessons from this distorted history. The PLO's Khalil al-Wazir generalized that Arab regimes "put on a show to pretend they supported our cause. But really their intention was to neutralize us." West Bank polemicist Daoud Kuttab reported that Palestinians regretted having let themselves for so long be "fooled by Arab [state] rhetoric." Faisal Abu Khadra, a PLO National Council member, vented his frustration in February 2023:

> Where are the Arabs and Arabhood? They convene and make decisions, but then fail to implement any of these decisions.... The Palestinian people are tired of the Arab summits that have divided the Arab nation. It is time that these leaders wake up and realize that Zionism, which is part of the Freemasons movement, is the greatest danger to the Arab states and that the only solution is thus to...end the [internal] conflict and for the Arab countries to make serious efforts to help the

> Palestinian people with money, weapons, tangible foreign diplomacy and everything else it needs.

Opportunity. Arab state leaders may have absorbed these insults in silence, not wanting to upset their populaces, but the accusations infuriated them. That fury gave Israel room for maneuver. The Temple Mount in Jerusalem, holy to Jews and Muslims alike, offers one example.

Although Israel enjoys complete sovereignty over the Temple Mount, it finds itself in a bind. In the intermediate aftermath of seizing the territory in 1967, its government put "status quo" regulations into effect that restrict Israeli governmental power over the holy esplanade, gave the waqf authority over Islamic sanctities, and limit visits by observant Jews. Over a half-century later, these concessions had hardened into established precedent that the PA exploits to create an insecure environment, wreck invaluable archeological remains, and humiliate observant Jewish visitors. The Palestinians and their Jordanian partners countenance no reasonable changes, and a global consensus endorses their rigidity.

But a possible escape exists for the Government of Israel to extricate itself from this self-inflicted problem: Mohammed bin Salman, the Saudi crown prince. Vulnerable to Iranian challenges to Saudi control over Mecca and Medina, this highly ambitious young man presumably would like nothing better than to add Al-Aqsa Mosque and the Dome of the Rock to his collection of Islamic sanctities. To take these away from the PA only renders the attraction greater. Israel could potentially negotiate this matter with Riyadh, offering the jewel in the PA's crown in exchange for altering the status quo on the Temple Mount and various diplomatic benefits. That a July 2023 survey found that 73 percent of Gazans want Saudi Arabia to have a role in determining the future of Jerusalem goes far to legitimize this possibility. Success here would have devastating implications for the PA.

• • •

Impact on the Palestinians. The Arab states' retreat offered Palestinians the chance to reprise their role as Israel's main enemy. They enthusiastically seized the opportunity and did a much better job of it.

Palestinians rush in. Palestinians had spearheaded the assault on Zionism before 1948 and they encouraged Arab states to make war on Israel after that date. During the era of 1948 to 1973, however, they mainly served as a tool of ambitious state leaders. For example, Egypt's Gamal Abdel Nasser steered the Arab League to set up the PLO in 1964. They rose to the fore again after the crushing of three Arab armed forces in 1967, a fiasco that caused Palestinians to give up on the Arab states as their saviors, re-assert the primacy of their struggle against Israel, and realize that only their self-help effort could destroy Israel. They were, as Shabtai Teveth notes, "in a hurry to resume the war against Israel in place of the defeated Arab armies."

State interests, however, remained paramount. Only in 1974 did the League of Arab States recognize the PLO as the "sole legitimate representative of the Palestinian people," grant it full membership, and defer to Palestinian primacy. After years of reluctance, the Jordanian government acceded to Palestinian leadership in 1988. The 1993 Oslo Accords then confirmed Palestinian centrality, which has ever since gone unchallenged.

Arab state and Palestinian records compared. The Palestinians' much lesser power, plus the Arab states' retreat might have reduced the conflict from Israel's perspective from an existential one to a dispute over borders; remarkably, that did not happen. Inspired by rejectionism, Palestinians continued to aspire to nothing less than Israel's destruction. More remarkably, while lacking the states' resources, Palestinians accomplished more than they did, both on the ground and in international public opinion.

Yes, Palestinians lost militarily every one of eight rounds of fighting (1982, 1987–1993, 2000–2005, 2008–2009, 2012, 2014, 2021, and 2023–) against the far more powerful IDF, but they lost less badly than the Arab states. Three Arab armed forces lost to Israel in six days in 1967, but the PLO managed to hang on against Israel for eighty-eight days in 1982. Hamas killed more Israelis on a single day, October 7, than huge armies ever managed to do. Israel conquered land from Arab states (the Sinai Peninsula, Gaza, East Jerusalem, the West Bank, and the Golan Heights) but turned territories over to the Palestinians (Gaza and parts of the West Bank). The latter even rejected two opportunities (in 2000 and 2008) for more territory, finding these inadequate. If Arab states felt constrained to observe treaties with Israel, however coldly, Palestinians with near impunity trashed the Oslo Accords and every other agreement. Arab states withdrew after just twenty-five years of leading the charge against Israel, but Palestinians keep going after fifty years.

The many and large Arab states howled about imperialist aggression directed against them but never convincingly portrayed themselves as victims of little Israel. In contrast, the even littler Palestinians have done so with great skill, winning themselves the coveted underdog status vis-à-vis Israel. Accordingly, Western governments and peoples largely disapproved of the Arab-state assault on Israel, but they more widely endorse Palestinian attacks on it. In the process, Palestinians achieved something unattainable by heavy-handed and lugubrious state dictators; they made themselves the darlings of international organizations and senior common rooms alike, giving them a unique global constituency. Israel may have won all its wars against Palestinians, but the latter made it look bad, enhancing their international support. Thus did Palestinians spread rejectionism to others, especially to Islamists and leftists.

American columnist Jonathan Tobin sums this up: "Israel's successes in wars of survival and the smart public-relations work of the Palestinians allowed the latter to play David to the Israeli Goliath." Or, in a historical irony, who a century ago would have imagined that Jews would become great warriors and Arabs great publicists?

• • •

A model for Palestinian defeat? The Arab-state defeat raises the question whether it contains implications for the Palestinians sensing themselves defeated. In small part, yes: If states with large Muslim-majority populations can be forced to give up, this shows that Islam does not make Muslims into super warriors immune from loss nor Jews into victims fated to experience perpetual hostility.

But in large part, no: State conflicts with Israel are more tractable and more prone to change than the Palestinian conflict. Israel is a far more remote issue for residents of Arab states than for Palestinians. Egyptians tend to care less about making Jerusalem the capital of "Palestine" than about installing proper sewer systems, while civil war has consumed Syrians since 2011. Also, states compromise more readily than ideological movements because their rulers have multiple and competing interests. Governments being hierarchical structures—and especially the Arabs' authoritarian regimes—a single individual (like Anwar al-Sadat or Mohammad bin Salman) can radically change policy. No one disposes of such power in the PA or Hamas. In addition, unlike state leaders, who can engage or withdraw from the battle on a whim, Palestinian leaders cannot simply walk away, being defined by rejectionism and Islamic Zionism. Finally, whereas battlefield losses eventually wore the states down, Palestinians seem to be the more outraged with each added death. Deterrence, which worked against the Arab states, seems not to work with Palestinians, who represent a much smaller but more impassioned and determined enemy.

Will Saudi acceptance of Israel push Palestinians also to come to terms? Israelis tend to believe so. Former Israeli parliamentarian Einat Wilf predicts that: "If the Palestinians realize they are alone, [they] will be forced to ditch their maximalist demands and accept the existence of a Jewish state while forgetting about the right of return." Israeli Colonel (res.) Eran Lerman agrees: "Saudi Arabia establishing diplomatic relations with Israel will be the ultimate signal to Palestinians that they have lost." A former senior Israeli security official predicts that: "When the Saudis enter the Abraham Accords, it's a drama that can change reality, it creates economic and financial levers, political opportunities and maybe a different atmosphere that will help lower the flames." Netanyahu expects that Saudi relations would "help us solve the Palestinian-Israeli conflict."

I disagree. Israel's agreements with Arab states have great intrinsic importance, but they hardly dent the perfervid hostility toward Israel among Palestinians, whose tenacious genocidal rejectionism demands a far deeper defeat. The long-ago peace treaties with Egypt and Jordan had little impact; the signature of an Egyptian dictator on a peace treaty changed few minds, while Amman commands little clout among Islamists, professors of English, or members of the United Nations. Likewise, the Abraham Accords failed to influence the Palestinians' groupies—Islamists, the Iranian and Turkish governments, global leftists—who disdain and ignore the accords. Sven Koopmans, EU special representative for the Middle East Peace Process, praises the "positive things" coming out of the accords but correctly notes that they have not "fundamentally changed the situation for the Palestinians." The Hebrew University's Elie Podeh adds that Israel's new ties to Arab states, "though certainly important, are not an alternative to resolution of the Palestinian problem."

Nevertheless, that problem may be soluble.

PALESTINIANS LESS TENACIOUS

Palestinians might appear unanimously to abhor Israel and seek its destruction but that is not the case. In fact, a significant percentage of them has either given up the fight; accepted Israel's existence; expressed appreciation of it; or chosen to *move to* it. Such overlooked persons have great importance, implying an unwonted receptivity to Israel and its messages.

• • •

Giving up the fight. Palestinians widely realize that they are getting nowhere. A January 2023 survey of Palestinian opinion found that 79 percent "are worried or very much worried about the future of the Palestinian people." Said Arikat of the Palestinian newspaper *Al-Quds* sums up the mood of despair: "It is probably easier to establish a colony on Mars than a state for the Palestinians."

This sense of despair causes some Palestinians to exit the battle. Zakaria Zubeidi, once Al-Aqsa Martyrs Brigade commander in Jenin, temporarily retired from killing Israelis after years of leading Palestinians in this pursuit. He explained why in 2008:

> It's perfectly clear to me that we won't be able to defeat Israel. My aim was for us, by means of the "resistance" [that is, violence], to get a message out to the world.... We failed entirely in the intifada. We haven't seen any benefit or positive result from it. We achieved nothing. It's a crushing failure. We failed at the political level—we didn't succeed in translating the military actions into political achievements.... We have been defeated.... We are marching in the direction of nowhere, toward total ruin. The Palestinian people is finished. Done for...

He drew personal conclusions from this predicament:

> I got tired. When you lose, what can you do? We, the activists, paid the heavy price. We've had family members killed, friends. They demolished our homes and we have no way of earning a living. And what is the result? Zero. Simply zero. And when that's the result, you don't want to be a part of it any more.

Zubeidi here articulates the essence of defeat: purposeless, hopelessness, giving up. Poll after poll shows that anti-Zionism ranks low down among Palestinian priorities. David Pollock of the Washington Institute for Near East Policy wrote about Gaza in 2018:

> The majority of its people actually oppose the violent Hamas border protests—and at least half would even support a formal cease-fire with Israel...most Gazans say they want direct personal dialogue with Israelis. Most would like Israeli companies to provide jobs for them inside their Hamas-ruled territory. Most also blame Hamas, the Palestinian Authority in Ramallah, the UN, or Egypt—rather than Israel—for their economic woes. Moreover, remarkably, a plurality of Palestinians in Gaza say they want Hamas to change its rejectionist position and agree to make peace with Israel.

The passage of time prompted Palestinian leaders from an earlier era—notorious figures, such as Nayef Hawatmeh, Ahmed Jibril, Leila Khaled, and Mohammed Oudeh—to acknowledge the error of their ways. Hawatmeh, leader of the Democratic Front for the Liberation of Palestine, noted in 2008 that, "After 60 years, we are struggling for what we could have had in 1947. We have missed many historic opportunities." Oudeh, planner of the Olympic games attack in 1972 that killed eleven Israeli athletes, observed that "maybe, just maybe, we should have shown some flexibility. Back in our days, it was 'the whole of Palestine or nothing.' But we should have accepted a Palestinian state next to Israel." Mkhaimer Abu Saada, an analyst in Gaza, generalizes: "I find it hard to say as a Palestinian, but we haven't achieved any of our national goals. Our leadership has failed to achieve anything."

While October 7 sparked anti-Zionism around the world, it had the opposite effect among Gazans themselves, as reported by the writer Tawfiq Abu Shomer: "Our people have lost their enthusiasm for resistance and struggle. Under the stress of hunger and displacement, struggle in the strictly military sense has become unpopular. The issues of Jerusalem and of prisoners [in Israeli jails] is no longer sacred for the majority of those who are hungry and displaced!" He concludes by observing, "How easy to decide to start a war, how difficult to endure its dangerous consequences?!"

In short, Palestinians are not supermen, impervious to failure.

• • •

Accepting Israel. For a century, about 20 percent of Palestinians have consistently accepted the Jewish state, worked with it, and wished to live in harmony with it.

Although this minority has never been in charge and its voice has always been buried under rejectionist bluster, it played a crucial role in history in building Israel, playing many roles for the Yishuv in the decades before independence. As shown by Hillel Cohen of the Hebrew University in *Army of Shadows: Palestinian Collaboration with Zionism, 1917–1948*,[1] this minority provided labor, engaged in commerce, sold land, sold arms, handed over state assets, provided intelligence about enemy forces, spread rumors and dissension, convinced fellow Palestinians to surrender, fought the Yishuv's enemies, and even operated behind enemy lines. So great was this cumulative assistance, the State of Israel likely could not have come into existence without its contribution. While Palestinian assistance remains important to Israeli security today (how else could the IDF foil so many attempted attacks coming out of the West Bank?), it is much less central.

Polling over the past twenty years confirms this rough but quite consistent 20 percent of Palestinians ready to live with Israel.

- 20.3 percent replied "yes" to a Palestinian Center for Policy and Survey Research survey of Palestine refugees in January 2003 that asked: "Are there conditions under which you could accept coexistence with Israeli Jews in peace and security?"
- 28.3 percent replied "yes" to a Najah University poll in April 2010 that asked: "Do you accept the creation of a Palestinian state within the 1967 borders with some land exchange as a final solution for the Palestinian problem?"
- 12 percent replied "yes" to an Arab World for Research & Development poll in October 2010 that asked: "If Palestinian negotiators delivered a peace settlement that includes a Palestinian State but had to make compromises on key issues (right of return, Jerusalem, borders, settlements, etc.) to do so would you support the result?"
- 11 percent replied "yes" to a Stanley Greenberg and Palestinian Center for Public Opinion survey in July 2011 in two parts: 34 percent accepted the statement that "there should be two states: Palestine as the homeland for the Palestinian people

1 Hillel Cohen, *Army of Shadows: Palestinian Collaboration with Zionism, 1917–1948* (Berkeley: University of California Press, 2008).

and Israel as the homeland for the Jewish people," of which a further 34 percent accepted a two-state solution as permanent. Taking 34 percent of 34 percent leaves 11 percent.

- 31.6 percent replied "yes" to the Washington Institute for Near Eastern Policy survey in June 2014 that asked: "If the Palestinian leadership is able to negotiate a two-state solution with Israel, do you think that this should be the end of the conflict with Israel?"
- Two-thirds of Gazans wanted "direct personal contacts and dialogue with Israelis" according to two polls taken in 2018.

Recent polling finds strikingly larger numbers, especially in Gaza, ready to end the conflict with Israel. A July 2023 Washington Institute poll of Gazans found:

- 42 percent hope that "someday we can be friends with Israelis, since we are all human beings after all."
- 44 percent agree that: "We should recognize that we will never defeat Israel and that fighting just makes things worse."
- 47 percent agree that "it would be better for us if we were part of Israel than in PA or Hamas ruled lands."
- 50 percent want Hamas to "stop calling for the destruction of Israel and instead accept a permanent two-state solution based on the 1967 borders."
- 50 percent agree that, "If Saudi Arabia normalizes relations with Israel, [the] Palestinian leadership should also normalize relations and end the conflict."
- 59 percent support "the Palestinian resumption of negotiations with Israel."
- 61 percent wish more Israeli jobs were offered in Gaza and the West Bank.
- 62 percent want Hamas to preserve the cease-fire with Israel.
- 63 percent seek direct personal contacts and dialogue with Israelis.

- 67 percent believe that, "Right now, the Palestinians should focus on practical matters like jobs, health care, education, and everyday stability, not on big political plans or resistance options."
- 79 percent believe that, "Right now, internal political and economic reform is more important for us than any foreign policy issue."
- 87 percent find that, "Many people are more preoccupied with their personal lives than with politics."

An Arab Barometer survey of Gazans completed the day before October 7 confirms these results, finding that: "Overall, 73 percent of Gazans favored a peaceful settlement to the Israeli-Palestinian conflict." In contrast, "just 20 percent of Gazans favored a military solution that could result in the destruction of the state of Israel." Arab Barometer pollsters concluded that, "Unlike Hamas, whose goal is to destroy the Israeli state, the majority of survey respondents favored a two-state solution with an independent Palestine and Israel existing side by side."

Much anecdotal evidence confirms this attitude. Rami Aman, who sponsored "Skype with Your Enemy" to create human relations with Israelis, estimates that most Gazans accept Israel's existence. The Center for Peace Communications' series "Whispered in Gaza" gives anonymized voice to a silenced and suffering people, many of whom call for an end to conflict. For example, Zainab says, "I don't want there to be wars and rockets. We and the Israelis are one people...all of us should live in peace."

Israel's Muslim citizens are also moving in this direction. Mansour Abbas, the leader of the Ra'am Islamist party, has provided important leadership. In 2021, while part of a coalition governing Israel, he made a historic statement: "The State of Israel was born as a Jewish state, and it will remain that." That is, Mansour did not demand Israel be a state of its citizens or in some other way try to eliminate its Jewish component. Although no other politicians have yet followed suit, Abbas' statement broke a taboo and will likely have long-term consequences.

• • •

Appreciating Israel. Palestinians have a first-hand awareness of the contrast between life in the West Bank or Gaza and in Israel. They have many reasons to express positive, even friendly, attitudes toward Israel: the rule of law, democracy, freedom of expression, the protection of minorities, security, restraints on violence, the absence of torture, and economic benefits. (Note the many PA and Hamas leaders quoted in this section.)

Rule of law. After two stints in Israeli prisons, Nabil Gheit served as mayor of Ras Khamis, a distant Palestinian neighborhood within Jerusalem. Over the cash register in his store, he displayed two posters of "the martyr Saddam Hussein." One might expect him to cheer the prospect of parts of eastern Jerusalem coming under PA control. But no, he dreads PA rule, rejecting it because, as he grudgingly acknowledged, "At least in Israel, there's law." Fayez Abu Shamaleh, a Gazan political analyst, noted that, "No one is above the law in Israel. The gates of the prisons [were] locked behind the president of the state [a reference to Moshe Katsav] and the former prime minister Olmert." He then added, sardonically, "Don't ask me why Israel achieved a victory over all the Arab countries." The opening in 2016 of a criminal investigation into Benjamin Netanyahu, the sitting prime minister, just like any other citizen, prompted admiring Palestinian comments. Sufian Abu Zaida, a former PA "minister" of prisoner affairs, saw in this "the real expression of a genuine state of law where everyone is equal before the law and not a state of counterfeit law."

Democracy. Nayef Hawatmeh wished that the PA made decisions more like Israel:

> We want the PNC [Palestine National Council] to discuss the developments since 1991, particularly the Oslo accords, which were concluded behind the back of the PNC contrary to what happened in Israel, for example, where the accords were presented to the Knesset and public opinion for voting.

His facts might not be completely accurate, but they do make his point. Israel's 1999 elections, which Netanyahu lost, impressed many Palestinian observers. Columnists remarked on the smooth transition in Israel and wanted the same for themselves; as one put it, he envied the Israelis and wants "a similar regime in my future state." Musa Abu Marzouk, a high-ranking Hamas official, scored points against Arafat in 2000 by comparing him unfavorably with the Jewish state: "We saw representatives of the Israeli opposition criticize [Israel's Prime Minister] Barak and they were not arrested...but in our case, the Palestinian Authority arrests people as the first order of business." Hassan al-Kashif, director-general of the PA's "information ministry," contrasted Netanyahu's immediate and graceful exit from office with the perpetual power of "several names in our leadership" who go on ruling in perpetuity.

Freedom of expression. After the PA police burned down the printing plant of *Al-Umma*, a Jerusalem weekly, its owner and editor Adnan Khatib bemoaned his troubles since the PA's heavy-handed leaders got power over him: "The measures they are taking against the Palestinian media, including the arrest of journalists and the closure of newspapers, are much worse than those taken by the Israelis against the Palestinian press." In an ironic turn of events, the PA arrested and jailed Na'im Salama, a lawyer living in Gaza, on charges that he slandered it by writing that Palestinians should adopt Israeli standards of democracy. Hanan Ashrawi acknowledged (reluctantly) that the Jewish state has something to teach the nascent Palestinian polity: "Freedom would have to be mentioned although it has only been implemented in a selective way, for example, the freedom of speech." Iyad as-Sarraj, a prominent psychiatrist and director of the Gaza Community Mental Health Program, confessed that "during the Israeli occupation, I was 100 times freer [than under the PA]."

Protection of minorities. Christians and secular Muslims particularly appreciate Israel's protection at a time when Palestinian politics has taken an increasingly Islamist cast. A Christian Palestinian worried that when the Palestinian state comes into existence, "the sacred union against the Zionist enemy will die. It will be time to settle accounts. We will undergo the same as our Lebanese brothers or the Copts in Egypt. It saddens me to say so, but Israeli laws protect us." His fear is in many ways too late, as the West Bank Christian population has precipitously declined under PA rule, to the point that one analyst asks if Christian life is "to be reduced to empty church buildings and a congregation-less hierarchy with no flock in the birthplace of Christianity?"

Security. Heidar Abdul-Shafi, head of the Palestinian delegation to the 1991 Madrid Conference, made a remarkable observation: "Can anyone imagine that a family would be happy to hear a knock at the door in the middle of the night from the Israeli army?" He continued: "When the infighting began in Gaza, the people were happy because the Israeli army imposed a curfew." Palestinian journalist Majed Azzam concludes from the mess in Gaza that: "The [only] thing that prevents the chaos and turmoil in Gaza from spreading to the West Bank is the presence of the Israeli occupation [in the West Bank...as opposed to] its absence from the Gaza Strip."

Restraints on violence. An opponent of Arafat's pointed out how Israeli soldiers "would first fire tear gas, and then fire rubber bullets, and only then shoot live ammunition. They never shot at us without a direct order to shoot, and then they only shot a few bullets. But these Palestinian police started shooting immediately, and they shot everywhere." After the PA police raided the house of a Hamas supporter in an after-midnight operation and roughed up both him and his seventy-year-old father, the father yelled at the police, "Even the Jews did not behave like you cowards." And the son, when he came out of the PA prison, declared his experience there much worse than in the Israeli jails.

No torture. Louai Faisal, twenty-seven, a Hebron resident and Hamas member who spent three periods in each of the Israeli and PA prisons, said he was never tortured in Israel but was by the PA, and called his experience in the latter's prisons "much worse." After a beating from a PA security agency, Emad Halayqa, a Hamas activist at Birzeit University in Ramallah, proclaimed, "Send me the Jews. I wish they would arrest me and save me from your violations." A young Palestinian spent thirty months in Israeli prisons for throwing stones at soldiers and ten days in a PA jail for obliquely insulting it on Facebook. Comparing the two experiences, he said that the Israelis "have rules. There's a law, a system. There's no law in the authority," where he was roughed up and humiliated during the daily interrogations. One West Bank man stated, "The [Israeli] soldier's military boots are preferable to Abu Mazen [Mahmoud Abbas] on my head." Another stated that, "The Israelis are a million times more compassionate than the PA" and that Israel's administration is "a million times better" than the PA's.

Economic benefits. Israel's GDP is twenty-seven times bigger than that of the West Bank and Gaza; its per capita income is fourteen times higher. In addition, Israel's insurance and pension plans have no Palestinian parallel. Not surprisingly, Palestinians living outside Israel admire what they are missing. In an unusual acknowledgment, *Al-Hayat Al-Jadida*, the PA's official daily, documented case after case of Palestinian workers in Israel not only making twice their West Bank and Gaza counterparts but also being treated much better, with commuting expenses, health insurance, and pension costs covered, plus a minimum wage and sick and vacation days—not to speak of assured payments for work done. "The Israelis are better than you," shouted a PA employee at a member of the Palestinian Legislative Council, distressed at not having been paid.

Riyad al-Laham, a father of eight who worked for a farm owned by Israelis in Gaza for nearly twenty years and became unemployed after Israel's withdrawal, wants them back and says everyone in his town does, as well. All of them "used to work in the settlements and make good money. Now there is nothing to do. Even our own agricultural land is barren." Israelis "used to take responsibility for us as occupiers. Neither [the PA nor Hamas] knocked on the doors to ask what we need. People are fed up.... We have become beggars." Economic problems led some Palestinians almost to utter the unmentionable: "I don't say [Israeli] occupation would be better," said a farmer in Jericho who let his peppers wilt on the vine, "But if they were occupying us, at least the city might be open," permitting his produce to get to market. Others do utter it: Salem al-Bahabsa complained, "We are all now unemployed and depend on charity for food. My sons were farmers in the greenhouses. We worked in the settlements and had resources. Now, I don't think I could survive without [the UN].... Before was better."

A Gazan named Ibrahim focused on electricity: "The Israelis are better. All talk on the street is about the [absence of] electricity. All the public talks about is how hard it is in Gaza." West Bank workers under PA administration formally requested that Israeli employment laws be applied to them, hoping to receive the greater rights in Israeli law. Sadly, for them, Israeli courts turned them down and even made them pay for the other side's legal fees.

In conclusion, a Palestinian worker recalled, to emphatic agreement among his listeners, about the situation in Hamas-controlled Gaza, "It wasn't like this when Israel controlled it. We had jobs and were safe. Now, Hamas has made Gaza into a mess. No one wants to live there." Instead, they want to live in Israel. Ismail Abu Shanab, a senior political leader of Hamas, criticized Palestinian self-rule: "When the Israelis were here, we lived our lives better than now, in every way. Believe me." Curiously, he then added, "Look how the streets of Gaza are not clean." These two are hardly alone; a September 2023 Palestinian Center for Public Opinion poll found that 47 percent of Gazans agree that "it would be better for us if we were part of Israel than in PA- or Hamas-ruled lands." That raises the topic of Palestinians who make themselves part of Israel by moving to it.

• • •

Moving to Israel. They may say horrible things about it, but Palestinians in numbers choose to live in Israel. They divide into two groups.

Eastern Jerusalemites, numbering about 350,000 and overwhelmingly not citizens but permanent residents of Israel, have it easy, as they may live anywhere they choose in Israel, whether majority Jewish areas of Jerusalem or pre-1967 Israel. They tend to move for three main reasons. Some wish to flee the city's tensions, high prices, and (in its remoter areas) paucity of city services. Others worry about having their Israeli identity cards revoked and losing access to the many advantages conferred by it, should Jerusalem be divided and they find themselves in the PA part. A final group moves in reaction to the separation fence that went up between Israel and the West Bank in 2004 and 2005, fearing exclusion from Israel. To avoid finding themselves in "Palestine," eastern Jerusalem non-citizens have moved in sizeable numbers to such predominantly Jewish areas as French Hill and Pisgat Ze'ev (areas which the PA, incidentally, considers illegal Israeli settlements).

As the Associated Press noted, the fence "stranded tens of thousands of Jerusalem Arabs on the 'West Bank side,' and many moved to Arab neighborhoods on the Jerusalem side for easier access to jobs and schools." Thus did a separation fence, ironically, spur Palestinian aliyah.

West Bankers and Gazans, the second group and our focus here, seek to flee PA or Hamas rule to live in Israel. Legally or illegally, they have voted with their feet, usually to take advantage of Israel's higher pay, greater work opportunities, and better services—education, health care, health insurance, pension, law enforcement, utilities (water, sewage, trash). In addition, they appreciate the rule of law, freedom of speech, and driving with an Israeli license plate.

Many share this aspiration. A West Bank woman estimated that about 80 percent of people in her village want Israeli citizenship and the other 20 percent do as well but will not admit so publicly. A West Bank man asserted that "everyone" wants Israeli papers. "Believe me, ask a child. Even he will tell you." West Bankers and Gazans subdivide into many types: husbands and wives, the beneficiaries of good-will gestures, PLO fighters, criminals, political murderers, homosexuals, and informants.

Husbands and wives. Under a family reunification program in place from 1967 until mid-2003, Israeli authorities permitted West Bankers and Gazans married to Israeli citizens—almost all Arab—to enter Israel, then granted them permanent residency. In one example, the wife of Ahmed

Tibi, a former Israeli Arab advisor to Yasir Arafat and currently a member of the Israeli parliament, moved to Israel and received citizenship. In another notable example, the three sisters (Kholidia, Laila, and Sabah) of Hamas leader Ismail Haniyeh married Israeli Muslim men and moved in the 1970s from Gaza to Tel Sheva, a mainly Bedouin town. "In a small community like ours there were not enough women to go round, so some of the men would go and look for wives elsewhere," explained a relative. Compounding the irony, they became Israeli citizens and some of their children served in the Israeli army.

Eventually, Israeli authorities realized that this seemingly minor humanitarian gesture had effectively opened the spigot to large movement of peoples, prompting the 2003 "Citizenship and Entry into Israel Law" that blocked such spouses from entering the country.

Beneficiaries of goodwill gestures. Ironically, the daughter of Ahmed Qurei, a top PLO negotiator, received an Israeli identification card on marrying a Jerusalemite after her father met with Israel's foreign minister, suggesting that this favor was intended to win his goodwill.

PA fighters. In 2007, the Fatah vs. Hamas fighting in Gaza prompted as many as 1,000 Fatah fighters to seek refuge in Israel; one of them, waiting at the border with his wife and children, explained to a reporter, "We cannot live in Gaza. Even if I have to sleep here for a year, I will."

Criminals. Salah Tarif, a Druze government minister for Arab affairs in the Labor government, was convicted in 2004 of "facilitating a bribe and breach of trust" for taking money to endorse the fictitious marriage between a Russian immigrant and a Palestinian criminal, enabling the latter to obtain Israeli citizenship.

Persecutees. In the West Bank and Gaza, conviction for sodomy brings a three- to ten-year jail term, and gay men tell of being tortured by the PA police. Some head for Israel where one estimate finds 300 of them, mostly males. Donatella Rovera of Amnesty International comments, "Going to Israel is a one-way ticket, and once there, their biggest problem is possibly being sent back." The West Bank Christian population has collapsed under PA rule, with many emigrants moving next door to Israel. Atheists who go public with their views quickly find life unbearable under Palestinian rule and often flee to Israel. The list goes on, including many disfavored groups.

Informants. Israeli intelligence depends on a wide network of informants, many of them Bedouin; when exposed or in danger of exposure, they may get moved to Israel. In perhaps the largest-scale operation of this sort, in 2005, as Israeli forces withdrew from Gaza, they evacuated about 250 of their agents from the village of Dahaniya in Gaza for resettlement in Israel.

In the aggregate, these indications point to many eastern Jerusalemites, West Bankers, and Gazans aware of the catastrophe of rejectionism and wanting to cast their lot with Israel. Palestinians who move show an appreciation for Israel that more than balances the horrid things said about it by their chieftains, even when those chieftains are their brother.

ISRAELIS TURN TO VICTORY

After the strategic fluff of the Oslo Era, trends are looking up for Israel. Voters support victory and leaders talk about it, especially after October 7.

• • •

Israeli public opinion. Repeated polling of Jewish Israelis finds wide but shallow support for Israel defeating the Palestinians: enthusiasm in the abstract, but hesitation when reminded of the short-term price. Also, the Left-Right divide presents challenges. Surveys conducted over five separate years found these results:

2017. A majority wants to push Palestinians into recognizing that the conflict is over and establish that Israel won. Fifty-eight percent agree that "A peace agreement with the Palestinians will only be possible once the Palestinian leadership recognizes the fact that it has been defeated in its struggle against Israel." But views are deeply polarized, with 69 percent on the Right agreeing and only 16 percent on the Left.

2018. Again, 58 percent of Jewish Israelis agrees with two statements: "It will only be possible to reach a peace agreement with the Palestinians when they recognize they have lost their war against Israel" and "Despite Israel's many victories over the Palestinians, most Palestinians continue to think they can eliminate the Jewish state of Israel." Fully 65 percent agree that: "None of the military conflicts to date with the Palestinians have produced an Israeli victory or a decisive result, and therefore the Israeli-Palestinian conflict perseveres." An even larger number, 70 percent, hold that "is it necessary for the Palestinian Authority to recognize Israel as the Jewish state before Israel agrees to continue negotiations with it." And 77 percent are ready, the next time Hamas attacks from Gaza or Hezbollah from Lebanon, to "Let the IDF win," meaning they want Israeli military operations to continue until the other side recognizes it has lost.

2019. A strikingly larger majority of Jewish Israelis support once-marginal ideas about a strong Israel defeating the Palestinians.

- 70 percent agrees that "It is time to stop managing the conflict and begin winning it."
- 76 percent agrees that "Negotiations with the Palestinians should take place only after they consistently show they accept Israel."
- 79 percent agrees that "Israel's security establishment is too timid vis-à-vis the Palestinians."
- 82 percent say the Israeli government is "too soft" in its policies toward Hamas.
- 82 percent agrees that "Palestinian rejection of Israel is the source of the conflict."
- 84 percent say that it is somewhat or very important "to achieve victory in the Israeli-Palestinian conflict." (Of that number, 58 percent deem it very important, 26 percent somewhat important.)
- 91 percent agrees that "Palestinians will benefit when they stop making war on Israel."

When 79 percent say that Israel's semi-sacrosanct security establishment is "too timid" and 82 percent say the government is "too soft," change is afoot.

But this exasperation does not automatically translate into policy preferences. When asked, "How do you define an Israeli victory in the Israeli-Palestinian conflict?" a mere 32 percent say, "Palestinians [must] give up their goal of eliminating the State of Israel." An equal number call for a peace agreement with the Palestinians to end the conflict—a reversion to the Oslo formula. Asked for their preference for ending the Palestinian-Israeli conflict, just 41 percent opt for "Palestinians giving up their dream of eliminating Israel" and only 49 percent consider the government "too soft" on the PA. These figures point to a sense among Jewish Israelis that Palestinian aggression must be more actively confronted, without agreeing on what that entails.

2021. Fully 70 percent of Jewish Israelis agree that, "There can be no deals with terrorist organizations, only defeat. Israel must use all its military, diplomatic and economic means to crush Hamas' will to continue fighting." Sentiment for this view is growing, as shown by the fact that only 54 percent of respondents agreed with this statement in January 2020; a 16 percent increase in sixteen months is noteworthy. These answers point to strong support in the abstract for Israel Victory and Palestinian defeat. The same 82 percent agree that, "There can be no appeasing Hamas; only by defeating it unequivocally can we bring this conflict to an end" and more generally on the importance "for Israel to defeat its enemies," not just Palestinians.

But then comes the kicker: Those lofty 70 and 82 percentages drop to 48 percent when respondents are reminded that crushing Hamas will lead to "a raised intensity of attacks on the home front and a possible significant loss of Israeli lives." They further descend to 37 percent when asked about Israel taking over Gaza "to root out Hamas once and for all." When asked about the main goal of a future round of fighting with Hamas, only 21 percent seek to break Hamas' will to continue to fight. This discrepancy implies that while roughly 80 percent of Jewish Israelis seek to defeat Hamas and other enemies, only about half that number are willing to pay the concomitant price.

2023. A poll taken ten days after October 7 found extraordinary support for the destruction of Hamas and for a ground operation to achieve this. Asked: "What should be Israel's primary objective" in the current war, 70 percent of the public answered to "eliminate Hamas," 15 percent answered to "secure the unconditional release of captives held by Hamas" and 13 percent "disarm Hamas completely." Given the option of a ground operation in Gaza to eradicate Hamas or avoiding a ground operation in favor another way to deal with Hamas, 68 percent chose the former and 25 percent the latter.

A survey of surveys reveals an ambivalence between wanting to achieve victory and a reluctance to pay the price for it. This points to the need for leadership to educate the public about the nature of warfare and how conflicts end, explaining that the pain required in decisively defeating Palestinians will ultimately prove a lesser price than a conflict without end.

• • •

Talking victory pre October 7. As public opinion shifts, so do Israeli leaders. Politicians, military officers, and others break with placation and become voluble on Israel needing to win. But how seriously should one take their statements?

Politicians. Uzi Landau, who filled various ministerial positions, called for victory in the Oslo Era, when doing so was a near taboo. In 2004, he stated that, "When you're in a war you want to win the war." When Israeli military officials speak, he added in 2009, "you don't want to hear things like 'quiet equals quiet.' You want them to speak in terms of victory."

Long-time Prime Minister Benjamin Netanyahu endorsed victory in several contexts: "We will succeed for Israel's victory." Israel, he stated, would not be deterred "from a struggle against those who strive for our annihilation. If we're required to defend ourselves, we will rise to the challenge and ensure Israel's victory." While visiting Gujarat, India, he proclaimed: "Jai Hind, Jai Bharat, Jai Israel" (Victory to India, victory to Israel). During one long, late-evening parliamentary debate, he whiled away the time reading John David Lewis' 2010 book, *Nothing Less than Victory: Decisive Wars and the Lessons of History*, an analysis (cited in Part III) arguing for victory in war.

The president and prime minister of Israel both emphasized victory in their April 2023 Holocaust remembrance speeches. Isaac Herzog celebrated Israel's existence as a seventy-five-year-long victory over Nazism. Netanyahu argued that despite the Nazi destruction, the people of Israel achieved a "unique victory," one revealed in many ways but especially by "a free, vibrant, democratic and high-achieving" Israel reaching its seventy-fifth anniversary. But the task is not over: "The victory of the past alone does not guarantee the victory of the future. The victory of the future requires constant determination and an uncompromising fight." Only by sustaining the spirit of the Warsaw Ghetto "will we continue to ensure Israel's victory."

Pre-October 7, no Israeli politician talked as often about Israel Victory as Naftali Bennett.

Naftali Bennett appears to be the Israeli politician who spoke most often of victory before October 7.

- As education minister in 2018, he complained that Israel stopped winning, demanding that it "start winning again," adding that, "When Israel decides to win, we will win."
- Out of government in 2019, he criticized former chief of staff and new political leader Benny Gantz for settling for "a tie" in the 2014 Gaza war, and not going for a decisive victory. Still out of government, he endorsed a Jabotinsky-style victory: "Israel's victory means taking away the capability of our enemies to harm us. I don't think there is anything that we can do to make them accept us or want us; we have to defeat them, and then they will understand that we are here to stay forever, and we have to disarm them from the ability to hurt us."
- As defense minister in 2020, he commented approvingly on a new military plan that, by "overcoming the enemy and bringing victory…puts the principle of victory back at the top of the list of priorities."

- As defense minister in 2021, he emotionally blessed the troops with "Strengthen the hands of those who defend our holy land, grant them deliverance, and adorn them in a mantle of victory."
- As prime minister in 2022: "The south [of Israel] and its region are greatly in demand, with new families coming and new houses being built—that is the true picture of victory."

Other Israeli politicians also spoke up. UN Ambassador Danny Danon asked, "What's wrong with Palestinian surrender? Surrender is the recognition that, in a contest, staying the course will prove costlier than submission." Former defense minister Liberman wanted to battle Hamas until it "loses the will to fight." Future minister Oded Forer correctly generalized that, "Wars have historically ended when one side wins and one loses." Deputy speaker of the Knesset Evgeny Sova complained that in Israel,

> terms like "victory" and "decisive win" have been replaced by a far milder and more elusive terminology of "deterrence," "containment," and "painful blow." That discourse must change and, with it, the goals. Israel must only go to war if it is determined to win a decisive victory and vanquish the enemy.

The Noam party stated that it "will work to make a government that requires the defense establishment to restore the value of victory as a central value of the IDF, in the education of commanders, in command training and in the considerations of building military and manpower." Yossi Dagan, head of the Samaria Regional Council, called on the government to "embark on a determined [military] operation that ends in victory," meaning "a decisive victory—certainly not a surgical strike. It is no longer possible to be satisfied with partial victories."

Israeli politicians are not always consistent. Reuven Rivlin, the president of Israel, has stated that: "An Israel that initiates is an Israel that wins" and a free people need "love of the homeland, dedication to mission, aiming for victory, comradeship, purpose, personal example and the purity of weapons." But at other times, he has offered an anti-victory point of view: "Ending decades of conflict requires firstly bringing people together, creating partnerships and strengthening shared interests." Which is it?

Military officers. IDF officers, mostly reserve but those also on active duty, increasingly spoke of operational and strategic victory. A trio of former chiefs of staff (Benny Gantz, Moshe Ya'alon, and Gabi Ashkenazi) joined forces in 2019 to form the Blue and White party, which called for tougher action. Major General (res.) Gershon Hacohen counsels political leaders not to let military leaders usurp their decisions.

Already in 2002, IDF Chief of Staff Moshe Ya'alon defined victory as "the very deep internalization by the Palestinians that terrorism and violence will not defeat us, will not make us fold." As the Oslo Accords fell into discredit, others picked up this theme. Former IDF Chief of Staff Benny Gantz published four videos titled "Only the strong win." Former Deputy Chief of Staff Uzi Dayan called on the armed forces "to return to the path of [tactical] victory" and to give the country's leaders the means to achieve strategic victory. Brigadier General (res.) Amir Avivi argued that Israel needs to "seek a victory over Palestinian violent rejectionism… it must make plans for victory. Only victory has ensured the endurance of the Jewish state." Brigadier General (res.) Moshe "Chico" Tamir stated that "achieving victory is not a political question. It's a matter of Israel's survival in this neighborhood." Even IDF Deputy Chief of Staff Yair Golan, infamous for comparing Israel to Nazi Germany, avowed that "Israel has no choice than to defeat its enemies."

IDF Chief of Staff Aviv Kochavi spoke often of victory. In April 2020, for example, he addressed Israel's enemies: "The IDF is there: ready, powerful, and aggressive. We will be there for every mission, prepared, and determined. We see victory as the only way to achieve our goal." In December 2020, he stressed victory as an essential component of military values. "We must see victory as a value. We must see it as a compass that guides us in every activity. The concept of victory isn't only applicable to war. It is an essential part of the soldier's identity and a unit's operation every day."

Others. The idea of victory spread. As media personality Ayalet Mitsch correctly notes, "even left-leaning Israelis think it's time to win again." Martin Sherman of the Israel Institute for Strategic Studies argued that the Palestinian-Israeli conflict "must be conceptualized as one between two irreconcilable collectives, with mutually exclusive foundational narratives.… Therefore, for one to prevail, the other must be prevailed upon. With antithetical and mutually exclusive core objectives, only one can emerge victorious, with the other vanquished." Israeli journalist Ron Ben-Yishai wrote that, "For the State of Israel to win, it must do all things, or some things, that will make it clear to the other side Hezbollah, Hamas, [Palestinian Islamic] Jihad or Iran—that it has been defeated." "We want victory!" proclaimed a sign when Israelis engaged in a revenge attack on Huwara, a West Bank town, in March 2023.

That victory and defeat became a topic for debate in Israel constituted a major step forward.

• • •

Talking victory post-October 7. Discussion of victory surged after the massacre.

Between October 7 and year's end, Netanyahu spoke at least twenty-one times of winning, victory, clear victory, total victory, complete victory, and absolute victory. He promised a message that would echo for generations, keeping to the highest standards of international law, winning for the sake of the civilized world, and continuing until the end, however long that takes.

Many others in government followed suit. Defense Minister Yoav Gallant quoted himself informing President Joe Biden that Israel's victory "is essential for us and for the United States." To his soldiers, Gallant declared, "I am responsible for bringing victory." Smotrich, the minister of finance, announced the halt "of all budgetary outlays and redirected them to one thing only: Israel's victory." He called the goal of Israel's war with Hamas to be "a crushing victory." Benny Gantz, a member of the War Cabinet, deemed it "the time for resilience and victory." Mark Regev, a senior adviser to the prime minister, called Israel's eventual victory "a victory for the people of Gaza and the entire Middle East, a victory for moderation and civilization."

Military leaders toed the line:

- Major General Yaron Finkelman, head of the Southern Command, to troops: "Southern Command stations, commander is speaking. We are launching an attack on Hamas and the terror groups in the Gaza Strip. Our goal is one: victory. No matter how long the fighting will be, how difficult, there is no other result but victory. We will fight professionally and powerfully in light of the IDF values we were raised on. Chief among them is sticking to the mission and striving for victory."

- Lieutenant Colonel Tomer Greenberg: "The enemy will challenge us but I'm sure victory will be ours."

Many other Israeli voices spoke out as well:

- Ohad Tal, member of parliament: "We will stand like an iron fist in front of you until victory."
- Amotz Asa-El, journalist: "At this stage of what will surely be a protracted and excruciating war, all our minds, resources, and efforts should be aimed at one thing, and at this one thing only: victory."
- Uri Dagon, journalist: "We will emerge victorious."
- Naftali Bennett: "Israel Victory is our only option."
- David Horovitz, editor, *Times of Israel*: Israel is in "a war that simply has to be won…the IDF…is not looking for victory pictures. It is looking for victory."
- Douglas Altabef, chairman of Im Tirtzu: "Netanyahu, Gallant and Gantz…. Bring us the victory that we, your citizens, demand. We will accept nothing less."
- Zvi Yehezkeli, analyst: "We need victory."
- The Gevurah Forum, an organization of families who lost relatives in the war on Hamas: "We trust in our forces to bring victory, with God's help. The nation is strong and its spirit is resolved, both on the front and at home. The citizens and heroic soldiers are determined to reach total victory…. There is no substitute for victory! All of Hamas must die, to the last of them."

Much favors Israel—Arab states retreating, the Palestinians faltering, Israelis rediscovering victory. Before moving on to how it can win, however, a problem needs addressing: that of Israeli overconfidence.

After Oct. 7, signs calling for victory proliferated in Israel. Top: At a shopping center. Bottom: A sushi restaurant.

11

ISRAELI OVERCONFIDENCE

IN ADDITION TO ENRICHMENT AND placation, already much discussed, the Jewish state suffers from an overconfidence that followed on its impressive economic and cultural triumphs after 1993. This led to three problems. During the first half of this period, or the Oslo Era (1993–2008), success encouraged a belief that Israel could reach decisions on its own, ignoring Palestinian views and actions. In the second half, or the Netanyahu Era (2009–), success spawned a brashness about Israel's strength in the world. Also roughly coterminous with the Netanyahu Era, since Hamas' seizure of power in Gaza in 2007, success spawned credence in the notion of "buying quiet."

MAKING THE KEY DECISIONS

New strengths led Israelis during the Oslo Era to believe that they could unilaterally end the conflict with Palestinians on their own terms, then impose peaceful relations by creating a State of Palestine. Israelis deluded themselves into thinking that they made the key decisions of war and peace; in fact, most of these were made in Ramallah, the de facto PA capital.[1] Foreign Minister Shimon Peres spoke for many of his countrymen when he airily dismissed Palestinian statements with "These are only words. Let them talk," a deeply condescending remark that encapsulated

1 Looking at Israel's major rounds of war confirms the point that its enemies make the key decisions. Hostilities with Arab states occurred five times (1948–1949, 1956, 1967, 1969–1970, and 1973); with the Palestinians seven times (1982, 1987–1993, 2000–2005, 2008–2009, 2012, 2014, and 2021); and with Hezbollah one time (2006). Israel initiated just four of those thirteen rounds (1956, 1967, 1982, and 2006).

an arrogant assumption that the mood, views, and actions of the other side hardly mattered.

• • •

Israel's success in 2000. Before the 1990s, Israel had been in constant danger; then came the safest era of its existence, with prosperity as a bonus. The Soviet Union imploded, the Arab-state threat diminished, while neither the Iranian nuclear buildup nor the invigorated Left had yet fully emerged. A snapshot of the country in early 2000, in the middle of the Oslo Era, helps to understand the sources of its overconfidence.

As the only country in the Middle East participating in the much-bruited "revolution in military affairs"—the application of high-tech to armaments—Israel built so great a lead in planes and tanks that Arab states had already conceded they could no longer compete. Peace treaties with two neighbors, Egypt and Jordan, and the near-universal expectation that negotiations with Syria would soon end with another treaty, created considerable optimism. Enemies like Iran turned their attention to forms of warfare lower (individual violent attacks) and higher (weapons of mass destruction). In those arenas, too, Israel was far from helpless, with formidable counterinsurgency capabilities, a missile-defense system in the works, and a major nuclear arsenal.

Israel had a powerful regional ally in Türkiye. A vestigial anti-Iraq commonality loosely tied the interests of Jerusalem and Tehran. More distant diplomatic ties flourished, with growing ties to China and India, and a warm, deep, personal, and reciprocal connection to the United States and its president. Thanks to Israel's position of strength, Prime Minister Ehud Barak could speak of an "end to wars" and his country finally being accepted as a permanent presence by its neighbors, sentiments widely echoed by politicians and the media.

Economically, Israel in 2000 enjoyed a per capita income of $18,000, placing it between Spain and Canada—in other words, in the big leagues. Better yet, it had shown a very impressive annual growth rate during the previous decade. "Silicon Wadi" had made the country a high-tech giant, with a computer and an internet sector larger in absolute terms than that of any other country in the world other than the United States. Demographically, a birth rate of 2.6 children per woman among Israeli Jews made it the highest in the West even as the country attracted significant immigration.

Articulating a general boisterousness, Barak called Israel a "modern and prosperous villa in the middle of the jungle."

Politically, Israel benefited from a lively and robust civic culture in which everyone had his say and no one bowed to politicians. However colorful and argumentative the public forum, when it came to key security issues, the major parties shared much common ground. In the 1999 elections, for example, the two candidates for prime minister, Barak and Netanyahu, differed in tone and pace but hardly in the substance of diplomacy with the Palestinians: yes, Palestinians should do more to live up to their promises; but no, their failings do not justify cutting off negotiations.

• • •

Going it alone. Multiple agreements with the PA, Israel's "partner for peace," suggested relations were going in the right direction. As the stronger party, Jerusalem pointedly refrained from demanding that the PA fulfill its many obligations, permitting it not to turn over criminals, not to cease inciting violence, and not to restrict the size of its armed forces. Stating that the PA violated every written promise made to Israel hardly exaggerates. Very few Israelis minded that the PA's logo brazenly showed a map of "Palestine" replacing Israel. To this and much else, the overconfident Israeli body politic paid almost no heed. An Israel so much mightier and more advanced than its Palestinian enemy could afford to overlook such peccadillos.

As Israel's edgy, on-the-go populace built a modern, democratic, affluent, and powerful country, it lost patience with the old, graduated policy of deterrence (defined as avoiding war by making it too expensive and painful for an enemy). That felt boring, difficult, erratic, expensive, frustrating, harsh, humiliating, indirect, passive, reactive, slow, and tedious. Rather than wear down an opponent, Israelis demanded a policy that boldly initiated. Of course, it was Israelis, specifically historians Yair Hirschfeld and Ron Pundak, who initiated the Oslo process.

Israelis experimented with such statecraft exotica as "painful concessions" and unilateral withdrawals. The Right developed elaborate schemes to finesse victory, the Center experimented with appeasement and unilateralism, and the Left wallowed in guilt and self-recrimination. Israelis relaxed their vigilance, permitted their enemies to create a quasi-governmental structure (the PA) and to amass a hoard of armaments (Hezbollah acquired an estimated 15,000 rockets in southern Lebanon). If their little, spunky country could repeatedly over decades beat far larger armed forces belonging to powerful states, what sort of threat were the Palestinians, lacking a real economy or a serious military?

Israelis largely ignored that Palestinians had revived an earlier ambition to destroy Israel, they underestimated the Islamist surge then in full swing, and they overlooked burgeoning worldwide leftist hostility. Israelis followed their own road to peace, and no "partners," however hostile, could deflect them from it. They hardly noticed that these many enemies lost their fears, coming to see Israel as a fatigued country and a paper tiger.

Paradoxically, overconfidence led both to an indulgence in expressions of fatigue and to a radical denunciation of Zionism.

• • •

Fatigue. Previously straightjacketed by a sense of emergency, Israelis in the Oslo Era permitted themselves finally to express public irritation about an unremitting state of war. Self-confidence translated into open complaints: enough with conscription, enough with huge military expenses, enough with military preparedness, enough with war. Time for a peace dividend. Yearning to close down an atavistic tribal war, they demanded to live like other Westerners; who else in the modern world faces an antediluvian enemy obsessed with harming it, the constant loss of life, the fear of sudden violence on the streets? As one Israeli put it to me, "My grandfather, father, myself, and my son have all fought the Arabs; I want to make sure my grandson does not also have to."

Israel's soaring economy gave many citizens a taste for the good life not easily reconciled with the patience, fortitude, and sacrifice needed to confront a tenacious enemy. Middle-aged Israeli men grumbled about going off to "play soldier" on reserve duty for several weeks a year, preferring to go to the office and increase their net worth, or enjoy what that net worth made possible. For those with an active social conscience, a number of long-deferred domestic problems—persistent poverty among Sephardim, Haredim (ultra-Orthodox Jews), and Arabs; a faulty educational system; worsening relations between secular and religious Israelis—seemed worthier of attention, and of state expenditure, than grappling ceaselessly with an incalcitrant opponent.

Many observers commented on this phenomenon. A reserve colonel summed up the mood with "the Israeli public is really tired of war." Future prime minister Ehud Barak noted the country's "accumulated weariness and cynicism." Israeli strategist Efraim Inbar wrote in 1996 how, "In recent years, Israeli society has shown signs of becoming increasingly beleaguered, war weary, and impatient for a 'solution' to the Arab-Israeli conflict.... Israeli society displays battle fatigue and clearly prefers butter to guns." Israeli philosopher Yoram Hazony famously called the Jews of Israel "an exhausted people, confused and without direction." Efraim Karsh wrote that "a militarily far stronger and economically more affluent Israeli society shows signs of fatigue and fragmentation and Palestinians appear to be on the offensive and holding their own."

Israel's enemies also watched and drew conclusions. In the pungent phrasing of Hezbollah's leader, Hassan Nasrallah, "Israel, which has both nuclear power and the strongest air force in the region, is weaker than a spider's web." But Israelis hardly noticed this mounting disrespect.

• • •

Switching sides. Success and optimism opened another new freedom, especially attractive to the elite: adopting the Palestinian narrative. Breaking loose from prior restraints, some leftists sought to escape the moral opprobrium that Israel suffers at the United Nations, in Western academic circles, and in editorial boardrooms by engaging in an orgy of self-flagellation. As they embraced such internationally popular policies as unilateral withdrawal and a State of Palestine, they lost all sense of comparison or context, ignored the enemy's intentions, and blamed themselves for Palestinian misdeeds.

For example, the school of "new historians" found the Jewish state guilty of an "original sin"—the alleged dispossession of Palestine's native inhabitants—that cast doubt on the country's legitimacy. "Post-Zionists" characterized Zionism as a nineteenth-century solution for twenty-first-century problems, an outdated and parochial ideology, if not a racist one, and no longer a proper basis of the country's public life. Some went further and denounced their country or even renounced their citizenship.

Such ideas, first incubated in prestigious fora and leading universities, became the stuff of educational textbooks and television documentaries, spreading throughout society. In the 2000 school year, ninth-graders no longer learned that Israel's war of independence in 1948–1949 was a battle of the few against the many but, to the contrary, that the Jews enjoyed military superiority over the Arabs. They also learned that many Palestinians fled the country in those war years not to clear the way for invading Arab armies expecting to be on their march to victory, but out of well-founded fears of Jewish brutality and terror.

Defection to the Palestinian side did win limited plaudits abroad, offering a way to be seen as "good Israelis" who should not be criticized or boycotted; it also offered a chance to flaunt a moral superiority over "bad Israelis." The process had a familiar feel, updating the earlier practice of Jews who, like the medieval scholar Moses Sephardi, converted to Christianity, then denounced their former religion and co-religionists. Now, comparing Israel to Nazi Germany became the rite of passage. Anyone—intellectual, politician, soldier—could engage in this outrage. A few examples:

Meron Benvenisti (1934–2020) served as deputy mayor of Jerusalem, wrote for the country's most prestigious newspaper, and taught at a leading university. *New York Times* columnist Thomas L. Friedman anointed him "the Middle East expert to whom Middle East experts go for advice." And what did Benvenisti advise? That Israel's treatment of the Palestinians constituted "legal violence…used indiscriminately against a dominated and defenseless ethnic group" comparable to the apartheid system in South Africa. He variously deemed Israeli rule over the West Bank and Gaza as "macabre," "absurd," "ludicrous," and "harsh." He called Israel "a master-nation democracy; in German, a *Herrenvolk* democracy. We are a country that behaves like a full-blooded democracy, but we have a group of serfs, the Arabs, to whom we do not apply democracy."

Avraham Burg (b. 1955) presents a more spectacular case. The son of a leading religious nationalist politician, he filled a great number of prestigious positions before the age of fifty: paratrooper, graduate of the Hebrew University, member of parliament, speaker of parliament, candidate for prime minister, chairman of the Jewish Agency, and Israel's interim president. Despite this illustrious and patriotic record, he switched sides. In his new role, he argued against Israel as defender of the Jewish people and wrote a book on the legacy of the Holocaust that included passages like this:

> We will never forgive the Arabs, for they are allegedly just like the Nazis, worse than the Germans. We have displaced our anger and revenge from one people to another, from an

> old foe to a new adversary, and so we allow ourselves to live comfortably with the heirs of the German enemy—representing convenience, wealth and high quality—while treating the Palestinians as whipping boys to release our aggression, anger and hysteria, of which we have plenty.

Burg found parallels between pre-Nazi Germany and contemporary Israel, both being paranoid, over-militarized, and inequitable. He joined the communist Hadash party while dispensing such rhetorical gems as Israel "is not a democracy, and all that remains is a hollow citizenship."

Major General Yair Golan (b. 1962), the IDF's deputy chief of staff, while still in uniform, speaking at the Massuah Institute for Holocaust Studies, no less, stated: "If there is one thing that frightens me about the memory of the Holocaust, it is identifying the revolting trends that occurred in Europe as a whole, and in Germany in particular, some 70, 80 and 90 years ago, and finding evidence of those trends here, among us, in 2016." Note, again, that he spoke this as the country's second-highest military officer at a Holocaust center.[2]

Israeli novelist Aharon Megged remarked in 1994 of Israel's Left: "We have witnessed a phenomenon which probably has no parallel in history: An emotional and moral identification by the majority of Israel's intelligentsia, and its print and electronic media, with people committed to our annihilation." So widespread had this identification become, Israeli-American analyst Meyrav Wurmser saw in it "a crisis of identity and values that strikes at the basic components and elements of [Israel's] identity: Judaism and nationalism."

Such moral preening brings to mind a Jewish joke:

> Moved by the solemnity of the Yom Kippur holiday, a rabbi threw himself on the synagogue floor, crying out, "Oh Lord, before You, I am nothing!" The synagogue president, inspired by this example, threw himself beside the rabbi, crying out, "Oh Lord, before You, I am nothing!" The town fool, also inspired, threw himself on the floor, crying out, "Oh Lord, before You,

2 Invoking the Nazis revived in early 2023, but now in the context of domestic politics (judicial reform especially). In this spirit, former Prime Minister Ehud Barak retweeted a video that compared Netanyahu to Hitler.

> I am nothing!" To which, the president nudged the rabbi and whispered, "Look who thinks he is nothing."

Self-flagellation, in other words, is not always what it seems to be. No one ever said that being Israeli is a simple matter.

INVULNERABILITY

When the Oslo-era fallacy that Israel makes the key decisions finally collapsed under its own implausible weight around 2008, Israelis awoke from years of wishful thinking and acknowledged Oslo's disastrous handiwork. They did not replace it, however, with a more sensible doctrine but with another conceit, this time a sense of invulnerability to outside pressure. Again, overconfidence followed a burst of success during which Israel made impressive economic and military advances.

• • •

Israel's success in 2023. Israel has an outsized military presence that includes powerful conventional force (ships, tanks, planes), a cutting-edge military-industrial complex, and many nuclear weapons. To take one example, the fifth-generation fighter aircraft: Its builder, Lockheed Martin, proudly informs that "Israel became the first [foreign] country to select the F-35 through the United States government's Foreign Military Sales process" in 2010. In 2016, Israel took the first foreign delivery and in 2017 it launched the first foreign operationally capable F-35 fleet.

The 2020 Abraham Accords with the United Arab Emirates, Bahrain, Morocco, and Sudan, with Saudi Arabia possibly following suit, built on Israel's 1979 peace treaty with Egypt and 1994 treaty with Jordan. Together, they confirm that Arab states no longer pose an existential threat. That all four of its immediate state neighbors—Egypt, Jordan, Syria, and Lebanon—have since 2011 faced major domestic problems further enhances that sense. The military balances of old, comparing the number of fighter jets and tanks on each side, have disappeared, presumably for good.

Israeli products—armaments, high-tech, medical supplies, agricultural methods, water technology—have found a global market. The Global Startup Ecosystem Report of June 2023 placed Tel Aviv at No. 5 in the world, following just Silicon Valley, New York City, London, and

Los Angeles. Natural gas production brought unprecedented financial and security stability. The Organization for Economic Cooperation and Development hailed Israel's economy as registering a "remarkable macro-economic and fiscal performance." The International Monetary Fund commended Israel's "remarkable economic performance."

Lopsided comparisons with Palestinians drive the point home. Israel's GDP of $482 billion is twenty-seven times bigger than the West Bank's and Gaza's $18 billion. Its per capita income of $55,000 is fourteen times higher than the latter's $3,700. The military contrast is yet more extreme. Global Firepower ranks Israel's armed forces as the eighteenth-strongest in the world out of 142; the Palestinians do not make the list. Their military innovation amounts to home-made explosives.

• • •

A sense of invulnerability. Palestinian rejectionism once weighed heavily on Israelis, but by the Netanyahu Era the unfinished business of winning Palestinian acceptance had become an almost non-issue. Inured by a lifetime of insults, Israelis tend to slough off delegitimization as business as usual, scorning Palestinians as impotent whiners, their vituperation dismissed as background noise. Rather than proclaim fatigue or switch sides, as they did previously, leading lights now express defiance. This takes two primary forms: dismissing the Palestinian challenge and assuming that the outside world needs Israel.

Scorning Palestinians. Israel's strengths make the unfinished business of winning over Palestinians rankle. Why must the Jewish people, with 4,000 years of history, win the favor of an opponent whose identity came into existence in 1920, and then, only in response to colonial arrangements? Why should dynamic Israel have to win the favor of its static neighbor? Already in 1977, Menachem Begin declared: "I don't need Palestinian recognition for my right to exist." Abba Eban echoed his view in 1981: "Nobody does Israel any service by proclaiming its 'right to exist.'" Benjamin Netanyahu added in 2007, "Our existence does not depend on the willingness of the Palestinians to make peace with us" and Naftali Bennett in 2018, the Jewish nation has "been around for 4,000 years and these folks [Palestinians] just a few decades. We're going to win."

The "peace process" that dominated the country's politics for decades receded; by 2013, only 10 percent of Jewish Israelis considered those negotiations the top priority. It played almost no role in the five Israeli elections between 2020 and 2022. For most Israelis, debating the fine points of Palestinian diplomacy became, a former Israeli prime ministerial aide commented, as irrelevant as "debating the color of the shirt you will wear when landing on Mars." This lack of interest leaves Palestinian developments somewhat neglected. As Emily Rose of Reuters understatedly observes, "In the greater scheme of Israeli media, there's not much television coverage of Palestinians." Summing up the general mood, Efraim Inbar dismisses Palestinians as a "strategic nuisance."

But scorn of the Palestinian issue makes sense if one looks only at violence, as Palestinians threaten less than Hezbollah and much less than the Islamic Republic of Iran. They present a danger that Hezbollah and Tehran do not, however, flogging an incalculably harmful anti-Zionist narrative to all the world. Israel's leaders downplay Palestinian anti-Zionism on the world stage, even though complaints by West Bank, Gaza, and eastern Jerusalem residents of ghastly maltreatment generates a toxic global anger. Like it or not, Palestinian acceptance must be a Zionist priority. The Palestinians and Iran pose opposite dangers to Israel: narrative, not violence; violence, not narrative.

Indispensable Israel. Whereas Israelis take very seriously mainstream Western opinion (as documented in "Western criticism," pp. 104-06) they tend to dismiss the international implications of anti-Zionism, believing the world's need for what Israel supplies renders it nearly irrelevant. In particular, hostile opinions concern less than previously because the BDS campaign has so far failed significantly to dent Israel's international trade.

Take the small but revealing case of academics: members of the Middle East Studies Association of North America (MESA), a professorial guild, by a 768 to 167 vote, 82 percent to 18 percent, "voted in favor of a resolution endorsing the Palestinian call for boycotts, divestment, and sanctions [BDS] of Israel as a way to hold the government accountable for ongoing human rights violations." In earlier times, this would have stung, but coming in 2022, it evinced scorn. Eyal Zisser, the vice rector of Tel Aviv University and himself a leading historian of the region, dismissed MESA and its scholars. For Israelis, it is "not as important as it used to be…they need us more than we need them…. Academically, as far as Israel is concerned, I don't think that this resolution has a real impact."

But this is wishful thinking. It is no small thing when the main body of Middle Eastern specialists in the United States and Canada—those who study the region for a living, who shape students' understanding of it, who influence policy toward it—have overwhelmingly adopted a position that aims (in the assessment of the Anti-Defamation League) "to dismantle the Jewish state and end the right to Jewish national self-determination on any portion of this contested land." MESA's members do not need Israel more than the other way around. To believe so amounts to overconfidence bordering on the negligent.

More broadly, just because Israel is not currently paying a heavy price for anti-Zionism does not protect it in the future. Should the West turn on Israel, the results would sting badly. Suffice to note that Vladimir Putin also thought Russia indispensable to the West, a not unreasonable assumption given that its economy is about four times bigger than Israel's and provides such essential commodities as oil, gas, wheat, semi-finished iron, nickel, and nitrogen-based fertilizers. In a matter of days in early 2022, however, Putin learned otherwise. Westerners outraged by Putin's invasion of Ukraine instantly and widely cut economic ties to Russia; some 1,000 of 1,200 corporations curtailed operations. The playbook of near-total cut-off having been written, it serves as the ready model for dealing with an Israel seen as breaching Western norms vis-à-vis the Palestinians.

Cutting economic ties would have more devastating consequences for Israel than for Russia, given its greater Western orientation, its smaller size, and the unique pre-existing obloquy and hatred that Palestinians can direct against it. Palestinians enjoy the support of a vast hinterland beyond the West, primarily among Muslims and leftists, meaning most media and the great majority of educators, but also among dictators. Think Iran, Türkiye, Cuba, Venezuela, Brazil, and Chile, all of which gladly already do or would forego the economic benefits of doing business with Israel.

Also, the international arena has generally grown inhospitable to Israel. Already in 2012, Israeli analyst Evelyn Gordon observed that:

> No honest appraisal could deny that Israel's international standing has deteriorated since it signed the Oslo Accords in 1993. Anti-Israel boycotts, once confined to the Arab world, are now routine agenda items for universities, certain Western churches, and trade unions. Courts in several European countries have considered indicting Israeli officials for war crimes, and European polls routinely deem Israel a prime threat to world peace. References to Israel as an "apartheid state" have

> become commonplace, and academics and journalists openly question its very right to exist.

Commentators on the Israeli Left go too far, but they offer a useful corrective to the "we don't need Palestinian recognition" conceit. Yair Golan of "revolting trends" fame and then a member of the Knesset for Meretz, calls the Palestinian issue "much more important than the Iranian issue. This is where our fate will be decided, not in Tehran. And we are running away from it." American editor Leon Wieseltier even predicted in 2013 that, "Unless there is a solution to the Israeli-Palestinian conflict, there will not be a Jewish state for very long."

Israel may sell what the world wants, but Palestinians purvey their highly valued victimhood. The one owns the worlds of finance and trade, the other the international organizations and legal fora. This means that Israel must avoid raising tensions with its many enemies, be they individuals, NGOs, or governments. For all of Israel's economic and military strength, therefore, severe restraints on that power render its conflict with the Palestinians surprisingly balanced.

BUYING QUIET

The future commission that inevitably will analyze Israel's unpreparedness on October 7, will no doubt blame that surprise in large part on what the Israelis call a *konceptzia,* "a concept." The term emerged in the late 1960s when IDF planners argued that Egypt's Anwar el-Sadat would not go to war until 1974, when his military would have acquired the advanced Soviet fighter jets needed to take on the Jewish state's air force. Israel's Agranat Commission, which investigated how the Egyptians and Syrians surprised Israel in the Yom Kippur War of October 1973, largely blamed this konceptzia for a blindness to the preparations taking place before Israel's very eyes.

• • •

The new konceptzia. A headline published days before October 7 captured the new prevailing konceptzia: "IDF and Shin Bet call on government to continue economic activities with Gaza. Senior security officials ask political echelon to increase work permits for Gazans to maintain calm on the border." *Maintain calm*. As Eran Lerman explained, also just ahead of October 7:

> The ruling center-right in Israel takes a "conflict management" approach to the Palestinian issue. They prefer to leave open the prospect that resolution of the Israeli-Palestinian conflict may yet be possible one day, as the region changes and new leaders emerge. But until then, they believe, what Israel should do is ease tensions and improve living conditions for Palestinians in the West Bank and Gaza, while reserving the right to hit back at terrorist activity in a selective and intelligence-driven manner.

In brief, the new konceptzia, like the old one, assumed that the enemy would not attack. It held, David Makovsky of the Washington Institute for Near East Policy explains, that

> under the heavy burden of governing the Gaza Strip, Hamas would feel the need to prove itself through economic performance. Specifically, economic inducements towards Hamas would moderate its foundational belief that Israel is an illegitimate entity whose very existence must be extinguished and its citizens killed.

This Israeli konceptzia, Makovsky argues, at its core held that "Hamas was undergoing an organizational evolution in which it would now value even modest increases in living standards in Gaza. Economic advancement would bring calm, as it gave Hamas something to lose." Note the words "something to lose," which summarize the new konceptzia, a belief that Hamas could be bought off or tempered through enrichment; or what came to be called "buying quiet."

The konceptzia miraculously transformed blood-curdling Hamas threats into empty words. Thus, the security establishment ignored Fathi Hammad luridly announcing in 2019:

> We are sharpening the knives.... If we die it will be when we are killing you [Jews], and we will cut off your heads, Allah willing...We must attack every Jew on the planet—slaughter and kill.... I will die as I blow up and cut—what? The

> throats of the Jews and their legs. We will tear them to shreds, Allah willing.

Hamas and its allies counted on konceptzia-induced blindness. They practiced their military maneuvers for three years, then publicly posted videos of their training exercises, exercises that almost exactly anticipated the tactics Hamas used on October 7. For example, they drilled in plain sight of Israelis, holding a live-fire exercise of blasting through a mock wall and raiding a mock town, then posted a video of the drill. Hamas also let Israeli intelligence pick up its boastful conclusion to an exercise against a mock Israeli village: "We have completed the killing of everyone on the kibbutz."

Only by completely disregarding such statements could Aryeh Deri, a senior Haredi politician, admit after October 7 that he "never imagined that we were dealing with such murderers who are capable of acting with such cruelty." Only blinding arrogance explains how, as summarized by a major *New York Times* investigation, "Israel had no battle plan for a massive Hamas invasion." Avichai Brodetz, whose family was taken hostage by Hamas, vented bitter frustration at a Likud member of parliament for the ineptitude that allowed October 7:

> The army could easily have destroyed them, but the entire konceptzia of the IDF [was wrong]. Hamas understood this, and they were far more clever than we were. They carried out an exceptional operation, raped our women, and killed our children because the IDF was not there. This did not happen because of Hamas but because of the konceptzia you used. It would have been so easy to destroy Hamas with tanks and planes—but they simply weren't there.

The buying-quiet konceptzia spread widely, even among those living closest to Gaza. Hanan Dann, a member of a kibbutz devastated on October 7, explains:

> We were glad that workers from Gaza were coming to Israel with work permits to have jobs to meet Israelis, to see that we're not all "those devils." We all really believed that things are changing, that Hamas has maybe matured from being this terrorist group to be the grown-up taking responsibility for its

> people, worrying for its welfare. And that concept really blew up in our face.

• • •

Warnings ignored. Israelis who rejected the konceptzia met with arrogance, scorn, and exclusion.

Forewarnings from the signal intelligence Unit 8200 met with contempt from a senior IDF officer ("fantasies") who refused to act on them. Israeli defense analyst Yoav Limor reports how Unit 8200 acquired an "absolute gem" and "genuine gold mine" in 2022, a Hamas document titled "The Plan for Defeating the IDF Gaza Division." It "contained everything: the IDF's deployment (with a chilling level of detail) and the methods of contending with it, how to breach the border obstacle and to carry out the attack, as well as the targets and objectives during the attack and thereafter." Disseminated to "everybody," including in the IDF and political policymakers, no one can claim ignorance. Yet, a *New York Times* investigation found that Israeli military and intelligence officials "dismissed the plan as aspirational, considering it too difficult for Hamas to carry out."

The same happened with reports from the front lines. A noncommissioned officer specializing in Hamas military doctrine wrote three analyses warning of Hamas' plans, emphasizing that its exercises simulate an invasion across the border into Israeli residences and reporting that senior Hamas officials personally supervised the exercises; her warnings went up the hierarchy, only to be met with a dismissive response: "You are imagining it." When IDF lookouts warned of the situation along the Gaza border ahead of October 7, *The Jerusalem Post* reports, they "were told to stop bothering their commanders and even threatened with a court-martial." A lookout reported seeing suspicious activities just a day before the attack but commanders "discounted" her concerns, telling her "Hamas is just a bunch of punks, they won't do anything."

The head of IDF's Southern Command, Major General Eliezer Toledano, argued in November 2022 to attack Hamas before it assaulted Israel in roughly the manner it actually did eleven months later: "Somewhere down the line along the enemy's progress, there will be a point where we have to launch a pre-emptive attack." Of course, he was ignored. The head of the IDF intelligence unit charged with questioning IDF assessments and conceptions, reports the *Times of Israel*, "warned four times in the three weeks leading up to October 7 that the Gaza terror group could soon launch an attack"; to no avail.

National Security Minister Itamar Ben-Gvir complained that his calls for the assassination of Hamas leaders caused him to be barred from cabinet discussions. Itai Hoffman, the chairman of a security organization near the Gaza border, accused the government: "We warned you about the situation. How can it be that you all sat here and kept silent?... You have abandoned us." A kibbutz member pointed out that his community had only four rifles, adding: "We have been screaming for years." Yehiel Zohar, the mayor of a town near Gaza, complained that senior security officials belittled his warnings, complete with maps, infiltration routes, and defense plans, about hundreds of murderers entering his town and killing its residents: "Forget about it, it won't happen."

The level of obtuseness staggers.

To summarize: Israel's leadership ignored the Islamist and jihadi nature of Hamas, believing that Israel's economic strength, military superiority, and technical advancement had moderated Hamas, rendering it less dangerous; and that enrichment—more work permits in Israel, a larger fishing zone, outside funding—gave Hamas something to lose, making it disinclined to take chances.

• • •

Peres' dismissive "These are only words. Let them talk" summed up the Left's ignoring what Palestinians said and did during the Oslo Era. Inbar's derisive "strategic nuisance" remark summed up the Right's ignoring the Palestinian issue during the Netanyahu Era. "Forget about it, it won't happen" sums up the buying-quiet error. All three reflect arrogance and point to the commonality of illusion across eras and across the political spectrum.

Note the ironic switch in errors: The Left underestimated Palestinians during the Oslo Era, wrongly assuming it could push them to end hostilities. The Right underestimated Palestinians during the Netanyahu Era, wrongly focusing on their violence rather than their message. Both sides underestimated Hamas' determination and viciousness.

The reader may note an apparent contradiction in my messages: to Palestinians, "You are losing to a mighty Israel"; to Israelis, "You face an existential threat in the Palestinian anti-Zionist message." Their resolution lies in the fact that Palestinians threaten only because Israelis do not fully appreciate their menace, paying too much attention to violence and not enough to narrative. Were Israelis to wake up to it, they could dispatch this danger. Therein lies the goal of this book's final part.

PART VI

Victory Attained

From the inception of Zionism until today, an Israel that initiates is an Israel that is victorious. Now is the time to initiate; now is the time for victory.

—Reuven Rivlin, president of Israel, 2019

We will fight until absolute victory—however long that takes.

—Benjamin Netanyahu, prime minister of Israel, December 2023

They tried to kill us, we won, let's eat.

—Alan King, American comedian, on the Jewish holidays, ca. 1985

REJECTIONISM—THE NEGATION, BY ANY MEANS necessary, of Judaism, Jews, Zionism, and Israel—harms both parties to the Palestinian-Israeli conflict. Israelis lose by being subjected to unremitting campaigns of violence and delegitimization. Palestinians lose by being yoked to a malign ideology that shackles them to nihilism, oppression, and evil. Both parties need the collapse of rejectionism. Ironically, that would bring even greater benefits to Palestinians than to Israelis. Israel's Muslim citizens would also gain.

Rejectionism, however, will not collapse on its own. It must be broken. Only one party, Israel, can achieve this. Doing so will require major changes, indeed, a paradigm shift: Israel's traditional tools of enrichment and placation having failed, their legacy needs to be renounced and a new approach adopted. That means abandoning conciliation and returning to the eternal verities of war. I call this *Israel Victory.*[1] More negatively but more accurately, it consists of Palestinian defeat. Summing up: Palestinians lose, Israel wins.

Put in mathematical terms, Israel faces the challenge to increase the roughly 20 percent of non-hostile Palestinians (see "Accepting Israel," pp. 206-09) to 40 percent, then 60 percent, and more, with the goal that this cohort eventually, with Israel's assistance, wrests control of the Palestinian national movement from rejectionists and turns Palestinians into a normal people.

1 In a 2019 opinion poll, 46 percent of Jewish Israelis found the term "Israel victory" (Hebrew: *nitzachon Yisrael*) sensible or inspiring, as opposed to 22 percent who found it dangerous or terrifying.

12

DEFEATING THE PALESTINIANS

AS THIS BOOK'S TITLE SUGGESTS, my primary purpose is to urge Israelis to seek victory. I would happily leave matters there. Inevitably, however, questions arise about ways to accomplish that. With some reluctance—not wanting to divert primary attention from the goal of victory nor eager to spur an argument over methods—I offer answers to those questions in this chapter.

CHOOSING A STRATEGY

The Palestinian-Israeli conflict exemplifies the classic description of insanity: "Doing the same thing over and over again and expecting different results." Understandably, Israelis tend toward conciliation, preferring to traditional remedies rather than risk greater Palestinian hostility and international condemnation. But time has come for Israel to try a radically different approach—no longer conciliating, but winning.

Reduced to a single sentence, Israel can win by identifying hope as the enemy's center of gravity, relentlessly focusing on it through a mix of demoralization and hasbara, achieving a change of heart, replacing rejectionism with normalization, eliminating the mainstays of rejectionism, and developing alternate ideas. Now, to unpack that sentence:

• • •

Introspection. While Jerusalem cannot unilaterally end the dismal sequence of aggression and retribution, it can relegate this to a sideshow. Instead of predictably responding to aggression, it can initiate its own program to convince Palestinians that their campaign is hopeless and unnecessary, that Israel is strong and benign, that a century-plus of fighting suffices, that good times beckon.

Developing such a program requires abandoning a deeply entrenched mentality, one with roots deep in diasporic and Zionist history. It assumes that rejectionism cannot be broken and therefore makes no efforts to confront it, instead appeasing it via conciliation. What made at least some sense pre-1948, when Zionists were few, isolated, weak, and poor, borders on the absurd when Israel is good-sized, networked, powerful, and rich. Conciliation has become wildly unsuited to the country's current needs; it limits Israel to waiting for its enemy to tire of wanting to destroy it, rather than doing something about it. A wing and a prayer do not constitute serious policy.

A major shift starts with the acknowledgment of historic errors—enrichment, placation, and overconfidence. This should come easily, for Zionism has always been a self-conscious, introspective movement. Ehud Luz of Haifa University explains how,

> due to the impact of the Jewish tradition on the one hand, and the unique historical position of the Jews in the modern age on the other, the moral dilemmas with which Zionists had been confronted were much sharper than for any other sovereign nation. To the best of my knowledge, no other national movement has been so tormented by painful inner wrestling. There is no doubt that it was the "Jewishness" of the Zionists which made their wrestling extremely acute: they were torn between their spiritual tradition and their historical experience.

That wrestling continues and needs to focus on the conciliatory mentality.

To abandon that mentality requires changes far more profound than government policy ones that reach into the population's psychological and societal bases. It means no more enrichment for goodwill, placation seeking quiet, delusions of compromise, dreamy offers of cooperation, lopsided collaborations, expressions of weariness, painful concessions, or unilateral withdrawals. It means acting like a military, not a police force, and ending the split in Israel's defense establishment with the return to a unitary force dedicated to winning.

Here, ancient Judaism, with its robust traditions, offers inspiration, for the Hebrew Bible refers often to victory. A priest addressed the Israelites (Deuteronomy 20:3–4) with: "Today you are going into battle against your enemies. Do not be fainthearted or afraid; do not panic or be terrified by them. For the Lord your God is the one who goes with you to fight for you against your enemies to give you victory." Jonathan spoke to his father Saul (1 Samuel 19:4–5) about David: "What he has done has benefited you greatly. He took his life in his hands when he killed the Philistine. The Lord won a great victory for all Israel, and you saw it and were glad." David himself spoke about God's support (Psalm 18:38): "I crushed them so that they could not rise; they fell beneath my feet." He also (2 Samuel 22:38) celebrated victory: "I have pursued mine enemies, and destroyed them; and turned not again until I had consumed them."

The Jewish holiday of Hanukkah commemorates the victory of the Jewish Hasmonean dynasty (c. 140 BCE–37 BCE) over the Greeks.[1] It seeks to keep that martial spirit alive, with the Hanukkah prayer thanking God "for the victories You made possible for our ancestors in their time and now do in this time." Alex Nachumson comments how, "This simple sentence demonstrates clearly that victory, a forcing of one's enemy into submission and achieving one's military aims, is a positive goal in Judaism and Jewish history." Likewise, the Hanukkah song *Mi Yi'malel* (Who Can Retell) includes the verses "In ancient days at this season, the Maccabees redeemed and delivered us/Therefore, in our day, Israel must unite, arise, to redeem ourselves!"

But the diaspora mentality subverted Hanukkah and other holidays through the centuries. "Hanukkah, Purim, and Passover are celebrations of victory over enemies who tried to destroy the Jews," notes Alex Selsky of the Middle East Forum, but diaspora Jews "turned these holidays into celebrations of light, donuts, costumes, spring, and renewal." Ending conciliation does not mean trying something new but a return to ancient ways, ones far older than Herzl or Ben-Gurion.

The time appears right for such a reconsideration. Palestinians' unquenchable demands and unconstrained violence have prompted some Israeli Jews to rethink their assumptions. Two self-professed leftists, Adi Schwartz and Einat Wilf, explain how this happened to them: "The fact that the Palestinians walked away from two concrete and recent opportunities—in 2000 and 2008—to establish their own state, free of settlements, in the West Bank and Gaza Strip, with a capital in East Jerusalem, started to plant serious seeds of doubt in both of our minds." Others have

1 Conversely, a sling bullet likely used by the Greeks against the Hasmoneans also bears the word "victory."

experienced different revelatory moments, such as the destruction of Israeli greenhouses in Gaza in 2005 or October 7.

The Israeli philosopher Yoram Hazony finds a "dramatic weakening" in the ways of thought that led to the Oslo delusion. He explains the change as "a return to political clarity and consensus on political basics." The rise to prominence of such voices as Itamar Ben-Gvir and Bezalel Smotrich points to this shift.

• • •

Extinguishing hope. Plenty of evidence (see Chapter 10, "Positive Developments") suggests a readiness for change among Arab states, Palestinians, and Israelis. Rejectionism is vulnerable and can be vanquished. But it requires the right approach, one that moves away from violence in favor of psychology and ideas. Israel Victory need not be exclusively or even primarily a *military* victory.

Where lies the Palestinian center of gravity, defined earlier as "the essential source of ideological and moral strength, which, if broken, makes it impossible to continue the war"? Not in the leadership, the militia, the economy, the land, or sanctities. Rather, it lies in hope: hope to fulfill the rejectionist vision, inspired by Islamic Zionism and supported by a global network, to destroy Israel and replace it with Palestine. Israel's goal must be to extinguish that hope.

Palestinian hope. Palestinians widely attribute their tenacity to suffering the most extreme deprivation of any peoples ever; in the memorable words of PA leader Mahmoud Abbas, Israel "perpetrated 50 Holocausts against the Palestinians people." This message resonates, with one poll finding that 84 percent of Palestinians believe that their suffering is "unique in human history." Such desolation has caused, again to quote Abbas, an "absence of hope and overwhelming despair [that] feed extremism." Eliminate those hardships, he implies, and Palestinians will become moderate, industrious, and exemplary citizens.

Most Israelis and nearly everyone else, including Western governments, accept this general explanation, even if many rebuff the Holocaust comparison. Thus does Israel's hard-boiled security establishment premise its policies on affluent Palestinians being less dangerous than impoverished ones. Assuming that economic well-being and political autonomy together will vest Palestinians in prosperity and moderation, making them true partners for peace, the outside world provides Palestinians with great dollops of money even as it pressures Israel to improve their conditions. Every major attempt at Palestinian-Israeli diplomacy, from Austrian chancellor Bruno Kreisky's in the 1970s to Biden's in late 2023, has promoted the same combination of free money and unearned concessions.

But this interpretation exactly reverses the role of hope among Palestinians, which actually inspires intransigence, extremism, and violence. Hope that the Jewish state can be destroyed keeps rejectionism alive, inspires continued murderous attacks, and motivates the international hate-campaign. Hope that hitting Israel hard and often enough will cause it to collapse motivates aggression. Hope that Israel will no longer exist on its hundredth anniversary (which Palestinians predicted will be the case by a ratio of 66 percent to 27 percent on its seventy-fifth anniversary) fundamentally impedes resolution.

Research strikingly confirms the link between more free money and greater malign hopes. American analyst Steve Stotsky in 2008 showed a striking correlation between funding for the Palestinian Authority and attacks on Israelis; each additional $1.25 million in aid, he graphed, translated into the killing of an additional Israeli. Maurice Hirsch of Palestinian Media Watch updated this research in March 2023, showing a similarly precise correlation between funding and violence between 2011 and 2022. His conclusion: "U.S. aid to the Palestinians fuels terror, not peace."

Non-financial steps have the same effect. When the Israeli government increases restrictions on Jewish access to the Temple Mount during Ramadan, so does Palestinian aggression. Tom Nisani of Israel's Beyadenu organization, explains that,

> every time when the Temple Mount was more restricted than usual or closed to Jews altogether, the closure or restriction was the spark of serious riots on the Temple Mount which, from there, very quickly brought the possibility of another military operation, such as in the Guardian of the Walls, or a wave of attacks in Jerusalem, or "only" another unprecedented destruction of antiquities on the Temple Mount.

Diplomatic isolation of Israel has a similar effect; nearly always losing votes at international organizations by lopsided margins lifts Palestinians' anticipations. Anything that buoys their hope—free money, unilateral Israeli concessions, academic endorsement, anti-Israel demonstrations—impedes resolution.

Some observers have noted this connection. Max Singer of the Hudson Institute has it right: "The fundamental obstacle to peace is the persistent Palestinian hope or belief that, despite Israel's military power, it can be defeated." Hillel Frisch concludes from his analysis that, "When Palestinians are hopeless, terror declines; when hopeful, terrorism increases." Richard Hanania of the Center for the Study of Partisanship and Ideology argues that "Israel must crush Palestinian hopes." Or, in Smotrich's iteration, "It is not desperation that motivates [Palestinian] terrorism, but hope."

Losing hope. Israeli and international actions can be judged on a simple scale: Do they encourage or discourage Palestinian hopes? Do they encourage rejectionism or undermine it?

Whatever causes Palestinians to lose hope in Israel's destruction makes them more inclined to moderate and accept their Zionist neighbor. Only that might turn them into temperate, industrious, and exemplary citizens. Pessimism about destroying Israel, the record shows, inspires them to take up the mundane tasks of earning a living and educating their children. Not coincidentally, the Palestinian economy peaked in 1992, at a moment of all-time despair in the aftermath of Palestinian loss in the Kuwait war and the Soviet collapse. Likewise, economic stress reduces military and other capabilities, depresses the mood, and so brings resolution closer.

Arguing for Palestinians to lose hope, admittedly, sounds unkind; this approach will not inspire greeting cards or Instagram memes. The nice approach, however, has been persistently tried for more than thirty years, and has always failed. As Putin's invasion of Ukraine reminds, some problems call for strong solutions, including defeat and humiliation.

It will not do, as Yifa Segal suggests, to differentiate among good and bad Palestinians. "Israel must set up more sophisticated carrot-and-stick mechanisms: yes, provide assistance, make life easier, and cultivate those who clearly reject the cycle of hatred and violence, but simultaneously impose harsher punishment for all acts of violence as well as manifestations of incitement and support." War does not permit such fine distinctions; that is like asking the air force to bomb only the houses of bad people. To repeat, the IDF is not a police force. Palestinian society as a whole must taste defeat.

How simple if Israel could induce Palestinians to drop rejectionism and experience a change of heart by emulating the Allies in World War II:

total war, as much time as needed, absolute victory, shattered countries, supine populations. But Israel fights within limits—geographic boundaries, time constraints, restrictions on punishment and violence—that it cannot ignore. After October 7, Jerusalem has more freedom of action in Gaza but even there it faces the task of engineering a soft landing, of breaking an enemy and changing hearts without full autonomy.

• • •

Demoralization. Palestinians being a nation of prospective "martyrs," Israel cannot induce them to give up their goals through violence and punishment. Rather, this requires affecting their mentality through a sustained and systematic effort to convince them of the hopelessness of their goals, showing that their self-sacrifice is useless and that rejectionism leads not to glorious triumph but to a miserable dead end. This calls for a policy of *demoralization.*

How it works. By way of illustration, imagine you work for the law-abiding Israeli state and are informed that someone has strapped a bomb to his body, has taken off to an unknown but crowded destination in Tel Aviv on a suicide mission, and carries a mobile telephone. You have his number and are assigned the task of dissuading him from carrying out his mission. How would you go about this? Obviously, the would-be suicide bomber is immune to personal threats. Almost as obviously, Israel's long history of blowing up the homes of political murderers suggests that this, too, will likely not deter him. Barred from collective punishment, you may not threaten his family or friends. In short, you dispose of no effective pressures.

But demoralization might succeed. You point out that, from every conceivable angle, his cause is hopeless. Forlorn. Forsaken. Futile. His sacrifice will make no difference, Israel being a powerful and determined country of nearly ten million, with a flourishing economy and a powerful military. The damage he can do amounts to a triviality that just wastes lives and causes grief without making a difference. Worse, as with all prior such murders, his attack will harden the Israeli electorate, making it more determined, more nationalistic, and tougher on the Palestinians.

That could stop the would-be martyr in his tracks, return home, and return the explosives to his handlers.

This small-scale example offers an insight into approaching the Palestinians writ large. Self-interest kicks in only when the cause no longer inspires. Who wants to suffer deprivation or give up one's life for a hopeless goal? Why endanger your family residence for a failed cause? Israel Victory requires convincing Palestinians that rejectionism cannot succeed. Their defeat will follow more from demoralization than from violence.

To those who hold Palestinians too fanatical to be defeated, I reply: If Germans and Japanese, comparably fanatic and vastly more powerful, could be defeated in World War II and transformed into democratic, law-abiding citizens, why not Palestinians? Other Muslims, faced with a determined and superior force, have given in to infidels, from Spain to the Balkans to India. The Arab states long ago withdrew from their military conflict with Israel.

A change of heart. A Palestinian change of heart—and here comes the central paragraph of this book—should be Israel's central war goal. That entails the end of rejectionism. This means not just the absence of violence and the ending of delegitimization but acknowledging definitively and unequivocally, fully and irrevocably, in deed as well as in word, consistently over a protracted period, Jews' historic ties to Jerusalem and the Land of Israel, recognition of Jews' right to live in their ancestral Jewish land, Israel's legitimacy, and its permanent identity as a Jewish state. That outcome entails Palestinians enduring the bitter crucible of defeat, accepting that further war on Israel is hopeless and inconceivable, and living in harmony with it. They must renounce the use of force and incitement, both domestic and international; drop the foul goal of destroying their Israeli neighbor; stop the demonization of Jews and Israel; and refute antisemitism. It requires closing down the machinery of warfare, including the channels of incitement, the suicide factories, the rhetoric glorifying death, and the campaign to delegitimize Israel. It means accepting Israel as just another member of international organizations and a presence on college campuses, not the object of undeserved, disproportionate, insane attention.

A change of heart implies a radical transformation for West Bankers, Gazans, and non-citizen Muslim eastern Jerusalemites. The sooner they start this process, the sooner a skilled and dignified people can move beyond its current barbarism and build a worthy economy, polity, society, and culture.

How to recognize a change of heart? When Palestinians show not a love of Israel but a respect for Israelis; not recognition of specific state boundaries but acceptance of the Jewish state; not a relinquishment of claims but their pursuit in a non-violent, legal way. Incitement stops, "normalization" becomes normal, with routine trade, tourism, study, cultural, and other human contacts. Incensed letters to the editor and sharply worded diplomatic démarches replace bloodshed. Walls separating Israel from the West Bank and Gaza come down with no resulting attacks on Israelis. Jews living in Hebron (in the West Bank) have no more need for security than do Israel's Muslim citizens living in Nazareth (in Israel).

The role of ideas. Richard Hanania provocatively encourages Israel to empty Gaza of its population and kill Palestinian aggressors until they give up, on the grounds that

> the more Israel makes clear that the Palestinians will never achieve their goals, the less trouble they will have with them. In addition to the direct benefit of eliminating terrorists and stopping them from attacking you, fewer are actually created by each one you kill, as long as it is clear you are willing to go as far as it takes to neutralize the threat.... If there was a way Israel could guarantee with 100% certainty that it wouldn't stop until Hamas was destroyed, I think Palestinian resistance would decline.

To the argument that deaths increase Palestinian enmity, Hanania retorts that they break the Palestinian will:

> Israel should just keep killing terrorists and trying to destroy Hamas because the increase in hatred among the Palestinians will be small. This war will probably end with Palestinians hating Israel a little bit more than before but having their ability to hurt the Jewish state degraded to an even larger degree, leading to a net gain in Israeli security.... In the long run, I think there is a good chance that Israel can end the conflict by breaking Palestinian will, which may require constant brutality towards Gaza and making everyone understand that the Palestinian cause is hopeless as every generation of Israelis is more hawkish than the one that came before.

Morality aside, following Hanania's advice would lead Israel to disaster. As with Kahane's "transfer" idea, but even more emphatically, such a step would prompt internal Israeli divisions, spread anti-Zionism, and inflate the ranks of Israel's enemies, to the point of endangering the very existence of the Jewish state.

Force has its role, of course, but as a tactic, not as a strategy. It addresses immediate problems; it cannot refute an ideology. Violence in itself cannot attain victory over rejectionism. Fighting an ideology requires an alternative set of ideas. One body of ideas can only be defeated with other, better, more compelling ideas. Their spread must be Israel's goal.

Two recommendations. Assuming that Israelis have abandoned conciliation, ended their awe of Palestinian resolve, adopted a victory mentality, made it their goal to break Palestinian hope, and settled on demoralization as the means, how do they replace rejectionism with a benign set of ideas? First, by eliminating the existing Palestinian quasi-sovereign institutions. Second, through a campaign to convince Palestinians to accept Israel. The one creates the conditions for the other.

These two proposals offer general guidelines, avoiding specifics. Partly, I wish to keep away from Israel's policy alternatives, for example, the ultimate disposition of the West Bank. Partly, too, I cannot predict in advance what might work. Will a certain tactic demoralize or incite, intimidate or infuriate, succeed or backfire? Which messages break Palestinian will, which strengthen the sense of resistance (*muqawama*) and steadfastness (sumud)? Answering such questions requires insight into the Palestinian psychology and sociology of the moment, closely studying the target person, group, and situation. Subtle factors might prompt one population to feel defeated while inspiring others to sacrifice their lives. Israel's security establishment needs to explore these and related issues as it chooses the best options for the political leadership. Without knowing precisely when a tactic might be productive or counterproductive, here are some broad ideas.

I. NO MORE HAMAS OR PA

Israelis and Palestinians alike have long reviled the dominant institutions in the West Bank and Gaza. But nothing challenged them before October 7 because Israel preferred the devils it knew while Palestinians lacked the strength to challenge Hamas or the PA. Spurred by October 7, the moment is nigh for revolution.

• • •

Hamas: Israeli changes. Despite persistent aggression coming out of Gaza, the pre-October 7 government of Israel showed great reluctance to do more than occasionally slap Hamas down. That changed in a matter of hours.

Netanyahu's caution. Analysts widely hold Prime Minister Benjamin Netanyahu personally responsible for not having brought down Hamas, ascribing alternate motives to him. One group blames political cowardice. Galit Distel-Atbaryan, a future Likud minister of information, wrote in 2019:

> It has to be said straight up: Netanyahu wants to keep Hamas standing and he's willing to pay an almost inconceivable price for it—half of the country paralyzed, children and parents post-trauma, homes bombarded, people killed. An alley cat is holding a nuclear leopard by the balls and Netanyahu, with outrageous and almost inconceivable restraint of sorts, isn't doing the thing that's the easiest to do—to topple this organization with the mere breath of the Israel Defense Forces.

Martin Kramer agrees:

> He promised to topple Hamas when it appeared electorally advantageous, but abandoned this pledge when it seemed politically risky. When his generals painted a pessimistic picture, he readily embraced it. His associates may even have leaked it, to justify his restraint.

A second group points to Netanyahu and the security establishment thinking Hamas sufficiently contained. Nadav Shragai of *Israel Hayom* holds Netanyahu "responsible for the misconception and its outcomes. He is its father, mother, and guardian." But to be fair, Shragai adds,

> almost all of Israel's highest political and military officials, right and left, and most of the media, too, lined up behind the separation policy, either as a systematic worldview or by acquiescing in it. Almost all of them backed Netanyahu when he refrained from crushing Hamas by land; almost all of them belittled the Hamas threat.

A third group points to Netanyahu's seeing Hamas as a block to "Palestine," pointing to his statement that, "Whoever wants to thwart the establishment of a Palestinian state must support bolstering Hamas and transferring money to it. This is part of our strategy of isolating Palestinians in Gaza from Palestinians in the West Bank." Thus, David Makovsky notes Netanyahu's "preference for maintaining the schism between Hamas in Gaza and the Palestinian Authority in the West Bank."

Each group focuses on a different explanation, but all agree, correctly, on Netanyahu being the key reason for Israel permitting Hamas to prosper as it did.

Consensus for destruction. October 7 brought Israeli caution to an end and created a sudden agreement that Hamas—but not the PA—had to be eliminated. Israel's new consensus congealed quickly and widely. Netanyahu spoke at least seven times on this subject, vowing that Hamas would be "defeated," "demolished," "destroyed," and "eliminated." A range of other high-ranking government figures seconded him:

- Yoav Gallant, defense minister: "There will be no situation in which Israeli children are murdered in the fields and in which Hamas will continue to exist."
- Gilad Erdan, United Nations ambassador: "Now is the time to obliterate Hamas terror infrastructure, to completely erase it."

Many formers also weighed in:

- Naftali Bennett, former prime minister: "It's time to destroy Hamas."
- Yaakov Amidror, former national security advisor: Hamas "should be killed and destroyed."
- Meir Ben Shabbat, former national security advisor: "Israel should destroy everything connected to Hamas."
- Chuck Freilich, former deputy national security advisor (in *Ha'aretz*): "Israel must now deal Hamas an unequivocal defeat."
- Tamir Heyman, former IDF intelligence chief: "We have to win."
- Amos Yadlin, former IDF intelligence chief: "We are going to destroy Hamas."
- Yossi Cohen, former head of Mossad: "Eliminating Hamas officials is a decision which needs to be made."

Public figures expressed unprecedented verbal aggressiveness. Gallant called Hamas "human animals" and Bennett called them "Nazis." The deputy parliamentary speaker called on Israel to "burn Gaza." An unnamed defense official announced that "Gaza will eventually turn into a city of tents. There will be no buildings." The minister for heritage endorsed attacking Gaza with nuclear weapons. Television news anchor Shay Golden went off-script to unload a tirade:

> We will destroy you. We keep telling you every day—we are coming. We are coming to Gaza, we are coming to Lebanon, we will come to Iran. We will come everywhere. You must take this into account. Can you imagine how many of you we are going to kill for every one of the 1,300 Israelis that you massacred? The death toll will reach numbers that you have never seen in the history of the Arab nations.... You will see numbers that you never imagined were possible.

A hip-hop anthem promising to rain hell on Israel's enemies jumped to the No. 1 spot. A pop singer called for Israel to "Erase Gaza. Don't leave a single person there" (implying expulsion, not murder).

In short, a ferociously anti-Hamas and anti-PA mood came to dominate Israeli politics, with only the two leftwing parties (Labor and Meretz) mildly in opposition. While the ultimate fate of Hamas remains unknown as of this writing, it clearly will not return to its former position of quasi-sovereignty in the whole of Gaza.

• • •

Hamas: Loathing in Gaza. Gazans widely despise their Hamas rulers.

Pre-October 7. Many indicators suggested a growing Gazan hatred of Hamas. A September 2022 poll found just 7 percent having good things to say about conditions in Gaza. Polling a year later found overwhelming support in Gaza for the statement that "Palestinians should push harder to replace their own political leaders with more effective and less corrupt ones." A Palestinian Center for Policy and Survey Research poll found support for Hamas in September 2023 at 38 percent; that is, most Gazans don't want to be ruled by it. The Arab Barometer survey completed on October 6 asked about the cause of food insecurity: 31 percent of respondents blamed Hamas mismanagement, 26 percent blamed inflation, and 16 percent blamed external economic sanctions. Tholfekar Swairjo, a Gazan political analyst, pointed to "boiling anger in the streets against the Hamas movement [which is] blamed for the very low quality of life in Gaza."

A thirty-two-year-old woman added that, "Most Gazans have stopped believing in Hamas and the others. You know why? Because they don't feed us, they don't provide anything. You have to depend on yourself. How can we build a future with these guys?" A PA-affiliated man complained about Hamas leaders, "These people profess Islam and claim to be religious, but they slaughtered [their own] people." Occasional discontent erupted against Hamas, as in 2019 and August 2023, producing further choice quotes about Hamas:

- Ramy: The Hamas security forces "barbarically attacked us even though the protests were completely peaceful.... They don't care. They don't even pretend to care about us. Their leaders ruined Gaza beyond hope and turned it into a place of misery, and yet they live luxurious lifestyles."
- Fadi: "Years of our lives are being wasted. We're suffering. We can't find work, we can't make any money, we can't get married, we can't put food on the table. We can't do anything in Gaza."
- Ahmed Hasan: "To this day, Hamas leaders don't act like they're the rulers of Gaza.... They're lazy, corrupt, careless and inhumane."

"Hamas has billions of dollars in investments in many countries, while people [in Gaza] starve to death and migrate in search of work," added Amer Balosha, a journalist.

Gazans also rejected Hamas by emigrating in droves. Interviewed while waiting in long lines seeking to enter to Egypt and on to the world, they expressed despair at life under Hamas. "All those who are seeking to emigrate want a dignified life...they are prepared to die." "I know I'm risking my life, but I want to leave, dead or alive." Palestinian political analyst Mahmoud al-Raqab concluded that, "Despite their exposure to the risks of drowning, loss, and death," Gazans were determined to flee their homeland. An estimated 250,000 to 350,000 young adults left the territory since Hamas' seizure of power in 2007.

Post-October 7. After October 7, more evidence of Gazan wrath against Hamas emerged. In the absence of polling, a sampling of views must suffice:

- H., a Gazan scared to give his name and now in exile: Gazans consider Yahya Sinwar "a fool and a madman" for October 7. "People are very tired of war. It's enough—how much more? Enough. We know that Hamas started this war."
- Quotes from the "Voices of Gaza" project of the Center for Peace Communications: "Hamas bears responsibility for all the wars, but we're the ones who pay the price." "Ending Hamas is the demand of young and old alike in Gaza." "We welcome any change that will save us from this indignation called Hamas."
- A young girl in Gaza: "Hamas is putting the people of Gaza in danger. Its fighters are hiding in the tunnels, while Gazan civilians are the victims."
- A young man with a bandaged wrist disrupted a televised press conference featuring a Hamas spokesman, shaking his wounded hand and yelling "May God hold you to account, Hamas!"
- Al Jazeera television interviewed a wounded old Palestinian man and he replied, "What's happening is criminal! Why is [Hamas] hiding among us? Why don't they go to hell and hide there?"
- Israel's Channel 12 cited conversations with Gazans who "are praying that Israel will destroy Hamas and are saying it out loud." Also, it reported that the greeting "May God take revenge upon Hamas" had become common.
- The *Daily Beast* quoted Hasan Ahmed, thirty-nine: "When you want to speak against Hamas.... They can easily kill us"; and Um Ahmed, fifty-five: "Hamas has lost support in Gaza."
- A former "communications minister" for Hamas, Yousef al-Mansi: "I have not seen anyone in the Gaza Strip who supports Sinwar; nobody likes Sinwar. There are people who, day and night, pray that God will free us from him."

- Muhammad Mansour, a Gazan interviewed on Hebron radio, addressed Hamas: "May God take revenge on you [and] curse your forefathers.... May God curse you, O Sinwar, you son of a dog."
- *The Wall Street Journal* quoted a fifty-six-year-old businessman from Gaza: "Hamas is the one that dragged us into this terrible vortex." Mkhaimar Abusada, a political scientist at Gaza's Al-Azhar University, generalized: "There is a lot of criticism among Palestinians that the October 7 attack...was a strategic mistake." "Damn Hamas," said a hairdresser.

Such sentiments suggest that the catastrophe that October 7 brought upon non-Hamas Gazans has much increased general rancor toward the organization in Gaza.

• • •

The PA: Pros and Cons. Jerusalem fumes at the violence and delegitimization directed at it by the PA but also tolerates and protects it. Netanyahu made this protection explicit in June 2023:

> We need the Palestinian Authority. We cannot allow it to collapse. We also do not want it to collapse. We are prepared to help it financially. We have an interest in the Authority continuing to work. In the areas which it manages to act, it does the work for us. And we have no interest in it collapsing.

Two weeks later, Israel's Security Cabinet formally resolved that "Israel will act to prevent the collapse of the Palestinian Authority." (To which the PA's "foreign ministry" showed its confidence and disdain by accusing Netanyahu of leading an "extreme right-wing government that wants to destroy the PA and harm it through the bloody escalation against the Palestinians and their lands.")

Pros. Several factors led to Israel's security establishment seeing this institution ruling the West Bank as a distasteful but necessary partner. First, the massive subventions it receives from abroad spare the Israeli taxpayer added expenses. (Pre-October 7, the same reasoning applied to Hamas, whose funding came primarily from Iran, taxes, Qatar, Türkiye, and the PA.)

Second, Netanyahu finds advantage in keeping the PA as a squabbling rival to the more powerful Hamas, thereby reducing pressure on him to permit the creation of a Palestinian state.

Third, the PA's joint security with the IDF "not only saves lives but also reduces the level of direct friction between the IDF and the population" according to Eran Lerman, for example, by the PA arresting suspects on Israel's behalf. The security coordination also includes deconfliction when the IDF moves in the West Bank and extricates Israelis who wandered into PA-controlled areas.

Fourth and most important, Israel's leadership dreads a return to the bad old days of directly administering hostile and restive populations in the West Bank. Serving as a police force dismays a self-respecting military; the misery of walking hostile city streets prompted the retreat from Gaza in 2005 and almost from the West Bank a few years later.

To keep the shambolic PA in business, Israel provides Ramallah with tax monies and encourages foreign donors to provide funds. It does not punish the PA severely, hoping to avoid another intifada or the PA's downfall. Therefore, it views dimly any initiative to deprive the PA of funds, infringe on its prerogatives, or diminish its stature.

Israel's backing manifests itself in other ways too. Some staff in COGAT pander to the PA by calling it the "Government of Palestine (GoP)." Jerusalem permitted the PA in 2022 to purchase two helicopters for use by its leadership to "strengthen Abbas' status" (in *Al-Monitor*'s explanation). It facilitated the transfer of ten armored vehicles and perhaps 1,500 guns in September 2023.

Cons. As for negatives, Israelis and West Bankers alike despise the PA, and for related reasons.

The PA incites, funds, and arms a wide range of low-level attacks on Israel, including stonings, knife stabbings, lynchings, car-rammings, shootings, bombings, arson, and intifadas. Suicide drones will soon likely join the battlefield. The PA also enjoys complete liberty to scream out any calumnies about its "partner for peace": that Jews descend from pigs and apes; that Zionism represents an imperialist movement of white supremacists subjugating an indigenous people; that Israel oppresses, exploits, and massacres a Christ-like victim population; that Gaza is an open-air concentration camp, that Benjamin Netanyahu is the new Hitler; and that Palestinians are experiencing fifty Holocausts. It blackens Israel's name around the world.

The vaunted PA security cooperation with Israel barely exists, forcing major Israeli incursions into PA-run areas, such as Jenin. As *The New York Times* acknowledges, the PA

> employs tens of thousands of security forces charged with law enforcement inside Palestinian communities. While the forces are expected to rein in Palestinian armed groups and keep them from attacking Israelis, they do so inconsistently, at least in part because their members sympathize with the fighters.

That an average of 5,000 annual attacks come out of the West Bank, however, makes one wonder about the utility of PA coordination. Yet more revealingly, a video boasts of the PA Security Forces' salaried employees, twenty-four in number, who did double duty as "martyrs" killed while carrying out murder operations against Israelis.

Plenty of Israelis see the PA for what it is. Yesha Council Chairman Shlomo Ne'eman called it "not the solution to security issues, but…the source of all the problems." National Security Minister Itamar Ben-Gvir can find "no greater absurdity" than the Israeli government supporting an organization that "encourages terrorism, pays salaries to terrorists and their families, encourages incitement of the murder of Jews in the education system, takes over territories in Judea and Samaria." Diaspora Affairs Minister Amichai Chikli calls the PA "the enemy of the State of Israel…an entity that is antisemitic to its core…a neo-Nazi entity in its essence and outlook." Smotrich observes that, "The PA's existence is not worth the diplomatic damage it causes us. It is better for Israel to work towards its collapse."

Public opinion polling and anecdotal evidence alike point to deep hostility among West Bankers toward their dictators. A March 2023 survey by the Palestinian Center for Policy and Survey Research found 52 percent wanting the collapse or dissolution of the PA. In June 2023, 63 percent saw the PA as a burden. A young protester at an anti-PA rally in Jerusalem called the organization "an enemy of the people" while Jerusalem prayer-goers at Al-Aqsa mosque denounced Mahmoud Abbas as "the traitor" due to his oppressive, corrupt, and ineffectual rule.

• • •

Post-PA. Once Israelis liberate themselves from conciliation, they can transform the West Bank, first by putting the PA on notice that it either undergoes fundamental reform by a date specific, say six months off, or it disappears. Reform means ending the violence, stopping the global campaign of calumny against Israel, and permanently accepting the Jewish state over a protracted period. Reform entails nothing exotic, just fulfilling the role of normal neighbor envisioned in the Oslo Accords. Israel could exert pressure by demanding reforms in return for supplying food, water, medicines, and energy. It can also deduct for material damages from the $2.5 billion in tax obligations the government of Israel annually collects and transfers to the PA. This, the ideal solution, should be given a chance, even though the record suggests that this particular leopard will not change its spots.

Assuming it does not, Israel has the option to eliminate it. Yossi Dagan, chairman of the Samaria Regional Council, calls on the IDF "to launch a determined military operation" to take down the PA. Force, however, is not necessary; economic and financial steps suffice to bankrupt it and cause its collapse. Specifically, Israel has the right to stop transferring tax monies to the PA on the grounds of massive Oslo Accords violations. Maurice Hirsch explains the legal basis for this step: "Israeli law says that the government can transfer funds, tax revenues that it collects on behalf of the PA, but this is not an absolute obligation. The funds are supposed to be given with the understanding that the PA fights terrorism and anti-Semitism and does not persecute IDF soldiers and Israeli leaders at the Hague courts"—none of which the PA does. That more than two-thirds of the PA's revenues in 2022 came from tax transfers means their denial would likely cause its quick collapse.

Further economic steps might include:

- Reducing economic interaction, for example by not purchasing produce from the West Bank.
- Shutting off Israeli-supplied water and electricity.
- Ending Israeli-provided hospital care.
- Lobbying against and otherwise obstructing foreign funding of the PA.
- Refusing the entry of people or goods beyond the minimum.

The PA's demise brings many benefits to Israel: An end to its ubiquitous incitement to violence, from school textbooks to wall posters to mosque sermons. No more rewards for murder, officially recognizing attackers of

Israelis as "soldiers" whose welfare and that of their families are looked after. No more international campaign of delegitimization coming out of Ramallah. The global Left is deprived of its mascot.

Perhaps most importantly, to quote Khalid Abu Toameh, the only way to "change the hearts and minds of the Palestinians…is by ending the anti-Israel rhetoric of Palestinian leaders and media outlets." The PA and Hamas must be eliminated to create the space for new, constructive ideas to replace rejectionism. Their continued existence virtually excludes such a possibility.

The disappearance of these two quasi-governments may bring a further benefit; the dissolution of Palestinian aspirations to full sovereignty. As Bishara A. Bahbah, vice president of the U.S.-Palestine Council, correctly observes,: "The collapse of the PA will end the hope of creating a Palestinian state." Ghaith al-Omari of the Washington Institute for Near East Policy goes further: "A collapse of the PA will likely usher the collapse of the Palestinian national movement."

• • •

Building a decent Gaza and West Bank. Palestinians have experienced generations of getting nowhere fast; some are ready for something new. However, Gaza is more ready than the West Bank.

Gaza vs. West Bank. The two regions have diverged since Egypt's Gamal Abdel Nasser and Jordan's King Hussein came to power within twenty days of each other in mid-1952; the former used anti-Zionism to mobilize his subject population far more than the latter, causing Gaza to become more radically anti-Zionist than the West Bank during the Egyptian and Jordanian occupations that lasted until 1967. So matters continued through fifty-five years, with Gaza's population always remaining the more extreme.

A reversal of this pattern began when Hamas took control of Gaza in mid-2007. That resulted from Hamas' historically unique torment of its subject population, exploiting its suffering for public relations purposes. Contrary to dictatorships around the world, which treat unengaged civilians with indifference, Hamas actively sacrificed their interests to gain foreign sympathy. Its perverse but savvy logic held that the more Gazans suffered, the more the leadership could accuse Israel of aggression and the wider and more vehement the support it won from antisemites of all persuasions—Islamists, Palestinian nationalists, far-leftists, and far-rightists.

Accordingly, Hamas wanted Gazans to be hungry, homeless, hopeless, injured, and dead. To ensure this outcome, it based troops and missiles in mosques, churches, schools, hospitals, and private homes, then attacked Israeli civilian targets. Hamas got its wish: repeated Israeli retaliations, from cutting off fuel deliveries to aerial bombing, won it massive and impassioned international backing.

Fifteen years of enduring this intentional suffering sobered Gazans, turned many of them against Hamas, and eroded their anti-Israel vehemence; they took on other priorities, such as their own welfare. The catastrophic destruction in Gaza following October 7 further heightened their rage at Hamas, and yet more so because Hamas made no provisions for civilians, but focused exclusively on the well-being of its own members.

West Bankers endured nothing comparable. To be sure, they had to cope with anarchy and Israeli operations, but on nothing like the scale of the Gazans. For all its many faults, the PA did not purposefully provoke Israel into harming its own population. This relatively favorable experience meant that West Bankers did not sober up but stayed steady in their anti-Zionism.

Polling reflects these trends. For example, asked in November 2023 by the Arab World for Research and Development: "How much do you support the military operation carried out by the Palestinian resistance led by Hamas on October 7th," a poll found the response "extremely support" much higher among West Bankers than among Gazans, 68 percent and 47 percent, respectively. Similarly, those condemning the attack numbered 7 percent and 21 percent, respectively.

This fits a pattern: Palestinians closest to the conflict and paying a price for it weary of rejectionism more than those far removed from it, for whom it is but occasional, voluntary, and costless. Indeed, the Arab-Israeli conflict writ large generates more intense partisanship among Americans than among Middle Easterners; the latter may die from the conflict but the former experience it with greater passion.[2] Thus did students in the West respond after October 7 with far more passion for Hamas than did those in Muslim-majority countries.

---

2 I document this phenomenon and draw conclusions in Daniel Pipes, "Americans Battle the Arab-Israeli Conflict," *Middle East Quarterly*, Vol. 22, No. 2 (Spring 2015).

Readiness for change. Their tribulations render Gazans surprisingly open to Israeli oversight. This came out with initial clarity in 2007, as the Hamas juggernaut seized Gaza but some freedom of expression still existed. Bassem Al-Nabris, a Gazan poet, speculated that were a referendum held in Gaza on the return of "the Israeli occupation," 70 percent or more would reply in the affirmative. Most people, a Gazan remarked at that time, "pray that Israel will come back and rule us again." An Israeli Arab publication reported at that time that Palestinian brutality prompts Gazans to

> say that, since the [start of intra-Palestinian] massacres, they [have begun to] miss the Israelis, since Israel is more merciful than [the Palestinian gunmen] who do not even know why they are fighting and killing one another. "It's like organized crime. Once, we resisted Israel together, but now we call for the return of the Israeli army to Gaza."

Gazans, the report went on, "are hoping that Israel will reenter the Gaza Strip, wipe out both Hamas and Fatah, and then withdraw again." *Al-Hayat Al-Jadida* columnist Yahya Rabah called on Israel to stay, "this time not as an occupier but as an international peace-keeping force."

Jumping ahead to 2023, Palestinian human rights activist Bassam Eid in January called for "corrupt Palestinian institutions [to] be completely abolished, and an entirely new framework envisioned." A June poll commissioned by the Washington Institute for Near East Policy found that three-quarters of Gazans support Arab governments taking "a more active role in Palestinian-Israeli peacemaking, offering incentives to both sides to take more moderate positions." Half of Gazans agreed that Hamas should "stop calling for the destruction of Israel and instead accept a permanent two-state solution based on the 1967 borders." Asked about a resumption of negotiations with Israel, 58 percent supported this. The polling organization Arab Barometer found that, "On the eve of Hamas's October 7 attack, just 20 percent of Gazans favored a military solution that could result in the destruction of the state of Israel."

The Palestinian Authority does not arouse the same contempt and loathing as Hamas, but it, too. has alienated many of its subjects. The eloquent Majdi Abd al-Wahhab wrote in a December 2023 article titled "O Israelis, Come and Work Together!":

> All but a few Palestinians believe that the PA is a catastrophe.... O Israelis, come let us work together to establish a polity...and let us agree that its mainstays will be building, economy, development, life, welfare, education and healthcare, which will lead to stability. Come, let us build this together, putting the individual in first place, permitting the Israeli and the Palestinian to live in peace and security.

Implementing change. Once the PA and Hamas are gone, Jerusalem can start over again, fixing the errors made following June 1967, when friendly and naïve Israelis entered the West Bank and Gaza, directed by Moshe Dayan to enrich the conquered peoples as a way to win their cooperation. Israel can draw on failed experiences and weary populaces to get it right this time. With generations of bitter experience behind them, their new counterparts should know much better what to do: finally extirpate the legacy of Amin al-Husseini by finding Palestinian allies, overseeing their every step, providing them with the means to govern, and—most of all—helping them to battle rejectionism.

In Gaza especially, Israel can reasonably expect to find a substantial cohort ready to work with it to establish a new authority that begins to return the territory to normal life. These Gazans will take on a wide range of tasks: policing, utilities, municipal services, administration, communications, teaching, urban planning, and more.

While this may sound like wishful thinking, it bears recalling that Gazans not that long ago led decent lives under Israeli rule. Unfortunately, Israel failed to cultivate relations with relatively friendly Gazans and lacked decent Gazan partners in its first period of rule, from 1967 to 2005. Then, in an act of historic stupidity, it handed the territory to the genocidal Yasir Arafat. In a further mistake, it not only permitted the even more horrific Hamas to control Gaza after 2007 but encouraged external funders, such as Qatar, to help it consolidate power.

The new entity must have no connection whatsoever to the execrable Palestinian Authority that rules parts of the West Bank. Nor should Arab or international bodies take part in its administration. Instead, it requires a tough Israeli military rule overseeing a tough police state along the lines of what exists in Egypt and Jordan, countries where one can lead a normal life so long as one stays out of trouble and never, ever criticizes the ruler. Gaza can become decent, not at war with its neighbor and economically viable. Will Israelis have the acumen and stamina to make this happen?

Once a model has been set up in Gaza, something similar can be implemented in the West Bank.

Removing Hamas and the PA only constitute Israel's first step; next comes an innovative approach to messaging.

II. A NEW HASBARA

Israel overwhelms Palestinians in military and economic power. That equation, however, is reversed when it comes to communications; for proof, review voting patterns in the UN General Assembly or the politics on campuses. These roughly asymmetrical situations shape Israel's challenge: first to degrade the messaging machinery of its enemy (bye, bye PA and Hamas) and then to redirect its own desultory efforts.

• • •

The limitations of violence. Enjoying a vast superiority in manpower, firepower, and technology, Israel has at its disposal a wide range of options to inflict violence on Palestinians, such as destroying infrastructure, blowing up houses, taking out operatives, and assassinating leaders. This is necessary, to be sure. But it faces a range of problems and limitations.

First, some initiatives have proven to be either inept or crude, such as the 1992 removal and return of 417 Palestinian leaders to Lebanon or the 1997 poisoning of Hamas leader Khaled Mashal.

Second, competent initiatives often fail to accomplish their goal. For example, increased violence in the West Bank in 2022 led to the large-scale Operation Wave Breaker that, Jonathan Schanzer of the Foundation for the Defense of Democracies observes, "resulted in numerous injured and dead jihadis. However, the Palestinian fighters were not deterred." On a larger scale, recall the eleven futile efforts (documented on pp. 95-96) to punish Hamas by withholding fuel and other imports. "Mowing the grass" likewise failed over a period of a decade and more.

Third, violence strengthens the Palestinians' argument of victimhood. As the *haka*, a New Zealand war dance, reminds us, combatants historically tried to intimidate their enemy. Now, however, aggressors usually compete to present themselves as innocent victims; think Hitler versus

Poland, Saddam Hussein versus Kuwait, or Vladimir Putin versus Ukraine. Palestinians seek the cherished mantle of victim, and more convincingly attain it due to their actual weakness. This amplifies their global message and endangers Israel's international stature.

Fourth, the growing number of Arabs and Palestinians open to working with Israel represents both an opportunity and a limitation, for their positive attitudes are based not just on Israel's strength but also on its decency. In the effort to break rejectionism, then, Israelis need to be on their best behavior and put forward their most appealing qualities. Put differently, whereas conciliation failed vis-à-vis the Palestinians, it works with Emiratis.

Fifth, military loss uniquely does not discredit or damage Palestinian leaders, who claim that losses are actually victories. Indeed, they can find disaster on the battlefield politically useful. (For details, see "Finessing defeat," pp. 47-48.)

Sixth, and most important, violence often has a counterproductive effect by multiplying the number of enemies. For example, a particularly large-scale January 2023 gunfight in Jenin killed at least nine Palestinians, including three PIJ members; the raid's tactical success notwithstanding, it had questionable utility. *The Jerusalem Post*'s Yonah Jeremy Bob rightly wondered whether the raid would not cause "relatives and friends of the nine Palestinians to turn to terrorism, even if previously they were staying on the sidelines. Put in mathematical terms: Before the operation, the IDF was worried about three terrorists; what if, afterward, there are 20–30 new terrorists acting out of personal fury and a desire for revenge?"

In other words, violence may have the intended effect of deterrence; or the contrary, unintended effect of creating new enemies. In and of itself, violence is an unpredictable tool. Inflicted in isolation, it can end up hurting Israel more than helping it. Indeed, Israel has historically focused too much on military methods; it needs to expand to the psychological. Israel's military power provides the necessary context but it best stays in the background, resorted to cautiously, sparingly.

Violence proves mutually and symmetrically counterproductive. Just as Palestinians murder Israelis intending to demoralize them but instead build more fury and resolve, so Israeli force against Palestinians also backfires. Israeli author Yossi Klein Halevi notes, "Rather than undermine our morale, the terrorist attacks only strengthen our resolve." To which, West Bank journalist Ahmed Melhem retorts that, "As Israel's raids grow in West Bank, so does Palestinian support for armed groups." Both sides come away confirmed in their views. More Palestinians hate Israel, more Israelis support a tougher approach.

Despite these undesired results, the two sides continue to bash away, blind to the inutility of their tactics, unable to find a better alternative. Thus, Israelis revert to alarming calls for more violence, hoping against hope that more of it will finally bring success. Thus, National Security Minister Itamar Ben-Gvir called on the government to kill "thousands of terrorists." Yitzhak Pundak, belatedly made a major general in the IDF at age one hundred in 2013, advised how to deal with Hamas missiles: "For every missile they fire, we reply with 20 artillery shells. If we kill 500, they'll calm down immediately." But the reverse is more likely. Those 500 have multiple relatives and friends who will swear vengeance, enlarging rather than diminishing Israel's pool of enemies. However emotionally appealing, such sentiments must be subjected to sober analysis.

Of course, Israel must use force; but it cannot look to force as the solution to rejectionism. Its power offers a wide range of levers with which to exert influence over Palestinians, from economics to religion. Based on its power and wealth, Israel can pivot to spreading ideas. After all, rejectionism will only be replaced by another set of views. Therefore, Israel's public diplomacy is central. Messaging is needed, but a better messaging than what exists at present.

• • •

The public diplomacy challenge. The Israeli effort to respond to foreign critics and convey a positive impression about the country is known in Hebrew as *hasbara*. Those campaigns tend to be ineffectual.

Misdirected hasbara. The Ministry of Foreign Affairs takes the lead in promoting hasbara. Gideon Meir, its deputy director-general for media and public affairs, explains why: "Because of its network of embassies and consulates abroad and its wide-ranging contacts all around the world, Israel's Ministry of Foreign Affairs is the government institution most intensely involved in public diplomacy and best suited to do it."

Two initiatives convey the flavor of existing hasbara: Brand Israel, started in 2005 by Israel's Prime Minister's Office, Foreign Ministry, and Finance Ministry, aimed to show Israel as where "cool, hip people" live, countering its reputation as "militaristic" and "religious." Voices of Israel (VOI), launched by the Foreign Ministry in 2022, had the goal of "strengthening positive perceptions of Israel and combating hate speech and incitement around the world…to strengthen Israel's legitimacy and to minimize the impact among key audiences of the delegitimization campaign against it." It encouraged "Israel's friends" to respond to "global social, demographic and political change; new worldviews and narratives that impact how Israel and Jews are perceived." VOI particularly targeted "young people and others who are susceptible to our enemies' distortions, by connecting on issues that they care about." It urged social media influencers to visit Israel.

Not addressing Palestinians. While useful, such international efforts largely ignore West Bankers, Gazans, and eastern Jerusalemites. For good measure, they also ignore Israel's Muslim citizens. Although Palestinians are the source of Israel's global delegitimization, the Foreign Ministry deals not with them but with foreign countries. It maintains, of course, no embassies or consulates in Ramallah or Gaza City, the PA and Hamas political centers.

Thus does Jerusalem's public diplomacy focus on the symptoms of rejectionism, not its causes; on the branches and leaves, not the roots; on the Left, not the Palestinians. Israel has effectively ceded any role in Palestinians' school books, print, electronic, and social media, mosque sermons, or wall posters. It tolerates ubiquitous incitement. Israel has even lost the battle in eastern Jerusalem schools, which it directly controls. A February 2023 study found that, of 118,000 non-citizen students attending twenty-six institutions, 47 percent are enrolled in public schools fully funded and run by Israel. While those schools do not explicitly incite violence, 85 percent teach the PA curriculum and teachers openly express anti-Israel views. According to one of them:

> Teachers sit in the teachers' room quite contently after terrorist attacks. They aren't concerned about the death of Israelis, and some of them even say "hopefully the wounded will die." … Many teachers identify with the Palestinian cause. Israel's existence is a technicality for them, that they put up with as they have no choice, but they do not feel any sentiment towards Israel. You might even overhear a teacher in the hallway say to him or herself "May God free us from the occupation, Israel must disappear." There are also extremist teachers teaching Islam in a way that brainwashes children.

Nor does the Israeli state address Israel's Muslim citizens in their schools, media, or the many other routes of delivering information. It even fails to use the tools available within its own prisons, where it has near-total control, instead, allowing them to serve as literal graduate schools in rejectionism.

This approach reflects the Israeli inclination pre-emptively to give up on Palestinians, seeing them as irredeemably hostile. A century and more of conciliation has had meager results. Content directed toward them, therefore, consists of routine announcements from government agencies like the Coordinator of Government Activities in the Territories (COGAT), a division of the Ministry of Defense. The creative and polemical Israelis addressing an Arabic-speaking audience, whether government employees (Avichay Adraee, Ofir Gendelman) or private individuals (Edi Cohen, Mordechai Kedar, Elhanan Miller), generally look beyond the Palestinians to the populations of Arab states.

Addressing Palestinians. Granted, changing Palestinian attitudes will not be easy. The PA and Hamas have subjected their populations to unprecedented and sustained barrages of messaging. Arguably, no other authoritarian or even totalitarian regimes have so assiduously and successfully pounded a mentality into their subject populations. Sermons inflame, media fabricate, posters celebrate, and politicians agitate. Life in the West Bank (and eastern Jerusalem to a lesser extent) comprises a series of propagandistic communications: the morning newspaper, posters on buildings, banners in streets, songs on the car radio, lessons at school, ads on the internet, sermons in mosques, products in stores. These many media unremittingly repeat the themes of Jews as descended from pigs and apes, Israel as satanic, and "martyrs" as heroes. The PA's school curriculum, according to the Israeli organization IMPACT-se, amounts to "education for war and against peace with Israel."

Israel needs to battle this messaging with a counteroffensive.

• • •

Normalization. *Normalization* (Arabic: *tatbi`*) offers the counter to rejectionism. This word has a decidedly negative connotation in Palestinian discourse; in a typical example, the PLO responded in 2020 to the news of Sudanese-Israeli normalization by calling it "a new stab in the back for the Palestinians." Instead, the PA and Hamas seek *denormalization* and its two objectives, as explained by Khaled Abu Toameh: "to intimidate and threaten Palestinians and Israelis who seek peace" and "to delegitimize and isolate Israel in the international community."

That negativity presents a challenge to Israel: It must convince Palestinians to accept normal relations with Israel, normal acceptance of it, and a normal role for it in international relations. Such a transformation will not happen by itself but depends on Israeli actions, on Israel devoting the bulk of its public relations efforts not to influencing the opinions of Americans, Africans, Iranians, or Lebanese, but to their closest and most deadly enemy. Rather than sponsor a float in New York City's gay pride parade, it should concentrate on the murderers stewing in its own prisons. Rather than focus on ignorant college students fooling around on TikTok or occupying campuses, it should fix on brainwashed Palestinian schoolchildren.

This entails a profound change from defense to offense: not showing Israel as a fun place with pretty women frolicking on beaches, but addressing Palestinians with an attitude of, "Let's figure out what went wrong for you." This effort, which I call the *New Hasbara*, develops smart and pervasive communications that saturate the Palestinians' mental environment with a mix of demoralizing and positive messages. Forget about destroying Israel, a strong, determined country. Further, you don't even want to because it's decent, normal, and your only lifeline out of oppression and poverty.

Herein lies the key to Israel Victory. Put most succinctly, it consists of minimal violence, maximal messaging.

Choose the messenger and audience. Palestinians and Israeli Arabic speakers who publicly call for an end to rejectionism and for acceptance of the Jewish state are the ideal messengers to explain why they appreciate Israel.[3] They know the issues, they have credibility, and they literarily speak the language. Their number includes such distinguished figures as writer Majdi Abd Al-Wahhab, journalist Khaled Abu Toameh, Gaza Youth Committee founder Rami Aman, professor Mohammed S. Dajani Daoudi, diplomat George Deek, human rights activist Bassam Eid, journalist Yoseph Haddad, businessman Ashraf Jabari, diplomat Ishmael Khaldi, former rock-thrower Mohammad Massad, social media influencer Noseir Yassin, activist Ziad Sabateen, former Hamas operative Mosab Hassan Yousef (aka the "Green

3 Non-Palestinians, such as Arabic-speaking Jews, lack their standing to influence Palestinians but can also help.

Prince"), outspoken gay activist Mohammad Zoabi, his mother Sarah Zoabi, and headmaster Nael Zoabi.

Israel should seek out and encourage, with suitable incentives, the many, many others to speak their minds who do not have a public stature but who gave up the fight against Israel, are sympathetic to it, praise it, want to live in it, and seek comity with it. They and their organizations (such as Haddad's Together Vouch for Each Other) should be funded, promoted, and celebrated so their voices are heard, their views widely known among Palestinians and Israel's Muslim citizens. If the rejectionists seek to intimidate, silence, and make examples of them, they and their families need to be protected.

Joseph Braude argues in his path-breaking book, *Reclamation: A Cultural Policy for Arab-Israeli Partnership*,[4] that all politicians, including autocrats, pay attention to the views of their populations, and therefore it pays to address those populations. He promotes three institutions as the best way to reach them: educational, religious, and media. Applied to our issue, this means developing strategies to use schools, mosques, and television to see Israel in a more benign light. When the masses accept this, they will pressure their autocratic PA and Hamas leaders to follow suit. The goal is, one century later, to undo the legacy of Amin al-Husseini and bring about the acceptance that did not take place in the 1920s.

Spread a message. Braude documents the phenomenon of non-Palestinian Arabic speakers who express benign views toward Israel, then offers ways to expand their reach and influence. Although specifically excluding Palestinians from his purview, his insights also apply to them. Pro-Israel Arabic speakers, he writes,

> merit scrutiny for who they are, how they came to their beliefs, and what role they might play in encouraging others. One can learn about them by following their activity on social media, watching them post comments to broadcasts, and of course meeting or working with them personally.

4 Joseph Braude, *Reclamation: A Cultural Policy for Arab-Israeli Partnership* (Washington, D.C.: Washington Institute for Near East Policy, 2019). The title word, *reclamation*, refers to positive Egyptian, Syrian, and other views of Zionism a century ago. Obviously, that aspect of Braude's argument does not apply to Palestinians. Nor does his hope that the U.S. government will work alongside Israel's.

In other words, learn what differentiates the 20 percent of Palestinians who accept Israel from the 80 percent who do not by interviewing, studying, and understanding them. Of the antis, how many are wavering, why, and which arguments will influence them? Sociologists, psychologists, pollsters, and marketers all have a role to play here.

• • •

Messages. Messaging, especially, requires a deep, contemporaneous, and detailed study. Substance, tone, and graphics need to be chosen with care. The geography, age, gender, religiosity, education, and income of the intended audience all come into play. Again, with due caution, I offer some ideas for Israel's message. It might have several components: anti-PA and -Hamas, anti-rejectionism, pro-Israel, and related to Islam.

First, publicizing intra-Palestinian differences, verbal and violent has an obvious appeal, exploiting the bonanza of horrible things the PA and Hamas have said about each other. This can include fanning the memory of hatreds from the Gaza civil war in 2007 or the intra-Palestinian battle over Islamic Zionism. The recall of embarrassing bits, such as rumors about Yasir Arafat's homosexuality or PA and Hamas corruption, would likely help.

Second, Israel's proxies can mount a campaign to undermine rejectionism, with messages such as:

- We are losing a century-long struggle, we are on the wrong track, our lives are miserable, we suffer from a death cult, our facts are wrong, our premises are evil, we are going nowhere.
- Our allies invariably end up in the trash heap of history: Ottomans, Nazis, Soviets, Gamal Abdel Nasser, and Saddam Hussein. The Islamic Republic of Iran is heading there, too.
- Resolutions from the United Nations and other international organizations sound great and feel good but carry no moral weight and bring no practical benefits.
- As Muslims, Jerusalem and Palestine have minor importance for us.
- A shared capital in Jerusalem is unworkable; give it up.

- The "right of return" of anyone claiming to be a Palestine refugee damages millions by impeding their full lives where they are.

Third, a pro-Zionist barrage:

- Israel is strong, tough, rich, determined, with powerful allies. (Amplify this with information on its scientific achievements, show video clips on its fighter jets, warships, and tanks, and statistics about Israel's integration in the world economy.)
- Many Palestinians praise the Jewish state and wish to live in it. (Quote them.)
- The Arab states have effectively abandoned you; the Abraham Accords are a roaring success.

Finally, the New Hasbara might include sponsoring the reconsideration of Koranic precepts. Two such possibilities concern the control of territory and the place of Jews in the Holy Land.

Control of territory. Islamic law asserts that Muslims must win back any Muslim-controlled territory which falls to non-Muslim control. This precept retains its power over long periods of time, so that Muslims widely assume that any possession, no longer how long ago lost, must revert to their control. This attitude has special power in Israel's case, partly because Jews were historically powerless, partly because of Jerusalem's Islamic sanctities. But that optimism about regaining any land under Muslim rule emerged over a millennium ago, in a period of Muslim expansion, when it was realistic to expect such a reconquest. It is mostly illusory in the modern era; Spain, Sicily, the Balkans, Greece, Cyprus, India, and Mindanao are not likely to revert to Muslim sovereignty (though being part of an empire, Xinjiang might). Islamic law needs a major overhaul and updating; Israeli's government can quietly commission Islamic scholars to rethink this assumption and reach a different conclusion that keeps with the temper of the times.

Zionist Koran. The Koran is a proto-Zionist document, with verses that endorse the Jewish presence in what it calls the Holy Land (*al-ard al-muqaddasa*), a territory that makes up roughly the northern half of today's Israel. The Koran refers to Jews as the "Children of Israel" while Verse 5:20-21 quotes Moses saying to the Jews, "O my people! Enter the

Holy Land which God [*Allah*] has ordained for you to enter." Likewise, Verse 7:137 states that, "We made those who were persecuted successors of the eastern and western lands [of the Jordan River], lands which We had blessed. In this way, your Lord's fair word was fulfilled for the Children of Israel." Other Koranic verses (2:40, 7:159–160, and 17:100–104)) confirm this theme, as do Hadith reports and some Koranic scholars of the premodern era.

Deep research into this issue has been carried out by such scholars as Nissim Dana of Ariel University, author of the 2013 book, in Hebrew, *To Whom Does This Land Belong? Reexamination of the Koran and Classical Islamic Sources on the People of Israel, Its Teachings, and Its Connection to Jerusalem*. On the Islamic side, key work has been done by Muhammad Al-Hussaini, formerly of Leo Baeck College, the late Khaleel Mohammed of San Diego State University, and Mohammad Tawhidi of the Islamic Association of South Australia. In Tawhidi's words, "It's in the Muslim consciousness that the land first belonged to the Jews." Another Muslim thinker, Abdul Hadi Palazzi, comes right out and states that "Allah Is a Zionist." Muhammad Khan Sherani, a former chairman of Pakistan's Council of Islamic Ideology, states that "Educated Muslims need to understand that the Quran and history prove to us that the Land of Israel belongs only to the Jews."

• • •

These practical steps offer a sketch of how Israel might non-violently but effectively respond to Palestinian violence and delegitimization. Israel should have taken the steps proposed here to mold and defang the territories it conquered in 1967, not waited until 2024, but better late than never. Mulligans are legal in politics.

That said, Israel Victory does not offer a quick fix. Were it immediately implemented, a Palestinian-Israeli resolution will likely take a generation, or occur around 2050.

Israel Victory is optimistic and non-violent. It calls for a rethinking of faulty assumptions, disproven methods, and failed results. Rejecting the stale duo of enrichment and placation, it offers a humane and hopeful approach. Conciliation assumes that Palestinians cannot be induced to change; Israel Victory presumes they can. The security establishment offers treasure to irredeemable enemies, hoping to distract them from further attacks; in contrast, this analysis foresees the possibility of real and positive change. Conciliation hopes to finesse rejectionism; Israel Victory confronts it, defeats it, and attains closure.

The final chapter points to the benefits that Israel Victory brings to all involved.

VICTORY'S BENEFITS

PALESTINIAN DEFEAT ADVANCES THE INTERESTS of three populations: Beyond the two main combatants—acceptance for Israelis, liberation for the Palestinians—it also offers an escape from the central dilemma of Israel's nearly two million Muslim citizens.

ZIONISTS ACCEPTED

Obviously, a Palestinian defeat brings two great advantages to Israel: a reduction in both violence and in the global anti-Zionist campaign. It also has the side-benefit of facilitating exciting new policies.

• • •

Ending violence and calumnies. Israelis (including Muslim Israelis) live well. Ranking fourth on the United Nations' happiness scale offers one indication, a poll finding 93 percent of Jewish Israelis proud to be Israeli offers another. Most persuasively, Israelis have a total fertility rate (the number of children per woman) of 3.0, making Israel the only advanced country to exceed the replacement rate of 2.1. (The next highest is New Zealand at 2.0; the lowest is South Korea at 0.8.) Israelis had a per capita income of $55,000 in 2022, placing them between Austrians and Canadians. Beyond numbers, Israel is a well-functioning society, with the rule of law, a boisterous democracy, a rowdy political life, and a vibrant culture.

But Israel is the only modern, democratic country to suffer from constant violence aimed at undermining its well-being as well as threats to its very existence.[1] Victory will finally permit Israelis to live fully normal lives,

1 Ukraine, Armenia, South Korea, and Taiwan also face existential threats but not the decades of violence nor the calumny.

not enduring security checks on entering a grocery store, not stopping conversations to listen to news on the hour.

The Palestinians' defeat also bestows a greater, if less obvious, gain, than ending violence; it also deals with their campaign of vilification and delegitimization against Israel that inspires groaning shelves of hostile studies, rounds of failed negotiations, lopsided United Nations resolutions, and global street demonstrations.

A vast hinterland heeds the Palestinians' calumnies. Closest at hand, Israel's Muslim citizens take their cue from them, challenging Israel's domestic peace and its Jewish nature. Other Arabic speakers enhance and expand the Palestinian cause, helping to turn it into a global issue. Iran has a unique place when it comes to violence, what with its building nuclear weapons directed firstly against Israel. Türkiye, standing firmly in NATO, presents a less violent, more diplomatic threat. Muslims around the world spread the anti-Zionist message far and wide. The global Left has become active in the delegitimization of Israel. As the Egyptian intellectual Mohamed Salmawy observes, those hostile to Israel around the world "are growing more numerous by the day." For example, the youngest cohort of Americans is the most liberal and also the most critical of Israel.

Israel cannot address all the manifestations of international rage; but it can go to the source and convince Palestinians to end their campaign of rejectionism. Palestinian defeat will mark the beginning of the end of the wider Islamist and leftist war on Israel. The hinterland will be left high and dry; how can it sustain the old animosity if those they fight for have acquiesced? Remove the Palestinians and hating Israel becomes a theoretical exercise. From Morocco to Indonesia, Muslim-majority states will likely back away, as will Western ones, as interest diminishes among Muslim populations. Many Islamists who take their cue from Palestinians will find other causes to take up as anti-Zionism tones down—perhaps those living in much more dire circumstances, such as those of the Uyghurs in Communist China and the Rohingyas in Myanmar. Leftist anti-Zionism will drop, if not end, as a serious force. That shift won't happen instantly, to be sure; but sustaining a more-Catholic-than-the-pope position becomes more implausible with time.

Palestinians are key. When they give up, the conflict will end, and only then.

The Left's anti-Zionism, it bears recalling, focuses almost exclusively on the supposed suffering of the 3.5 million inhabitants of the West Bank,

Gaza, and eastern Jerusalem. In contrast, it hardly cares about other issues, such as Israel's income inequality, its tensions with Iran and Türkiye, or its nuclear weapons. This implies that solving the Palestinian issue effectively ends the Left's hostility to Israel.

Israel finds itself in the fortunate position of not needing to fight the great body of its haters—Islamists, Iranian and Turkish regimes, the global Left, and beyond—but only the Palestinians, the ultimate enemy of roughly the same size demographically while much weaker in economic and military terms.

Two main objections to this argument arise. One holds that this dynamic is precisely the wrong way around: Palestinians will not influence far-flung Arabs, Muslims, Islamists, and leftists, but will be influenced by them. Any Palestinian entity that follows surrender, writes Martin Sherman, "is certain to be branded as illegitimate by much of the Arab/Muslim world, to which the bulk of Palestinian-Arabs, exposed to the perspectives of their ethnic kinfolk beyond their borders, see themselves as belonging." To this, I reply: This view is stuck in the pre-1973 era, when Arabs stood together in opposition to Israel. But now, when the most important Arab states have largely reconciled to Israel's existence, the Palestinians who join them will be welcomed. Indeed, their abandoning rejectionism eases the Arab states' position vis-à-vis their own radicalized populations.

Palestinians have long driven the process. Note the dynamic already from 1992 to 1994, when they seemed to accept Israel. The governments of Syria and Iran, among others, could not prevent Arafat from signing the Oslo Accords and failed in their efforts to assume his leadership of the anti-Zionist cause. After holding off for more than forty years, both China and India established diplomatic relations with Israel within days on each other in 1992 (on January 24 and January 29, respectively). Within a year, Israel had diplomatic relations with 146 states, thirty more than before the White House signing.

The second objection maintains that the "world's oldest hatred" will surely survive a Palestinian defeat, especially given the near-ubiquity of antisemitism among Palestinians and its general appeal to Muslims. True, but bigotry does not imply genocidal war. Further, antisemitism is superficial among Muslims, based less in Islamic doctrine or history than in tactical needs for battling Israel. Under the right circumstances—that is, with Palestinians quiescent and the battle ended—antisemitism could well diminish, as recent trends, especially in the United Arab Emirates, suggest.

For the Jewish state to become a normal country requires an end to Palestinian rejectionism. This makes a Palestinian change of heart as important to Israel as dispatching the Iranian nuclear threat.

• • •

Solution agnostic. Some find the idea of Israel Victory shocking; the American J Street organization calls it "medieval" and "truly terrifying." With apologies for terrifying those gentle progressives, Israel Victory actually reduces contention over final status arrangements. Further, it is solution agnostic, with no implications for the debate over what happens after a Palestinian change of heart. It favors no Palestinian-Israeli final-status dispensation. Whatever one's preferred outcome, whether J Street's complete withdrawal from the West Bank or Americans for a Safe Israel's annexing it, Israel Victory takes a step toward reaching either goal. The same applies to the one-state or two-state solution.[2] All who want a safe and secure Israel can agree on ending rejectionism. As former Israeli politician Einat Wilf puts it, "Victory is on the path to peace; it is not an end point."

Supporters of this approach are free to promote their preferred solutions. I, however, choose neutrality on final-status issues, and for two reasons: First, until victory has become policy, arguing over policies is premature and distracts attention from the priority, the need for victory. Second, advocating a specific policy risks alienating those who disagree with it, reducing the number of potential supporters for victory.

Palestinian-Israeli trust opens up new possible arrangements, including what are now pie-in-the-sky mutual concessions, sweeping aside today's intractable issues:

- *Adjusted borders*: What should be the borders of a Palestinian state? As many Israeli politicians have suggested, the "Triangle" area of Israel, with its large Muslim population, can become part of a Palestinian state (more on this below, under "Israel's Muslim citizens released," pp. 290-96.)

2 This solution-agnostic approach contrasts with other like-minded plans, each of which entails a very specific course of action: Jordan-is-Palestine, the New State Solution (Benjamin Anthony), the One-State Solution (Caroline Glick), Palestinian Emirates (Mordechai Kedar), and the Humanitarian Paradigm (Martin Sherman).

- *Palestinian sovereignty*: Jews in the West Bank can live under Palestinian rule. Israeli towns in the West Bank lose their contention when Palestinians accept Jews living among them and treat them fairly, on the model of Israel's Muslim citizens. Indeed, their percentages are roughly similar.
- *Israeli sovereignty*: Jews living outside Israel proper in the West Bank can live under Israeli rule. No imperative requires that sovereignty be contiguous.
- *A two state solution*, or the creation of a Palestinian state: This prospect rightly arouses intense opposition at present because it represents an absurdity, demanding of Israel to reward rejectionism and strengthen its mortal enemy. But a Palestinian state becomes acceptable when hostilities, physical and verbal, are long past and Palestinians have in a full and protracted way accepted Israel to the satisfaction of Israelis. In other words, it remains a very distant prospect but not an impossibility.

If Israel already ranks No. 4 on the world happiness list, Palestinian acceptance could catapult it to No. 1.

PALESTINIANS LIBERATED

When Palestinians give up their goal of destroying Israel, they can leave today's troubles behind, fulfill their potential, build their polity, economy, society, and culture, and live the good life. Ironically, they need Israel Victory to redirect them onto this path. It is win-win. Who is truly pro-Palestinian should advise Palestinians to give up and acknowledge defeat: "The game is over, accept the Jewish state, bargain with it, and benefit from its dynamism."

• • •

Today's misery. West Bank and Gaza residents live in conditions fluctuating between chaos and despotism, assailed by insecurity and corruption, surrounded by nihilism and lies, living under repressive and malign dictatorships. Little wonder they constitute the world's most radicalized and genocidal population. Less wonder that they are growing weary of their exceptional status.

The West Bank, nominally ruled by the Palestinian Authority, is partially anarchic—an even more harrowing circumstance than despotism—with curfews, road blocks, and violence defining its population's immediate parameters. Effective rule had already broken down under Yasir Arafat, with gangs and clans taking PA's place. "He doesn't control anything anymore" said one top Israeli official in 2003; "Right now, only God is in charge" observed a top Palestinian. Then, things got even worse under Mahmoud Abbas, as indicated by a *Los Angeles Times* report from early 2005:

> Feuds among rival security chiefs, who often command loyalty based on patronage or clan ties, regularly spill over into shootouts and abductions, particularly in the Gaza Strip. Some branches of the service so loathe one another that straying into the wrong patch of territory without a full complement of armed escorts would be deadly. Particularly at odds are the preventive security and militant intelligence branches, which have attacked one another with grenades and gunfire.

Despite an attempted crackdown by Abbas, anarchy has remained a problem. In a 2016 analysis, Israeli reporter Pinhas Inbari found that the Ramallah-based administration's

> loss of control over the West Bank districts raises questions about its ability to run a state and play its part in ensuring not only Israel's and Jordan's security...but even its own security.... The fragmented Palestinian West Bank will be a weaker entity than the weak states that collapsed in the Arab Spring. When the Palestinian entity collapses, the vacuum will be filled by the negative forces that have become the nightmare of the world.

The problem continues. Late 2022 saw an area from Jenin to Nablus becoming nearly lawless as the corrupt and weak PA faced no-go zones and other forms of intimidation. A July 2023 assessment by Haviv Rettig Gur found that:

> The northern West Bank, everyone now understands, has disintegrated into a power vacuum. The Palestinian Authority no longer rules there. Israeli security forces rarely enter (at least until recently) and entire areas and neighborhoods in

> both of its major cities have come under the control of newborn militias.

Gaza, seized by Hamas from the PA in a bloody insurrection between 2005 and 2007, suffers yet more, with an even more repressive regime engaged in intermittent rocket and missile attacks on Israel purposefully intended to lead to retribution in the form of air attacks on Gaza's infrastructure, homes, and lives. Typically, *The New York Times* reported in 2013:

> Raw sewage has flooded streets in a southern Gaza City neighborhood in recent days, threatening a health disaster, after a shortage of electricity and cheap diesel fuel from Egypt led the Hamas government to shut down Gaza's lone power plant, causing a pump station to flood. Three more sewage stations in Gaza City and 10 others elsewhere in the Gaza Strip are close to overflowing, sanitation officials here said, and 3.5 million cubic feet of raw sewage is seeping into the Mediterranean Sea daily. The sanitation department may soon no longer be able to pump drinking water to Gaza homes....
>
> The sewage crisis is the most acute of an array of problems since the Islamist Hamas movement that governs Gaza shut down the power plant on Nov. 1. Four months earlier Egypt's new military-backed government closed the smuggling tunnels that were used to transport around one million liters (about 260,000 gallons) of diesel here each day.... Having gotten used to years of scheduled blackouts, generally eight hours without electricity two of every three days, Gaza's 1.7 million residents are now facing daily power failures of 12 or even 18 hours.

According to the large-scale Palestinian Psychological Conditions Survey carried out in 2022 by the World Bank and other institutions, 58 percent of Palestinian adults "exhibit symptoms consistent with depression." In the assessment of a sympathetic observer, Harvard University's Sara Roy, Palestinians have been "ravaged by widespread poverty, declining health status, eroding education, physical and environmental destruction, and the absence of hope."

Then came October 7 and the destruction that followed, unmeasurable at the time of this writing but clearly catastrophic.

Making the situation yet more tenuous, the West Bank and Gaza economies both depend, probably more than any other territories in the world, on free money flowing in from abroad. By one estimate, more than 70 percent of Gaza's residents pre-October 7 depended on international aid. This creates the twin evils of dependence and resentment, manifested among elite and ordinary recipients alike who whine about insufficient amounts of gratis cash, wanting ever more of it. One PA leader, Nabil Shaath, demanded that donors be ready to give "massive economic support" to the PA. When Israel cut off some PA funding, a PA spokesman responded by asserting, "either Israel pays the tax money to the [PA] or the international donors try to fund the salaries." When Israel did make unilateral concessions to the PA, a senior official dismissed those as "a bad joke...not serious." Salam Fayyad, the PA's so-called prime minister, petulantly complained about the slow delivery of promised donations: "We need to see an acceleration in the receipt of aid that has been committed."

The same avarice applies to individuals, especially when it comes to free housing. As the Associated Press explains:

> The United Nations suspended a construction project in [the Jenin] refugee camp after Palestinian gunmen threatened crews rebuilding houses destroyed by Israeli forces, a U.N. official said Thursday. Many residents of the Jenin camp are complaining that their new houses, replacing those destroyed in Israeli incursions, are not big enough.... In the most recent attack, five Palestinians from one family barged into the U.N. office in Jenin on Tuesday and opened fire with M-16 and Kalashnikov assault rifles.... One gunman, who identified himself as Abu Maher, said he took action because the house promised to him was only half the size of the one Israeli forces destroyed. He said dissatisfaction in the camp was widespread, with some residents saying the wait for a new home was too long.... Raed Karawi said the agency gave him an apartment of 600 square feet. "This is not enough for me and my wife to live. We will have children soon. This is not fair," he said, threatening to buy 20 old cars and block the new roads.

The rejected homes, it bears noting, were built to European construction standards and came outfitted with ceramic floor tiles and Italian marble kitchen tops.

Worse, Palestinian mores are backward and becoming more medieval with time. Opinion surveys consistently show a tendency toward nihilism. Which other parents celebrate their children becoming suicide bombers? Which other people prefers to harm its neighbor than improve its own lot? Bassam Eid ponders the damage that rejectionism has wrought on his people:

> It's time to admit that Palestinian institutions are broken, and that they have developmentally harmed generations of Palestinian men and women, boys and girls, by whipping them into a constant froth with violently antisemitic educational and media content that celebrate "martyrdom" attacks against Israelis.... The Palestinian people's immersion in a culture of violence now spans generations.

The cause of this failure and frustration is clear: rejectionism. As Hussain Abdul-Hussain of the Foundation for the Defense of Democracies explains, until the Palestinians accept "that Israel is here to stay and that the only way out is genuine peace, not half-peace that will create Palestine alongside half-conflict that will destroy Israel, Palestinians will keep suffering, a sorry situation of their own doing."

Defeat permits improvements in two main ways: by allowing Palestinians to move ahead with their lives and to enter productive negotiations with Israel.

• • •

Moving ahead. Israeli future success in crushing the Palestinians' war morale will unburden them from ugly ambitions, a cult of death, and genocidal fantasies. To become a normal people, one whose parents do not encourage their children to become suicide killers, Palestinians need to undergo the trauma of defeat, which permits them to terminate their irredentist fantasies and close down the empty rhetoric of revolution. Sloughing off their current oppression, extremism, and violence, they can become a positive influence rather than today's destructive force.

When they accept the permanence of Israel, Palestinians can finally give up their foul irredentist fantasies and instead focus on their own welfare, to begin what Arafat once deceitfully spoke of as the "process of economic, social, and cultural growth." This opens the way to fulfilling their considerable potential by building a stable country, a prosperous economy, an open political system, and an attractive culture commensurate with their dignity and talent. With the end of conflict, they can finally work with and gain from Israel rather than fight it.

"They must accept defeat, and accept it constructively," writes South African novelist J.M. Coetzee of the Palestinians. "The alternative, unconstructive way is to go on nourishing revanchist dreams of a tomorrow when all wrongs, by some miracle, will be righted. For a constructive way of accepting defeat they might look to Germany post-1945." Indeed, post-1945 Germany and Japan, transformed by defeat from menace to solid citizen, offer a model for Palestinians through an acknowledgment of lies, evil, and folly, plus a de-rejectionism comparable to de-Nazification. Sudanese columnist Osama Di Al-Naim Muhammad agrees, recalling that Germany and Japan in 1945 "were defeated and destroyed.... The enemies of yesterday [now] coexist, trade and cooperate on mutual interests." Walter Russell Mead elaborates on this analogy:

> Palestinians today don't need a Nelson Mandela who can lead the struggle for equal political rights in one state. They need a Konrad Adenauer: a leader who can accept military defeat and painful territorial losses while building a prosperous future through reconciliation with the victors. As Adenauer's postwar West Germany showed, it is possible to recover from crushing defeats, but defeat must be accepted before it can be overcome. A new generation, instead of following its elders down the rabbit hole of eternally futile resistance, could instead work toward competent governance, and ultimately reconciliation and renewal.

To repeat, "defeat must be accepted before it can be overcome."

Between the twin afflictions of seventeen years under Hamas and the post-October 7 devastation, Gazans have endured a hard landing roughly comparable to what Germans and Japanese suffered in World War II. Drawing on that analogy, these circumstances may make it easier for them to move ahead. In contrast, West Bankers have had a relatively easy time of it, so their evolution is likely to be more protracted.

Therein lies the essential challenge to the Palestinians. Their transformation will be neither easy nor quick. As they repudiate the filthy legacy of Amin al-Husseini and acknowledge their century-long error, they must pass through the harsh ordeal of defeat. There is no shortcut.

• • •

Negotiations. Until Palestinians undergo a change of heart, negotiations with Israel remain not just futile but counterproductive. Futile, because they cannot usefully be undertaken so long as one party still aims to destroy the other. Counterproductive, because Israeli concessions inflame Palestinian aggression, violence, and calumnies.

Israelis in turn will need plenty of time to become confident about the reality of that change of heart. As the Taliban and Russian resurgences of 2021 and 2022 made clear, giving up can be reversed. This means that the Palestinians must remain on probation for years or even decades. A century of genocidal rejectionism implies a long period of recovery to ensure that the body politic is rid of toxins.

When Israelis recognize a change of heart, it means that Palestinians will finally have accepted defeat and become a normal people. Good things will follow. Released from a murderous obsession, Palestinians can gain from their long-time enemy. Negotiations can re-open. Issues raised in the Oslo Accords and subsequent agreements—borders, water, other resources, armaments, sanctities, Jerusalem, Jewish residents in the West Bank, and the "Palestine refugees"—can be taken up anew, this time in earnest. The talks might reach similar conclusions as in 1993, but now workable and realistic. Uri Dromi, the Rabin-Peres government spokesman from 1992 to 1996, hopes that "having seen once again the futility of trying to defeat Israel on the battlefield, a Palestinian leadership will emerge that will, like Sadat, and as Jabotinsky predicted, begin 'bargaining with us on practical matters, such as guarantees against pushing them out, and equality of civil and national rights.'"

No longer aspiring to destroy Israel, Palestinians become eligible for money and other signs of approval. Those many plans discussed in Chapter 6 can now be dusted off and seriously reviewed. Indeed, to encourage resolution, Israelis can provide benefits and inducements. They, Alex Nachumson explains,

> need to show how much can be gained from defeat. Once a group has accepted defeat, they should be given assistance to help their community, to see how the seeds of defeat can be sown for the betterment of the defeated. Once the weapons, rhetorical or otherwise, have been laid down, the victor can be magnanimous. Defeat does not need to involve violence; it can also be incentivized through benefits.

As the Middle East Forum's Cliff Smith notes, Israel Victory "need not look like the destruction left in the wake of the [2021] conflict in Gaza, but like the skyscrapers of Dubai." Rejectionism abandoned, Palestinians will naturally begin to forge a new identity, one independent of Zionism, Israel, and especially of that ignominious fraud, Islamic Zionism.

The contrast between Israeli success and Palestinian misery has a striking implication: Palestinians suffer more from rejectionism than Israelis, and Israel Victory benefits Palestinians even more than Israelis. In a cosmic irony, Palestinians gain more from defeat than do Israelis from victory.

ISRAEL'S MUSLIM CITIZENS RELEASED

Israel's Muslim citizens make up nearly one-fifth of the country's population. Although they appreciate many aspects of Israeli life, they also have deep reservations about living as a minority in a Jewish state. Their status as citizens means that the State of Israel cannot treat them as it does West Bankers, Gazans, and eastern Jerusalemites; a democratic government cannot make war on or defeat its own citizens. A Palestinian change of heart offers a way for them to avoid living in Israel by making the West Bank and Gaza newly attractive places to live.

• • •

Appreciation. The Arabic-speaking population of Israel began small, amounting to 158,000 persons in 1949, 15 percent of Israel's population. Its leadership had mostly fled, it lived under military rule, and it had a minimal role in the country's life. For understandable reasons, Israeli Jews initially looked at their Muslim neighbors with great suspicion, worried that they would rise up against the new state. When this did not happen, fears diminished and military rule eventually ceased in 1966.

Two processes then made Israeli Arabs less marginal. First, their numbers increased dramatically, multiplying thirteen-fold, to 2.02 million in 2022, increasing to 21 percent of the country's population. (Adding the Arab residents of Jerusalem, who overwhelmingly hold permanent resident status, but not Israeli citizenship, the Arab population expands to 2.37 million, 24 percent of the population.) About two-thirds of this increase resulted from reproduction and one-third from immigration. Early on, Muslims had a birthrate many times higher than that of Jews, but that evolved to the point that the two are effectively equal, with the Jewish rate marginally higher. Barring massive immigration or emigration, the proportion of about one-fifth will likely remain stable.

Second, Israeli Muslim citizens integrated into the larger society. Children learned Hebrew, went to Hebrew-language universities, and used Hebrew at work. They took advantage of Israel's open, modern society to evolve from a small, docile, and leaderless population into a robust, assertive community. Its leaders have included Supreme Court justices Abdel Rahman Zuabi and Khaled Kabub, Knesset Committee Chairman Mansour Abbas, ambassadors Ali Yahya and Ishmael Khaldi, government minister Raleb Majadele, his son, journalist Muhamad Majadele, journalist Lucy Aharish, vice president and dean of research at University of Haifa Mouna Maroun, banker Samer Haj-Yehia, surgeon Ahmed Eid, writer Sayed Kashua, football player Bibras Nathko, plus academics, entrepreneurs, and others.

Israel's Muslim citizens appreciate, sometimes eloquently, the country's economic success, standard of healthcare, rule of law, and functioning democracy. Opinion surveys and a substantial record of statements and actions suggest that, despite their anti-Zionist swagger, Israel's most intimate opponents perceive its virtues. Survey research confirms this attitude:

- A 2004 poll found that Israeli Arab respondents preferred by a ten-to-one ratio to remain Israeli citizens.
- Two polls in December 2007 agreed on a 4.5-to-one ratio for Israeli Arabs who want to remain Israeli citizens.
- A 2008 poll found that Israeli Arabs preferred Israel to "any other country in the world" by a 3.5-to-one ratio.

- A 2011 survey found 53 percent proud to be Israeli.
- A 2012 poll found similar results to the 2008 poll.
- A 2015 poll found pride in being Israeli by a two-to-one ratio.
- A 2022 poll found that 49 percent have a "sense of belonging to the state and its problems."

When given a choice of living under Zionist or Palestinian rule, Israel's Muslim citizens decidedly prefer the former. This becomes especially clear when Israeli leaders raise the idea of moving the country's border to include more West Bank Jews and exclude Israel's Muslim citizens by putting them under PA control, as suggested by prime ministers Ariel Sharon in February 2004, Ehud Olmert in October 2007, and Benjamin Netanyahu in January 2014, as well as Avigdor Liberman in June 2010, November 2014, and September 2016. The inevitable howls of protest assured these proposals' quick and ignominious death.

Sharon's initiative raised special objections. The Islamist mayor of Umm al-Fahm, the largest predominantly Muslim town in Israel, responded with "the democracy and justice in Israel is better than the democracy and justice in Arab and Islamic countries." Ahmed Tibi, a viciously anti-Zionist member of the Knesset called PA control "a dangerous, antidemocratic suggestion."

The 2020 Trump plan also created a furor because it contemplated "the possibility, subject to agreement of the parties, that the borders of Israel will be redrawn such that the Triangle Communities become part of the State of Palestine." ("The Triangle" is a region of Israel's Galilee region bordering the West Bank and predominantly inhabited by some 300,000 Muslims.) In other words, no one will be evicted but Israel's border will be moved, to exclude the Triangle, transferring it to become part of today's Palestinian Authority and (perhaps) tomorrow's State of Palestine.

Reactions came fast and furious. Ayman Odeh, head of the Joint List party defiantly announced that: "No one will deprive us of citizenship in the homeland where we were born." Mayors of three towns mentioned by name in the plan slammed the idea of being included in a future Palestine and demonstrations erupted. Israeli Arab media reactions were "without exception" opposed to the plan. The Trump plan also had an emotional impact, according to Rodayna Badir of Hebrew University: "If you ask Israeli Arabs, they will say that part of their identity is Israeli. The younger generation feels more Israeli than Palestinian, but now they feel the state is accusing them of being traitors." Khaled Abu Toameh (who lives in what the PA calls a "settlement" and humorously calls himself an "Arab settler") explains that, like him, Israeli Arabs are mainly afraid of becoming Palestinian citizens "because they know that the Palestinian state will be anything but democratic."

Anger at this aspect of the Trump plan apparently increased Israeli Muslim turnout in the next election, in March 2020, and may have affected the outcome. According to Yousef Makladeh of the Statnet Research Institute, Arab turnout was 49.2 percent in April 2019, 59.2 percent in September 2019, and 64.7 percent in March 2020.

Nor was the response confined to words. Should the prospect of a border move become real, Israel's Muslim citizens can and will exercise their right as citizens of Israel to remove themselves from the Triangle and live in a region not slated to be turned over to Mahmoud Abbas & Co. Journalist Jalal Bana reports that, "almost entirely under the radar, we have seen an interesting phenomenon where many Triangle residents have bought property in Jewish cities.... Some have even moved in.... This trend could really take off now: young couples...will prefer to purchase apartments in [majority-Jewish] places like Harish and Netanya and live there."

So, while transferring the Galilee Triangle from Israeli to Palestinian control appears like an elegant and simple win-win solution, it is infeasible.

• • •

Hostility. Despite wanting to live in the Jewish state, Israel's Muslim citizens tend to feel limited, or no, loyalty to it. They resent Judaism as the country's privileged religion, the Law of Return that permits only Jews to immigrate at will, Hebrew as the primary language of state, the Star of David on the flag, and mention of the "Jewish soul" in the national anthem.

Over the years, various external factors—Israel's wars with the Arab states and Palestinians, increased contact with the West Bank and Gaza, the surge of Islamism—radicalized many of Israel's Muslim citizens, leading them to push away their Israeli identity. Rejectionist innovations such as the "right of return," Land Day, and Nakba Day increasingly appeal to them.

A 2006 document, "The Future Vision of the Palestinian Arabs in Israel," codified this hostility. Issued by the Mossawa Center in Haifa and endorsed by many establishment figures, it rejects the Jewish nature of Israel, insisting that the country become a binational state in which Palestinian culture and power enjoy complete equality. The document's notion of a "joint homeland" involves Jewish and Arab sectors which run their own affairs and have the right of veto over some of the other's decisions. "Future Vision" demands elevating Arabic to the equal of Hebrew, canceling the Law of Return, and adjusting the flag and anthem. It seeks separate Arab representation in international fora. Most profoundly, the vision would terminate the Zionist achievement of a sovereign Jewish state. Foreign Minister Avigdor Liberman called this document "deeply troubling." Indeed, its extremism marked a turning point for Israel's Muslim citizens.

Other than the members of Ra'am, a Muslim party, since 2021, all Israeli Muslim parliamentarians are hotheads spewing rank anti-Zionism. Some go beyond words actively to aid Israel's enemies. For example, Ahmed Tibi advised Yasir Arafat and Mahmoud Abbas how best to confront and defeat Israel even while receiving a salary from Israeli taxpayers as a member of the Knesset. Azmi Bishara resigned from the Knesset and fled the country in 2007, days before being accused of treason and espionage for selling Hezbollah information that helped it to aim rockets at Israeli targets in the 2006 war.

Large demonstrations regularly take place in Muslim-majority cities throughout Israel, sometimes accompanied by pictures of Hamas and Hezbollah leaders and rhythmic shouts of "Death to the Jews." Muslim-on-Jewish violence within Israel culminated (so far) in the violent disturbances that erupted during the "Aqsa Intifada" of October 2000 and the Israel-Hamas war of May 2021.

In all, this situation suggests that Israel's Muslim citizens will emerge as an ever-greater concern, perhaps the ultimate obstacle to establishing securely the Jewish homeland, the one that remains after foreign states and Palestinians have been neutralized. Indeed, an internal Shin Bet document in 2007 called Israel's Arabs a "genuine long-range danger to the Jewish character and very existence of the State of Israel." In this sense, they pose an existential danger to the Jewish state.

Many discussions about Israel's Muslim citizens conclude that such discontents would ease if only the government offered more respect and more money; the 2003 Orr Commission looking into Israel's Muslim citizen violence inevitably resorted to enrichment as the solution. Likewise, the head of Shin Bet, Ronen Bar, warned that reducing government funds to Israel's Muslim citizens "will increase motivation for violent nationalistic acts."

This polite, default position blames the alienation of Israeli Muslims on Zionists and inevitably calls for more enrichment to remedy the problem.

In fact, hopes for enrichment are factually and conceptually wrong. Factually wrong because Israeli Arabs take in magnitudes more than they pay out; in 2012, for example, they received twenty-seven times more (11 billion vs. 0.4 billion shekels) in government benefits than they paid in taxes. That lopsided ratio goes far to explain the massive rejection of the opportunity to live under PA or Hamas rule. Conceptually wrong because, as Efraim Karsh notes, the socioeconomic argument needs to be reversed: "The more prosperous, affluent, and better educated [Israeli Arabs] became, the stronger and more vociferous their leaders' incitement against their state of citizenship, to the point of open rejection of the fundamental principles underpinning its very existence." To which Gershon Hacohen adds, referring to the May 2021 riots, that those were a nationalist and Islamist uprising "stemming not from the lack of rights or opportunities but from the rejection of a minority status that is regarded as unlawful domination by an alien invader who must be supplanted." Enrichment fails within Israel's borders no less than in the West Bank and in Gaza.

• • •

Resolution. Appreciation and hostility present a set of profoundly conflicted feelings and attitudes. Only Israel Victory can resolve them.

Confliction. Survey research confirms the conflicted views of Israel's Muslim citizens about living in a Jewish polity. A 2017 poll found that 46 percent identify as Israeli Arabs, 42 percent as Palestinians, and 3 percent as Israelis. Despite this, 60 percent are "very proud" or "fairly proud" to be Israeli, while 37 percent are "not proud" to be Israeli. They scream discrimination (note the extremists who serve as their parliamentary representatives) but fully recognize their greater rights and privileges than any Muslim populace living in a Muslim-majority country (think Egypt or Syria), much less in the West Bank or in Gaza.

Israel's Muslim citizens live in the country that their fellow Muslims most malign and even threaten with annihilation. As their numbers, skills, and confidence grow, they become simultaneously more integral to the country's life and more impatient to throw off Jewish sovereignty. The same Israeli Muslim citizens who bluster contempt for the Jewish state and praise the murderers of Jewish children also desperately hope to stay in it rather than become part of "Palestine." They dislike the Jewish state but much prefer living in to subjecting themselves to the tender mercies of the PA or Hamas. They appreciate the practical benefits of living in Israel—the rights, freedoms, economic advantages—but are alienated by its identity. They like it practically, hate it theoretically. Their views are as unequivocal as they are paradoxical. They wish to remain disloyal citizens of Israel rather than become loyal citizens of Palestine.

Moving. Does an option exist to reconcile these contradictory urges? Yes, after the Palestinians experience a change of heart.

Educated in excellent schools, versed in democratic ways, accomplished and ambitious, Israel's Muslim citizens have the skills and outlook to build a new society in the West Bank and in Gaza. But only when a Palestinian change of heart takes place will these territories become attractive places to live, places that today's Israeli Muslim citizens might move to of their own volition, potentially offering both an Israeli-style quality of life and a Palestinian identity, where they can enjoy the many practical benefits Israel offers while living under their own people's rule. No more Jewish state, Law of Return, Hebrew, Star of David, or *Hatikvah*; but also no political repression, failed institutions, and a culture celebrating delusion, extremism, and self-destruction. Thus can the inner dissonance of Israel's Muslim citizens potentially be resolved.

Jewish Israelis will welcome the prospect of their Muslim co-nationals voluntarily moving to the West Bank and Gaza, as both their security and their identity favor minimizing the number of non-Jews in Israel. Existing measures—building fences along the frontiers, implementing stringent family reunification policies, and carefully scrutinizing refugee applications—limit the Muslim population without reducing it. Other policies, including pro-natalist ones, actually encourage Muslim population growth. The more radical idea of adjusting Israel's borders, as we have seen, will not work. Kahane-style deportations would be an unmitigated disaster.

Accordingly, the government of Israel would likely fund and provide other support to facilitate the exit for those intending to move. Indeed, Avigdor Liberman has already proposed that Israel provide "a system of economic incentives" for those "who decide that their identity is Palestinian... forfeit their Israeli citizenship and move and become citizens of the future Palestinian state."

Thus does Israel Victory offer a possible solution to the otherwise insoluble problem of the Jewish state and its reluctant Muslim citizens.

CONCLUSION

THE IMPACT OF OCTOBER 7

I am so damn depressed.... I hardly hear any talk of victory anymore [in Israel].

—American novelist Jack Engelhard, November 2023

Your war cabinet is made up of people still stuck in the konceptzia of October 6.

—Minister of Economy Nir Barkat to Netanyahu, December 2023

"EVERYTHING CHANGED" IN ISRAEL ON October 7, they said.

Indeed, the massacre of 1,200 Israelis and more than 200 taken hostage caused dramatic changes. The judicial reform dispute that had wracked Israeli public life evaporated. Destroying Hamas, a distant prospect, instantly became a matter of consensus. Talk of victory became ubiquitous (as documented on pp. 223-24) among politicians, military officers, journalists, and commentators. The prime minister invoked victory every few days, sometimes echoing Winston Churchill or Douglas MacArthur. Long-ignored figures such as Major General (res.) Yitzhak Brik became media sensations.

In one practical example of change, prisoners captured on October 7 did not enjoy the "five-star" accommodations of old; in Itamar Ben-Gvir's concise formulation, "What was in the past will not be in the future." Or, as he elaborated, "eight terrorists are kept cuffed in a dark cell, iron beds, facilities are a hole in the ground, and the National Anthem, Hatikvah, is constantly playing in the background." Mattresses on the floor replaced beds. For once, the prison service did not contradict him, with its head, Katy Perry, adding "They are kept 4-by-8 in a cell, locked up all day...they are in solitude and receive only the basic necessities."

But did the mistakes that led to the Hamas massacre—enrichment, conciliation, punishment, konceptzia, poor messaging—change? Some expressed optimism. Bezalel Smotrich opined that: "The konceptzia that withdrawals and money can 'buy peace' has collapsed. The vast majority of Israeli citizens understand the dangers."

I am skeptical. Israel's errors are deep-seated, in some cases going back to the origins of Zionism, and a single shock, such as the massacre, will not instantly reverse them. In retrospect, the month of ferocity following October 7 signified less a fundamental shift in outlook than a passing surge in emotions. Rhetoric about victory continued, but with increasing hollowness as Israel's officialdom and public hastily reverted to the errors that had led to October 7.

We begin by reviewing this shift and then focusing on the hostage deal.

• • •

Symptoms. In September 2005, a month after his unilateral withdrawal from Gaza, Ariel Sharon acceded to American pressure and also unilaterally withdrew from the Philadelphi Corridor, a 14-kilometer long and 100-meter wide area between Gaza and Egypt. With this, Israel gave up control of Gaza's borders, hoping that a mix of European and Egyptian policing would protect its interests. That decision led to smuggling that eventually culminated in missiles that can reach Jerusalem and even Ramallah. Despite assurances by Netanyahu that the corridor would be retaken (it "has to be in our hands"), by the end of 2023 he made only a single, failed effort to seize it. Egyptian opposition to such an operation makes it doubtful that this, the Hamas lifeline, will be severed.

Before October 7, Israel supplied Gaza with forty-nine million liters of water per day, 9 percent of the territory's consumption, through three pipelines. It cut off all electricity, water, and fuel supplies on October 7 and formalized this as policy on October 12. On October 15, UNRWA Commissioner General Philippe Lazzarini confirmed that, "Not one drop of water, not one grain of wheat, not a liter of fuel has been allowed in the Gaza Strip for the last eight days." But that policy quickly fell apart under international pressure, and by October 28, Israel had reinstated 28.5 million liters per day through two pipelines. Why not all three? Because Hamas had damaged the third on October 7, necessitating repairs. Not to fear: IDF Colonel Elad Goren announced that his office had "assembled a team of experts who assess the humanitarian situation in Gaza on a daily basis."

Fuel supplies also resumed, followed by 200 trucks per day of "humanitarian aid." Netanyahu reportedly agreed to allow that aid into Gaza in return for Joe Biden visiting Israel. Israel also reached an agreement with Cyprus to establish a "humanitarian corridor" through which water, food, medicine, and other supplies enter Gaza via its port at Mawasi, so not having to go through Israel.

That thousands of workers from Gaza had spied on Israel, down to the level of mapping out individual homes, seemed to be forgotten when the security establishment approved the entry of 8,000 West Bank workers to Israel. It did so after Israel's agriculture minister (a former head of Shin Bet) gave assurances that they had been vetted and posed no danger. Ben Gvir called for the cancellation of these permits but to no avail, and up to 10,000 West Bank workers entered Israel or Israeli towns in the West Bank in late December. Reports indicated that the security services, ever concerned with enrichment, pressured reluctant Israeli municipalities to hire these West Bankers.

Israel's commanding general in the West Bank issued oxymoronic orders limiting Arab access that appeared tough but changed very little. As explained by the Binyamin Regional Council, "There is no entry into Israeli towns for Arab workers. They will be permitted to enter industrial areas at night only." Do marauders and murderers carry out their crimes only in daylight?

Enrichment lives on in another important way. When discussing the future of Gaza, Israeli politicians widely speak of its economic revival. Netanyahu: "We have to...rebuild Gaza." Danny Danon called for the "economic rehabilitation for Gazans within Gaza on the premise of the renunciation of incitement and terror." Michael Oren hoped the Arab states would help build

> a modern infrastructure for Gaza—transportation systems, water desalination and waste treatment plants, and electrical grids—along with state-of-the-art hospitals and healthcare centers.... The refugee camps will be disbanded and replaced by new neighborhoods complete with parks and commercial centers. A harbor and an airport will be opened. The farm-

> lands that, prior to Israel's disengagement from Gaza in 2005, exported organic vegetables to the world, will be revived.

Organic vegetables! Israeli faith in enrichment appears infinite.

The Regavim organization warned that the Palestinian Authority has built close to 20,000 structures close by the Green Line, its border with the part of the West Bank under full Israeli control (Area C); it called this phenomenon "frightening and threatening...a real danger; a ticking bomb." When presented with this information, the security establishment responded much as it had to the threat from Gaza, preferring either to ignore the issue or dismiss the buildings as innocent construction by individuals.

The Alma Research & Education Center published an analysis arguing that, "Hezbollah's Radwan unit is capable of carrying out an invasion of the Galilee at any given moment." When added to the Hamas invasion and the Regavim report, this means that three of Israel's six land borders are in imminent danger of invasion. (Ironically, Israel's borders with police states—Egypt, Jordan, Syria—are relatively safe, despite reports of increased Iranian activity in Jordan.)

The Palestinian Authority not only offered full-throated support for the Hamas massacre, but the Fatah movement headed by PA President Abbas boasted of having a role in it. Referring to October 7, a top Fatah official vowed that: "The next and more violent explosion will be in the West Bank." The PA required mosques within its jurisdiction to instruct congregants that exterminating Jews constitutes an Islamic duty.

Despite this, the Israeli cabinet continued to send tax monies to the PA. Gallant endorsed this decision, saying: "It is appropriate to transfer, and transfer immediately, the funds to the Palestinian Authority so that they will be used by its forces who help prevent terrorism." Beyond such funds, Jerusalem actively wants the PA to survive, seeing it as a bulwark against Hamas. Netanyahu explained this reasoning in December 2023: "We cooperate with [the PA] against Hamas when it serves both their interest and ours, and up to a certain limit. We decided several months ago that we do not want them to collapse so that Hamas does not rise up in Judea and Samaria as well."

Ben-Gvir tried to loosen the rules of engagement for police officers, permitting them in emergencies to shoot at the legs of aggressors, but

Gantz managed to deflect a vote, thereby keeping the more restrictive regulations in place.

Five days after October 7, Israel shuttered its Public Diplomacy Ministry, providing a perfect symbol of Israel's historically hapless and low-priority messaging efforts.

Contrarily, Israel's communications minister called Al Jazeera, the Qatari television channel, a "propaganda mouthpiece" that incites against Israel, and attempted to close down its office in Israel. The government rejected his recommendation, wanting not to upset the Qatari government, which had helped to mediate the release of some hostages, thereby ignoring its role in perpetrating October 7. Yossi Cohen, the former head of Mossad, went further; he favored "refraining from criticizing Qatar."

Talk of victory did not stop negativism from quickly rearing its head. Israeli military correspondent Yoav Limor found that the very idea of victory has become "elusive and controversial." A senior IDF officer said that two years hence "it is possible that the residents of the Gaza envelope will hear Red Alert alarms," meaning that Israelis living near Gaza will still be attacked by rockets from there. Former IDF chief of staff Dan Halutz already proclaimed in late December 2023 that, "We lost the war against Hamas." "I don't see any kind of victory going out of this mess," commented Avi Issacharoff, creator of the hit TV series *Fauda*. Orly Noy of B'Tselem informed her Israeli co-nationals, "I have no interest in the victory you're offering me.... I'm ready to admit defeat."

The principal of a public high school in Tel Aviv devoted forty-five minutes to talking to three students who had come to school patriotically wrapped in Israeli flags. During the conversation, one student reported, the principal pointed out that other students objected to such a display, adding that "if a large number of students came to school wrapped in Israeli flags, he would end this immediately." So bad had the mood become that even the far-left *Ha'aretz* newspaper ran a story under the headline, "Stop Applauding Hamas for Its 'Humanity.'"

Polls show a massive softening of public opinion within a month of the massacre. If mid-October polling by the Middle East Forum showed 70 percent wanting to "eliminate Hamas," in mid-November polling by The Jewish People Policy Institute, a mere 38 percent defined victory as "Gaza is no longer under Hamas control," a huge drop. Asked in November by Hebrew University researchers about the war's most important objective, 34 percent of Israeli Jews replied, incapacitating Hamas, and 46 percent, the hostages' return. Asked about making "painful concessions" to secure the hostages' release, 61 percent expressed a readiness, a near-tripling of the 21 percent ready to do so six weeks earlier. A poll by Israel's Channel 14 reported a 52 percent approval of the hostage agreement with Hamas versus 32 percent opposed. The percentages for victory—38, 34, 32—are impressively consistent and low.

Turned around, the mid-October poll found that 15 percent prioritized hostages, and a *Maariv* poll two months later saw that number increase to 67 percent.

Politicians and the security establishment had driven previous flights from strategic reality (such as the Oslo Accords and the 2005 retreat from Gaza) but not this one. Here, the public pushed the destruction of Hamas aside in favor of rescuing the hostages. In the words of one October 7 survivor, Nadav Peretz, "We want two things. To see Hamas destroyed and to free the hostages. And right now, the latter outweighs the former." A mid-November *Maariv* poll found that the National Unity party headed by Gantz, a former chief of staff and the personification of the security establishment, jumped from twelve seats in the prior election to forty-three seats in the next one. According to Nimrod Nir, a psychologist who led the Hebrew University survey research, "Our polling shows that the Israeli people were consistently ahead of the decision makers on this. As they learned about who Hamas was holding and under what conditions, the pressure to do something grew."

Politicians began seeking ways to catch up and square the circle. Michael Oren suggested changing the war goal "from annihilating Hamas to securing Hamas's unconditional surrender," thereby allowing Hamas to continue to exist. More specifically, he advocated offering Hamas "free passage from Gaza...in return for the hostages' release." *The Wall Street Journal* reported on discussions underway for Hamas members to leave Gaza.

• • •

The hostage deal. The biggest reversion to old thinking concerned the hostages seized by Hamas. Initially, this seemed out of the question, with Israel's President Isaac Herzog calling Hamas "absolute evil" and a consensus that Israel must not have any dealings with it. (Friends like Republican presidential candidate Tim Scott echoed this view: "You cannot negotiate with evil. You have to destroy it").

But pressure to bring the hostages home quickly broke this consensus, as symbolized by Major General (res.) Noam Tibon telling a rally, "The release of all hostages is the supreme mission of the war, before any other mission! And at the top of our priorities." Major General (res.) Amos Gilad echoed him at another rally: "No victory is possible over Hamas if it later turns out that not everything possible was done to retrieve [the hostages]. An exchange is a matter of national security." IDF spokesman Daniel Hagari nearly echoed them in stating that: "We will do everything, everything, to bring all the hostages home—whether during the operational pause or through continued fighting."

Thus it was, just one and a half months after the massacre and after an avalanche of calls for the destruction of Hamas, that the government of Israel reached a deal with the jihadi group.

The contents of the deal only made matters worse, for a desperate Israel made a majority of the concessions. In return for fewer than one-quarter of Israeli hostages being freed, all of them women and children, Israel agreed to: free 150 female and underage security prisoners (prisoners arrested in connection with offenses bearing on national security); permit an increase in water, food, medicine, and fuel to Gaza; and for four days not to send warplanes over southern Gaza or engage in drone aerial surveillance during six hours each day or attack Hamas.

Consider some implications of these terms:

1. Just a fraction of the hostages implies that the bargaining process will continue indefinitely, with multiple breaks. This suits Hamas' needs while disrupting the Israeli military campaign. As Israeli Colonel (res.) Shai Shabtai explains, Hamas' "continued hold on the hostages has one object: to use endless negotiation in order to undermine the dismantling of its political and military power."
2. Negotiations hamper IDF operations. According to a report in *Ha'aretz*, "the army presented political officials with operations aimed at retrieving the hostages but were not approved for fear that they would complicate the negotiations with Hamas for their return."
3. Interrupting surveillance permits Hamas fighters to escape their besieged tunnels or bring supplies into the tunnels.

4. The deal signaled Israel's return to the bargaining table with Hamas, undercutting the many promises to destroy the organization. For Edy Cohen, an Israeli analyst, this nurtured a widespread Muslim perception that "Israel has lost and Hamas has won."
5. Trading Palestinian security prisoners for October 7 victims confirms Hamas' argument that a moral equivalency exists between criminals and innocent civilians violently abducted.

In brief, the negotiations undercut Israel's tactical, diplomatic, and moral position, signaling its relapse into the errors that had brought about October 7. As the French politician Talleyrand said of the Bourbon dynasty, *Ils n'ont rien appris, ni rien oublié* (They have learnt nothing, and forgotten nothing).

It bears noting, however, that not all Israelis placed personal concerns over the national interest. Eliahu Liebman, father of the hostage Elyakim Liebman, summed up the dilemma in his valorous protest against the proposed deal: "We want all of our hostages released, and the only way to do that is by attacking the enemy with all of our strength, without interruption and without surrendering to their demands, as if they are the victors." Tikvah, an organization of families related to hostages, concurs: "The most correct and effective way of retrieving the hostages is by applying uncompromising pressure on Hamas, until the hostages become a liability for Hamas instead of an asset." But supplications drowned out such voices.

• • •

Contrary to the initial impression that "everything changed," at the time of this writing—the last day of 2023—little had changed. The abrupt and radical shift toward a sudden emphasis on victory over Hamas lasted about a month, quickly giving way to old patterns of economic concessions to and negotiations with Hamas. "The State of Israel which fought and was the spearhead in fighting terrorism," Likud Knesset member Moshe Saada commented, "has surrendered to it." Liberman perceived a "konceptzia coalition" conducting the war on Hamas. Ben-Gvir concurred: "We are still prisoners of the konceptzia."

This reversion fits a much larger pattern. From 1882 until the present, the two feuding parties to this conflict have compiled extraordinary records of sterile continuity. The Palestinians maintain a mentality of rejectionism (no, no, and never to everything Jewish and Israeli), while Zionists stick to conciliation (accept us and we will enrich you). The two go around and around, hardly evolving or making progress. A mistaken approach to Palestinians will remain in place until Israelis accept the need for something radically different, when they break with the traditional Zionist mentality of conciliation and seek Israel Victory.

APPENDICES

A. TERMINOLOGY

Linguistic simplicity and precision contradict each other; precision must win out when dealing with a topic so fraught as this one.

Several words and phrases have my own, specialized meanings:

- *Change of heart*: When the Palestinians abandon rejectionism.
- *Conciliation*: Israel's policies of enriching and placating Palestinians.
- *Demoralization*: Breaking the Palestinian will to sustain rejectionism.
- *Eastern Jerusalem*: The part of the West Bank seized by Israel in 1967 and incorporated into the Jerusalem municipality.
- *Enrichment*: Winning acceptance by Palestinians through economic benefits.
- *Israel Victory*: Inducing Palestinians to give up rejectionism and accept the permanent existence of the Jewish state.
- *Netanyahu Era*: The period 2009–.
- *New Hasbara*: An Israeli communications policy to saturate the Palestinian mental environment.
- *Oslo Era*: The period from 1993 to 2008.
- *Placation*: Winning acceptance by Palestinians through caution and timidity.
- *Rejectionism*: The Palestinian negation by any means necessary of Jews, Judaism, Zionism, and Israel.
- *Zionist*: pre-May 1948, a Jewish resident of the Land of Israel; post-May 1948, a Jewish Israeli.

Depending on context, *Israelis* means either Jewish Israelis or all Israelis. *Israel* serves as short-hand for the *government of Israel* or the *State of Israel*, and the same goes for other country names.

I use *West Bank* rather than *Judea and Samaria* because the latter is only a vague approximation of the former. I accept the newly preferred term *Türkiye* for the country long known in English as *Turkey*. *Allah* is Arabic for *God*.

Palestinian-Israeli conflict neutrally implies that both sides are equally responsible for the problem. It is, therefore, a deceptive label; the *Palestinian war on Israel* is more accurate. Nonetheless, not wanting endlessly to belabor the point, I generally use the neutral term.

Scare quotes indicate my distancing from certain unavoidable terms. Thus, international organizations include "Palestine" as a member. Some individuals who never stepped foot in Mandatory Palestine are "Palestine refugees" who live in "refugee camps." The Palestinian Authority (PA) has a "prime minister" and a "council of ministers" with attendant "ministers." The PA militia has ranks like "colonel." Palestinian-Israeli diplomacy constitutes a "peace process." Palestinian murderers who lose their lives are "martyrs." Israeli towns in the West Bank are "settlements." One strain of Zionism seeks to "transfer" Palestinians, a euphemism for *expulsion*. "Islamophobia" turns anti-Islamic views into a psychological condition.

I avoid ambiguous words like *peace*, *terrorist*, and *terrorism* that raise contentious and irrelevant problems of definition; *quiet*, *murderer*, and *violence* prompt no debate. Where animus toward the Jewish state primarily motivates, I write *anti-Israel*, not *pro-Palestinian*. I use *he* in the traditional, generic sense. Dollars are U.S. dollars. The affiliations of individuals refer to their positions at the time of a quotation or an action. Well-known Arabic names appear in their usual Anglicized form; obscure ones are transliterated more systematically. Dates are given in years except for 2023; before and after October 7 being vitally different, I supply the months, too.

B. *PALESTINE* AND RELATED WORDS

Palestine and related words require special attention because they have evolved, acquiring different and even contrary meanings.

Palestine: Variants of the name go back to the Ancient Egyptian language as early as 1150 BCE, which was later picked up by users of several other languages, including Hebrew. Initially, it referred to the coastal region north and south of Gaza where Philistines lived. It became an official place name in about 135 CE, when the Roman Empire called the province of Judea *Syria Palæstina*. Over the next centuries, Rome divided and re-divided this area, using variants of *Palæstina*, and these survived for yet longer as a place name.

When Arabians conquered the area in 634, they adopted this name. Arabic lacking a "p" sound, they replaced it with "f," making *Filastin*. The Arabians inherited and kept the Roman divisions for several centuries, specifically creating a military district called *Jund Filastin* with its capital in Ramla (not Jerusalem). Filastin referred to a geographic area roughly corresponding to what Jews call *Eretz Yisrael*, Christians *Terra Sancta*, and Muslims *al-Ard al-Muqaddasa*.

Christians in modern times increasingly used *Palestine* as a substitute for *Terra Sancta*. To press their claim among Christians, therefore, Zionists adopted the term *Palestine*. Jewish history contained many boundaries for *Eretz Yisrael*; so, on adopting *Palestine* to define their aspiration, early Zionists gave it an expansive definition that included much of today's Jordan.

Zionists won a singular success in November 1917, when the British government issued the Balfour Declaration promising to "view with favor the establishment in Palestine of a national home for the Jewish people." At that point, in bears emphasizing, Palestine was territorially undefined. A month later, British troops conquered this territory, making the promise operational.

The British then struggled to define Palestine's boundaries. The British-controlled "Mandate for Palestine" came into existence in April 1920. By 1921, for political reasons, London excluded the region east of the Jordan River, which it renamed Transjordan, from the mandate.

Zionists, Pinhas Inbari notes, reveled in the name Palestine:

> The term *Palestine* was Western and was regularly used by Jews who immigrated to the country; the Zionists called themselves *Palestinians* while the Arabs simply identified themselves as *Arabs*. The Zionist institutions—such as the Anglo-Palestine Bank, the *Palestine Post*, and so on—were "Palestinian," whereas the Arab institutions, such as the Arab Higher Committee, were simply "Arab."

Other Jewish institutions with *Palestine* in the name included the Palestine Electric Corporation, Palestine Jewish Colonisation Association, Palestine Foundation Fund, Palestine Land Development Corporation, Palestine

Potash Company, Palestine Salt Company, Ltd., and the Palestine Symphony Orchestra.

In contrast, Arabs resisted *Palestine* during British rule precisely because it had acquired Zionist political and religious significance. Instead, they preferred to view that territory as almost anything else: a part of Greater Syria or the Arab nation or the Muslim *umma* (the Islamic community). Reflecting this resistance, Princeton historian Philip Hitti testified in 1946 that: "There is no such thing as Palestine in history, absolutely not."

In 1948, however, Zionists abandoned the term *Palestine* in favor of *Israel*, making *Palestine* available to Arabs, who picked it up, made it exclusively theirs, and built a vast nationalist myth around it. By now, the very invocation of *Palestine* implies hostility to Israel.

Confusingly, then, *Palestine* began the twentieth century as a Zionist term and ended it as an anti-Zionist term.

Palestinian: Today, this means Arabic-speaking residents of the West Bank and Gaza, that is, Palestinian Arabs. This definition, admittedly, is anachronistic when applied before 1948, but using it greatly simplifies nomenclature. The term here does not refer to (1) the pre-1948 use of *Palestinian* as applied to Zionists, or (2) Israel's Muslim citizens.

Palestinian-origin person: A Palestinian Arab or his descendants who emigrated, whether to nearby Jordan, remote Australia, or anywhere in between.

Palestinian nation: Israel's Prime Minister Golda Meir said in 1976 that, "There is no Palestinian people." Former speaker of the U.S. House of Representatives Newt Gingrich said in 2011 that "there was no Palestine as a state.... We have invented the Palestinian people." Bezalel Smotrich used nearly the same wording in March 2023: "There is no such thing as Palestinians because there's no such thing as the Palestinian people." Florida's Governor Ron DeSantis added in April 2023: "There's never been a Palestinian Arab entity." Are they right?

They have a point: No Palestinian people existed through the centuries. But, starting in 1920, with the imposition of a geographical unit later to be called the British Mandate for Palestine, Arabic speakers of that territory slowly and reluctantly began adopting the Palestinian identity. As noted above, that identification has grown spectacularly. By now, it is futile, even silly, to deny the existence of a distinct Palestinian Arab people. At the same time, the Palestinian identity emerged due to the nature of British rule a century ago, and so, it may not last; the primacy of Palestinian nationalism could be temporary.

Israeli Arabs: Arabic speakers living within Israel's 1948–1967 boundaries and their descendants, including Muslims, Christians, and Druze.

Israel's Muslim citizens: Palestinian Muslims living within Israel's 1948–1967 boundaries and their descendants. Where possible, I prefer this term to the more common *Israeli Arab* because Muslims dominate that population (making up about 85 percent of it). Further, Christians and Druze tend to view Israel more favorably than Muslims.

Thus, the population of what was the Mandate for Palestine now has three main elements: Zionists or Israelis, Israel's Muslim citizens, and Palestinians.

C. THE ISRAEL VICTORY PROJECT

The idea: Israel Victory has evolved over one-third of a century. In 1990, I offered an "outside-in plan" for the Palestinian issue based on the idea that "when the Arab states give Israel something it wants, Israelis should then—and only then—be expected to give something in turn to the Palestinians." The Oslo Accords of 1993, which ignored the Arab states, shunted this approach aside.

Israel Victory germinated in the battles of the Oslo Era, 1993–2008, a time when Israelis blinded themselves to normal national self-interest. Concluding that the "peace process" had gone deeply awry, I sought from 1997 to apply the lessons of history to the Palestinian-Israeli conflict. This approach reached full formulation in 2001. It draws in particular on the global experience of victory and defeat, on Revisionist Zionism, and on Israel's defeat of the Arab states.

The project: The Middle East Forum (MEF), where I am president, launched the Israel Victory Project (IVP) in January 2017. It fit within MEF's existing approach of "finding the path to victory" against radical and destructive forces in the Middle East. IVP benefited from Gregg Roman, with his activist skills, joining the staff in 2015 and two years later, the coming to office of Donald Trump, with his idiosyncratic approach to policy ("I would love to be able to be the one that made peace with Israel and the Palestinians. I would love that, that would be such a great achievement because nobody's been able to do it").

The project had two areas of activity, the United States and Israel.

The United States: The forum organized a bipartisan Congressional Israel Victory Caucus with thirty-three members in the U.S. House of Representatives in 2017; Ron DeSantis and Juan Vargas served as two of its co-chairs. Outside Congress, however, we found an insipid response. A Carnegie Endowment event in 2018 showed the typical inside-the-beltway attitude; as MEF Fellow Andrew E. Harrod reported, "the panelists' refusal to consider the just concept of an Israel Victory typifies the diplomatic establishment's atrophied thinking." Even those sympathetic to the goal kept their distance. One deemed it "chest-pounding" and another defers to an Israel that "maybe knows what it's doing." Concluding that Israel Victory was a small idea in a big country, we focused on Israel, where it is a big idea in a small country.

Israel: The Knesset Israel Victory Caucus, with twenty-six members, stood out as the second-largest caucus of almost one hundred in the twentieth Knesset (2015–2019). It also had a wide representation of parties, seven, making it at one point the Knesset's most politically diverse caucus. Among its other accomplishments, it convened the first-ever combined Knesset-U.S. Congress event dealing with security issues, complete with a joint declaration of principles.

IVP built on this parliamentary success by engaging in a wide variety of activities, some serious and others attention seeking. At the serious end of the spectrum, staff spoke with prime ministers, many other ministers, members of parliament, as well as other politicians, former, present, and future. We led university seminars, gave interviews on television and radio, organized webinars, and gave public talks. We focused on border towns, pre-military academies, and victims of Palestinian violence. We wrote articles, blogs, and social media messages.

As for attention-seeking activities, IVP engaged in a range of gimmicks. A rented 10-meter-tall rubber chicken appeared outside Israel's parliament and Ministry of Defense. Man-hole covers showed realistic decals of armed Palestinians emerging. Supporters changed street signs in Tel Aviv, for example turning Ben-Gurion Boulevard temporarily into "Yasir Arafat Boulevard."

The Israel Victory Project's February 2020 billboard in Tel Aviv showing two Palestinian leaders photoshopped giving up on a battlefield along with a slogan in Hebrew, "Peace can ONLY be made with defeated enemies." After one day, the mayor illegally had the graphic removed.

Provocative billboards appeared in Tel Aviv. One showed Hamas leader Ismail Haniyeh in an immodest swimsuit on the beach with a suitcase of cash and a cluster of firebomb balloons, cheerfully declaring: "Thank you Israel, I love you, Ismail." Another graphic showed blindfolded Palestinian Authority and Hamas leaders, Mahmoud Abbas and Haniyeh, photo-shopped against a battlefield scene. Abbas' hands are raised high while Haniyeh's hold a white flag. The graphic carried a slogan in Hebrew, "Peace can ONLY be made with defeated enemies." A day later, the mayor of Tel Aviv ordered the billboards removed, ignoring our right of free speech and despoiling our property. We sued the mayor and won in Israel's Supreme Court. Others also reacted strongly to the poster showing Abbas and Haniyeh giving up on the battlefield, with Hagai El Ad, the head of B'Tselem, calling it "this election's victory image" and, in a backhanded compliment, declaring the pictures "etched in the collective consciousness" of Israel.

IVP's work led to considerable discussion and returned *victory* to the Israeli lexicon after an absence of decades, with its full fruition as a near-universal mantra coming after October 7. This culminated a years-long process; as Matan Peleg and Douglas Altabef of Im Tirtzu, an Israeli organization, explained in 2018: "After a lengthy disappearance from Israeli social and political discourse, the idea of victory, of triumph, has once again surfaced and is quickly gaining attention and traction" due to "frustration with accommodation...and the realization that halfway measures are tantamount to eventual defeat.... Victory is not a plan, but a mindset that will eventually lead to a plan...the path to peace in our region lies through Israeli victory."

ABOUT THE AUTHOR

DANIEL PIPES TAUGHT HISTORY AT Harvard University and the University of Chicago, served on the State Department's Policy Planning Staff under President Reagan, administered Fulbright Fellowships, and founded the Middle East Forum. *Israel Victory* is his nineteenth book. Prior books of note include *In the Path of God*, *Greater Syria*, and *The Rushdie Affair*.

A top Al-Qaeda figure publicly invited him to convert to Islam. Pipes has also been recognized as one of Harvard University's 100 most influential living graduates and has been listed in Marquis' *Who's Who in the World*.

The *New York Times* calls him "smart and well-informed," the *Wall Street Journal*, "an authoritative commentator," and the *Washington Post*, "perhaps the most prominent U.S. scholar on radical Islam." Egypt's *Al-Ahram* deems him the neo-conservative movement's "leading thinker" and the *Toronto Star* labels him "wildly controversial." *Le Monde Diplomatique* considers him "one of the most unconditionally pro-Israel propagandists," and, finally, *Counterpunch* denounces him as "an infamous charlatan."